An Introduction to Literature

DRAMA

An Introduction to Literature

DRAMA

EDITED BY

Edmond L. Volpe AND *Marvin Magalaner*

FICTION

EDITED BY

Theodore Gross AND *Norman Kelvin*

POETRY

EDITED BY

Edmond L. Volpe AND *Marvin Magalaner*

Selected from these three volumes
A one-volume omnibus anthology

POETRY, DRAMA, FICTION:

An Introduction to Literature

EDITED BY

Edmond L. Volpe, Marvin Magalaner,
Norman Kelvin AND *Theodore Gross*

An
Introduction to
Literature

DRAMA

Edited by

Edmond L. Volpe
and Marvin Magalaner

The City College of
The City University of New York

RANDOM HOUSE New York

PN
6112
.V6

ACKNOWLEDGMENTS

Oedipus Rex by Sophocles. An English Version by Dudley Fitts and Robert Fitzgerald, copyright, 1949, by Harcourt, Brace and Company, Inc. Reprinted by permission of the publisher.

Tartuffe by Molière. From *Eight Plays by Molière*, translated by Morris Bishop. © Copyright 1957 by Morris Bishop. Reprinted by permission of Random House, Inc.

The Wild Duck by Henrik Ibsen. From *The Wild Duck and Other Plays*, by Henrik Ibsen, translated by Eva Le Gallienne. © Copyright 1961 by Eva Le Gallienne. Reprinted by permission of Random House, Inc.

The Cherry Orchard by Anton Chekhov. From *Best Plays of Chekhov*, Modern Library Edition, translated by Stark Young. Copyright, 1939, 1941, 1947 and 1950 by Stark Young. © 1956 by Stark Young. Reprinted by permission of The Estate of Stark Young.

Desire under the Elms by Eugene O'Neill. Copyright 1924 and renewed 1952 by Eugene O'Neill. Reprinted from *Nine Plays by Eugene O'Neill* by permission of Random House, Inc.

Contents

An Introduction to Literature

DRAMA

Introduction

~~~~~~

Anyone who has ever orally recounted an experience is prepared to understand drama. The two essentials of dramatic communication are present in this everyday occurrence—a story-teller who wants to share an experience, and a listener. Some people, as everyone knows, are dreadful story-tellers, mainly because they are insensitive to their listeners. They become so absorbed in their own thoughts that they go off on tangents, dwell on irrelevant details, and lose the point of their story. Because a good story-teller is aware of his listener's response, he is as concerned with the manner in which he tells the story as with the story itself. The major difference between the amateur describing an experience and the artist telling a story is that the artist deliberately works to evoke responses. Audience response is related to the degree of involvement in the story. When a listener begins to feel shock or terror, love or hate, when he begins to wonder what will happen next, ponder the meaning of a statement or an event, see the relevance of the story to his own life, he is involved because he is reacting emotionally and intellectually. He is undergoing a real experience. The kind and intensity of his reactions will be a measure of success of the story-teller.

When we speak, therefore, of dramatic techniques, what we mean are the various devices the story-teller uses to evoke response and involve his audience. Consider, for instance, how effective a speaker can be if he varies the tone and pitch of his voice and uses facial expressions and hand gestures to emphasize what he is saying. Such devices are means of communication, and the more techniques that can be employed the more effective the communication. If a story-teller is relating a conversation between two people, he can create for his listener a greater illusion of reality by altering his voice for each character. The next logical step toward more effective presentation, having two people speak the lines, is the beginning of drama.

A story rendered in this way by actors is more effective because greater audience involvement is required. The listener now becomes a witness and must form his own judgments about the characters from the way they speak and the way they gesture and move, and draw his own conclusions about the meaning of their speeches. Telling a story through the use of actors has, therefore, many advantages in terms of evoking audience response. But by choosing this form of presentation, the story-teller also accepts many limitations. He can no longer, for instance, describe a setting, tell his listener what is going on in the mind of a character, or relate what the character feels. He cannot say that one character is good and another is mean and cruel. He cannot explain the significance of the story he is telling. Everything must be done through dialogue which creates the illusion that real people are undergoing a real experience.

Presenting a story through actors requires a stage and a place for an audience to congregate. The very structure of this place and stage will affect the manner in which the story can be told. The ancient Greeks congregated in huge outdoor amphitheaters with excellent acoustics. But because a portion of the audience was seated far from the actors, facial expressions and slight physical gestures could not be seen. Greek dramatists, therefore, had to depend almost exclusively upon the spoken word to evoke audience response. Shakespeare's theater was much smaller. The stage projected into the pit where some of the audience stood. The proximity of audience and actors made the use of asides and soliloquies more natural than their use on the modern stage, which separates the actors from the audience. No scenery was used on Shakespeare's stage, so he could dramatize his stories with many diverse scenes. The use of expensive, realistic sets tends to limit the number of scenes a modern playwright can use to present his story.

Such limitations as these actually define the art of story-telling called the drama, and much of the excitement of drama is created by the ability of the great dramatist to transcend these limitations and still create intense emotions, moods, and profound thoughts in an audience. To create such responses the playwright interfuses story, characters, and theme. The story tells what happens, the characters reveal to whom it happens and why, and the theme expresses the significance of these events.

Story is the heart of drama. The progression of events taking place on stage develops and sustains audience interest and involvement. Every story is basically a clash of forces. The story begins when the forces are identified and come into conflict; it develops as these forces struggle for supremacy, and it ends when one of the forces is defeated. The opposing forces can take any form. On the simplest level, the hero struggles against the villain, but the more significant human struggles are frequently against intangible forces such as conscience, social traditions and mores, or fate, the very conditions of human existence. The task of the playmaker, at the opening of the drama, is to make the audience aware, as soon as possible, what form the conflict will take, who the protagonist is, and what he will be battling. Most such struggles have their beginnings sometime in the past, and in the opening scenes the dramatist must present this background as quickly and unobtrusively as possible. Once the antagonists are identified, each scene is designed to move the plot forward, that is, to reveal to the audience the progress of the struggle. At a certain point, the battle reaches its climax, or turning point. Something crucial has occurred that makes the defeat or victory of the protagonist inevitable. The rest of the story, the dénouement, presents this defeat or victory and its effects.

The effectiveness of a story cannot be truly isolated from character. If the antagonistic forces are not almost equally matched, there is no contest and hence no drama. A weak protagonist who feels confined, say, by the demands of his domineering mother for financial support and for companionship would provide no conflict. But a personality capable of intense filial love coupled with a very strong sense of filial responsibility could be torn in two by an equally intense desire to live his own life. His conflict occurs because he is the kind of person he is. Stories are about people, and the dramatist must create these people so that his audience accepts them as real, driven by recognizable motives, and expressing recognizable needs and feelings. To become involved in their story, the audience must come to know the major character well enough to want him to succeed.

In his characterizations, the playwright mirrors the manner in which people generally view those around them. People whom we know casually, who are on the periphery of our lives, we tend to recognize and remember by a few obvious characteristics. We frequently classify them by the work they do, a habit of speech, some physical characteristic—superficial aspects of personality. But the people we know best, including ourselves, cannot be characterized so easily. There are too many conflicting traits and forces at work in any personality, and the better we know someone the more complex his character appears. The dramatist recreates this situation on stage. The minor characters he makes identifiable by superficial characteristics. The major characters are presented in depth. And when a dramatist has really succeeded in creating a character, the audience knows him well, which means it is confronted by the baffling complexity of the human character. Just as the dramatist develops the plot with each successive scene, so he reveals in each episode more and more about his major characters. As the audience comes to know the protagonist better, the more emotionally involved it becomes in his struggle.

This kind of involvement in the fate of a character prepares the audience to understand the thematic significance of the story. No human experience, felt deeply enough, lacks meaning. Our ideas, our attitudes about life are constantly being shaped and changed by the experiences we undergo. The more intense the experience the greater will be its impact upon our thinking and feeling. Watching or reading a great drama can be an intense and vital experience, and when we speak of the theme of a drama, what we mean is the meaning for us of the experience the dramatist has provided—the revelations about the human being or society, or about the conditions of existence.

The excitement produced by such an experience gives impetus to the kind of discussion and analysis that will engage any class studying drama. We mull over experiences that excite us; we try to understand what happened, how it happened, why it happened, what it all means —in short, analyze it. When a poem or story or drama makes an impression upon us and we begin to think about it in this way, we enter the realm of literary criticism. A critic watching or reading a tragedy, for instance, feels a growing sense of impending doom. When he first experiences the feeling, he simply lets himself go and enjoys it; but then, because he has been made to respond, he wants to discover how the dramatist succeeded in evoking this mood, what techniques he used. The critic then begins to notice details: the dark images that recur in the speeches of the protagonist, symbolic statements or actions, the emotions expressed in individual scenes, the attitudes of various characters, the structure and pacing of the episodes. All such details are making their contributions to the dramatic effect.

This kind of attention to detail should occupy the student of drama, but only after he has read through the play once and experienced it on an emotional level. The second reading should be critical. Perhaps the best approach to this second reading is to imagine oneself as the director of the play who must know and understand the characters well enough to help the actors interpret their roles, who must coordinate the acting and the pacing of the scenes to create mood, and who must seek the meaning of the experience and be certain that it is conveyed by the production. Such an imaginative and careful reading will make the student aware of the challenge and excitement of the dramatic art and inevitably intensify the experience these great dramas can provide.

Sophocles

Nearly 2,500 years ago, about 495 B.C., one of the greatest playwrights in history was born in Colonus, a suburb of Athens. Sophocles, the son of Sophillus, lived for ninety years, during which he won fame and honor. The year of his death is generally assigned as 406 B.C., not because the date was officially recorded, but because Aristophanes alluded to the recent death of the poet in *The Frogs*, which was produced in 406 B.C. From such references scholars have garnered a few facts about Sophocles' life and career.

His father, apparently, was a man of fairly substantial means and provided his son with the good education enjoyed by upper-class Athenian boys of the period. Under the guidance of Lamprus, a well-known musician, he studied music, an important asset to Greek dramatists. Sophocles was a good enough pupil to be chosen to lead a boys' chorus in a hymn sung at the victory celebration in 480 B.C. when the Greeks defeated the Persians at Salamis. Twelve years later, in 468 B.C., he is recorded as the winner of the first prize in the annual tragedy contest. Though only in his twenties, Sophocles had defeated the leading dramatist of the age—Aeschylus. During the next sixty years, Sophocles wrote over a hundred plays and won first prize about eighteen times. The quality of playwrights against whom he competed in the tragedy contests is perhaps indicated by the fact that *Oedipus Rex* won only a second prize. We have fragments of many of Sophocles' plays, but only seven complete plays have come down to us. Several of these can be assigned production dates: *Ajax, Antigone*

(442 B.C.), *Oedipus Rex* (between 430 and 411 B.C.), *Electra, Trachiniae* (about 420 B.C.), *Philoctetes* (409 B.C.), and *Oedipus at Colonus* (produced after the playwright's death).

In the Age of Pericles, dramatists were honored public figures. When he was fifty-five, Sophocles was appointed to serve as a general under Pericles during the Samian War (440–439 B.C.). He, like most Athenian citizens, took his civic responsibilities seriously, and he is recorded as one of the treasurers who managed the tribute paid to Athens by her allies. He also held other public positions, among which was membership on a Committee of Thirty to modify the Athenian constitution. Despite his obvious sensitivity to the horrors of human existence, Sophocles was not a morose, embittered man as was his younger contemporary, the dramatist Euripides, who became almost a recluse. Most allusions to Sophocles' character reveal him as an amiable, witty, even-tempered man who was held in high esteem by his fellow Athenians not only for his greatness as a playwright, but also for his gentleness and affability.

To appreciate fully the significance of Sophocles' personal achievement as a dramatist and his contribution to the drama, it is necessary to know something about the early history of the drama and also about the stage conditions and the dramatic conventions with which the Greek playwrights worked.

The most remarkable thing about Greek drama is that it seems to have gone through no period of development. Almost without predecessors, Aeschylus (525–455 B.C.) produced tragedies which were unmatched during the next twenty centuries of dramatic creation. How it happened that men began to tell stories by acting them out we do not know. What does seem to be clear about the origin of Greek drama is that it developed from rituals performed at religious ceremonies. The tragedy contests of the fifth century B.C. were held at the annual festival honoring Dionysus (later called Bacchus), the god of vegetation and wine. It is therefore conjectured that the drama developed from ancient ceremonies honoring Dionysus. What these ceremonies might have been, we can only guess, but the tragedies provide a clue. The chorus in these dramas, we know, sang their odes and accompanied their singing with some kind of dance. (The word "Chorus" actually derives from the Greek word meaning "dance.") If the ancient ceremonies honoring the god of wine did consist of singing and dancing by a chorus, then what may have happened was that a composer decided to incorporate a solo part. And as soon as the chorus began to respond to the soloist rather than accompany him, dialogue was created and the drama was born.

The actor Thespis is credited with the initial step of separating an actor from the chorus. The number of singers in the chorus in his time was about fifty. Aeschylus reduced the number to fifteen and in his plays used two actors. Sophocles worked with a chorus of twelve and introduced a third actor. This third actor was an important innovation. With only two characters with speaking roles on stage at one time, the playwright was forced to create his characters in broad, stylized form. Aeschylus, for example, in *Agammemnon*, does not strive for subtlety in the characterization of the warrior king who sacrificed his daughter Iphigenia to appease the gods and who, when he returned triumphant from the Trojan War, was murdered by his wife Clytemnestra. Such characters, drawn on a scale much larger than life, are suited for their heroic roles in the religious dramas of Aeschylus. Sophocles also cast his characters from a heroic mold, but because he was interested in presenting them as recognizable human beings as well as legendary heroes, his third actor became necessary. With three speaking characters on stage at one time, the reactions and responses of the second and third characters to the protagonist permit greater depth and subtlety in characterization. And since the chorus also reacts to the actions and words of the main personages, the dramatist can create complex characters. This emphasis by Sophocles upon the human quality of his characters within the framework of the mythic, poetic, religious drama he inherited from Aeschylus gives to his tragedies a dual level of significance—man and his relation to the gods, and man as a complex product of emotional drives and needs, of loyalties and moral codes.

Though Sophocles is credited with introducing a bit of realism into the drama through painted scenery, he wrote for a theater which was quite different from the modern box stage and which, therefore, set different requirements for the playwright. The ancient amphitheater in Athens was built upon the southeastern slope of the Acropolis, with stone benches placed in rows on three sides. In the center of this tiered semicircle was a circular area called the "orchestra," in which the chorus danced. Beyond this area was a raised platform on which the actors stood, and beyond the stage, a structure in which the actors changed their costumes and masks and from which they made their entrances.

The open-air theater outside of Athens held about eighteen thousand spectators, and though the acoustics are believed to have been excellent, the actors necessarily had to project their voices. Such a theater demanded stately sonorous poetry rather than the intimate, realistic dialogue of the modern drama. The distance of much of the audience from the stage also limited the amount of stage business a dramatist could use. The actors had to move and gesture slowly and melodramatically. The stances and gestures of modern opera singers probably approximate the acting on the Greek stage. Ancient actors wore long, flowing gowns, high-soled shoes, and leggings called "buskins" which gave them added height. They used large masks which some scholars believe served not only to identify the characters, but also acted as megaphones. In contrast, for example, to television drama which can depend upon closeups of the actor's face to register his feelings and reactions, Greek drama was completely dependent upon words to set the scenes, create character, evoke mood, and tell the story. For this reason, the ancient dramatists were not only makers of plays but poets who could express profound emotions in a few words set in rhythmic patterns and who could evoke in the audience moods of despair or exaltation, terror, or peace.

The important role of poetry in the ancient drama is perhaps most evident in the odes of the chorus. To a modern audience, the Greek chorus seems imposed and artificial, but if one examines the role of the chorus and the odes it sings, its dramatic function and effect become obvious. Sophocles, particularly, strove to incorporate the chorus into the story. In *Oedipus Rex,* the entire town of Thebes is suffering from the plague; thus the presence of the group of elders at the king's palace and their interest in the fate of their king are logical. Greek dramatists did not have a curtain to bring down when they ended a scene or wanted a change of scene; the odes of the chorus served these purposes. When all the actors left the stage, the chorus sang and danced. Their odes, however, were more than interludes. With them the poet created mood and put into words the emotional responses of the audience. Some of the most beautiful poetry in Sophocles' plays is recited by the chorus, and there can be no question that the thousands of Athenians in the audience responded to the exquisite imagery and the beauty of these odes.

They must have responded, because they were willing to sit on hard stone seats not merely through one play, but through four plays in one day. When Sophocles began to write, the annual festival of Dionysus was a well-established function. The festival lasted for five days, the last three of which were devoted to tragedy. On each of these days, a dramatist, who had competed for the honor, presented a trilogy, three separate tragedies with a common theme and often a related story, and then a satyr play, a drama in a lighter mood but on a similar theme. Most of the townspeople, and many from other towns, turned out for the three days of drama, bringing with them food and wine to be consumed between plays. So important was the drama to the Athenians that provision was made to provide free tickets to those who could not afford the modest entrance fee. Unfortunately, none of the trilogies which Sophocles presented for the entertainment and edification of his fellow Athenians has survived, but we do have *Orestia* of Aeschylus which dramatizes the story of Agammemnon and his children; and three of Sophocles' surviving plays, though written at widely spaced intervals in his career, do form a trilogy. *Oedipus Rex* depicts the fall of Oedipus; *Oedipus at Colonus* sets forth his peaceful death after twenty long years of suffering; and *Antigone* deals with the children of Oedipus, the death of his two sons by each other's hand and Antigone's struggle to bury her brother.

In these three plays, which, because they were written at different periods, have many inconsistencies in details of the story, in characterizations, and in the author's attitude toward his characters, there is a common view of human existence that provides an insight into Sophocles' themes and philosophy. In *Antigone* (Grene and Latimore's translation), the chorus chants:

> *Words of wisdom it was when someone said,*
> *"The bad becomes the good*
> *to him a god would doom."*
> *Only briefly is that one from under doom.*

The final line of *Oedipus Rex* declares, "Count no mortal happy till he has passed the final limit of his life secure from pain." And in the posthumously produced *Oedipus at Colonus,* Sophocles writes:

> *Not to be born surpasses thought and speech*
> *The second best is to have seen the light*
> *And then to go back quickly whence we came.*

Human life is filled with anguish and pain. If a man, momentarily, enjoys happiness and serenity, terror and horror are never far below the surface. As king of Thebes, Oedipus knew years of peace and success, but the horror which he had tried to escape remained coiled to strike. Such a view of the human lot, however, does not in itself produce tragedy. What elevates Sophocles' violent dramas of patricide and incest, revolt and fratricide to the heights of tragedy is his belief in the power of the human being to accept the horrors of existence with strength and nobility. In the face of the most dire catastrophe—for instance, King Oedipus' discovery that it is he who is causing the plague because he had unknowingly murdered his father and married his mother—the hero rises to pity-evoking grandeur in his acceptance of the unrelieved spiritual and physical suffering that he must endure.

Sophocles' belief in man's dignity is accompanied by another optimistic note—that life is not simply ruled by chance. There is a rational pattern of justice in the universe. In *Oedipus at Colonus,* Oedipus defends himself by declaring that he was a victim; he did not knowingly kill his father and marry his mother. But Oedipus acknowledges that he must have been paying for some crime of an ancestor. A crime disturbs the moral balance and the balance, sooner or later, must be restored by punishment and suffering. Because an individual's view is limited, the fundamental justice of the universe may not be apparent to him, but if he gains sufficient perspective, the law of the gods is manifest. No matter, therefore, how painful and tragic the fate of one individual may be, there is a rational and meaningful pattern in existence.

Of great importance in understanding Sophocles is his view of the role of the gods in human affairs. As H. D. Kitto points out in *Greek Tragedy,* the gods know the destiny of individual men, but such knowledge is not equivalent to ordaining that destiny. The oracles declare that Oedipus will kill his father and marry his mother because they voice what the gods know will happen. But Oedipus is no puppet. He is a human being with certain characteristics and drives which govern his actions, and he must therefore bear the ultimate responsibility for his crime.

Sophocles' view of existence contributed much to the creation of his tragedies. But such a view does not by itself produce that unique type of drama that is labeled "tragedy." Exactly what does constitute tragedy is a very complex and very difficult question. It has preoccupied some of our greatest philosophers and produced no single theory that satisfies everyone and that fully explains the experience a tragedy provides. Aristotle began the discussion when he set down in *Poetics* his thoughts about the nature of tragedy. His ideas have served as the touchstone for all future discussions. Aristotle's observations about tragedy typify his philosophic approach; he did not formulate a theory and then apply it to existing dramas. He studied the tragedies of the great writers of the fifth century B.C. and generalized from his observations of specific details. And though Aristotle's conclusions do not encompass comfortably the many variations in the styles of Aeschylus, Sophocles, and Euripides, nor of many of the later writers of tragedy, they are particularly useful to the student of *Oedipus Rex* because Aristotle was a great admirer of Sophoclean drama and particularly of *Oedipus Rex,* to which he refers frequently in his essay.

Aristotle places much emphasis upon plot, by which he means the way in which a story is developed. On stage, a story must be presented in a series of scenes or incidents, and if the plot is well constructed, every incident is essential to the development of the story. If a dramatist includes scenes that are not essential, his drama lacks unity. A good plot has two parts, divided by the climax, or what Aristotle calls the change in fortune. In the first part all the action leads directly to the climax; in the second part the action depicts the result of the change in fortune. Aristotle's ideas about plot are, of course, valid for any well-constructed play or story. But what makes a particular plot suitable for tragedy? The Greek philosopher lists several essentials among which the most important is that the major character be a man of high station "who is not eminently good or just, yet whose misfortune is brought about not by vice or depravity, but by some error or frailty." The story of this character must excite in the audience the emotions of fear and pity, and the kind of story that best does that will be one in which the tragic incidents occur "between those who are near or dear to one another—if, for example, a brother kills, or intends to kill, a brother, a son his father, a mother her son, a son his mother, or any other deed of the kind. . . ."

The pity and fear experienced by the audience should reach its peak at the climax of the play when the change of fortune occurs. To achieve this peak of emotional response, the change of fortune should be accompanied by "Reversal or by Recognition or by both." As Aristotle defines these terms,

> Reversal of the Situation is a change by which the action veers around to its opposite. . . . Thus in *Oedipus*, the messenger comes to cheer Oedipus and free him from his alarms about his mother, but by revealing who he is, he produces the opposite effect. . . . Recognition, as the name indicates, is a change from ignorance to knowledge, producing love or hate between the persons destined by the poet for good or bad fortune. The best form of recognition is coincident with a Reversal of the Situation as in the *Oedipus*.

In the second part of the plot, the dénouement, the audience is released from the grip of pity and fear. Aristotle does not detail the means by which this purgation is achieved, but it would seem generally to be affected by the hero's nobility in suffering.

Though he does not insist upon unity of time and place, Aristotle does indicate that a story in which the lapse of time approximates the time it takes the story to be enacted and a story which can be dramatized in one setting enhances the effectiveness of the drama. Aside from plot and character, Aristotle also mentions Diction, Thought, Spectacle, and Song as essential elements in tragedy. The diction, or poetry, which the author provides for his characters must be appropriate to the elevated mood of tragedy without being excessively ornate. The thought, which we today generally speak of as theme, is the expression of the dramatist's perceptions about life and about his fellow man. Spectacle and Song—the costumes of the actors, the dramatic incidents enacted on stage, and the dances and songs of the chorus—all contribute to the effect that the tragic poet creates in his audience.

What Aristotle's observations indicate is that *tragedy* is not to be equated with *tragic*. The tragic incidents that we witness or read about daily—the death of an innocent child, murders and suicides, patricides and matricides—do not constitute tragedy. What does constitute tragedy is a dramatic presentation in which tragic incident, heroic character, elevated theme, and poetry are uniquely combined. As Edith Hamilton wrote in *The Greek Way,* "None but a poet can write a tragedy. For tragedy is nothing less than pain transmuted into exaltation by the alchemy of poetry." The unusual sensitivity and perceptiveness of a poet, his power to evoke intense responses in others, and his ability to create beauty with words are essential to tragedy. And yet not all great poets can write tragedy and not all ages can produce great writers of tragedy. Perhaps what a poet-dramatist needs to create tragedy is a period in history in which men can believe, as did Sophocles, that though existence is filled with horror, the human being is strong enough and great enough to accept and endure the direst calamities and even rise above his afflictions with heroic grace.

Certainly it is this kind of vision, in part at least, which enabled Sophocles to transform an ancient legend into a great tragedy. Today, the legend which he used in *Oedipus Rex* has a psychological significance that the Greeks did not attach to it; but it may very well be, as some thinkers argue, that such myths do articulate man's unconscious, and that much of the power of Greek tragedy lies in its expression of our deepest fears and needs. Perhaps that is why through a combination of instinct and tradition, the Greek writers of tragedy returned again and again to stories their audience knew as well as Americans do the story of John Kennedy's death. When Sophocles chose the Oedipus legend, he automatically deprived himself of one of the most valued devices of the dramatist—surprise and novelty. With typical ingenuity, however, Sophocles made use of his audience's knowledge of the tale. One of his most powerful dramatic devices in this play is irony, which, simply defined, is the difference between what is and what seems to be. Because the audience knows what Oedipus does not know, the actions and statements of the doomed king—his cursing the murderer of Laius, his relief at the announcement of the death of Polybus—create dramatic irony. We know he is cursing himself and that his relief is unfounded. The modern reader's appreciation of *Oedipus Rex* can be enhanced, as was the ancient Greeks', by knowing the Oedipal legend.

King Laïos, the ruler of Thebes, and his wife Iocastè were warned by Apollo that their son would kill his father and marry his mother. When a son was born to the royal couple, Laïos drove a pin through the infant's ankles and ordered a faithful shepherd to take the child to Kithairon, a nearby mountain, and leave him to die. The shepherd took pity on the child and gave it instead to a shepherd from Corinth who also grazed his sheep on Kithairon. The Corinthian brought the child with the injured feet (the word Oedipus means "swollen foot") to his childless king and queen, Polybus and Merope, who adopted him as their own.

As Oedipus in the drama tells Iocastè, when he reached young manhood he was told by a man who had drunk too much at a banquet that Polybus and Merope were not his parents. Though he was advised by the king and queen to ignore the statement, Oedipus was troubled. He set out for Delphi to ask the oracle of Apollo who his parents were. The oracle did not answer his question but warned him that he would kill his father and marry his mother. To avoid this fate, Oedipus decided not to return to Corinth. On his way from Delphi, at a crossroads where three roads met, Oedipus was ordered out of the way to permit the passage of a chariot in which the King of Thebes, who was unknown to him, was riding. Oedipus refused and a fight ensued. The young man killed four of the five travelers in the group; the fifth, an attendant of the king, escaped. Continuing on his way, Oedipus reached Thebes which was besieged by the Sphinx—a monster, part bird, part lion, part woman. The Sphinx was killing the young men of the city and demanded, as the price of leaving, the answer to her riddle. So many Theban youths had been killed by the monster that Queen Iocastè offered the throne of Thebes and herself in marriage to the man who could solve the riddle: "What two-footed animal with one voice also goes on four feet and on three feet and goes most slowly when he goes on most feet?" Oedipus correctly replied that the two-footed animal is man who goes on four feet as a creeping child and limps with the aid of a cane in old age. Thebes was freed and Oedipus became its king and married Iocastè. The prophecy of Apollo was now fulfilled. During the years in which Oedipus ruled Thebes well and wisely, Iocastè bore him four children, two boys and two girls. Then suddenly a plague broke out: the crops rotted, animals and people died, and as a delegation of elders approaches Oedipus' castle to appeal to their king for help, the play begins.

❧❧

BIBLIOGRAPHY

Adams, Sinclair. *Sophocles the Playwright*. Toronto: University of Toronto Press, 1957.

Bowra, Cecil. *Sophoclean Tragedy*. Oxford: The Clarendon Press, 1945.

Kitto, H. D. F. *Greek Tragedy*. New York: Doubleday, 1955.

Waldock, Arthur. *Sophocles the Dramatist*. Cambridge: Cambridge University Press, 1951.

Oedipus Rex

AN ENGLISH VERSION

By Dudley Fitts and Robert Fitzgerald

CHARACTERS

OEDIPUS	*King of Thebes*
A PRIEST	
CREON	*brother of Iocastê*
TEIRESIAS	*a blind seer*
IOCASTÊ	*the Queen, wife of Oedipus*
MESSENGER	
SHEPHERD OF LAÏOS	
SECOND MESSENGER	
CHORUS OF THEBAN ELDERS	
ANTIGONE	*}daughters of Oedipus*
ISMENE	

THE SCENE: *Before the palace of Oedipus, King of Thebes. A central door and two lateral doors open onto a platform which runs the length of the façade. On the platform, right and left, are altars; and three steps lead down into the "orchestra," or chorus-ground. At the beginning of the action these steps are crowded by suppliants who have brought branches and chaplets of olive leaves and who lie in various attitudes of despair.* OEDIPUS *enters.*

PROLOGUE

OEDIPUS: My children, generations of the living
    In the line of Kadmos,[1] nursed at his ancient hearth:
    Why have you strewn yourselves before these altars
    In supplication, with your boughs and garlands?
    The breath of incense rises from the city
    With a sound of prayer and lamentation.

                         Children,
    I would not have you speak through messengers,
    And therefore I have come myself to hear you—
    I, Oedipus, who bear the famous name.
    (*To a* PRIEST)
    You, there, since you are eldest in the company,
    Speak for them all, tell me what preys upon you,
    Whether you come in dread, or crave some blessing:
    Tell me, and never doubt that I will help you
    In every way I can; I should be heartless
    Were I not moved to find you suppliant here.
PRIEST: Great Oedipus, O powerful King of Thebes!
    You see how all the ages of our people
    Cling to your altar steps: here are boys
    Who can barely stand alone, and here are priests
    By weight of age, as I am a priest of God,
    And young men chosen from those yet unmarried;
    As for the others, all that multitude,
    They wait with olive chaplets in the squares,
    At the two shrines of Pallas, and where Apollo
    Speaks in the glowing embers.

                         Your own eyes
    Must tell you: Thebes is in her extremity
    And can not lift her head from the surge of death.
    A rust consumes the buds and fruits of the earth;
    The herds are sick; children die unborn,
    And labor is vain. The god of plague and pyre
    Raids like detestable lightning through the city,
    And all the house of Kadmos is laid waste,

---

[1] *Kadmos:* founder of Thebes.

All emptied, and all darkened: Death alone
Battens upon the misery of Thebes.

You are not one of the immortal gods, we know;
Yet we have come to you to make our prayer
As to the man of all men best in adversity
And wisest in the ways of God. You saved us
From the Sphinx, that flinty singer, and the tribute
We paid to her so long; yet you were never
Better informed than we, nor could we teach you:
It was some god breathed in you to set us free.

Therefore, O mighty King, we turn to you:
Find us our safety, find us a remedy,
Whether by counsel of the gods or men.
A king of wisdom tested in the past
Can act in a time of troubles, and act well.
Noblest of men, restore
Life to your city! Think how all men call you
Liberator for your triumph long ago;
Ah, when your years of kingship are remembered,
Let them not say *We rose, but later fell—*
Keep the State from going down in the storm!
Once, years ago, with happy augury,
You brought us fortune; be the same again!
No man questions your power to rule the land:
But rule over men, not over a dead city!
Ships are only hulls, citadels are nothing,
When no life moves in the empty passageways.
OEDIPUS: Poor children! You may be sure I know
All that you longed for in your coming here.
I know that you are deathly sick; and yet,
Sick as you are, not one is as sick as I.
Each of you suffers in himself alone
His anguish, not another's; but my spirit
Groans for the city, for myself, for you.

I was not sleeping, you are not waking me.
No, I have been in tears for a long while
And in my restless thought walked many ways.
In all my search, I found one helpful course,

And that I have taken: I have sent Creon,
Son of Menoikeus, brother of the Queen,
To Delphi, Apollo's place of revelation,
To learn there, if he can,
What act or pledge of mine may save the city.
I have counted the days, and now, this very day,
I am troubled, for he has overstayed his time.
What is he doing? He has been gone too long.
Yet whenever he comes back, I should do ill
To scant whatever hint the god may give.
PRIEST: It is a timely promise. At this instant
   They tell me Creon is here.
OEDIPUS: O Lord Apollo!
   May his news be fair as his face is radiant!
PRIEST: It could not be otherwise: he is crowned with bay,
   The chaplet is thick with berries.
OEDIPUS: We shall soon know;
   He is near enough to hear us now.

(*Enter* CREON)

                                O Prince:
Brother: son of Menoikeus:
What answer do you bring us from the god?
CREON: It is favorable. I can tell you, great afflictions
   Will turn out well, if they are taken well.
OEDIPUS: What was the oracle? These vague words
   Leave me still hanging between hope and fear.
CREON: Is it your pleasure to hear me with all these
   Gathered around us? I am prepared to speak,
   But should we not go in?
OEDIPUS: Let them all hear it.
   It is for them I suffer, more than for myself.
CREON: Then I will tell you what I heard at Delphi.

   In plain words
   The god commands us to expel from the land of Thebes
   An old defilement that it seems we shelter.
   It is a deathly thing, beyond expiation.
   We must not let it feed upon us longer.
OEDIPUS: What defilement? How shall we rid ourselves of it?
CREON: By exile or death, blood for blood. It was

Murder that brought the plague-wind on the city.

OEDIPUS: Murder of whom? Surely the god has named him?

CREON: My lord: long ago Laïos was our king,
Before you came to govern us.

OEDIPUS: I know;
I learned of him from others; I never saw him.

CREON: He was murdered; and Apollo commands us now
To take revenge upon whoever killed him.

OEDIPUS: Upon whom? Where are they? Where shall we find a clue
To solve that crime, after so many years?

CREON: Here in this land, he said.

                                    If we make enquiry,
We may touch things that otherwise escape us.

OEDIPUS: Tell me: Was Laïos murdered in his house,
Or in the fields, or in some foreign country?

CREON: He said he planned to make a pilgrimage.
He did not come home again.

OEDIPUS: And was there no one,
No witness, no companion, to tell what happened?

CREON: They were all killed but one, and he got away
So frightened that he could remember one thing only.

OEDIPUS: What was that one thing? One may be the key
To everything, if we resolve to use it.

CREON: He said that a band of highwaymen attacked them,
Outnumbered them, and overwhelmed the King.

OEDIPUS: Strange, that a highwayman should be so daring—
Unless some faction here bribed him to do it.

CREON: We thought of that. But after Laïos' death
New troubles arose and we had no avenger.

OEDIPUS: What troubles could prevent your hunting down the
killers?

CREON: The riddling Sphinx's song
Made us deaf to all mysteries but her own.

OEDIPUS: Then once more I must bring what is dark to light.
It is most fitting that Apollo shows,
As you do, this compunction for the dead.
You shall see how I stand by you, as I should,
To avenge the city and the city's god,
And not as though it were for some distant friend,
But for my own sake, to be rid of evil.
Whoever killed King Laïos might—who knows?—

Decide at any moment to kill me as well.
By avenging the murdered king I protect myself.

Come, then, my children: leave the altar steps,
Lift up your olive boughs!
                                    One of you go
And summon the people of Kadmos to gather here.
I will do all that I can; you may tell them that.

                                                    (*Exit a Page.*)

So, with the help of God,
We shall be saved—or else indeed we are lost.
PRIEST: Let us rise, children. It was for this we came,
And now the King has promised it himself.
Phoibos² has sent us an oracle; may he descend
Himself to save us and drive out the plague.
(*Exeunt* OEDIPUS *and* CREON *into the palace by the central door. The*
PRIEST *and the* SUPPLIANTS *disperse R. and L. After a short pause the*
CHORUS *enters the orchestra.*)

PÁRODOS

CHORUS: What is the god singing in his profound   STROPHE I³
    Delphi of gold and shadow?
    What oracle for Thebes, the sunwhipped city?

    Fear unjoints me, the roots of my heart tremble.

    Now I remember, O Healer, your power, and wonder:
    Will you send doom like a sudden cloud, or weave it
    Like nightfall of the past?

    Ah no: be merciful, issue of holy sound:
    Dearest to our expectancy: be tender!

                                                    ANTISTROPHE I⁴

    Let me pray to Athenê, the immortal daughter of Zeus,
    And to Artemis her sister
    Who keeps her famous throne in the market ring,
    And to Apollo, bowman at the far butts of heaven—

                                        .   .   .

---

² *Phoibos:* Apollo.
³ *Strophe:* indicates the movement of the chorus on the stage from right to
left as it chants.
⁴ *Antistrophe:* chorus moves from left to right.

O gods, descend! Like three streams leap against
The fires of our grief, the fires of darkness;
Be swift to bring us rest!

As in the old time from the brilliant house
Of air you stepped to save us, come again!

Now our afflictions have no end.   STROPHE 2
Now all our stricken host lies down
And no man fights off death with his mind;

The noble plowland bears no grain,
And groaning mothers can not bear—

See, how our lives like birds take wing,
Like sparks that fly when a fire soars,
To the shore of the god of evening.

The plague burns on, it is pitiless,   ANTISTROPHE 2
Though pallid children laden with death
Lie unwept in the stony ways,

And old gray women by every path
Flock to the strand about the altars

There to strike their breasts and cry
Worship of Zeus in wailing prayers:
Be kind, God's golden child! [5]

There are no swords in this attack by fire,   STROPHE 3
No shields, but we are ringed with cries.

Send the besieger plunging from our homes
Into the vast sea-room of the Atlantic
Or into the waves that foam eastward of Thrace—

For the day ravages what the night spares—

Destroy our enemy, lord of the thunder!
Let him be riven by lightning from heaven!

Phoibos Apollo,[6] stretch the sun's bowstring,   ANTISTROPHE 3
That golden cord, until it sing for us,

[5] *God's golden child*: Athenê, daughter of Zeus.
   [6] *Apollo*: god of light and truth; the oracle of Apollo serves to connect man
and the gods.

Flashing arrows in heaven!

                      Artemis, Huntress,
Race with flaring lights upon our mountains!

O scarlet god, O golden-banded brow,
O Theban Bacchos in a storm of Maenads,[7]

          (*Enter* OEDIPUS, *center.*)

Whirl upon Death, that all the Undying hate!
Come with blinding cressets, come in joy!

SCENE I

OEDIPUS: Is this your prayer? It may be answered. Come,
Listen to me, act as the crisis demands,
And you shall have relief from all these evils.

Until now I was a stranger to this tale,
As I had been a stranger to the crime.
Could I track down the murderer without a clue?
But now, friends,
As one who became a citizen after the murder,
I make this proclamation to all Thebans:
If any man knows by whose hands Laïos, son of Labdakos,
Met his death, I direct that man to tell me everything,
No matter what he fears for having so long withheld it.
Let it stand as promised that no further trouble
Will come to him, but he may leave the land in safety.

Moreover: If anyone knows the murderer to be foreign,
Let him not keep silent: he shall have his reward from me.
However, if he does conceal it; if any man
Fearing for his friend or for himself disobeys this edict,
Hear what I propose to do:

I solemnly forbid the people of this country,
Where power and throne are mine, ever to receive that man
Or speak to him, no matter who he is, or let him
Join in sacrifice, lustration,[8] or in prayer.

    [7] *Theban Bacchos . . . Maenads:* according to the myth, the god of wine
was born in Thebes. He was attended by dancing and singing women, called
Maenads.
    [8] *lustration:* a sacrificial rite of purification.

I decree that he be driven from every house,
Being, as he is, corruption itself to us: the Delphic
Voice of Zeus has pronounced this revelation.
Thus I associate myself with the oracle
And take the side of the murdered king.

As for the criminal, I pray to God—
Whether it be a lurking thief, or one of a number—
I pray that that man's life be consumed in evil and wretchedness.
And as for me, this curse applies no less
If it should turn out that the culprit is my guest here,
Sharing my hearth.

      You have heard the penalty.
I lay it on you now to attend to this
For my sake, for Apollo's, for the sick
Sterile city that heaven has abandoned.
Suppose the oracle had given you no command:
Should this defilement go uncleansed for ever?
You should have found the murderer: your king,
A noble king, had been destroyed!

        Now I,
Having the power that he held before me,
Having his bed, begetting children there
Upon his wife, as he would have, had he lived—
Their son would have been my children's brother,
If Laïos had had luck in fatherhood!
(But surely ill luck rushed upon his reign)—
I say I take the son's part, just as though
I were his son, to press the fight for him
And see it won! I'll find the hand that brought
Death to Labdakos' and Polydoros' child,[9]
Heir of Kadmos' and Agenor's line.
And as for those who fail me,
May the gods deny them the fruit of the earth,
Fruit of the womb, and may they rot utterly!
Let them be wretched as we are wretched, and worse!

For you, for loyal Thebans, and for all
Who find my actions right, I pray the favor
Of justice, and of all the immortal gods.

[9] *child:* Laïos, the murdered king.

CHORAGOS:[10] Since I am under oath, my lord, I swear
    I did not do the murder, I can not name
    The murderer. Might not the oracle
    That has ordained the search tell where to find him?
OEDIPUS: An honest question. But no man in the world
    Can make the gods do more than the gods will.
CHORAGOS: There is one last expedient—
OEDIPUS: Tell me what it is.
    Though it seem slight, you must not hold it back.
CHORAGOS: A lord clairvoyant to the lord Apollo,
    As we all know, is the skilled Teiresias.
    One might learn much about this from him, Oedipus.
OEDIPUS: I am not wasting time:
    Creon spoke of this, and I have sent for him—
    Twice, in fact; it is strange that he is not here.
CHORAGOS: The other matter—that old report—seems useless.
OEDIPUS: Tell me. I am interested in all reports.
CHORAGOS: The King was said to have been killed by highwaymen.
OEDIPUS: I know. But we have no witnesses to that.
CHORAGOS: If the killer can feel a particle of dread,
    Your curse will bring him out of hiding!
OEDIPUS: No.
    The man who dared that act will fear no curse.

(Enter the blind seer TEIRESIAS, *led by a Page.)*

CHORAGOS: But there is one man who may detect the criminal.
    This is Teiresias, this is the holy prophet
    In whom, alone of all men, truth was born.
OEDIPUS: Teiresias: seer: student of mysteries,
    Of all that's taught and all that no man tells,
    Secrets of Heaven and secrets of the earth:
    Blind though you are, you know the city lies
    Sick with plague; and from this plague, my lord,
    We find that you alone can guard or save us.

    Possibly you did not hear the messengers?
    Apollo, when we sent to him,
    Sent us back word that this great pestilence
    Would lift, but only if we established clearly
    The identity of those who murdered Laïos.

[10] *Choragos:* leader of the chorus.

They must be killed or exiled.

Can you use

Birdflight or any art of divination
To purify yourself, and Thebes, and me
From this contagion? We are in your hands.
There is no fairer duty
Than that of helping others in distress.

TEIRESIAS: How dreadful knowledge of the truth can be
   When there's no help in truth! I knew this well,
   But did not act on it: else I should not have come.

OEDIPUS: What is troubling you? Why are your eyes so cold?

TEIRESIAS: Let me go home. Bear your own fate, and I'll
   Bear mine. It is better so: trust what I say.

OEDIPUS: What you say is ungracious and unhelpful
   To your native country. Do not refuse to speak.

TEIRESIAS: When it comes to speech, your own is neither temperate
   Nor opportune. I wish to be more prudent.

OEDIPUS: In God's name, we all beg you—

TEIRESIAS: You are all ignorant.
   No; I will never tell you what I know.
   Now it is my misery; then, it would be yours.

OEDIPUS: What! You do know something, and will not tell us?
   You would betray us all and wreck the State?

TEIRESIAS: I do not intend to torture myself, or you.
   Why persist in asking? You will not persuade me.

OEDIPUS: What a wicked old man you are! You'd try a stone's
   Patience! Out with it! Have you no feeling at all?

TEIRESIAS: You call me unfeeling. If you could only see
   The nature of your own feelings . . .

OEDIPUS: Why,
   Who would not feel as I do? Who could endure
   Your arrogance toward the city?

TEIRESIAS: What does it matter!
   Whether I speak or not, it is bound to come.

OEDIPUS: Then, if "it" is bound to come, you are bound to tell me.

TEIRESIAS: No, I will not go on. Rage as you please.

OEDIPUS: Rage? Why not!

And I'll tell you what I think:

   You planned it, you had it done, you all but
   Killed him with your own hands: if you had eyes,
   I'd say the crime was yours, and yours alone.

TEIRESIAS: So? I charge you, then,
   Abide by the proclamation you have made:
   From this day forth
   Never speak again to these men or to me;
   You yourself are the pollution of this country.

OEDIPUS: You dare say that! Can you possibly think you have
   Some way of going free, after such insolence?

TEIRESIAS: I have gone free. It is the truth sustains me.

OEDIPUS: Who taught you shamelessness? It was not your craft.

TEIRESIAS: You did. You made me speak. I did not want to.

OEDIPUS: Speak what? Let me hear it again more clearly.

TEIRESIAS: Was it not clear before? Are you tempting me?

OEDIPUS: I did not understand it. Say it again.

TEIRESIAS: I say that you are the murderer whom you seek.

OEDIPUS: Now twice you have spat out infamy. You'll pay for it!

TEIRESIAS: Would you care for more? Do you wish to be really angry?

OEDIPUS: Say what you will. Whatever you say is worthless.

TEIRESIAS: I say that you live in hideous love with her
   Who is nearest you in blood. You are blind to the evil.

OEDIPUS: It seems you can go on mouthing like this for ever.

TEIRESIAS: I can, if there is power in truth.

OEDIPUS: There is:
   But not for you, not for you,
   You sightless, witless, senseless, mad old man!

TEIRESIAS: You are the madman. There is no one here
   Who will not curse you soon, as you curse me.

OEDIPUS: You child of endless night! You can not hurt me
   Or any other man who sees the sun.

TEIRESIAS: True: it is not from me your fate will come.
   That lies within Apollo's competence,
   As it is his concern.

OEDIPUS: Tell me:
   Are you speaking for Creon, or for yourself?

TEIRESIAS: Creon is no threat. You weave your own doom.

OEDIPUS: Wealth, power, craft of statesmanship!
   Kingly position, everywhere admired!
   What savage envy is stored up against these,
   If Creon, whom I trusted, Creon my friend,
   For this great office which the city once
   Put in my hands unsought—if for this power
   Creon desires in secret to destroy me!

                              .   .   .

He has bought this decrepit fortune-teller, this
Collector of dirty pennies, this prophet fraud—
Why, he is no more clairvoyant than I am!

                                    Tell us:

Has your mystic mummery ever approached the truth?
When that hellcat the Sphinx was performing here,
What help were you to these people?
Her magic was not for the first man who came along:
It demanded a real exorcist. Your birds—
What good were they? or the gods, for the matter of that?
But I came by,
Oedipus, the simple man, who knows nothing—
I thought it out for myself, no birds helped me!
And this is the man you think you can destroy,
That you may be close to Creon when he's king!
Well, you and your friend Creon, it seems to me,
Will suffer most. If you were not an old man,
You would have paid already for your plot.

CHORAGOS: We can not see that his words or yours
    Have been spoken except in anger, Oedipus,
    And of anger we have no need. How can God's will
    Be accomplished best? That is what most concerns us.

TEIRESIAS: You are a king. But where argument's concerned
    I am your man, as much a king as you.
    I am not your servant, but Apollo's.
    I have no need of Creon to speak for me.

    Listen to me. You mock my blindness, do you?
    But I say that you, with both your eyes, are blind:
    You can not see the wretchedness of your life,
    Nor in whose house you live, no, nor with whom.
    Who are your father and mother? Can you tell me?
    You do not even know the blind wrongs
    That you have done them, on earth and in the world below.
    But the double lash of your parents' curse will whip you
    Out of this land some day, with only night
    Upon your precious eyes.
    Your cries then—where will they not be heard?
    What fastness of Kithairon [11] will not echo them?
    And that bridal-descant of yours—you'll know it then,

---

[11] *Kithairon:* the mountain where the infant Oedipus was to be left to die.

The song they sang when you came here to Thebes
And found your misguided berthing.
All this, and more, that you can not guess at now,
Will bring you to yourself among your children.

Be angry, then. Curse Creon. Curse my words.
I tell you, no man that walks upon the earth
Shall be rooted out more horribly than you.

OEDIPUS: Am I to bear this from him?—Damnation
Take you! Out of this place! Out of my sight!

TEIRESIAS: I would not have come at all if you had not asked me.

OEDIPUS: Could I have told that you'd talk nonsense, that
You'd come here to make a fool of yourself, and of me?

TEIRESIAS: A fool? Your parents thought me sane enough.

OEDIPUS: My parents again!—Wait: who were my parents?

TEIRESIAS: This day will give you a father, and break your heart.

OEDIPUS: Your infantile riddles! Your damned abracadabra!

TEIRESIAS: You were a great man once at solving riddles.

OEDIPUS: Mock me with that if you like; you will find it true.

TEIRESIAS: It was true enough. It brought about your ruin.

OEDIPUS: But if it saved this town?

TEIRESIAS (*to the Page*): Boy, give me your hand.

OEDIPUS: Yes, boy; lead him away.

                                        —While you are here
We can do nothing. Go; leave us in peace.

TEIRESIAS: I will go when I have said what I have to say.
How can you hurt me? And I tell you again:
The man you have been looking for all this time,
The damned man, the murderer of Laïos,
That man is in Thebes. To your mind he is foreign-born,
But it will soon be shown that he is a Theban,
A revelation that will fail to please.

                                        A blind man,
Who has his eyes now; a penniless man, who is rich now;
And he will go tapping the strange earth with his staff.
To the children with whom he lives now he will be
Brother and father—the very same; to her
Who bore him, son and husband—the very same
Who came to his father's bed, wet with his father's blood.

Enough. Go think that over.
If later you find error in what I have said,

You may say that I have no skill in prophecy.

(*Exit* TEIRESIAS, *led by his Page.* OEDIPUS *goes into the palace.*)

ODE I

CHORUS: The Delphic stone [12] of prophecies   STROPHE 1
Remembers ancient regicide
And a still bloody hand.
That killer's hour of flight has come.
He must be stronger than riderless
Coursers of untiring wind,
For the son of Zeus armed with his father's thunder
Leaps in lightning after him;
And the Furies follow him, the sad Furies.

Holy Parnassos [13] peak of snow   ANTISTROPHE 1
Flashes and blinds that secret man,
That all shall hunt him down:
Though he may roam the forest shade
Like a bull gone wild from pasture
To rage through glooms of stone.
Doom comes down on him; flight will not avail him;
For the world's heart calls him desolate,
And the immortal Furies follow, for ever follow.

But now a wilder thing is heard   STROPHE 2
From the old man skilled at hearing Fate in the wingbeat of a bird.
Bewildered as a blown bird, my soul hovers and can not find
Foothold in this debate, or any reason or rest of mind.
But no man ever brought—none can bring
Proof of strife between Thebes' royal house,
Labdakos' line, and the son of Polybos;[14]
And never until now has any man brought word
Of Laïos' dark death staining Oedipus the King.

Divine Zeus and Apollo hold   ANTISTROPHE 2
Perfect intelligence alone of all tales ever told;
And well though this diviner works, he works in his own night;
No man can judge that rough unknown or trust in second sight,

[12] *Delphic stone:* the Delphic oracle.
[13] *Parnassos:* a mountain, sacred to Apollo.
[14] *son of Polybos:* Oedipus, who was adopted by that king of Corinth.

For wisdom changes hands among the wise.
Shall I believe my great lord criminal
At a raging word that a blind old man let fall?
I saw him, when the carrion woman [15] faced him of old,
Prove his heroic mind! These evil words are lies.

SCENE II

CREON: Men of Thebes:
　　I am told that heavy accusations
　　Have been brought against me by King Oedipus.

　　I am not the kind of man to bear this tamely.

　　If in these present difficulties
　　He holds me accountable for any harm to him
　　Through anything I have said or done—why, then,
　　I do not value life in this dishonor.
　　It is not as though this rumor touched upon
　　Some private indiscretion. The matter is grave.
　　The fact is that I am being called disloyal
　　To the State, to my fellow citizens, to my friends.
CHORAGOS: He may have spoken in anger, not from his mind.
CREON: But did you not hear him say I was the one
　　Who seduced the old prophet into lying?
CHORAGOS: The thing was said; I do not know how seriously.
CREON: But you were watching him! Were his eyes steady?
　　Did he look like a man in his right mind?
CHORAGOS:　　　　　　　　　　　　　　I do not know.
　　I can not judge the behavior of great men.
　　But here is the King himself.

(*Enter* OEDIPUS.)

OEDIPUS:　　　　　　　　　　　So you dared come back.
　　Why? How brazen of you to come to my house,
　　You murderer!

　　　　　　　　Do you think I do not know
　　That you plotted to kill me, plotted to steal my throne?
　　Tell me, in God's name: am I coward, a fool,
　　That you should dream you could accomplish this?

---

[15] *carrion woman:* the Sphinx.

A fool who could not see your slippery game?
A coward, not to fight back when I saw it?
You are the fool, Creon, are you not? hoping
Without support or friends to get a throne?
Thrones may be won or bought: you could do neither.

CREON: Now listen to me. You have talked; let me talk, too.
You can not judge unless you know the facts.

OEDIPUS: You speak well: there is one fact; but I find it hard
To learn from the deadliest enemy I have.

CREON: That above all I must dispute with you.

OEDIPUS: That above all I will not hear you deny.

CREON: If you think there is anything good in being stubborn
Against all reason, then I say you are wrong.

OEDIPUS: If you think a man can sin against his own kind
And not be punished for it, I say you are mad.

CREON: I agree. But tell me: what have I done to you?

OEDIPUS: You advised me to send for that wizard, did you not?

CREON: I did. I should do it again.

OEDIPUS: Very well. Now tell me:
How long has it been since Laïos—

CREON: What of Laïos?

OEDIPUS: Since he vanished in that onset by the road?

CREON: It was long ago, a long time.

OEDIPUS: And this prophet,
Was he practicing here then?

CREON: He was; and with honor, as now.

OEDIPUS: Did he speak of me at that time?

CREON: He never did;
At least, not when I was present.

OEDIPUS: But . . . the enquiry?
I suppose you held one?

CREON: We did, but we learned nothing.

OEDIPUS: Why did the prophet not speak against me then?

CREON: I do not know; and I am the kind of man
Who holds his tongue when he has no facts to go on.

OEDIPUS: There's one fact that you know, and you could tell it.

CREON: What fact is that? If I know it, you shall have it.

OEDIPUS: If he were not involved with you, he could not say
That it was I who murdered Laïos.

CREON: If he says that, you are the one that knows it—
But now it is my turn to question you.

OEDIPUS: Put your questions. I am no murderer.

CREON: First, then: You married my sister?

OEDIPUS: I married your sister.

CREON: And you rule the kingdom equally with her?

OEDIPUS: Everything that she wants she has from me.

CREON: And I am the third, equal to both of you?

OEDIPUS: That is why I call you a bad friend.

CREON: No. Reason it out, as I have done.

Think of this first: Would any sane man prefer
Power, with all a king's anxieties,
To that same power and the grace of sleep?
Certainly not I.
I have never longed for the king's power—only his rights.
Would any wise man differ from me in this?
As matters stand, I have my way in everything
With your consent, and no responsibilities.
If I were king, I should be a slave to policy.

How could I desire a scepter more
Than what is now mine—untroubled influence?
No, I have not gone mad; I need no honors,
Except those with the perquisites I have now.
I am welcome everywhere; every man salutes me,
And those who want your favor seek my ear,
Since I know how to manage what they ask.
Should I exchange this ease for that anxiety?
Besides, no sober mind is treasonable.
I hate anarchy
And never would deal with any man who likes it.

Test what I have said. Go to the priestess
At Delphi, ask if I quoted her correctly.
And as for this other thing: if I am found
Guilty of treason with Teiresias,
Then sentence me to death! You have my word
It is a sentence I should cast my vote for—
But not without evidence!
                              You do wrong
When you take good men for bad, bad men for good.
A true friend thrown aside—why, life itself
Is not more precious!
                    In time you will know this well:

For time, and time alone, will show the just man,
　　Though scoundrels are discovered in a day.
CHORAGOS: This is well said, and a prudent man would ponder it.
　　Judgments too quickly formed are dangerous.
OEDIPUS: But is he not quick in his duplicity?
　　And shall I not be quick to parry him?
　　Would you have me stand still, hold my peace, and let
　　This man win everything, through my inaction?
CREON: And you want—what is it, then? To banish me?
OEDIPUS: No, not exile. It is your death I want,
　　So that all the world may see what treason means.
CREON: You will persist, then? You will not believe me?
OEDIPUS: How can I believe you?
CREON:　　　　　　　　　　Then you are a fool.
OEDIPUS: To save myself?
CREON:　　　　　　　　In justice, think of me.
OEDIPUS: You are evil incarnate.
CREON:　　　　　　　　　　But suppose that you are wrong?
OEDIPUS: Still I must rule.
CREON:　　　　　　　　But not if you rule badly.
OEDIPUS: O city, city!
CREON:　　　　　　It is my city, too!
CHORAGOS: Now, my lords, be still. I see the Queen,
　　Iocastê, coming from her palace chambers;
　　And it is time she came, for the sake of you both.
　　This dreadful quarrel can be resolved through her.

(*Enter* IOCASTÊ.)

IOCASTÊ: Poor foolish men, what wicked din is this?
　　With Thebes sick to death, is it not shameful
　　That you should rake some private quarrel up?
　　(*To* OEDIPUS)
　　Come into the house.
　　　　　　　　　—And you, Creon, go now:
　　Let us have no more of this tumult over nothing.
CREON: Nothing? No, sister: what your husband plans for me
　　Is one of two great evils: exile or death.
OEDIPUS: He is right.
　　　　　　　　Why, woman I have caught him squarely
　　Plotting against my life.
CREON:　　　　　　　No! Let me die.

Accurst if ever I have wished you harm!

IOCASTÊ: Ah, believe it, Oedipus!

In the name of the gods, respect this oath of his
For my sake, for the sake of these people here!   STROPHE 1

CHORAGOS: Open your mind to her, my lord. Be ruled by her, I beg
you!

OEDIPUS: What would you have me do?

CHORAGOS: Respect Creon's word. He has never spoken like a fool,
And now he has sworn an oath.

OEDIPUS: You know what you·ask?

CHORAGOS: I do.

OEDIPUS: Speak on, then.

CHORAGOS: A friend so sworn should not be baited so,
In blind malice, and without final proof.

OEDIPUS: You are aware, I hope, that what you say
Means death for me, or exile at the least.

CHORAGOS: No, I swear by Helios,[16] first in Heaven!   STROPHE 2
     May I die friendless and accurst,
The worst of deaths, if ever I meant that!
                    It is the withering fields
                         That hurt my sick heart:
                    Must we bear all these ills,
                         And now your bad blood as well?

OEDIPUS: Then let him go. And let me die, if I must,
Or be driven by him in shame from the land of Thebes.
It is your unhappiness, and not his talk,
That touches me.
                    As for him—
Wherever he is, I will hate him as long as I live.

CREON: Ugly in yielding, as you were ugly in rage!
Natures like yours chiefly torment themselves.

OEDIPUS: Can you not go? Can you not leave me?

CREON: ·   I can.
You do not know me; but the city knows me,
And in its eyes I am just, if not in yours.

                                        (*Exit* CREON.)

                                                  ANTISTROPHE 1

CHORAGOS: Lady Iocastê, did you not ask the King to go to his
chambers?

[16] *Helios:* the sun-god.

IOCASTÊ: First tell me what has happened.

CHORAGOS: There was suspicion without evidence; yet it rankled
  As even false charges will.

IOCASTÊ: On both sides?

CHORAGOS: On both.

IOCASTÊ: But what
  was said?

CHORAGOS: Oh let it rest, let it be done with!
  Have we not suffered enough?

OEDIPUS: You see to what your decency has brought you:
  You have made difficulties where my heart saw none.

                                        ANTISTROPHE 2

CHORAGOS: Oedipus, it is not once only I have told you—
      You must know I should count myself unwise
    To the point of madness, should I now forsake you—
            You, under whose hand,
              In the storm of another time,
            Our dear land sailed out free.
              But now stand fast at the helm!

IOCASTÊ: In God's name, Oedipus, inform your wife as well:
  Why are you so set in this hard anger?

OEDIPUS: I will tell you, for none of these men deserves
  My confidence as you do. It is Creon's work,
  His treachery, his plotting against me.

IOCASTÊ: Go on, if you can make this clear to me.

OEDIPUS: He charges me with the murder of Laïos.

IOCASTÊ: Has he some knowledge? Or does he speak from hearsay?

OEDIPUS: He would not commit himself to such a charge,
  But he has brought in that damnable soothsayer
  To tell his story.

IOCASTÊ: Set your mind at rest.
  If it is a question of soothsayers, I tell you
  That you will find no man whose craft gives knowledge
  Of the unknowable.
                    Here is my proof:

An oracle was reported to Laïos once
(I will not say from Phoibos himself, but from
His appointed ministers, at any rate)
That his doom would be death at the hands of his own son—

His son, born of his flesh and of mine!
Now, you remember the story: Laïos was killed
By marauding strangers where three highways meet;
But his child had not been three days in this world
Before the King had pierced the baby's ankles
And had him left to die on a lonely mountain.

Thus, Apollo never caused that child
To kill his father, and it was not Laïos' fate
To die at the hands of his son, as he had feared.
This is what prophets and prophecies are worth!
Have no dread of them.
                              It is God himself
Who can show us what he wills, in his own way.

OEDIPUS: How strange a shadowy memory crossed my mind,
    Just now while you were speaking; it chilled my heart.

IOCASTÊ: What do you mean? What memory do you speak of?

OEDIPUS: If I understand you, Laïos was killed
    At a place where three roads meet.

IOCASTÊ: So it was said;
    We have no later story.

OEDIPUS: Where did it happen?

IOCASTÊ: Phokis, it is called: at a place where the Theban Way
    Divides into the roads toward Delphi and Daulia.

OEDIPUS: When?

IOCASTÊ: We had the news not long before you came
    And proved the right to your succession here.

OEDIPUS: Ah, what net has God been weaving for me?

IOCASTÊ: Oedipus! Why does this trouble you?

OEDIPUS: Do not ask me yet.
    First, tell me how Laïos looked, and tell me
    How old he was.

IOCASTÊ: He was tall, his hair just touched
    With white; his form was not unlike your own.

OEDIPUS: I think that I myself may be accurst
    By my own ignorant edict.

IOCASTÊ: You speak strangely.
    It makes me tremble to look at you, my King.

OEDIPUS: I am not sure that the blind man can not see.
    But I should know better if you were to tell me—

IOCASTÊ: Anything—though I dread to hear you ask it.

OEDIPUS: Was the King lightly escorted, or did he ride
　　With a large company, as a ruler should?
IOCASTÊ: There were five men with him in all: one was a herald;
　　And a single chariot, which he was driving.
OEDIPUS: Alas, that makes it plain enough!

　　　　　　　　　　　　　　　But who—
　　Who told you how it happened?
IOCASTÊ:　　　　　　　　　A household servant,
　　The only one to escape.
OEDIPUS:　　　　　　　And is he still
　　A servant of ours?
IOCASTÊ:　　　　No; for when he came back at last
　　And found you enthroned in the place of the dead king,
　　He came to me, touched my hand with his, and begged
　　That I would send him away to the frontier district
　　Where only the shepherds go—
　　As far away from the city as I could send him.
　　I granted his prayer; for although the man was a slave,
　　He had earned more than this favor at my hands.
OEDIPUS: Can he be called back quickly?
IOCASTÊ:　　　　　　　　　　Easily.
　　But why?
OEDIPUS:　　I have taken too much upon myself
　　Without enquiry; therefore I wish to consult him.
IOCASTÊ: Then he shall come.

　　　　　　　　　But am I not one also
　　To whom you might confide these fears of yours?
OEDIPUS: That is your right; it will not be denied you,
　　Now least of all; for I have reached a pitch
　　Of wild foreboding. Is there anyone
　　To whom I should sooner speak?

　　Polybos of Corinth is my father.
　　My mother is a Dorian: Meropê.
　　I grew up chief among the men of Corinth
　　Until a strange thing happened—
　　Not worth my passion, it may be, but strange.

　　At a feast, a drunken man maundering in his cups
　　Cries out that I am not my father's son!

　　I contained myself that night, though I felt anger
　　And a sinking heart. The next day I visited

My father and mother, and questioned them. They stormed,
Calling it all the slanderous rant of a fool;
And this relieved me. Yet the suspicion
Remained always aching in my mind;
I knew there was talk; I could not rest;
And finally, saying nothing to my parents,
I went to the shrine at Delphi.

The god dismissed my question without reply;
He spoke of other things.

               Some were clear,
Full of wretchedness, dreadful, unbearable:
As, that I should lie with my own mother, breed
Children from whom all men would turn their eyes;
And that I should be my father's murderer.

I heard all this, and fled. And from that day
Corinth to me was only in the stars
Descending in that quarter of the sky,
As I wandered farther and farther on my way
To a land where I should never see the evil
Sung by the oracle. And I came to this country
Where, so you say, King Laïos was killed.

I will tell you all that happened there, my lady.

There were three highways
Coming together at a place I passed;
And there a herald came towards me, and a chariot
Drawn by horses, with a man such as you describe
Seated in it. The groom leading the horses
Forced me off the road at his lord's command;
But as this charioteer lurched over towards me
I struck him in my rage. The old man saw me
And brought his double goad down upon my head
As I came abreast.

           He was paid back, and more!
Swinging my club in this right hand I knocked him
Out of his car, and he rolled on the ground.

                  I killed him.

I killed them all.
Now if that stranger and Laïos were—kin,

Where is a man more miserable than I?
More hated by the gods? Citizen and alien alike
Must never shelter me or speak to me—
I must be shunned by all.

                    And I myself
Pronounced this malediction upon myself!
Think of it: I have touched you with these hands,
These hands that killed your husband. What defilement!

Am I all evil, then? It must be so,
Since I must flee from Thebes, yet never again
See my own countrymen, my own country,
For fear of joining my mother in marriage
And killing Polybos, my father.

                    Ah,
If I was created so, born to this fate,
Who could deny the savagery of God?

O holy majesty of heavenly powers!
May I never see that day! Never!
Rather let me vanish from the race of men
Than know the abomination destined me!

CHORAGOS: We too, my lord, have felt dismay at this.
But there is hope: you have yet to hear the shepherd.

OEDIPUS: Indeed, I fear no other hope is left me.

IOCASTÊ: What do you hope from him when he comes?

OEDIPUS: This much:
If his account of the murder tallies with yours,
Then I am cleared.

IOCASTÊ: What was it that I said
Of such importance?

OEDIPUS: Why, "marauders," you said,
Killed the King, according to this man's story.
If he maintains that still, if there were several,
Clearly the guilt is not mine: I was alone.
But if he says one man, singlehanded, did it,
Then the evidence all points to me.

IOCASTÊ: You may be sure that he said there were several;
And can he call back that story now? He can not.
The whole city heard it as plainly as I.
But suppose he alters some detail of it:
He can not ever show that Laïos' death

Fulfilled the oracle: for Apollo said
My child was doomed to kill him; and my child—
Poor baby!—it was my child that died first.
No. From now on, where oracles are concerned,
I would not waste a second thought on any.

OEDIPUS: You may be right.

But come: let someone go
For the shepherd at once. This matter must be settled.

IOCASTÊ: I will send for him.

I would not wish to cross you in anything,
And surely not in this.—Let us go in.

(Exeunt into the palace.)

ODE II

CHORUS: Let me be reverent in the ways of right,   STROPHE 1
Lowly the paths I journey on;
Let all my words and actions keep
The laws of the pure universe
From highest Heaven handed down.
For Heaven is their bright nurse,
Those generations of the realms of light;
Ah, never of mortal kind were they begot,
Nor are they slaves of memory, lost in sleep:
Their Father is greater than Time, and ages not.

The tyrant is a child of Pride   ANTISTROPHE 1
Who drinks from his great sickening cup
Recklessness and vanity,
Until from his high crest headlong
He plummets to the dust of hope.
That strong man is not strong.
But let no fair ambition be denied;
May God protect the wrestler for the State
In government, in comely policy,
Who will fear God, and on His ordinance wait.

Haughtiness and the high hand of disdain   STROPHE 2
Tempt and outrage God's holy law;
And any mortal who dares hold
No immortal Power in awe
Will be caught up in a net of pain:

The price for which his levity is sold.
Let each man take due earnings, then,
And keep his hands from holy things,
And from blasphemy stand apart—
Else the crackling blast of heaven
Blows on his head, and on his desperate heart;
Though fools will honor impious men.
In their cities no tragic poet sings.

Shall we lose faith in Delphi's obscurities,   ANTISTROPHE 2
We who have heard the world's core
Discredited, and the sacred wood
Of Zeus at Elis praised no more?
The deeds and the strange prophecies
Must make a pattern yet to be understood.
Zeus, if indeed you are lord of all,
Throned in light over night and day,
Mirror this in your endless mind:
Our masters call the oracle
Words on the wind, and the Delphic vision blind!
Their hearts no longer know Apollo,
And reverence for the gods has died away.

SCENE III

(Enter IOCASTÊ.*)*

IOCASTÊ: Princes of Thebes, it has occurred to me
    To visit the altars of the gods, bearing
    These branches as a suppliant, and this incense.
    Our King is not himself: his noble soul
    Is overwrought with fantasies of dread,
    Else he would consider
    The new prophecies in the light of the old.
    He will listen to any voice that speaks disaster,
    And my advice goes for nothing.
    (She approaches the altar, R.)
                        To you, then, Apollo,
    Lycean lord, since you are nearest, I turn in prayer.
    Receive these offerings, and grant us deliverance
    From defilement. Our hearts are heavy with fear

When we see our leader distracted, as helpless sailors
Are terrified by the confusion of their helmsman.

(*Enter* MESSENGER.)

MESSENGER: Friends, no doubt you can direct me:
Where shall I find the house of Oedipus,
Or, better still, where is the King himself?
CHORAGOS: It is this very place, stranger; he is inside.
This is his wife and mother of his children.
MESSENGER: I wish her happiness in a happy house,
Blest in all the fulfillment of her marriage.
IOCASTÊ: I wish as much for you: your courtesy
Deserves a like good fortune. But now, tell me:
Why have you come? What have you to say to us?
MESSENGER: Good news, my lady, for your house and your husband.
IOCASTÊ: What news? Who sent you here?
MESSENGER: I am from Corinth.
The news I bring ought to mean joy for you,
Though it may be you will find some grief in it.
IOCASTÊ: What is it? How can it touch us in both ways?
MESSENGER: The people of Corinth, they say,
Intend to call Oedipus to be their king.
IOCASTÊ: But old Polybos—is he not reigning still?
MESSENGER: No. Death holds him in his sepulchre.
IOCASTÊ: What are you saying? Polybos is dead?
MESSENGER: If I am not telling the truth, may I die myself.
IOCASTÊ (*to a Maid-servant*): Go in, go quickly; tell this to your
master.

O riddlers of God's will, where are you now!
This was the man whom Oedipus, long ago,
Feared so, fled so, in dread of destroying him—
But it was another fate by which he died.

(*Enter* OEDIPUS, *center.*)

OEDIPUS: Dearest Iocastê, why have you sent for me?
IOCASTÊ: Listen to what this man says, and then tell me
What has become of the solemn prophecies.
OEDIPUS: Who is this man? What is his news for me?
IOCASTÊ: He has come from Corinth to announce your father's death!
OEDIPUS: Is it true, stranger? Tell me in your own words.

MESSENGER: I can not say it more clearly: the King is dead.

OEDIPUS: Was it by treason? Or by an attack of illness?

MESSENGER: A little thing brings old men to their rest.

OEDIPUS: It was sickness, then?

MESSENGER: Yes, and his many years.

OEDIPUS: Ah!

> Why should a man respect the Pythian hearth,[17] or
> Give heed to the birds that jangle above his head?
> They prophesied that I should kill Polybos,
> Kill my own father; but he is dead and buried,
> And I am here—I never touched him, never,
> Unless he died of grief for my departure,
> And thus, in a sense, through me. No. Polybos
> Has packed the oracles off with him underground.
> They are empty words.

IOCASTÊ: Had I not told you so?

OEDIPUS: You had; it was my faint heart that betrayed me.

IOCASTÊ: From now on never think of those things again.

OEDIPUS: And yet—must I not fear my mother's bed?

IOCASTÊ: Why should anyone in this world be afraid,
> Since Fate rules us and nothing can be foreseen?
> A man should live only for the present day.

> Have no more fear of sleeping with your mother:
> How many men, in dreams, have lain with their mothers!
> No reasonable man is troubled by such things.

OEDIPUS: That is true; only—
> If only my mother were not still alive!
> But she is alive. I can not help my dread.

IOCASTÊ: Yet this news of your father's death is wonderful.

OEDIPUS: Wonderful. But I fear the living woman.

MESSENGER: Tell me, who is this woman that you fear?

OEDIPUS: It is Meropê, man; the wife of King Polybos.

MESSENGER: Meropê? Why should you be afraid of her?

OEDIPUS: An oracle of the gods, a dreadful saying.

MESSENGER: Can you tell me about it or are you sworn to silence?

OEDIPUS: I can tell you, and I will.

> Apollo said through his prophet that I was the man
> Who should marry his own mother, shed his father's blood
> With his own hands. And so, for all these years

[17] *Pythian hearth:* the Delphic oracle.

I have kept clear of Corinth, and no harm has come—
Though it would have been sweet to see my parents again.

MESSENGER: And is this the fear that drove you out of Corinth?

OEDIPUS: Would you have me kill my father?

MESSENGER: As for that
You must be reassured by the news I gave you.

OEDIPUS: If you could reassure me, I would reward you.

MESSENGER: I had that in mind, I will confess: I thought
I could count on you when you returned to Corinth.

OEDIPUS: No: I will never go near my parents again.

MESSENGER: Ah, son, you still do not know what you are doing—

OEDIPUS: What do you mean? In the name of God tell me!

MESSENGER: —If these are your reasons for not going home.

OEDIPUS: I tell you, I fear the oracle may come true.

MESSENGER: And guilt may come upon you through your parents?

OEDIPUS: That is the dread that is always in my heart.

MESSENGER: Can you not see that all your fears are groundless?

OEDIPUS: How can you say that? They are my parents, surely?

MESSENGER: Polybos was not your father.

OEDIPUS: Not my father?

MESSENGER: No more your father than the man speaking to you.

OEDIPUS: But you are nothing to me!

MESSENGER: Neither was he.

OEDIPUS: Then why did he call me son?

MESSENGER: I will tell you:
Long ago he had you from my hands, as a gift.

OEDIPUS: Then how could he love me so, if I was not his?

MESSENGER: He had no children, and his heart turned to you.

OEDIPUS: What of you? Did you buy me? Did you find me by chance?

MESSENGER: I came upon you in the crooked pass of Kithairon.

OEDIPUS: And what were you doing there?

MESSENGER: Tending my flocks.

OEDIPUS: A wandering shepherd?

MESSENGER: But your savior, son, that day.

OEDIPUS: From what did you save me?

MESSENGER: Your ankles should tell you that.

OEDIPUS: Ah, stranger, why do you speak of that childhood pain?

MESSENGER: I cut the bonds that tied your ankles together.

OEDIPUS: I have had the mark as long as I can remember.

MESSENGER: That was why you were given the name [18] you bear.

---

[18] *the name:* Oedipus means "swollen foot."

OEDIPUS: God! Was it my father or my mother who did it?
  Tell me!
MESSENGER: I do not know. The man who gave you to me
  Can tell you better than I.
OEDIPUS: It was not you that found me, but another?
MESSENGER: It was another shepherd gave you to me.
OEDIPUS: Who was he? Can you tell me who he was?
MESSENGER: I think he was said to be one of Laïos' people.
OEDIPUS: You mean the Laïos who was king here years ago?
MESSENGER: Yes; King Laïos; and the man was one of his herdsmen.
OEDIPUS: Is he still alive? Can I see him?
MESSENGER: These men here
  Know best about such things.
OEDIPUS: Does anyone here
  Know this shepherd that he is talking about?
  Have you seen him in the fields, or in the town?
  If you have, tell me. It is time things were made plain.
CHORAGOS: I think the man he means is that same shepherd
  You have already asked to see. Iocastê perhaps
  Could tell you something.
OEDIPUS: Do you know anything
  About him, Lady? Is he the man we have summoned?
  Is that the man this shepherd means?
IOCASTÊ: Why think of him?
  Forget this herdsman. Forget it all.
  This talk is a waste of time.
OEDIPUS: How can you say that,
  When the clues to my true birth are in my hands?
IOCASTÊ: For God's love, let us have no more questioning!
  Is your life nothing to you?
  My own is pain enough for me to bear.
OEDIPUS: You need not worry. Suppose my mother a slave,
  And born of slaves: no baseness can touch you.
IOCASTÊ: Listen to me, I beg you: do not do this thing!
OEDIPUS: I will not listen; the truth must be made known.
IOCASTÊ: Everything that I say is for your own good!
OEDIPUS: My own good
  Snaps my patience, then; I want none of it.
IOCASTÊ: You are fatally wrong! May you never learn who you are!
OEDIPUS: Go, one of you, and bring the shepherd here.
  Let us leave this woman to brag of her royal name.
IOCASTÊ: Ah, miserable!

That is the only word I have for you now.
That is the only word I can ever have.

(Exit into the palace.)

CHORAGOS: Why has she left us, Oedipus? Why has she gone
In such a passion of sorrow? I fear this silence:
Something dreadful may come of it.

OEDIPUS: Let it come!
However base my birth, I must know about it.
The Queen, like a woman, is perhaps ashamed
To think of my low origin. But I
Am a child of Luck; I cannot be dishonored.
Luck is my mother; the passing months, my brothers,
Have seen me rich and poor.

                          If this is so,
How could I wish that I were someone else?
How could I not be glad to know my birth?

ODE III

CHORUS: If ever the coming time were known   STROPHE
To my heart's pondering,
Kithairon, now by Heaven I see the torches
At the festival of the next full moon,
And see the dance, and hear the choir sing
A grace to your gentle shade:
Mountain where Oedipus was found,
O mountain guard of a noble race!
May the god who heals us lend his aid,
And let that glory come to pass
For our king's cradling-ground.

Of the nymphs that flower beyond the years,   ANTISTROPHE
Who bore you, royal child,
To Pan of the hills or the timberline Apollo,
Cold in delight where the upland clears,
Or Hermês [19] for whom Kyllenê's heights are piled?
Or flushed as evening cloud,
Great Dionysos, roamer of mountains,
He—was it he who found you there,
And caught you up in his own proud

[19] *Hermês:* (Mercury) was born in a cave on Mount Kyllenê.

Arms from the sweet god-ravisher
Who laughed by the Muses' fountains?

SCENE IV

OEDIPUS: Sirs: though I do not know the man,
I think I see him coming, this shepherd we want:
He is old, like our friend here, and the men
Bringing him seem to be servants of my house.
But you can tell, if you have ever seen him.

(*Enter* SHEPHERD *escorted by servants.*)

CHORAGOS: I know him, he was Laïos' man. You can trust him.
OEDIPUS: Tell me first, you from Corinth: is this the shepherd
We were discussing?
MESSENGER: This is the very man.
OEDIPUS (*to* SHEPHERD): Come here. No, look at me. You must
answer
Everything I ask.—You belonged to Laïos?
SHEPHERD: Yes: born his slave, brought up in his house.
OEDIPUS: Tell me: what kind of work did you do for him?
SHEPHERD: I was a shepherd of his, most of my life.
OEDIPUS: Where mainly did you go for pasturage?
SHEPHERD: Sometimes Kithairon, sometimes the hills near-by.
OEDIPUS: Do you remember ever seeing this man out there?
SHEPHERD: What would he be doing there? This man?
OEDIPUS: This man standing here. Have you ever seen him before?
SHEPHERD: No. At least, not to my recollection.
MESSENGER: And that is not strange, my lord. But I'll refresh
His memory: he must remember when we two
Spent three whole seasons together, March to September,
On Kithairon or thereabouts. He had two flocks;
I had one. Each autumn I'd drive mine home
And he would go back with his to Laïos sheepfold.—
Is this not true, just as I have described it?
SHEPHERD: True, yes; but it was all so long ago.
MESSENGER: Well, then: do you remember, back in those days,
That you gave me a baby boy to bring up as my own?
SHEPHERD: What if I did? What are you trying to say?
MESSENGER: King Oedipus was once that little child.
SHEPHERD: Damn you, hold your tongue!

OEDIPUS: No more of that!
It is your tongue needs watching, not this man's.
SHEPHERD: My King, my Master, what is it I have done wrong?
OEDIPUS: You have not answered his question about the boy.
SHEPHERD: He does not know . . . He is only making trouble . . .
OEDIPUS: Come, speak plainly, or it will go hard with you.
SHEPHERD: In God's name, do not torture an old man!
OEDIPUS: Come here, one of you; bind his arms behind him.
SHEPHERD: Unhappy king! What more do you wish to learn?
OEDIPUS: Did you give this man the child he speaks of?
SHEPHERD: I did.
And I would to God I had died that very day.
OEDIPUS: You will die now unless you speak the truth.
SHEPHERD: Yet if I speak the truth, I am worse than dead.
OEDIPUS: Very well; since you insist upon delaying—
SHEPHERD: No! I have told you already that I gave him the boy.
OEDIPUS: Where did you get him? From your house? From some-
where else?
SHEPHERD: Not from mine, no. A man gave him to me.
OEDIPUS: Is that man here? Do you know whose slave he was?
SHEPHERD: For God's love, my King, do not ask me any more!
OEDIPUS: You are a dead man if I have to ask you again.
SHEPHERD: Then . . . Then the child was from the palace of Laïos.
OEDIPUS: A slave child? or a child of his own line?
SHEPHERD: Ah, I am on the brink of dreadful speech!
OEDIPUS: And I of dreadful hearing. Yet I must hear.
SHEPHERD: If you must be told, then . . .
                                          They said it was Laïos' child;
But it is your wife who can tell you about that.
OEDIPUS: My wife!—Did she give it to you?
SHEPHERD: My lord, she did.
OEDIPUS: Do you know why?
SHEPHERD: I was told to get rid of it.
OEDIPUS: An unspeakable mother!
SHEPHERD: There had been prophecies . . .
OEDIPUS: Tell me.
SHEPHERD: It was said that the boy would kill his own father.
OEDIPUS: Then why did you give him over to this old man?
SHEPHERD: I pitied the baby, my King,
And I thought that this man would take him far away
To his own country.

He saved him—but for what a fate!
For if you are what this man says you are,
No man living is more wretched than Oedipus.

OEDIPUS: Ah God!
It was true!
All the prophecies!
—Now,
O Light, may I look on you for the last time!
I, Oedipus,
Oedipus, damned in his birth, in his marriage damned,
Damned in the blood he shed with his own hand!

(He rushes into the palace.)

ODE IV

CHORUS: Alas for the seed of men.   STROPHE I

What measure shall I give these generations
That breathe on the void and are void
And exist and do not exist?

Who bears more weight of joy
Than mass of sunlight shifting in images,
Or who shall make his thought stay on
That down time drifts away?

Your splendor is all fallen.

O naked brow of wrath and tears,
O change of Oedipus!
I who saw your days call no man blest—
Your great days like ghósts góne.

That mind was a strong bow.   ANTISTROPHE I

Deep, how deep you drew it then, hard archer,
At a dim fearful range,
And brought dear glory down!

You overcame the stranger—
The virgin with her hooking lion claws—
And though death sang, stood like a tower
To make pale Thebes take heart.

Fortress against our sorrow!

.   .   .

Divine king, giver of laws,
Majestic Oedipus!
No prince in Thebes had ever such renown,
No prince won such grace of power.

And now of all men ever known   STROPHE 2
Most pitiful is this man's story:
His fortunes are most changed, his state
Fallen to a low slave's
Ground under bitter fate.

O Oedipus, most royal one!
The great door that expelled you to the light
Gave at night—ah, gave night to your glory:
As to the father, to the fathering son.

All understood too late.

How could that queen whom Laïos won,
The garden that he harrowed at his height,
Be silent when that act was done?

But all eyes fail before time's eye,   ANTISTROPHE 2
All actions come to justice there.
Though never willed, though far down the deep past,
Your bed, your dread sirings,
Are brought to book at last.

Child by Laïos doomed to die,
Then doomed to lose that fortunate little death,
Would God you never took breath in this air
That with my wailing lips I take to cry:

For I weep the world's outcast.

Blind I was, and cannot tell why;
Asleep, for you had given ease of breath;
A fool, while the false years went by.

EXODOS

(*Enter, from the palace,* SECOND MESSENGER.)

2ND MESSENGER: Elders of Thebes, most honored in this land,
What horrors are yours to see and hear, what weight

Of sorrow to be endured, if, true to your birth,
You venerate the line of Labdakos!
I think neither Istros nor Phasis, those great rivers,
Could purify this place of the corruption
It shelters now, or soon must bring to light—
Evil not done unconsciously, but willed.

The greatest griefs are those we cause ourselves.
CHORAGOS: Surely, friend, we have grief enough already;
     What new sorrow do you mean?
2ND MESSENGER: The Queen is dead.
CHORAGOS: Iocastè? Dead? But at whose hand?
2ND MESSENGER: Her own.
     The full horror of what happened you cannot know,
     For you did not see it; but I, who did, will tell you
     As clearly as I can how she met her death.

     When she had left us,
     In passionate silence, passing through the court,
     She ran to her apartment in the house,
     Her hair clutched by the fingers of both hands.
     She closed the doors behind her; then, by that bed
     Where long ago the fatal son was conceived—
     That son who should bring about his father's death—
     We heard her call upon Laïos, dead so many years,
     And heard her wail for the double fruit of her marriage,
     A husband by her husband, children by her child.
     Exactly how she died I do not know:
     For Oedipus burst in moaning and would not let us
     Keep vigil to the end: it was by him
     As he stormed about the room that our eyes were caught.
     From one to another of us he went, begging a sword,
     Cursing the wife who was not his wife, the mother
     Whose womb had carried his own children and himself.
     I do not know: it was none of us aided him,
     But surely one of the gods was in control!
     For with a dreadful cry
     He hurled his weight, as though wrenched out of himself,
     At the twin doors: the bolts gave, and he rushed in.
     And there we saw her hanging, her body swaying
     From the cruel cord she had noosed about her neck.

A great sob broke from him, heartbreaking to hear,
As he loosed the rope and lowered her to the ground.

I would blot out from my mind what happened next!
For the King ripped from her gown the golden brooches
That were her ornament, and raised them, and plunged them down
Straight into his own eyeballs, crying, "No more,
No more shall you look on the misery about me,
The horrors of my own doing! Too long you have known
The faces of those whom I should never have seen,
Too long been blind to those for whom I was searching!
From this hour, go in darkness!" And as he spoke,
He struck at his eyes—not once, but many times;
And the blood spattered his beard,
Bursting from his ruined sockets like red hail.
So from the unhappiness of two this evil has sprung,
A curse on the man and woman alike. The old
Happiness of the house of Labdakos
Was happiness enough: where is it today?
It is all wailing and ruin, disgrace, death—all
The misery of mankind that has a name—
And it is wholly and for ever theirs.

CHORAGOS: Is he in agony still? Is there no rest for him?

2ND MESSENGER: He is calling for someone to lead him to the gates
So that all the children of Kadmos may look upon
His father's murderer, his mother's—no,
I can not say it!
                      And then he will leave Thebes,
Self-exiled, in order that the curse
Which he himself pronounced may depart from the house.
He is weak, and there is none to lead him,
So terrible is his suffering.
                      But you will see:
Look, the doors are opening; in a moment
You will see a thing that would crush a heart of stone.

(*The central door is opened; OEDIPUS, blinded, is led in.*)

CHORAGOS: Dreadful indeed for men to see.
Never have my own eyes
Looked on a sight so full of fear.

.   .   .

Oedipus!
What madness came upon you, what daemon
Leaped on your life with heavier
Punishment than a mortal man can bear?
No: I cannot even
Look at you, poor ruined one.
And I would speak, question, ponder,
If I were able. No.
You make me shudder.

OEDIPUS: God.   God.
Is there a sorrow greater?
Where shall I find harbor in this world?
My voice is hurled far on a dark wind.
What has God done to me?

CHORAGOS: Too terrible to think of, or to see.

OEDIPUS: O cloud of night,   STROPHE I
Never to be turned away: night coming on,
I can not tell how: night like a shroud!

My fair winds brought me here.
                                   O God. Again
The pain of the spikes where I had sight,
The flooding pain
Of memory, never to be gouged out.

CHORAGOS: This is not strange.
You suffer it all twice over, remorse in pain,
Pain in remorse.

OEDIPUS: Ah dear friend   ANTISTROPHE I
Are you faithful even yet, you alone?
Are you still standing near me, will you stay here,
Patient, to care for the blind?
                                   The blind man!
Yet even blind I know who it is attends me,
By the voice's tone—
Though my new darkness hide the comforter.

CHORAGOS: Oh fearful act!
What god was it drove you to rake black
Night across your eyes?

OEDIPUS: Apollo. Apollo. Dear   STROPHE 2
Children, the god was Apollo.

He brought my sick, sick fate upon me.
But the blinding hand was my own!
How could I bear to see
When all my sight was horror everywhere?
CHORAGOS: Everywhere; that is true.
OEDIPUS: And now what is left?
Images? Love? A greeting even,
Sweet to the senses? Is there anything?
Ah, no, friends; lead me away.
Lead me away from Thebes.

                    Lead the great wreck
And hell of Oedipus, whom the gods hate.
CHORAGOS: Your fate is clear, you are not blind to that.
Would God you had never found it out!

OEDIPUS: Death take the man who unbound   ANTISTROPHE 2
My feet on that hillside
And delivered me from death to life! What life?
If only I had died,
This weight of monstrous doom
Could not have dragged me and my darlings down.
CHORAGOS: I would have wished the same.
OEDIPUS: Oh never to have come here
With my father's blood upon me! Never
To have been the man they call his mother's husband!
Oh accurst! Oh child of evil,
To have entered that wretched bed—

                      the selfsame one!
More primal than sin itself, this fell to me.
CHORAGOS: I do not know how I can answer you.
You were better dead than alive and blind.
OEDIPUS: Do not counsel me any more. This punishment
That I have laid upon myself is just.
If I had eyes,
I do not know how I could bear the sight
Of my father, when I came to the house of Death,
Or my mother: for I have sinned against them both
So vilely that I could not make my peace
By strangling my own life.

                Or do you think my children,
Born as they were born, would be sweet to my eyes?

Ah never, never! Nor this town with its high walls,
Nor the holy images of the gods.

For I,

Thrice miserable!—Oedipus, noblest of all the line
Of Kadmos, have condemned myself to enjoy
These things no more, by my own malediction
Expelling that man whom the gods declared
To be a defilement in the house of Laïos.
After exposing the rankness of my own guilt,
How could I look men frankly in the eyes?
No, I swear it,
If I could have stifled my hearing at its source,
I would have done it and made all this body
A tight cell of misery, blank to light and sound:
So I should have been safe in a dark agony
Beyond all recollection.

Ah Kithairon!

Why did you shelter me? When I was cast upon you,
Why did I not die? Then I should never
Have shown the world my execrable birth.

Ah Polybos! Corinth, city that I believed
The ancient seat of my ancestors: how fair
I seemed, your child! And all the while this evil
Was cancerous within me!

For I am sick

In my daily life, sick in my origin.

O three roads, dark ravine, woodland and way
Where three roads met: you, drinking my father's blood,
My own blood, spilled by my own hand: can you remember
The unspeakable things I did there, and the things
I went on from there to do?

O marriage, marriage!

The act that engendered me, and again the act
Performed by the son in the same bed—

Ah, the net

Of incest, mingling fathers, brothers, sons,
With brides, wives, mothers: the last evil
That can be known by men: no tongue can say
How evil!

No. For the love of God, conceal me

Somewhere far from Thebes; or kill me; or hurl me
Into the sea, away from men's eyes for ever.

Come, lead me. You need not fear to touch me.
Of all men, I alone can bear this guilt.

(*Enter* CREON.)

CHORAGOS: We are not the ones to decide; but Creon here
   May fitly judge of what you ask. He only
   Is left to protect the city in your place.
OEDIPUS: Alas, how can I speak to him? What right have I
   To beg his courtesy whom I have deeply wronged?
CREON: I have not come to mock you, Oedipus,
   Or to reproach you, either.
   (*To Attendants*)
                              —You, standing there:
   If you have lost all respect for man's dignity,
   At least respect the flame of Lord Helios:
   Do not allow this pollution to show itself
   Openly here, an affront to the earth
   And Heaven's rain and the light of day. No, take him
   Into the house as quickly as you can.
   For it is proper
   That only the close kindred see his grief.
OEDIPUS: I pray you in God's name, since your courtesy
   Ignores my dark expectation, visiting
   With mercy this man of all men most execrable:
   Give me what I ask—for your good, not for mine.
CREON: And what is it that you would have me do?
OEDIPUS: Drive me out of this country as quickly as may be
   To a place where no human voice can ever greet me.
CREON: I should have done that before now—only,
   God's will had not been wholly revealed to me.
OEDIPUS: But his command is plain: the parricide
   Must be destroyed. I am that evil man.
CREON: That is the sense of it, yes; but as things are,
   We had best discover clearly what is to be done.
OEDIPUS: You would learn more about a man like me?
CREON: You are ready now to listen to the god.
OEDIPUS: I will listen. But it is to you
   That I must turn for help. I beg you, hear me.

. . .

The woman in there—
Give her whatever funeral you think proper:
She is your sister.
                          —But let me go, Creon!
Let me purge my father's Thebes of the pollution
Of my living here, and go out to the wild hills,
To Kithairon, that has won such fame with me,
The tomb my mother and father appointed for me,
And let me die there, as they willed I should.
And yet I know
Death will not ever come to me through sickness
Or in any natural way: I have been preserved
For some unthinkable fate. But let that be.

As for my sons, you need not care for them.
They are men, they will find some way to live.
But my poor daughters, who have shared my table,
Who never before have been parted from their father—
Take care of them, Creon; do this for me.
And will you let me touch them with my hands
A last time, and let us weep together?
Be kind, my lord,
Great prince, be kind!
                          Could I but touch them,
They would be mine again, as when I had my eyes.

(*Enter* ANTIGONE *and* ISMENE, *attended.*)

Ah, God!
Is it my dearest children I hear weeping?
Has Creon pitied me and sent my daughters?
CREON: Yes, Oedipus: I knew that they were dear to you
    In the old days, and know you must love them still.
OEDIPUS: May God bless you for this—and be a friendlier
    Guardian to you than he has been to me!

Children, where are you?
Come quickly to my hands: they are your brother's—
Hands that have brought your father's once clear eyes
To this way of seeing—
                          Ah dearest ones,
I had neither sight nor knowledge then, your father
By the woman who was the source of his own life!

And I weep for you—having no strength to see you—,
I weep for you when I think of the bitterness
That men will visit upon you all your lives.
What homes, what festivals can you attend
Without being forced to depart again in tears?
And when you come to marriageable age,
Where is the man, my daughters, who would dare
Risk the bane that lies on all my children?
Is there any evil wanting? Your father killed
His father; sowed the womb of her who bore him;
Engendered you at the fount of his own existence!

That is what they will say of you.

                         Then, whom
Can you ever marry? There are no bridegrooms for you,
And your lives must wither away in sterile dreaming.

O Creon, son of Menoikeus!
You are the only father my daughters have,
Since we, their parents, are both of us gone for ever.
They are your own blood: you will not let them
Fall into beggary and loneliness;
You will keep them from the miseries that are mine!
Take pity on them; see, they are only children,
Friendless except for you. Promise me this,
Great Prince, and give me your hand in token of it.
(CREON *clasps his right hand.*)
Children:
I could say much, if you could understand me,
But as it is, I have only this prayer for you:
Live where you can, be as happy as you can—
Happier, please God, than God has made your father!

CREON: Enough. You have wept enough. Now go within.
OEDIPUS: I must; but it is hard.
CREON: Time eases all things.
OEDIPUS: But you must promise—
CREON: Say what you desire.
OEDIPUS: Send me from Thebes!
CREON: God grant that I may!
OEDIPUS: But since God hates me . . .
CREON: No, he will grant your wish.

OEDIPUS: You promise?

CREON: I can not speak beyond my knowledge.

OEDIPUS: Then lead me in.

CREON: Come now, and leave your children.

OEDIPUS: No! Do not take them from me!

CREON: Think no longer
That you are in command here, but rather think
How, when you were, you served your own destruction.

> (*Exeunt into the house all but the* CHORUS; *the* CHORAGOS
> *chants directly to the audience.*)

CHORAGOS: Men of Thebes: look upon Oedipus.
This is the king who solved the famous riddle
And towered up, most powerful of men.
No mortal eyes but looked on him with envy,
Yet in the end ruin swept over him.

Let every man in mankind's frailty
Consider his last day; and let none
Presume on his good fortune until he find
Life, at his death, a memory without pain.

William Shakespeare

The private life of England's greatest dramatist has been the object of countless conjectures, ranging from the reasonable to the grotesque. Three hundred years of painstaking research have produced a substantial body of facts—far more than generally realized—about Shakespeare's life and environment. All this research, however, has done nothing to illuminate the character of the man. Much frustration has resulted from the understandably intense desire of readers and scholars to know the kind of personality that could write such remarkable plays. Some scholars have refused to accept the idea that so great a writer was not acclaimed as a literary man by most of his contemporaries, and various famous men of the era have been proposed as the true author of Shakespeare's works. The historical facts, however, refuse to yield to this sort of speculation. Though we shall probably never know much more than we now do about the character of the dramatist, all the available facts indicate that the William Shakespeare who was born in 1564 in Stratford-upon-Avon deserves the honor that three centuries of playgoers and readers have heaped upon his name and his dramas.

The public documents of Stratford reveal that the dramatist's father was a glover who became a magistrate of that small village. Shakespeare probably attended the local grammar school where he would have received a thorough grounding in Latin literature and particularly in the works of Ovid, the Roman poet he was later to use so extensively as a source. In 1582, at the age of eighteen, the records note, he married Anne Hathaway, the daughter of a neighboring farmer. Six months later she gave birth to a daughter Susanna, and two years after that, in 1585, to a set of twins christened Hamnet and Judith.

Between 1585 and 1592 absolutely nothing is known of Shakespeare's activities. Sometime during this period he must have gone to London and joined one of the acting companies, for in 1592 a contemporary refers to him as an actor and playwright. In 1594, he joined the acting group with which he remained throughout his career, the newly formed Lord Chamberlain's Men, later called the King's Men.

By the time Shakespeare joined the Lord Chamberlain's Men he had already written at least six plays, two long poems, *Venus and Adonis* and *The Rape of Lucrece,* and some (if not all), of his sonnets. His apprenticeship could not have been longer than the nine years about which we know nothing, but it was enough and at the age of thirty, Shakespeare was ready to begin perfecting his craft. He served as the Lord Chamberlain's Men's chief playwright, and they soon became the leading acting company in London. They appeared before Queen Elizabeth and her court on numerous occasions and by 1599 were prosperous enough to build their own theater, the Globe, on the south bank of the Thames River.

During this period Shakespeare learned to mold the lyricism of his poetry to the demands of drama in such plays as *A Midsummer Night's Dream, Richard II,* and *Romeo and Juliet.* He had also created some of his greatest characters, including Shylock and Falstaff. The opening of the Globe, however, marked a new phase in his career. His comedies acquired richness of texture and maturity of expression, best exemplified in the subtly modulated romanticism of *As You Like It* and *Twelfth Night.* These comedies were succeeded by his so-called "problem plays," sensitive probings of complex moral and ethical issues. This group of plays, chief among which are *Measure for Measure* and *Troilus and Cressida,* were long neglected by critics and audiences, but recently they have begun to receive recognition as an important aspect of Shakespeare's total achievement. Simultaneously with the problem plays he produced his tragic masterpieces, probably the most significant achievement in all literature.

Of his personal life during this period, little is known. His wife and family continued to live in Stratford. In 1596 his only son, Hamnet, died at the age of eleven. Five years later his father died after having secured for the family a coat of arms entitling William to sign himself "Gentleman." Shakespeare's attachment to his native town was apparently deeply rooted; extant records show that he made a number of purchases of Stratford property. The nature of these purchases enables us to infer one thing about his personality: he was a shrewd and careful businessman.

In London, too, he and his fellow actors revealed business acumen by purchasing, in 1608, a playhouse in the Blackfriars' district of London. This Blackfriars theater, a "private" theater as opposed to the Globe which was "public," was a small indoor theater that catered to a more restricted clientele, generally wealthier and more sophisticated. Catering to the tastes of his new audience, Shakespeare began experimenting with a new type of play, variously designated as "romances" or "tragicomedies." These final plays represent Shakespeare's attempt to go beyond tragedy, to present, through the themes of reconciliation and reunion, values which affirm life and impose a pattern of meaning on the disorder of human experience.

About 1613, Shakespeare retired and moved back to Stratford. His remaining years were presumably serene. He died on April 23, 1616 and was buried two days later in the Stratford church. A monument was erected to him by his family and friends, but a far more enduring monument was that produced by his two fellow actors, John Heminges and Henry Condell, who after his death brought together manuscript copies of his plays and oversaw the printing of his collected work in the First Folio of 1623.

Though the biographical facts available to us make it impossible to determine the influence of Shakespeare's personal life and character upon his plays, we do know enough about the era in which he lived and about the theater of the period to recognize that he responded to his environment and that his plays reflect the dramatic influences that shaped Elizabethan drama.

When the playwright was born in 1564, Queen Elizabeth I had already been on the throne for six years. Her forty-five-year reign was a brilliant era in English history. Shakespeare's early history plays mirror the intense and optimistic patriotism that was evoked in Englishmen by the great victory over the Spanish Armada, the establishment of comparative peace and prosperity, and, perhaps of most importance, the emergence of England as one of the great nations of Europe. Intellectually, the Age of Elizabeth was characterized by vitality and by the belief that life was an ordered, harmonious experience. The Elizabethan accepted as a scientific fact, provable with mathematical precision and not simply as a matter of faith, that the human being had a significant and established role in the order of the cosmos. To a large extent, this vision was responsible for such great literary masterpieces as Spenser's *The Faerie Queene* and Shakespeare's *A Midsummer Night's Dream*.

During the closing years of Elizabeth's reign, however, this harmonious, affirmative vision began to fade. New discoveries in science and astronomy began to question the foundations of the Ptolemaic universe, and as a result to "call all in doubt" as John Donne put it. The bold and daring spirits who had symbolized Elizabeth's reign—the Earl of Essex, Sir Walter Raleigh, Sir Francis Drake—were either dead or in prison. When the childless Elizabeth died in 1603, she was succeeded by Scotland's James I, a pedantic man who had neither the political skill nor the charismatic impact of the Virgin Queen.

The new mood of the Jacobean era had its effect upon literature. The literary style of Jacobean writers reflected the mood of disenchantment, and it was less expansive and elaborate than the style of the Elizabethans. Satire became the dominant literary form, and the pervasive theme of the period was human corruption, generally symbolized by sexual corruption. It was during this Jacobean period that Shakespeare, then at the peak of his creative powers, produced those profound explorations of the human spirit: *Hamlet, Othello, King Lear,* and *Macbeth*.

Shakespeare was responsive not only to the moods and themes of his era but also to the dramatic techniques and traditions of the Elizabethan theater. Elizabethan drama was the heir of two great theatrical traditions—Roman drama and native English drama. From the classical Roman drama (represented by Seneca in tragedy and Plautus and Terence in comedy), Elizabethan dramatists learned the rules of structure and form. The division of a play into five acts, for instance, was a classical convention which Elizabethans adopted. They also incorporated into their comedies many of the comical types, such as the braggart, cowardly soldier (Falstaff) of the Roman comedies. The Senecan theme of revenge became a dominant theme in Elizabethan tragedy. Although the heritage of classical drama was significant, perhaps, to Shakespeare and his contemporaries, their own English theatrical background was more influential.

English drama began with the enactment on religious holidays of scenes from the Bible. These amateur performances, called "miracle" or "mystery" plays, were sponsored by various craft organizations throughout the Middle Ages. In time, these enactments of Biblical stories gave way to a less explicitly religious but more allegorical drama, known as the "morality" play, the finest example of which is *Everyman*. The plot of such dramas evolved from the conflict between specific virtues and vices, which were personified. These morality plays, and a later development of them called interludes, were performed by troupes of professional actors that toured the countryside, performing in the castles of noblemen and in the courtyards of inns.

These early, primitive plays have little resemblance to the elaborate, imaginative, Elizabethan dramas that succeeded them, but they prepared the way for the sudden flowering of drama. They provided what no playwright can do without, an audience receptive and eager for dramatic entertainment. They also provided an audience accustomed to drama written in verse and one that would lend its imagination to drama without realistic stage settings.

The first designers of Elizabethan theaters, in fact, simply copied the design of the inn courtyards in which touring actors set up a platform at one end and the audience congregated along the galleries of the rectangular inn or stood in the courtyard. The stage for which Shakespeare wrote was a platform about three feet high that jutted out from one wall of the roofless circular building into the center of the yard. The dimensions and shape of this stage are not certain, but we do know that it was an "open" stage, that is, the audience surrounded it on three sides. Actors made their entrances and exits through two doors at the rear of the stage and, when the occasion demanded, through a trap door in the stage floor. Above the doors at the rear of the stage was a gallery which served for balcony scenes. Some scholars have argued that below the gallery was an inner stage enclosed by a curtain that could be drawn back for interior scenes. But the general opinion of most modern scholars is that there was no such inner stage and that an interior scene such as that in Desdemona's bedroom (Act V, Scene II) in *Othello* was prepared for simply by pushing Desdemona's bed onto the stage, in full view of the audience since there was no curtain. But the audience did not object to witnessing such an action as would a modern audience accustomed to realistic drama. Elizabethans were prepared to use their imaginations—to envision an empty stage as a battlefield, to accept the passage of hours or days between the exit of one actor and the entrance of another, to react promptly to the hints in the speeches about the change of scene and the passage of time. The popular picture of Shakespeare's audience as a collection of brawling, noisy, primitive "groundlings" interested only in low comedy and sensational bloodletting is a gross caricature which the sophisticated poetic dramas of Elizabethan dramatists contradict. The apprentices and shopkeepers of London, who presumably formed the bulk of the Elizabethan audience, were highly sophisticated, critical theatergoers who recognized the genius of Shakespeare and returned again and again to the Globe.

The acting companies which served this audience were repertory groups, performing under the aegis of one of the powerful noblemen of Queen Elizabeth's court. Technically, the actors were servants of the nobleman, the Lord Chamberlain or the Lord Admiral, whose name the company bore. The companies needed the protection of a nobleman because the magistrates of London during this period were Puritans who considered drama immoral, dangerous, and unhealthy. Because the noblemen were beyond the jurisdiction of the London magistrates, their servants were also safe. But the Puritans could and did forbid theatrical performances within London proper, so the theaters had to be built beyond the confines of the city.

Today, the successful among those connected with the theater enjoy economic security and social acceptance, but in the Age of Elizabeth, the actors and the men who wrote for them lived on the fringes of society. Only the more successful actors who were part owners of theaters had good incomes. The playwrights, on the other hand, had no such advantage. "The play's the thing," Hamlet observes, and the man who writes the play is of little significance. The Elizabethan playwright was a free-lancer peddling his wares to the highest bidder, and the bidding was usually very low, even by the standards of the time. Writers for the Elizabethan stage were barely able to make a living, and many of the dramatists who made significant contributions to English drama—Christopher Marlowe, George Peele, Robert Greene, Thomas Lodge, and Thomas Nashe—lived and died in poverty. Only Shakespeare achieved financial success, and only because he was a full-time member of an acting company which he helped to make the most successful company in London.

Comparable to the precarious social and economic position of the Elizabethan dramatist was his literary position. Shakespeare won literary acknowledgment as a poet, but few of his contemporaries considered his dramatic works as literary productions. Many of the dramas of his contemporaries were never preserved, and we are very lucky that two of Shakespeare's friends decided to collect the manuscript copies and print them.

Despite all of these economic, social, and literary harassments, Elizabethan drama managed to survive and to flourish (largely but not exclusively as a result of Shakespeare) and eventually to emerge as one of the greatest eras in the history of the drama, surpassed only, perhaps, by the Golden Age of Greece, which produced, as did the Elizabethan era, some of the greatest tragedies of the world.

As a writer of tragedy, Shakespeare followed many of the principles of the Greek dramatists. All tragedy springs from the effort of the human imagination to confront the fact of death. It represents man's attempt to wrest from the awareness of his own death a value that transcends mortality. The tragic hero explores the limits of human experience. His exploration inevitably ends in his death, but not before he is able to achieve insight—either about himself or about his world—which makes his death seem almost unimportant by comparison. The audience shares the triumph of the tragic hero and leaves the theater, as Aristotle suggests, purged of the terror of death.

The tragedies of Shakespeare follow this basic pattern but they are also uniquely Shakespearean in that they reflect the ideas and pressures of the Jacobean age. The skepticism, which was previously noted as characteristic of this period, was due in some measure to the new discoveries in science and astronomy, but it had deeper, more historical, roots. The seventeenth century was a pivotal point for Englishmen in the transition from the medieval period to the modern. It chronicled the shift in human experience and human thought from a religious to a secular emphasis, from concentration upon the group—the family or the state—as the center of society to emphasis upon individual man. One aspect of Shakespeare's greatness is that he had an intuitive sense of this development. His four greatest tragedies (*Hamlet, Othello, King Lear,* and *Macbeth*), all written within the first decade of the seventeenth century, are pervaded by the sense that the old ordering principles of life—the relationship of children to their father; of a husband to his wife; of subjects to a king; of men to God; the congruence of appearance to reality; the dominance of reason over passion—were undergoing a severe transformation. His tragic heroes are men who, victims either of fate or of their own illusions, are forced to face the reality of a changing order and to seek answers to questions they had never faced before. They are the first examples of modern men who can no longer feel secure with the idea of an established order of existence, no longer fully accept the traditional laws of God and society, and, thus, must seek within themselves for the answers to the mystery of life and death. In this shift from the external and codified to the internal and individual, Shakespeare's tragic heroes are uniquely suited to express the needs of the modern reader.

Hamlet is our representative "born to set right" the rottenness that infects Denmark, to explore the problem of how to act in a world in which there exists a vast disparity between appearance and reality, and ultimately to explore the basic question of the deeply troubled and lost soul—"to be or not to be." Macbeth is our agent in Hell, pursuing a commitment which none of us dares make and discovering at the end of that pursuit a terrifying vision of Life as Absurdity "full of sound and fury/Signifying nothing." Lear discovers to us those human values which stubbornly cling to a man even after he has been systematically stripped of everything else, including his own sanity. And Othello, apparently secure in the reality of his high position and his great love, veers toward madness as the thin line between reality and illusion is erased by Iago.

This kind of twentieth-century interpretation of seventeenth-century drama reveals the depth and scope of Shakespeare's achievement. Each era finds mirrored in these powerful dramatizations of the human tragedy its own malaise. During the past three centuries, *Othello,* which was first performed on November 1, 1604, has been variously interpreted. Some scholars have viewed it as a morality play, a struggle between the forces of good and evil for the soul of Everyman (Othello). Many commentators consider it a study of sexual jealousy; others a drama of love. Othello has been described as a savage with a thin veneer of civilization that Iago is easily able to peel away; he has also been characterized as Shakespeare's noblest, most unblemished tragic hero. Some actors have portrayed Iago as the incarnation of evil; others have interpreted him as a likeable, wronged character seeking justifiable vengeance. Both Othello the man and *Othello* the drama are large enough to contain such contradictions. New interpretations of the play's meaning will undoubtedly continue to be offered by critics not yet born, but one element shall remain a constant in the experience the drama provides—the intense emotional response to the elemental passions that Shakespeare has dramatized.

❦❦

BIBLIOGRAPHY

Allardyce, Nicoll. *Shakespeare: An Introduction.* New York: Oxford University Press, 1952.

Beckerman, Bernard. *Shakespeare at the Globe.* New York: Macmillan, 1962.

Bradley, A. C. *Shakespearean Tragedy.* Cleveland: The World Publishing Co., 1955.

Chute, Marchette. *Shakespeare of London.* New York: E. P. Dutton, 1949.

Granville-Barker, Harley. *Preface to Othello.* Princeton, N.J.: Princeton University Press, 1958.

Harbage, Alfred. *William Shakespeare: A Reader's Guide.* New York: Farrar, Straus & Giroux, 1963.

Thorndike, Ashley. *Shakespeare's Theater.* New York: Macmillan, 1960.

The Tragedy of Othello, The Moor of Venice

CHARACTERS

DUKE OF VENICE

BRABANTIO *a Senator, father to Desdemona*

SENATORS

GRATIANO *brother to Brabantio* } *two noble*

LODOVICO *kinsman to Brabantio* } *Venetians*

OTHELLO *the Moor*

CASSIO *Othello's honorable Lieutenant*

IAGO *Othello's Ancient, a villain*

RODERIGO *a gulled gentleman*

MONTANO *retiring Governor of Cyprus*

CLOWN *servant to Othello*

DESDEMONA *daughter to Brabantio and wife to Othello*

EMILIA *wife to Iago*

BIANCA *a courtesan*

SAILOR, MESSENGER, HERALD, OFFICERS, GENTLEMEN, MUSICIANS, ATTENDANTS

SCENE: *Venice; Cyprus.*

ACT I
SCENE I

(*Venice. A street.*)

(*Enter* RODERIGO *and* IAGO.)

RODERIGO: Tush, never tell me! I take it much unkindly
    That thou, Iago, who hast had my purse
    As if the strings were thine, shouldst know of this.
IAGO: 'Sblood, but you'll not hear me!
    If ever I did dream of such a matter,
    Abhor me.
RODERIGO: Thou told'st me thou didst hold him in thy hate.
IAGO: Despise me if I do not. Three great ones of the city,
    In personal suit to make me his lieutenant,
    Off-capped to him; and, by the faith of man,   10
    I know my price, I am worth no worse a place.
    But he, as loving his own pride and purposes,
    Evades them with a bombast circumstance,
    Horribly stuffed with epithets of war;
    And, in conclusion,
    Nonsuits my mediators; for, "Certes," says he,
    "I have already chose my officer."
    And what was he?
    Forsooth, a great arithmetician,
    One Michael Cassio, a Florentine   20
    (A fellow almost damned in a fair wife),
    That never set a squadron in the field,
    Nor the division of a battle knows
    More than a spinster; unless the bookish theoric,
    Wherein the toged consuls can propose

l. 4. *'Sblood:* by God's blood.
l. 10. *Off-capped to him:* took off their caps before him, i.e., pleaded for Iago.
l. 13. *bombast circumstance:* pompous circumlocution.
l. 16. *Nonsuits:* rejects
l. 19. *arithmetician:* student of theoretical military tactics.
l. 25. *toged consuls:* toga-wearing councilors.

(76)

As masterly as he. Mere prattle, without practice,
Is all his soldiership. But he, sir, had th' election;
And I (of whom his eyes had seen the proof
At Rhodes, at Cyprus, and on other grounds
Christian and heathen) must be be-leed and calmed   30
By debitor and creditor, this counter-caster.
He (in good time!) must his lieutenant be,
And I (God bless the mark!) his Moorship's ancient.

RODERIGO: By heaven, I rather would have been his hangman.

IAGO: Why, there's no remedy; 'tis the curse of service.
Preferment goes by letter and affection,
And not by old gradation, where each second
Stood heir to the first. Now, sir, be judge yourself,
Whether I in any just term am affined
To love the Moor.

RODERIGO: I would not follow him then.   40

IAGO: O, sir, content you.
I follow him to serve my turn upon him.
We cannot all be masters, nor all masters
Cannot be truly followed. You shall mark
Many a duteous and knee-crooking knave
That, doting on his own obsequious bondage,
Wears out his time, much like his master's ass,
For naught but provender; and when he's old, cashiered.
Whip me such honest knaves! Others there are
Who, trimmed in forms and visages of duty,   50
Keep yet their hearts attending on themselves;
And, throwing but shows of service on their lords,
Do well thrive by them, and when they have lined their coats,
Do themselves homage. These fellows have some soul;
And such a one do I profess myself. For, sir,
It is as sure as you are Roderigo,
Were I the Moor, I would not be Iago.
In following him, I follow but myself.
Heaven is my judge, not I for love and duty,
But seeming so, for my peculiar end;   60

l. 30. *be-leed and calmed:* stopped.
l. 31. *counter-caster:* an accountant, a reference to Cassio's book knowledge.
l. 33. *ancient:* ensign.
l. 47. *cashiered:* dismissed.

For when my outward action doth demonstrate
The native act and figure of my heart
In compliment extern, 'tis not long after
But I will wear my heart upon my sleeve
For daws to peck at. I am not what I am.

RODERIGO: What a full fortune does the thick-lips owe
If he can carry't thus!

IAGO: Call up her father:
Rouse him, make after him, poison his delight,
Proclaim him in the streets, incense her kinsmen,
And though he in a fertile climate dwell,   7
Plague him with flies; though that his joy be joy,
Yet throw such changes of vexation on't
As it may lose some color.

RODERIGO: Here is her father's house. I'll call aloud.

IAGO: Do, with like timorous accent and dire yell
As when, by night and negligence, the fire
Is spied in populous cities.

RODERIGO: What, ho, Brabantio! Signior Brabantio, ho!

IAGO: Awake! What, ho, Brabantio! Thieves! thieves! thieves!
Look to your house, your daughter, and your bags!   8
Thieves! thieves!

(Enter BRABANTIO *above, at a window.)*

BRABANTIO: What is the reason of this terrible summons?
What is the matter there?

RODERIGO: Signior, is all your family within?

IAGO: Are your doors locked?

BRABANTIO: Why, wherefore ask you this?

IAGO: 'Zounds, sir, y'are robbed! For shame, put on your gown!
Your heart is burst; you have lost half your soul.
Even now, now, very now, an old black ram
Is tupping your white ewe. Arise, arise!
Awake the snorting citizens with the bell,   9
Or else the devil will make a grandsire of you.
Arise, I say!

BRABANTIO: What, have you lost your wits?

RODERIGO: Most reverend signior, do you know my voice?

BRABANTIO: Not I. What are you?

RODERIGO: My name is Roderigo.

l. 87. *'Zounds:* by God's wounds.
l. 89. *snorting:* snoring.

BRABANTIO: The worser welcome!
　I have charged thee not to haunt about my doors.
　In honest plainness thou hast heard me say
　My daughter is not for thee; and now, in madness,
　Being full of supper and distemp'ring draughts,
　Upon malicious knavery dost thou come   100
　To start my quiet.
RODERIGO: Sir, sir, sir—
BRABANTIO: But thou must needs be sure
　My spirit and my place have in their power
　To make this bitter to thee.
RODERIGO: Patience, good sir.
BRABANTIO: What tell'st thou me of robbing? This is Venice;
　My house is not a grange.
RODERIGO: Most grave Brabantio,
　In simple and pure soul I come to you.
IAGO: 'Zounds, sir, you are one of those that will not serve God if the
　devil bid you. Because we come to do you service, and you think
　we are ruffians, you'll have your daughter covered with a Barbary   110
　horse; you'll have your nephews neigh to you; you'll have coursers
　for cousins, and jennets for germans.
BRABANTIO: What profane wretch art thou?
IAGO: I am one, sir, that comes to tell you your daughter and the
　Moor are now making the beast with two backs.
BRABANTIO: Thou art a villain.
IAGO: You are a senator.
BRABANTIO: This thou shalt answer. I know thee, Roderigo.
RODERIGO: Sir, I will answer anything. But I beseech you,
　If't be your pleasure and most wise consent
　(As partly I find it is) that your fair daughter,   120
　At this odd-even and dull watch o' the night,
　Transported, with no worse nor better guard
　But with a knave of common hire, a gondolier,
　To the gross clasps of a lascivious Moor—
　If this be known to you, and your allowance,
　We then have done you bold and saucy wrongs;
　But if you know not this, my manners tell me
　We have your wrong rebuke. Do not believe

l. 106. *grange:* isolated farmhouse.
ll. 111–112. *nephews . . . germans:* Moorish horses for near relations.
l. 121. *odd-even:* between midnight and morning.
l. 125. *allowance:* with permission.

That, from the sense of all civility,
I thus would play and trifle with your reverence.   13(
Your daughter, if you have not given her leave,
I say again, hath made a gross revolt,
Tying her duty, beauty, wit, and fortunes
In an extravagant and wheeling stranger
Of here and everywhere. Straight satisfy yourself.
If she be in her chamber, or your house,
Let loose on me the justice of the state
For thus deluding you.

BRABANTIO: Strike on the tinder, ho!
Give me a taper! Call up all my people!
This accident is not unlike my dream: 14(
Belief of it oppresses me already.
Light, I say! light!   (*Exit above.*)

IAGO: Farewell, for I must leave you.
It seems not meet, nor wholesome to my place,
To be produced (as, if I stay, I shall)
Against the Moor. For I do know, the state,
However this may gall him with some check,
Cannot with safety cast him; for he's embarked
With such loud reason to the Cyprus wars,
Which even now stand in act, that for their souls
Another of his fathom they have none   15(
To lead their business; in which regard,
Though I do hate him as I do hell pains,
Yet, for necessity of present life,
I must show out a flag and sign of love,
Which is indeed but sign. That you shall surely find him,
Lead to the Sagittary the raised search;
And there will I be with him. So farewell.   (*Exit.*)

(*Enter, below,* BRABANTIO, *in his nightgown, and* SERVANTS
with torches.)

BRABANTIO: It is too true an evil. Gone she is;
And what's to come of my despised time

l. 129. *from:* in spite of.
l. 134. *extravagant and wheeling stranger:* a roving stranger.
l. 150. *fathom:* capacity.
l. 156. *Sagittary:* the name of an inn.
l. 159. *despised time:* old age.

Is naught but bitterness. Now, Roderigo,   160
Where didst thou see her?—O unhappy girl!—
With the Moor, say'st thou?—Who would be a father?—
How didst thou know 'twas she?—O, she deceives me
Past thought!—What said she to you?—Get more tapers!
Raise all my kindred!—Are they married, think you?
RODERIGO: Truly I think they are.
BRABANTIO: O heaven! How got she out? O treason of the blood!
Fathers, from hence trust not your daughters' minds
By what you see them act. Is there not charms
By which the property of youth and maidhood   170
May be abused? Have you not read, Roderigo,
Of some such thing?
RODERIGO: Yes, sir, I have indeed.
BRABANTIO: Call up my brother.—O, would you had had her!—
Some one way, some another.—Do you know
Where we may apprehend her and the Moor?
RODERIGO: I think I can discover him, if you please
To get good guard and go along with me.
BRABANTIO: Pray you lead on. At every house I'll call;
I may command at most.—Get weapons, ho!
And raise some special officers of night.—   180
On, good Roderigo. I'll deserve your pains.

                                              (*Exeunt.*)

SCENE II

(*Venice. Before the Sagittary.*)

(*Enter* OTHELLO, IAGO, ATTENDANTS, *with torches.*)

IAGO: Though in the trade of war I have slain men,
Yet do I hold it very stuff o' the conscience
To do no contrived murder. I lack iniquity
Sometimes to do me service. Nine or ten times
I had thought t' have yerked him here under the ribs.
OTHELLO: 'Tis better as it is.
IAGO: Nay, but he prated,

l. 170. *property*: nature.
l. 181. *deserve*: reward.
l. 5. *yerked*: stabbed.

And spoke such scurvy and provoking terms
Against your honor,
That with the little godliness I have
I did full hard forbear him. But I pray you, sir,   10
Are you fast married? Be assured of this,
That the magnifico is much beloved,
And hath in his effect a voice potential
As double as the Duke's. He will divorce you,
Or put upon you what restraint and grievance
The law, with all his might to enforce it on,
Will give him cable.

OTHELLO: Let him do his spite.
My services which I have done the signiory
Shall out-tongue his complaints. 'Tis yet to know—
Which, when I know that boasting is an honor,   20
I shall promulgate—I fetch my life and being
From men of royal siege; and my demerits
May speak (unbonneted) to as proud a fortune
As this that I have reached. For know, Iago,
But that I love the gentle Desdemona,
I would not my unhoused free condition
Put into circumscription and confine
For the sea's worth.

(*Enter* CASSIO, *and* OFFICERS *with torches.*)

                    But look what lights come yond.
IAGO: Those are the raised father and his friends.
You were best go in.

OTHELLO: Not I. I must be found.   30
My parts, my title, and my perfect soul
Shall manifest me rightly. Is it they?
IAGO: By Janus, I think no.
OTHELLO: The servants of the Duke? and my lieutenant?
The goodness of the night upon you, friends!

l. 11. *fast:* securely.
l. 12. *the magnifico:* Brabantio.
l. 14. *double:* more influential than the Duke.
l. 18. *signiory:* government of Venice.
l. 19. *yet to know:* still unknown.
l. 22. *demerits:* deserts.
l. 31. *perfect soul:* clear conscience.
l. 33. *Janus:* the two-faced Roman god.

What is the news?

CASSIO:　　　　　　　The Duke does greet you, General;
And he requires your haste-post-haste appearance
Even on the instant.

OTHELLO:　　　　　　　What's the matter, think you?

CASSIO:　Something from Cyprus, as I may divine.
It is a business of some heat. The galleys　　　　　　　40
Have sent a dozen sequent messengers
This very night at one another's heels;
And many of the consuls, raised and met,
Are at the Duke's already. You have been hotly called for;
When, being not at your lodging to be found,
The Senate hath sent about three several quests
To search you out.

OTHELLO:　　　　　'Tis well I am found by you.
I will but spend a word here in the house,
And go with you.　　　　　　　　　　　(*Exit.*)

CASSIO:　　　　　　Ancient, what makes he here?

IAGO:　Faith, he tonight hath boarded a land carrack.　　50
If it prove lawful prize, he's made for ever.

CASSIO:　I do not understand.

IAGO:　　　　　　　He's married.

CASSIO:　　　　　　　　　　To who?

(*Enter* OTHELLO.)

IAGO:　Marry, to—Come, Captain, will you go?

OTHELLO:　　　　　　　　Have with you.

CASSIO:　Here comes another troop to seek for you.

(*Enter* BRABANTIO, RODERIGO, *and* OFFICERS *with torches
and weapons.*)

IAGO:　It is Brabantio. General, be advised;
He comes to bad intent.

OTHELLO:　　　　　Holla! stand there!

RODERIGO:　Signior, it is the Moor.

BRABANTIO:　　　　　Down with him, thief!

(*Both parties draw swords.*)

IAGO:　You, Roderigo! Come, sir, I am for you.

l. 41. *sequent:* consecutive.
l. 50. *carrack:* cargo ship.

OTHELLO: Keep up your bright swords, for the dew will rust them.
Good signior, you shall more command with years   6
Than with your weapons.

BRABANTIO: O thou foul thief, where hast thou stowed my daughter?
Damned as thou art, thou hast enchanted her!
For I'll refer me to all things of sense,
If she in chains of magic were not bound,
Whether a maid so tender, fair, and happy,
So opposite to marriage that she shunned
The wealthy curled darlings of our nation,
Would ever have (t' incur a general mock)
Run from her guardage to the sooty bosom   7
Of such a thing as thou—to fear, not to delight.
Judge me the world if 'tis not gross in sense
That thou hast practiced on her with foul charms,
Abused her delicate youth with drugs or minerals
That weaken motion. I'll have't disputed on.
'Tis probable, and palpable to thinking.
I therefore apprehend and do attach thee
For an abuser of the world, a practicer
Of arts inhibited and out of warrant.
Lay hold upon him. If he do resist,   8
Subdue him at his peril.

OTHELLO: Hold your hands,
Both you of my inclining and the rest.
Were it my cue to fight, I should have known it
Without a prompter. Where will you that I go
To answer this your charge?

BRABANTIO: To prison, till fit time
Of law and course of direct session
Call thee to answer.

OTHELLO: What if I do obey?
How may the Duke be therewith satisfied,
Whose messengers are here about my side
Upon some present business of the state   9
To bring me to him?

OFFICER: 'Tis true, most worthy signior.
The Duke's in council, and your noble self,

l. 72. *gross in sense:* obvious.
l. 75. *motion:* common sense.
l. 77. *attach:* arrest.

I am sure, is sent for.

BRABANTIO: How? The Duke in council?
In this time of the night? Bring him away!
Mine's not an idle cause. The Duke himself,
Or any of my brothers of the state,
Cannot but feel this wrong as 'twere their own;
For if such actions may have passage free,
Bondslaves and pagans shall our statesmen be.

(Exeunt.)

SCENE III

(Venice. A chamber in the Senate House.)

(Enter DUKE *and* SENATORS, *set at a table, with lights and*
ATTENDANTS.*)*

DUKE: There is no composition in these news
That gives them credit.
I SENATOR: Indeed they are disproportioned.
My letters say a hundred and seven galleys.
DUKE: And mine a hundred forty.
2 SENATOR: And mine two hundred.
But though they jump not on a just account
(As in these cases where the aim reports
'Tis oft with difference), yet do they all confirm
A Turkish fleet, and bearing up to Cyprus.
DUKE: Nay, it is possible enough to judgment.
I do not so secure me in the error   10
But the main article I do approve
In fearful sense.
SAILOR *(within)*:   What, ho! what, ho! what, ho!

(Enter SAILOR.*)*

OFFICER: A messenger from the galleys.
DUKE: Now, what's the business?

l. 1. *composition:* consistency.
l. 5. *jump:* agree.
l. 6. *the aim:* conjecture.
l. 10. *secure me in:* feel safe.
l. 11. *approve:* accept.

SAILOR: The Turkish preparation makes for Rhodes.
    So was I bid report here to the state
    By Signior Angelo.
DUKE: How say you by this change?
I SENATOR: This cannot be
    By no assay of reason. 'Tis a pageant
    To keep us in false gaze. When we consider
    Th' importancy of Cyprus to the Turk,   2
    And let ourselves again but understand
    That, as it more concerns the Turk than Rhodes,
    So may he with more facile question bear it,
    For that it stands not in such warlike brace,
    But altogether lacks th' abilities
    That Rhodes is dressed in—if we make thought of this,
    We must not think the Turk is so unskilful
    To leave that latest which concerns him first,
    Neglecting an attempt of ease and gain
    To wake and wage a danger profitless.   3
DUKE: Nay, in all confidence he's not for Rhodes.
OFFICER: Here is more news.

                (*Enter a* MESSENGER.)

MESSENGER: The Ottomites, reverend and gracious,
    Steering with due course toward the isle of Rhodes,
    Have there injointed them with an after fleet.
I SENATOR: Ay, so I thought. How many, as you guess?
MESSENGER: Of thirty sail; and now they do re-stem
    Their backward course, bearing with frank appearance
    Their purposes toward Cyprus. Signior Montano,
    Your trusty and most valiant servitor,
    With his free duty recommends you thus,   4
    And prays you to believe him.
DUKE: 'Tis certain then for Cyprus.
    Marcus Luccicos, is not he in town?
I SENATOR: He's now in Florence.
DUKE: Write from us to him; post-post-haste dispatch.

l. 18. *assay:* test.
l. 23. *more facile . . .* : capture it more easily.
l. 35. *injointed:* joined.
ll. 37–38. *re-stem . . . course:* turn back.
l. 38. *with frank appearance:* making no attempt to hide.
l. 41. *recommends:* reports.

(*Enter* BRABANTIO, OTHELLO, CASSIO, IAGO, RODERIGO,
and OFFICERS.)

1 SENATOR: Here comes Brabantio and the valiant Moor.
DUKE: Valiant Othello, we must straight employ you
    Against the general enemy Ottoman.
    (*To* BRABANTIO)
    I did not see you. Welcome, gentle signior.   50
    We lacked your counsel and your help tonight.
BRABANTIO: So did I yours. Good your Grace, pardon me.
    Neither my place, nor aught I heard of business,
    Hath raised me from my bed; nor doth the general care
    Take hold on me; for my particular grief
    Is of so floodgate and o'erbearing nature
    That it engluts and swallows other sorrows,
    And it is still itself.
DUKE: Why, what's the matter?
BRABANTIO: My daughter! O, my daughter!
ALL: Dead?
BRABANTIO: Ay, to me!
    She is abused, stol'n from me, and corrupted   60
    By spells and medicines bought of mountebanks;
    For nature so prepost'rously to err,
    Being not deficient, blind, or lame of sense,
    Sans witchcraft could not.
DUKE: Whoe'er he be that in this foul proceeding
    Hath thus beguiled your daughter of herself,
    And you of her, the bloody book of law
    You shall yourself read in the bitter letter
    After your own sense; yea, though our proper son
    Stood in your action.
BRABANTIO: Humbly I thank your Grace.   70
    Here is the man—this Moor, whom now, it seems,
    Your special mandate, for the state affairs,
    Hath hither brought.
ALL: We are very sorry for't.
DUKE (*to* OTHELLO): What, in your own part, can you say to this?

l. 55. *particular*: personal.
l. 57. *engluts*: devours.
l. 64. *Sans*: without.
l. 70. *Stood in your action*: were accused by you.

BRABANTIO: Nothing, but this is so.

OTHELLO: Most potent, grave, and reverend signiors,
My very noble, and approved good masters:
That I have ta'en away this old man's daughter,
It is most true; true I have married her.
The very head and front of my offending   8
Hath this extent, no more. Rude am I in my speech,
And little blessed with the soft phrase of peace;
For since these arms of mine had seven years' pith
Till now some nine moons wasted, they have used
Their dearest action in the tented field;
And little of this great world can I speak
More than pertains to feats of broil and battle;
And therefore little shall I grace my cause
In speaking for myself. Yet, by your gracious patience,
I will a round unvarnished tale deliver   9
Of my whole course of love—what drugs, what charms,
What conjuration, and what mighty magic
(For such proceeding am I charged withal)
I won his daughter.

BRABANTIO: A maiden never bold;
Of spirit so still and quiet that her motion
Blushed at herself; and she—in spite of nature,
Of years, of country, credit, everything—
To fall in love with what she feared to look on!
It is a judgment maimed and most imperfect
That will confess perfection so could err   10
Against all rules of nature, and must be driven
To find out practices of cunning hell
Why this should be. I therefore vouch again
That with some mixtures pow'rful o'er the blood,
Or with some dram, conjured to this effect,
He wrought upon her.

DUKE: To vouch this is no proof,
Without more certain and more overt test
Than these thin habits and poor likelihoods

l. 77. *approved:* proved.
l. 90. *round:* plain.
l. 95. *motion:* emotion.
l. 102. *practices:* plots.
l. 108. *thin habits:* thin clothing, i.e., small evidence.

Of modern seeming do prefer against him.

1 SENATOR: But, Othello, speak.   110
  Did you by indirect and forced courses
  Subdue and poison this young maid's affections?
  Or came it by request, and such fair question
  As soul to soul affordeth?

OTHELLO: I do beseech you,
  Send for the lady to the Sagittary
  And let her speak of me before her father.
  If you do find me foul in her report,
  The trust, the office, I do hold of you
  Not only take away, but let your sentence
  Even fall upon my life.

DUKE: Fetch Desdemona hither.   120

OTHELLO: Ancient, conduct them; you best know the place.

        (*Exeunt* IAGO *and two or three* ATTENDANTS.)

  And till she come, as truly as to heaven
  I do confess the vices of my blood,
  So justly to your grave ears I'll present
  How I did thrive in this fair lady's love,
  And she in mine.

DUKE: Say it, Othello.

OTHELLO: Her father loved me, oft invited me;
  Still questioned me the story of my life
  From year to year—the battles, sieges, fortunes   130
  That I have passed.
  I ran it through, even from my boyish days
  To the very moment that he bade me tell it.
  Wherein I spake of most disastrous chances,
  Of moving accidents by flood and field;
  Of hairbreadth scapes i' th' imminent deadly breach;
  Of being taken by the insolent foe
  And sold to slavery; of my redemption thence
  And portance in my travel's history;
  Wherein of antres vast and deserts idle,   140
  Rough quarries, rocks, and hills whose heads touch heaven,

l. 109. *modern:* ordinary.
l. 111. *indirect:* illegal.
l. 129. *Still:* continually.
l. 139. *portance:* conduct.
l. 140. *antres:* caves.

It was my hint to speak—such was the process;
And of the Cannibals that each other eat,
The Anthropophagi, and men whose heads
Do grow beneath their shoulders. This to hear
Would Desdemona seriously incline;
But still the house affairs would draw her thence;
Which ever as she could with haste dispatch,
She'd come again, and with a greedy ear
Devour up my discourse. Which I observing,   15
Took once a pliant hour, and found good means
To draw from her a prayer of earnest heart
That I would all my pilgrimage dilate,
Whereof by parcels she had something heard,
But not intentively. I did consent,
And often did beguile her of her tears
When I did speak of some distressful stroke
That my youth suffered. My story being done,
She gave me for my pains a world of sighs.
She swore, in faith, 'twas strange, 'twas passing strange;   16
'Twas pitiful, 'twas wondrous pitiful.
She wished she had not heard it; yet she wished
That heaven had made her such a man. She thanked me;
And bade me, if I had a friend that loved her,
I should but teach him how to tell my story,
And that would woo her. Upon this hint I spake.
She loved me for the dangers I had passed,
And I loved her that she did pity them.
This only is the witchcraft I have used.
Here comes the lady: let her witness it.   17

(*Enter* DESDEMONA, IAGO, ATTENDANTS.)

DUKE: I think this tale would win my daughter too.
    Good Brabantio,
    Take up this mangled matter at the best.
    Men do their broken weapons rather use

l. 144. *Anthropophagi:* cannibals.
l. 151. *pliant:* favorable.
l. 153. *dilate:* tell fully.
l. 154. *parcels:* bits.
l. 155. *intentively:* with undivided attention.
l. 163. *her:* for her

Than their bare hands.

BRABANTIO: I pray you hear her speak.
If she confess that she was half the wooer,
Destruction on my head if my bad blame
Light on the man! Come hither, gentle mistress.
Do you perceive in all this noble company
Where most you owe obedience?

DESDEMONA: My noble father,   180
I do perceive here a divided duty.
To you I am bound for life and education;
My life and education both do learn me
How to respect you: you are the lord of duty;
I am hitherto your daughter. But here's my husband;
And so much duty as my mother showed
To you, preferring you before her father,
So much I challenge that I may profess
Due to the Moor my lord.

BRABANTIO: God be with you! I have done.
Please it your Grace, on to the state affairs.   190
I had rather to adopt a child than get it.
Come hither, Moor.
I here do give thee that with all my heart
Which, but thou hast already, with all my heart
I would keep from thee. For your sake, jewel,
I am glad at soul I have no other child;
For thy escape would teach me tyranny,
To hang clogs on them. I have done, my lord.

DUKE: Let me speak like yourself and lay a sentence
Which, as a grise or step, may help these lovers   200
Into your favor.
When remedies are past, the griefs are ended
By seeing the worst, which late on hopes depended.
To mourn a mischief that is past and gone
Is the next way to draw new mischief on.
What cannot be preserved when fortune takes,
Patience her injury a mock'ry makes.

l. 186. *hint*: opportunity.
l. 191. *get*: beget.
l. 195. *For your sake*: because of you.
l. 197. *escape*: escapade.
l. 199. *like yourself*: as you should.
l. 200. *grise*: a step or degree.

The robbed that smiles steals something from the thief;
He robs himself that spends a bootless grief.

BRABANTIO: So let the Turk of Cyprus us beguile: 2**
We lose it not, so long as we can smile.
He bears the sentence well that nothing bears
But the free comfort which from thence he hears;
But he bears both the sentence and the sorrow
That to pay grief must of poor patience borrow.
These sentences, to sugar, or to gall,
Being strong on both sides, are equivocal.
But words are words: I never yet did hear
That the bruised heart was pierced through the ear.
I humbly beseech you, proceed to the affairs of state.   22

DUKE: The Turk with a most mighty preparation makes for Cyprus. Othello, the fortitude of the place is best known to you; and though we have there a substitute of most allowed sufficiency, yet opinion, a sovereign mistress of effects, throws a more safer voice on you. You must therefore be content to slubber the gloss of your new fortunes with this more stubborn and boist'rous expedition.

OTHELLO: The tyrant custom, most grave senators,
Hath made the flinty and steel couch of war
My thrice-driven bed of down. I do agnize
A natural and prompt alacrity   23
I find in hardness; and do undertake
These present wars against the Ottomites.
Most humbly, therefore, bending to your state,
I crave fit disposition for my wife;
Due reference of place, and exhibition,
With such accommodation and besort
As levels with her breeding.

DUKE: If you please,
Be't at her father's.

BRABANTIO: I'll not have it so.

l. 209. *bootless*: futile.
l. 217. *equivocal*: equal.
l. 223. *allowed sufficiency*: recognized ability.
l. 225. *slubber*: make dull.
l. 226. *stubborn*: dangerous.
l. 229. *agnize*: acknowledge, confess.
l. 231. *hardness*: hardship.
l. 235. *exhibition*: subsistence allowance.
l. 236. *besort*: suitable company.

OTHELLO: Nor I.

DESDEMONA: Nor would I there reside,
To put my father in impatient thoughts   240
By being in his eye. Most gracious Duke,
To my unfolding lend your prosperous ear,
And let me find a charter in your voice,
T' assist my simpleness.

DUKE: What would you, Desdemona?

DESDEMONA: That I did love the Moor to live with him,
My downright violence, and storm of fortunes,
May trumpet to the world. My heart's subdued
Even to the very quality of my lord.
I saw Othello's visage in his mind,   250
And to his honors and his valiant parts
Did I my soul and fortunes consecrate.
So that, dear lords, if I be left behind,
A moth of peace, and he go to the war,
The rights for which I love him are bereft me,
And I a heavy interim shall support
By his dear absence. Let me go with him.

OTHELLO: Let her have your voice.
Vouch with me heaven, I therefore beg it not
To please the palate of my appetite,   260
Nor to comply with heat, the young affects
In my defunct and proper satisfaction;
But to be free and bounteous to her mind.
And heaven defend your good souls that you think
I will your serious and great business scant
For she is with me. No, when light-winged toys
Of feathered Cupid seel with wanton dullness
My speculative and officed instruments,
That my disports corrupt and taint my business,
Let housewives make a skillet of my helm,   270
And all indign and base adversities

l. 242. *prosperous ear:* listen with favor.
l. 243. *charter:* privilege.
l. 251. *parts:* qualities.
l. 261. *young affects:* passion.
l. 262. *defunct:* postponed.
l. 267. *seel:* blinded like a hunting hawk that has its eyelids sewn.
l. 268. *speculative and officed instruments:* eyes whose duty is to watch.
l. 271. *indign:* unworthy.

Make head against my estimation!

DUKE: Be it as you shall privately determine,
Either for her stay or going. Th' affair cries haste,
And speed must answer it. You must away tonight.

OTHELLO: With all my heart.

DUKE: At nine i' th' morning here we'll meet again.
Othello, leave some officer behind,
And he shall our commission bring to you;
With such things else of quality and respect   28
As doth import you.

OTHELLO: So please your Grace, my ancient.
A man he is of honesty and trust.
To his conveyance I assign my wife,
With what else needful your good Grace shall think
To be sent after me.

DUKE: Let it be so.
Good night to every one.
(*To* BRABANTIO)
                            And, noble signior,
If virtue no delighted beauty lack,
Your son-in-law is far more fair than black.

I SENATOR: Adieu, brave Moor. Use Desdemona well.

BRABANTIO: Look to her, Moor, if thou hast eyes to see.   29
She has deceived her father, and may thee.
                    (*Exit with* DUKE, SENATORS, OFFICERS, *etc.*)

OTHELLO: My life upon her faith!—Honest Iago,
My Desdemona must I leave to thee.
I prithee let thy wife attend on her,
And bring them after in the best advantage.
Come, Desdemona. I have but an hour
Of love, of worldly matters and direction,
To spend with thee. We must obey the time.
                            (*Exeunt* MOOR *and* DESDEMONA.)

RODERIGO: Iago.

IAGO: What say'st thou, noble heart?   30

RODERIGO: What will I do, think'st thou?

l. 272. *Make head . . . estimation*: attack my reputation.
l. 281. *import*: concern.
l. 283. *conveyance*: escort.
l. 287. *delighted*: delightful.
l. 295. *advantage*: opportunity.

IAGO: Why, go to bed and sleep.

RODERIGO: I will incontinently drown myself.

IAGO: If thou dost, I shall never love thee after. Why, thou silly gentleman!

RODERIGO: It is silliness to live when to live is torment; and then have we a prescription to die when death is our physician.

IAGO: O villainous! I have looked upon the world for four times seven years; and since I could distinguish betwixt a benefit and an injury, I never found man that knew how to love himself. Ere I would say   310
I would drown myself for the love of a guinea hen, I would change my humanity with a baboon.

RODERIGO: What should I do? I confess it is my shame to be so fond, but it is not in my virtue to amend it.

IAGO: Virtue? a fig! 'Tis in ourselves that we are thus or thus. Our bodies are our gardens, to the which our wills are gardeners; so that if we will plant nettles or sow lettuce, set hyssop and weed up thyme, supply it with one gender of herbs or distract it with many—either to have it sterile with idleness or manured with in-dustry—why, the power and corrigible authority of this lies in our   320
wills. If the balance of our lives had not one scale of reason to poise another of sensuality, the blood and baseness of our natures would conduct us to most prepost'rous conclusions. But we have reason to cool our raging motions, our carnal stings, our unbitted lusts; whereof I take this that you call love to be a sect or scion.

RODERIGO: It cannot be.

IAGO: It is merely a lust of the blood and a permission of the will. Come, be a man! Drown thyself? Drown cats and blind puppies! I have professed me thy friend, and I confess me knit to thy deserv-ing with cables of perdurable toughness. I could never better stead   330
thee than now. Put money in thy purse. Follow thou the wars; defeat thy favor with an usurped beard. I say, put money in thy purse. It cannot be that Desdemona should long continue her love

l. 303. *incontinently:* at once.
l. 317. *hyssop:* an herb.
l. 319. *manured:* cultivated.
l. 320. *corrigible:* corrective.
l. 321. *poise:* counterbalance.
l. 324. *unbitted:* unbridled.
l. 325. *sect or scion:* cutting or graft.
l. 330. *perdurable:* enduring.
     stead: support.
l. 332. *defeat thy favor . . . beard:* spoil your looks with a false beard.

to the Moor—put money in thy purse—nor he his to her. It was a violent commencement, and thou shalt see an answerable sequestration. Put but money in thy purse. These Moors are changeable in their wills. Fill thy purse with money. The food that to him now is as luscious as locusts shall be to him shortly as bitter as coloquintida. She must change for youth. When she is sated with his body, she will find the error of her choice. She must have 340 change, she must. Therefore put money in thy purse. If thou wilt needs damn thyself, do it a more delicate way than drowning. Make all the money thou canst. If sanctimony and a frail vow betwixt an erring barbarian and a supersubtle Venetian be not too hard for my wits and all the tribe of hell, thou shalt enjoy her. Therefore make money. A pox of drowning thyself! It is clean out of the way. Seek thou rather to be hanged in compassing thy joy than to be drowned and go without her.

RODERIGO: Wilt thou be fast to my hopes, if I depend on the issue?

IAGO: Thou art sure of me. Go, make money. I have told thee often, 350 and I re-tell thee again and again, I hate the Moor. My cause is hearted; thine hath no less reason. Let us be conjunctive in our revenge against him. If thou canst cuckold him, thou dost thyself a pleasure, me a sport. There are many events in the womb of time, which will be delivered. Traverse! go! provide thy money! We will have more of this tomorrow. Adieu.

RODERIGO: Where shall we meet i' the morning?

IAGO: At my lodging.

RODERIGO: I'll be with thee betimes.

IAGO: Go to, farewell.—Do you hear, Roderigo?   360

RODERIGO: What say you?

IAGO: No more of drowning, do you hear?

RODERIGO: I am changed. I'll go sell all my land.   (*Exit.*)

IAGO: Thus do I ever make my fool my purse;
    For I mine own gained knowledge should profane
    If I would time expend with such a snipe

---

ll. 335–336. *answerable sequestration:* corresponding estrangement.
l. 338. *locusts:* locust fruit.
ll. 338–339. *coloquintida:* a medicine.
l. 345. *erring:* wandering.
l. 346. *clean out of the way:* wrong course of action.
l. 347. *compassing:* achieving.
l. 352. *hearted:* heartfelt.
     conjunctive: united.
l. 355. *Traverse:* about face.

But for my sport and profit. I hate the Moor;
And it is thought abroad that 'twixt my sheets
'Has done my office. I know not if't be true;
Yet I, for mere suspicion in that kind,   370
Will do as if for surety. He holds me well;
The better shall my purpose work on him.
Cassio's a proper man. Let me see now:
To get his place, and to plume up my will
In double knavery—How, how? Let's see.
After some time, to abuse Othello's ear
That he is too familiar with his wife.
He hath a person and a smooth dispose
To be suspected—framed to make women false.
The Moor is of a free and open nature   380
That thinks men honest that but seem to be so,
And will as tenderly be led by the nose
As asses are.
I have't! It is engend'red! Hell and night
Must bring this monstrous birth to the world's light.

                                                              (*Exit.*)

✁✁

ACT II

SCENE I

(*A seaport in Cyprus. An open place near the harbor.*)

(*Enter* MONTANO *and two* GENTLEMEN.)

MONTANO: What from the cape can you discern at sea?
I GENTLEMAN: Nothing at all, it is a high-wrought flood;
    I cannot 'twixt the heaven and the main
    Descry a sail.
MONTANO: Methinks the wind hath spoke aloud at land;
    A fuller blast ne'er shook our battlements.

l. 369. *'Has:* he (i.e., Othello) has.
l. 373. *proper:* handsome.
l. 378. *dispose:* disposition.

If it hath ruffianed so upon the sea,
What ribs of oak, when mountains melt on them,
Can hold the mortise? What shall we hear of this?
2 GENTLEMAN: A segregation of the Turkish fleet.
For do but stand upon the foaming shore,
The chidden billow seems to pelt the clouds;
The wind-shaked surge, with high and monstrous mane,
Seems to cast water on the burning Bear
And quench the Guards of th' ever-fixed pole.
I never did like molestation view
On the enchafed flood.
MONTANO: If that the Turkish fleet
Be not ensheltered and embayed, they are drowned.
It is impossible they bear it out.

(Enter a third GENTLEMAN.*)*

3 GENTLEMAN: News, lads! Our wars are done.
The desperate tempest hath so banged the Turks
That their designment halts. A noble ship of Venice
Hath seen a grievous wrack and sufferance
On most part of their fleet.
MONTANO: How? Is this true?
3 GENTLEMAN: The ship is here put in,
A Veronesa; Michael Cassio,
Lieutenant to the warlike Moor Othello,
Is come on shore; the Moor himself at sea,
And is in full commission here for Cyprus.
MONTANO: I am glad on't. 'Tis a worthy governor.
3 GENTLEMAN: But this same Cassio, though he speak of comfort
Touching the Turkish loss, yet he looks sadly
And prays the Moor be safe, for they were parted
With foul and violent tempest.
MONTANO: Pray heaven he be;
For I have served him, and the man commands
Like a full soldier. Let's to the seaside, ho!

l. 14. *burning Bear*: Ursa Minor.
l. 15. *Guards*: stars pointing to the North Pole.
l. 16. *molestation*: storm.
l. 17. *enchafed*: raging.
l. 18. *ensheltered and embayed*: at anchor in some bay.
l. 19. *bear*: ride.
l. 23. *sufferance*: disaster.

As well to see the vessel that's come in
As to throw out our eyes for brave Othello,
Even till we make the main and th' aerial blue
An indistinct regard.

3 GENTLEMAN: Come, let's do so;   40
For every minute is expectancy
Of more arrivance.

(*Enter* CASSIO.)

CASSIO: Thanks, you, the valiant of this warlike isle,
That so approve the Moor! O, let the heavens
Give him defense against the elements,
For I have lost him on a dangerous sea!
MONTANO: Is he well shipped?
CASSIO: His bark is stoutly timbered, and his pilot
Of very expert and approved allowance.
Therefore my hopes (not surfeited to death)   50
Stand in bold cure.
(*Within "A sail, a sail, a sail!"*)

(*Enter a* MESSENGER.)

CASSIO: What noise?
MESSENGER: The town is empty; on the brow o' the sea
Stand ranks of people, and they cry "A sail!"
CASSIO: My hopes do shape him for the Governor.
(*A shot*)
2 GENTLEMAN: They do discharge their shot of courtesy.
Our friends at least.
CASSIO: I pray you, sir, go forth
And give us truth who 'tis that is arrived.
2 GENTLEMAN: I shall.   (*Exit.*)
MONTANO: But, good Lieutenant, is your general wived?   60
CASSIO: Most fortunately. He hath achieved a maid
That paragons description and wild fame;
One that excels the quirks of blazoning pens,

ll. 39–40. *Even . . . regard:* until it is so dark that we can no longer distinguish between sea and sky.
l. 42. *arrivance:* arrivals (of ships).
l. 49. *approved allowance:* proven skill.
l. 51. *Stand . . . cure:* have hope for the best.
l. 55. *shape . . . Governor:* imagine that it is the Governor, Othello.
l. 62. *paragons:* surpasses.

And in th' essential vesture of creation
Does tire the ingener.

(*Enter* SECOND GENTLEMAN.)

How now? Who has put in?

2 GENTLEMAN: 'Tis one Iago, ancient to the General.

CASSIO: H'as had most favorable and happy speed.
Tempests themselves, high seas, and howling winds,
The guttered rocks and congregated sands,
Traitors ensteeped to clog the guiltless keel,   7
As having sense of beauty, do omit
Their mortal natures, letting go safely by
The divine Desdemona.

MONTANO: What is she?

CASSIO: She that I spake of, our great captain's captain,
Left in the conduct of the bold Iago,
Whose footing here anticipates our thoughts
A se'nnight's speed. Great Jove, Othello guard,
And swell his sail with thine own pow'rful breath,
That he may bless this bay with his tall ship,
Make love's quick pants in Desdemona's arms,   8
Give renewed fire to our extincted spirits,
And bring all Cyprus comfort!

(*Enter* DESDEMONA, IAGO, RODERIGO, *and* EMILIA *with*
ATTENDANTS.)

O, behold!
The riches of the ship is come on shore!
You men of Cyprus, let her have your knees.
Hail to thee, lady! and the grace of heaven,
Before, behind thee, and on every hand,
Enwheel thee round!

DESDEMONA: I thank you, valiant Cassio.
What tidings can you tell me of my lord?

CASSIO: He is not yet arrived; nor know I aught
But that he's well and will be shortly here.   9

DESDEMONA: O, but I fear! How lost you company?

CASSIO: The great contention of the sea and skies

l. 65. *ingener*: contriver.
l. 70. *ensteeped*: sunken.
l. 77. *se'nnight's*: a week's.
l. 87. *Enwheel thee round*: encompass you.

Parted our fellowship.
(*Within* "*A sail, a sail!*" *A shot*)
But hark. A sail!
2 GENTLEMAN: They give their greeting to the citadel.
This likewise is a friend.
CASSIO: See for the news.
(*Exit* GENTLEMAN.)

Good ancient, you are welcome.
(*To* EMILIA)
Welcome, mistress.
Let it not gall your patience, good Iago,
That I extend my manners. 'Tis my breeding
That gives me this bold show of courtesy.
(*Kisses her.*)
IAGO: Sir, would she give you so much of her lips   100
As of her tongue she oft bestows on me,
You would have enough.
DESDEMONA: Alas, she has no speech!
IAGO: In faith, too much.
I find it still when I have list to sleep.
Marry, before your ladyship, I grant,
She puts her tongue a little in her heart
And chides with thinking.
EMILIA: You have little cause to say so.
IAGO: Come on, come on! You are pictures out of doors,
Bells in your parlors, wildcats in your kitchens,   110
Saints in your injuries, devils being offended,
Players in your housewifery, and housewives in your beds.
DESDEMONA: O, fie upon thee, slanderer!
IAGO: Nay, it is true, or else I am a Turk.
You rise to play, and go to bed to work.
EMILIA: You shall not write my praise.
IAGO: No, let me not.
DESDEMONA: What wouldst thou write of me, if thou shouldst praise
me?
IAGO: O gentle lady, do not put me to't,
For I am nothing if not critical.
DESDEMONA: Come on, assay.—There's one gone to the harbor?   120

l. 104. *still . . . list:* always when I wish.
ll. 106–107. *She puts . . . chides with thinking:* Emilia holds her tongue
before Desdemona and only scolds in her thoughts.
l. 120. *assay:* try.

IAGO: Ay, madam.

DESDEMONA: I am not merry; but I do beguile
    The thing I am by seeming otherwise.
    Come, how wouldst thou praise me?

IAGO: I am about it; but indeed my invention
    Comes from my pate as birdlime does from frieze—
    It plucks out brains and all. But my Muse labors,
    And thus she is delivered:
            If she be fair and wise, fairness and wit—
            The one's for use, the other useth it.   13(

DESDEMONA: Well praised! How if she be black and witty?

IAGO: If she be black, and thereto have a wit,
    She'll find a white that shall her blackness fit.

DESDEMONA: Worse and worse!

EMILIA: How if fair and foolish?

IAGO: She never yet was foolish that was fair,
    For even her folly helped her to an heir.

DESDEMONA: These are old fond paradoxes to make fools laugh i' th'
alehouse. What miserable praise hast thou for her that's foul and
foolish?   14(

IAGO: There's none so foul, and foolish thereunto,
    But does foul pranks which fair and wise ones do.

DESDEMONA: O heavy ignorance! Thou praisest the worst best. But
what praise couldst thou bestow on a deserving woman indeed—
one that, in the authority of her merit, did justly put on the vouch
of very malice itself?

IAGO: She that was ever fair, and never proud;
        Had tongue at will, and yet was never loud;
        Never lacked gold, and yet went never gay;
        Fled from her wish, and yet said "Now I may";   15(
    She that, being angered, her revenge being nigh,
    Bade her wrong stay, and her displeasure fly;
        She that in wisdom never was so frail
    To change the cod's head for the salmon's tail;
    She that could think, and ne'er disclose her mind;
        See suitors following, and not look behind:
    She was a wight (if ever such wight were)—

l. 126. *birdlime:* sticky paste.
    frieze: rough paste.
l. 138. *fond:* foolish.
ll. 145–146. *put . . . malice:* make even malice vouch for her merit.
l. 157. *wight:* person; note Iago's pun on "wight-white" in ll. 132–133.

DESDEMONA: To do what?

IAGO: To suckle fools and chronicle small beer.

DESDEMONA: O most lame and impotent conclusion! Do not learn of   160
him, Emilia, though he be thy husband. How say you, Cassio? Is
he not a most profane and liberal counsellor?

CASSIO: He speaks home, madam. You may relish him more in the
soldier than in the scholar.

IAGO (*aside*): He takes her by the palm. Ay, well said, whisper! With
as little a web as this will I ensnare as great a fly as Cassio. Ay,
smile upon her, do! I will gyve thee in thine own courtship. You
say true; 'tis so, indeed! If such tricks as these strip you out of your
lieutenantry, it had been better you had not kissed your three fingers so oft—which now again you are most apt to play the sir in.   170
Very good! well kissed! an excellent curtsy! 'Tis so, indeed. Yet
again your fingers to your lips? Would they were clyster pipes for
your sake! (*Trumpet within*) The Moor! I know his trumpet.

CASSIO: 'Tis truly so.

DESDEMONA: Let's meet him and receive him.

CASSIO: Lo, where he comes!

(*Enter* OTHELLO *and* ATTENDANTS.)

OTHELLO: O my fair warrior!

DESDEMONA: My dear Othello!

OTHELLO: It gives me wonder great as my content
To see you here before me. O my soul's joy!
If after every tempest come such calms,   180
May the winds blow till they have wakened death!
And let the laboring bark climb hills of seas
Olympus-high, and duck again as low
As hell's from heaven! If it were now to die,
'Twere now to be most happy; for I fear
My soul hath her content so absolute
That not another comfort like to this
Succeeds in unknown fate.

DESDEMONA: The heavens forbid
But that our loves and comforts should increase
Even as our days do grow!

OTHELLO: Amen to that, sweet powers!   190

l. 159. *chronicle small beer:* keep household accounts.
l. 167. *gyve:* tie up.
l. 172. *clyster pipes:* syringes.

I cannot speak enough of this content;
It stops me here; it is too much of joy.
And this, and this, the greatest discords be
(*They kiss.*)
That e'er our hearts shall make!

IAGO (*aside*):   O, you are well tuned now!
But I'll set down the pegs that make this music,
As honest as I am.

OTHELLO: Come, let us to the castle.
News, friends! Our wars are done; the Turks are drowned.
How does my old acquaintance of this isle?—
Honey, you shall be well desired in Cyprus;
I have found great love amongst them. O my sweet,   20
I prattle out of fashion, and I dote
In mine own comforts. I prithee, good Iago,
Go to the bay and disembark my coffers.
Bring thou the master to the citadel.
He is a good one, and his worthiness
Does challenge much respect.—Come, Desdemona,
Once more well met at Cyprus.

                    (*Exeunt all but* IAGO *and* RODERIGO.)

IAGO: Do thou meet me presently at the harbor. Come hither. If thou
be'st valiant (as they say base men being in love have then a nobility in their natures more than is native to them), list me. The Lieu-   21
tenant tonight watches on the court of guard. First, I must tell thee
this: Desdemona is directly in love with him.

RODERIGO: With him? Why, 'tis not possible.

IAGO: Lay thy finger thus, and let thy soul be instructed. Mark me
with what violence she first loved the Moor, but for bragging and
telling her fantastical lies; and will she love him still for prating?
Let not thy discreet heart think it. Her eye must be fed; and what
delight shall she have to look on the devil? When the blood is
made dull with the act of sport, there should be, again to inflame it
and to give satiety a fresh appetite, loveliness in favor, sympathy in   22
years, manners, and beauties; all which the Moor is defective in.
Now for want of these required conveniences, her delicate tenderness will find itself abused, begin to heave the gorge, disrelish and
abhor the Moor. Very nature will instruct her in it and compel her
to some second choice. Now, sir, this granted (as it is a most preg-

l. 195. *set down the pegs:* untune.
l. 203. *coffers:* baggage.

nant and unforced position), who stands so eminent in the degree of this fortune as Cassio does? A knave very voluble; no further conscionable than in putting on the mere form of civil and humane seeming for the better compass of his salt and most hidden loose affection? Why, none! why, none! A slipper and subtle knave; a finder of occasion; that has an eye can stamp and counterfeit advantages, though true advantage never present itself; a devilish knave! Besides, the knave is handsome, young, and hath all those requisites in him that folly and green minds look after. A pestilent complete knave! and the woman hath found him already.   230

RODERIGO: I cannot believe that in her. She's full of most blessed condition.

IAGO: Blessed fig's-end! The wine she drinks is made of grapes. If she had been blessed, she would never have loved the Moor. Blessed pudding! Didst thou not see her paddle with the palm of his hand? Didst not mark that?   240

RODERIGO: Yes, that I did; but that was but courtesy.

IAGO: Lechery, by this hand! an index and obscure prologue to the history of lust and foul thoughts. They met so near with their lips that their breaths embraced together. Villainous thoughts, Roderigo! When these mutualities so marshal the way, hard at hand comes the master and main exercise, th' incorporate conclusion. Pish! But, sir, be you ruled by me. I have brought you from Venice. Watch you tonight; for the command, I'll lay't upon you. Cassio knows you not. I'll not be far from you. Do you find some occasion to anger Cassio, either by speaking too loud, or tainting his discipline, or from what other course you please which the time shall more favorably minister.   250

RODERIGO: Well.

IAGO: Sir, he is rash and very sudden in choler, and haply with his truncheon may strike at you. Provoke him that he may; for even out of that will I cause these of Cyprus to mutiny; whose qualification shall come into no true taste again but by the displanting of Cassio. So shall you have a shorter journey to your desires by the

l. 228. *conscionable:* conscientious.
l. 229. *salt:* lechery.
l. 230. *slipper:* slippery.
l. 246. *mutualities:* exchanges.
l. 247. *incorporate:* carnal, bodily.
l. 251. *tainting:* disparaging.
l. 257. *qualification:* appeasement.
l. 258. *true taste:* satisfactory state.

means I shall then have to prefer them; and the impediment most   260
profitably removed without the which there were no expectation of
our prosperity.

RODERIGO: I will do this if I can bring it to any opportunity.

IAGO: I warrant thee. Meet me by-and-by at the citadel. I must fetch
his necessaries ashore. Farewell.

RODERIGO: Adieu.   (*Exit.*)

IAGO: That Cassio loves her, I do well believe it;
That she loves him, 'tis apt and of great credit.
The Moor (howbeit that I endure him not)
Is of a constant, loving, noble nature,   270
And I dare think he'll prove to Desdemona
A most dear husband. Now I do love her too;
Not out of absolute lust (though peradventure
I stand accountant for as great a sin)
But partly led to diet my revenge,
For that I do suspect the lusty Moor
Hath leaped into my seat; the thought whereof
Doth, like a poisonous mineral, gnaw my inwards;
And nothing can or shall content my soul
Till I am evened with him, wife for wife;   280
Or failing so, yet that I put the Moor
At least into a jealousy so strong
That judgment cannot cure. Which thing to do
If this poor trash of Venice, whom I trace
For his quick hunting, stand the putting on,
I'll have our Michael Cassio on the hip,
Abuse him to the Moor in the right garb
(For I fear Cassio with my nightcap too),
Make the Moor thank me, love me, and reward me
For making him egregiously an ass   290
And practicing upon his peace and quiet
Even to madness. 'Tis here, but yet confused.
Knavery's plain face is never seen till used.

                                                              (*Exit.*)

l. 260. *prefer:* proffer, advance.
l. 275. *diet:* feed.
l. 284. *trace:* hold back.
l. 285. *stand the putting on:* react to my inciting.
l. 286. *on the hip:* at my mercy.
l. 287. *right garb:* gross manner.
l. 291. *practicing upon:* plotting against.

SCENE II

(Cyprus. Before Othello's Castle.)

(Enter Othello's HERALD, *with a proclamation; people following.)*

HERALD: It is Othello's pleasure, our noble and valiant general, that, upon certain tidings now arrived, importing the mere perdition of the Turkish fleet, every man put himself into triumph; some to dance, some to make bonfires, each man to what sport and revels his addiction leads him. For, besides these beneficial news, it is the celebration of his nuptial. So much was his pleasure should be proclaimed. All offices are open, and there is full liberty of feasting from this present hour of five till the bell have told eleven. Heaven bless the isle of Cyprus and our noble general Othello!

(Exeunt.)

SCENE III

(Cyprus. Within the Castle.)

(Enter OTHELLO, DESDEMONA, CASSIO, *and* ATTENDANTS.*)*

OTHELLO: Good Michael, look you to the guard tonight.
　　Let's teach ourselves that honorable stop,
　　Not to outsport discretion.
CASSIO: Iago hath direction what to do;
　　But notwithstanding, with my personal eye
　　Will I look to't.
OTHELLO:　　　　　　Iago is most honest.
　　Michael, good night. Tomorrow with your earliest
　　Let me have speech with you.—Come, my dear love.
　　The purchase made, the fruits are to ensue;
　　That profit's yet to come 'tween me and you.—　　　　　10
　　Good night.
　　　　　　(Exeunt OTHELLO *and* DESDEMONA *with* ATTENDANTS.*)*

ii, l. 2. *mere perdition:* total destruction.
ii, l. 7. *offices:* kitchens and storage rooms.
iii, l. 3. *outsport discretion:* let the celebration go too far.

(*Enter* IAGO.)

CASSIO: Welcome, Iago. We must to the watch.

IAGO: Not this hour, Lieutenant; 'tis not yet ten o' the clock. Our general cast us thus early for the love of his Desdemona; who let us not therefore blame. He hath not yet made wanton the night with her, and she is sport for Jove.

CASSIO: She's a most exquisite lady.

IAGO: And I'll warrant her, full of game.

CASSIO: Indeed, she's a most fresh and delicate creature.

IAGO: What an eye she has! Methinks it sounds a parley to provocation.   20

CASSIO: An inviting eye; and yet methinks right modest.

IAGO: And when she speaks, is it not an alarum to love?

CASSIO: She is indeed perfection.

IAGO: Well, happiness to their sheets! Come, Lieutenant, I have a stoup of wine, and here without are a brace of Cyprus gallants that would fain have a measure to the health of black Othello.

CASSIO: Not tonight, good Iago. I have very poor and unhappy brains for drinking. I could well wish courtesy would invent some other custom of entertainment.   30

IAGO: O, they are our friends. But one cup! I'll drink for you.

CASSIO: I have drunk but one cup tonight, and that was craftily qualified too; and behold what innovation it makes here. I am unfortunate in the infirmity and dare not task my weakness with any more.

IAGO: What, man! 'Tis a night of revels. The gallants desire it.

CASSIO: Where are they?

IAGO: Here at the door. I pray you call them in.

CASSIO: I'll do't, but it dislikes me.   (*Exit.*)

IAGO: If I can fasten but one cup upon him
With that which he hath drunk tonight already,   40
He'll be as full of quarrel and offense
As my young mistress' dog. Now my sick fool Roderigo,
Whom love hath turned almost the wrong side out,
To Desdemona hath tonight caroused
Potations pottle-deep; and he's to watch.
Three lads of Cyprus—noble swelling spirits,

l. 14. *cast:* dismissed.
l. 26. *stoup:* a tankard holding two quarts.
l. 33. *qualified:* diluted
    innovation: disturbance.
ll. 44–45. *caroused . . . pottle-deep:* drunk healths "bottoms up."

That hold their honors in a wary distance,
The very elements of this warlike isle—
Have I tonight flustered with flowing cups,
And they watch too. Now, 'mongst this flock of drunkards   50
Am I to put our Cassio in some action
That may offend the isle.

    (*Enter* CASSIO, MONTANO, *and* GENTLEMEN;
      SERVANT *with wine.*)

         But here they come.
If consequence do but approve my dream,
My boat sails freely, both with wind and stream.
CASSIO: Fore God, they have given me a rouse already.
MONTANO: Good faith, a little one; not past a pint, as I am a soldier.
IAGO: Some wine, ho!
 (*Sings.*)
    And let me the canakin clink, clink;
    And let me the canakin clink.
     A soldier's a man;   60
     A life's but a span,
    Why then, let a soldier drink.
 Some wine, boys!
CASSIO: Fore God, an excellent song!
IAGO: I learned it in England, where indeed they are most potent in
  potting. Your Dane, your German, and your swag-bellied Hol-
  lander—Drink, ho!—are nothing to your English.
CASSIO: Is your Englishman so expert in his drinking?
IAGO: Why, he drinks you with facility your Dane dead drunk; he
  sweats not to overthrow your Almain; he gives your Hollander a   70
  vomit ere the next pottle can be filled.
CASSIO: To the health of our General!
MONTANO: I am for it, Lieutenant, and I'll do you justice.
IAGO: O sweet England!
 (*Sings.*)
  King Stephen was and a worthy peer;
   His breeches cost him but a crown;
  He held 'em sixpence all too dear,

l. 47. *hold their honors . . . distance:* are sensitive about their honor.
l. 55. *rouse:* a great deal to drink.
l. 70. *Almain:* German.

With that he called the tailor lown.
He was a wight of high renown,
  And thou art but of low degree.   8(
'Tis pride that pulls the country down;
  Then take thine auld cloak about thee.

Some wine, ho!

CASSIO: Fore God, this is a more exquisite song than the other.

IAGO: Will you hear't again?

CASSIO: No, for I hold him unworthy of his place that does those
    things. Well, God's above all; and there be souls must be saved,
    and there be souls must not be saved.

IAGO: It's true, good Lieutenant.

CASSIO: For mine own part—no offense to the General, nor any man   9(
    of quality—I hope to be saved.

IAGO: And so do I too, Lieutenant.

CASSIO: Ay, but, by your leave, not before me. The lieutenant is to be
    saved before the ancient. Let's have no more of this; let's to our af-
    fairs. God forgive us our sins! Gentlemen, let's look to our business.
    Do not think, gentlemen, I am drunk. This is my ancient. This is
    my right hand, and this is my left. I am not drunk now. I can stand
    well enough, and speak well enough.

ALL: Excellent well!

CASSIO: Why, very well then. You must not think then that I am   10(
    drunk.   (*Exit.*)

MONTANO: To the platform, masters. Come, let's set the watch.

IAGO: You see this fellow that is gone before.
    He is a soldier fit to stand by Caesar
    And give direction; and do but see his vice.
    'Tis to his virtue a just equinox,
    The one as long as th' other. 'Tis pity of him.
    I fear the trust Othello puts him in,
    On some odd time of his infirmity,
    Will shake this island.

MONTANO: But is he often thus?   11(

IAGO: 'Tis evermore the prologue to his sleep.
    He'll watch the horologe a double set

l. 78. *lown:* rascal.
l. 106. *just equinox:* exact equivalent.
l. 109. *some odd time:* at some time or another.
l. 112. *horologe a double set:* stay awake twice around the clock, i.e.,
twenty-four hours.

If drink rock not his cradle.

MONTANO: It were well
The General were put in mind of it.
Perhaps he sees it not, or his good nature
Prizes the virtue that appears in Cassio
And looks not on his evils. Is not this true?

(*Enter* RODERIGO.)

IAGO (*aside to him*): How now, Roderigo?
I pray you after the Lieutenant, go!   (*Exit* RODERIGO.)
MONTANO: And 'tis great pity that the noble Moor   120
Should hazard such a place as his own second
With one of an engraffed infirmity.
It were an honest action to say
So to the Moor.
IAGO: Not I, for this fair island!
I do love Cassio well and would do much
To cure him of this evil.
(*Within "Help! Help!"*)
                         But hark! What noise?

(*Enter* CASSIO, *driving in* RODERIGO.)

CASSIO: 'Zounds, you rogue! you rascal!
MONTANO: What's the matter, Lieutenant?
CASSIO: A knave teach me my duty?
I'll beat the knave into a twiggen bottle.
RODERIGO: Beat me?
CASSIO: Dost thou prate, rogue?
(*Strikes him.*)
MONTANO: Nay, good lieutenant!   130
(*Takes his arm.*)
I pray you, sir, hold your hand.
CASSIO: Let me go, sir,
Or I'll knock you o'er the mazzard.
MONTANO: Come, come, you're drunk!
CASSIO: Drunk?
(*They fight.*)
IAGO (*aside to* RODERIGO): Away, I say! Go out and cry a mutiny!
                              (*Exit* RODERIGO.)

l. 122. *engraffed:* ingrained.
l. 129. *twiggen bottle:* bottle covered with wicker.
l. 132. *mazzard:* head.

Nay, good Lieutenant. God's will, gentlemen!
Help, ho!—Lieutenant—sir—Montano—sir—
Help, masters!—Here's a goodly watch indeed!
(*A bell rung.*)
Who's that which rings the bell? Diablo, ho!
The town will rise. God's will, Lieutenant, hold!
You will be shamed for ever.   140

(*Enter* OTHELLO *and* ATTENDANTS.)

OTHELLO: What is the matter here?
MONTANO: I bleed still. I am hurt to the death. He dies!
OTHELLO: Hold for your lives!
IAGO: Hold, hold! Lieutenant—sir—Montano—gentlemen!
     Have you forgot all sense of place and duty?
     Hold! The General speaks to you. Hold, hold, for shame!
OTHELLO: Why, how now, ho? From whence ariseth this?
     Are we turned Turks, and to ourselves do that
     Which heaven hath forbid the Ottomites?
     For Christian shame put by this barbarous brawl!   150
     He that stirs next to carve for his own rage
     Holds his soul light; he dies upon his motion.
     Silence that dreadful bell! It frights the isle
     From her propriety. What's the matter, masters?
     Honest Iago, that looks dead with grieving.
     Speak. Who began this? On thy love, I charge thee.
IAGO: I do not know. Friends all but now, even now,
     In quarter, and in terms like bride and groom
     Devesting them for bed; and then, but now
     (As if some planet had unwitted men)   160
     Swords out, and tilting one at other's breast
     In opposition bloody. I cannot speak
     Any beginning to this peevish odds,
     And would in action glorious I had lost
     Those legs that brought me to a part of it!
OTHELLO: How comes it, Michael, you are thus forgot?
CASSIO: I pray you pardon me; I cannot speak.
OTHELLO: Worthy Montano, you were wont be civil;
     The gravity and stillness of your youth

l. 151. *carve:* use his sword.
l. 158. *In quarter:* friendly.
l. 163. *peevish odds:* silly quarrel.

The world hath noted, and your name is great   170
In mouths of wisest censure. What's the matter
That you unlace your reputation thus
And spend your rich opinion for the name
Of a night-brawler? Give me answer to't.

MONTANO: Worthy Othello, I am hurt to danger.
Your officer, Iago, can inform you—
While I spare speech, which something now offends me—
Of all that I do know; nor know I aught
By me that's said or done amiss this night,
Unless self-charity be sometimes a vice,   180
And to defend ourselves it be a sin
When violence assails us.

OTHELLO: Now, by heaven,
My blood begins my safer guides to rule,
And passion, having my best judgment collied,
Assays to lead the way. If I once stir
Or do but lift this arm, the best of you
Shall sink in my rebuke. Give me to know
How this foul rout began, who set it on;
And he that is approved in this offense,
Though he had twinned with me, both at a birth,   190
Shall lose me. What! in a town of war,
Yet wild, the people's hearts brimful of fear,
To manage private and domestic quarrel?
In night, and on the court and guard of safety?
'Tis monstrous. Iago, who began 't?

MONTANO: If partially affined, or leagued in office,
Thou dost deliver more or less than truth,
Thou art no soldier.

IAGO: Touch me not so near.
I had rather have this tongue cut from my mouth
Than it should do offense to Michael Cassio.   200
Yet I persuade myself, to speak the truth

l. 171. *censure:* judgment.
l. 173. *rich opinion:* good reputation.
l. 177. *offends:* pains.
l. 183. *blood:* passion.
l. 184. *collied:* blackened.
l. 189. *approved in:* proved guilty.
l. 193. *manage:* engage in.
l. 196. *partially affined:* prejudiced by friendship.

Shall nothing wrong him. Thus it is, General.
Montano and myself being in speech,
There comes a fellow crying out for help,
And Cassio following him with determined sword
To execute upon him. Sir, this gentleman
Steps in to Cassio and entreats his pause.
Myself the crying fellow did pursue,
Lest by his clamor (as it so fell out)
The town might fall in fright. He, swift of foot,   210
Outran my purpose; and I returned the rather
For that I heard the clink and fall of swords,
And Cassio high in oath; which till tonight
I ne'er might say before. When I came back
(For this was brief) I found them close together
At blow and thrust, even as again they were
When you yourself did part them.
More of this matter cannot I report;
But men are men; the best sometimes forget.
Though Cassio did some little wrong to him,   220
As men in rage strike those that wish them best,
Yet surely Cassio I believe received
From him that fled some strange indignity,
Which patience could not pass.

OTHELLO: I know, Iago,
Thy honesty and love doth mince this matter,
Making it light to Cassio. Cassio, I love thee;
But never more be officer of mine.

(*Enter* DESDEMONA, *attended.*)

Look if my gentle love be not raised up!
I'll make thee an example.

DESDEMONA: What's the matter, dear?

OTHELLO: All's well now, sweeting; come away to bed.   230
(*To* MONTANO)
Sir, for your hurts, myself will be your surgeon.
Lead him off.   (*Exit* MONTANO, *attended.*)
Iago, look with care about the town
And silence those whom this vile brawl distracted.
Come, Desdemona. 'Tis the soldiers' life

l. 206. *execute upon him:* enforce his will.
l. 225. *mince:* make small.

To have their balmy slumbers waked with strife.

(*Exeunt all but* IAGO *and* CASSIO.)

IAGO: What, are you hurt, Lieutenant?

CASSIO: Ay, past all surgery.

IAGO: Marry, God forbid!

CASSIO: Reputation, reputation, reputation! O, I have lost my reputa-   240
tion! I have lost the immortal part of myself, and what remains is
bestial. My reputation, Iago, my reputation!

IAGO: As I am an honest man, I thought you had received some bodily
wound; there is more sense in that than in reputation. Reputation
is an idle and most false imposition; oft got without merit and lost
without deserving. You have lost no reputation at all unless you re-
pute yourself such a loser. What, man! there are ways to recover the
General again. You are but now cast in his mood—a punishment
more in policy than in malice, even so as one would beat his of-
fenseless dog to affright an imperious lion. Sue to him again, and   250
he's yours.

CASSIO: I will rather sue to be despised than to deceive so good a com-
mander with so slight, so drunken, and so indiscreet an officer.
Drunk? and speak parrot? and squabble? swagger? swear? and discourse fustian with one's own shadow? O thou invisible spirit of
wine, if thou hast no name to be known by, let us call thee devil!

IAGO: What was he that you followed with your sword? What had he
done to you?

CASSIO: I know not.

IAGO: Is't possible?   260

CASSIO: I remember a mass of things, but nothing distinctly; a quarrel, but nothing wherefore. O God, that men should put an enemy
in their mouths to steal away their brains! that we should with joy,
pleasance, revel, and applause transform ourselves into beasts!

IAGO: Why, but you are now well enough. How came you thus recovered?

CASSIO: It hath pleased the devil drunkenness to give place to the devil
wrath. One unperfectness shows me another, to make me frankly
despise myself.

IAGO: Come, you are too severe a moraler. As the time, the place, and   270
the condition of this country stands, I could heartily wish this had

l. 248. *cast in his mood:* discharged because of his anger.
l. 254. *speak parrot:* gabble senselessly.
l. 255. *fustian:* silly nonsense.
l. 264. *applause:* desire to be pleasant.

not so befall'n; but since it is as it is, mend it for your own good.

CASSIO: I will ask him for my place again: he shall tell me I am a drunkard! Had I as many mouths as Hydra, such an answer would stop them all. To be now a sensible man, by-and-by a fool, and presently a beast! O strange! Every inordinate cup is unblest, and the ingredient is a devil.

IAGO: Come, come, good wine is a good familiar creature if it be well used. Exclaim no more against it. And, good Lieutenant, I think you think I love you.   28

CASSIO: I have well approved it, sir. I drunk?

IAGO: You or any man living may be drunk at a time, man. I'll tell you what you shall do. Our General's wife is now the General. I may say so in this respect, for that he hath devoted and given up himself to the contemplation, mark, and denotement of her parts and graces. Confess yourself freely to her. Importune her help to put you in your place again. She is of so free, so kind, so apt, so blessed a disposition she holds it a vice in her goodness not to do more than she is requested. This broken joint between you and her husband entreat her to splinter; and my fortunes against any lay   29 worth naming, this crack of your love shall grow stronger than 'twas before.

CASSIO: You advise me well.

IAGO: I protest, in the sincerity of love and honest kindness.

CASSIO: I think it freely; and betimes in the morning will I beseech the virtuous Desdemona to undertake for me. I am desperate of my fortunes if they check me here.

IAGO: You are in the right. Good night, Lieutenant; I must to the watch.

CASSIO: Good night, honest Iago.   (*Exit.*)   30

IAGO: And what's he then that says I play the villain,
When this advice is free I give and honest,
Probal to thinking, and indeed the course
To win the Moor again? For 'tis most easy
Th' inclining Desdemona to subdue
In any honest suit. She's framed as fruitful
As the free elements. And then for her

l. 274. *Hydra:* many-headed monster.
l. 287. *free:* generous.
l. 290. *splinter:* bind with splints.
        lay: bet.
l. 303. *Probal to thinking:* probable-sounding.

To win the Moor—were't to renounce his baptism,
All seals and symbols of redeemed sin—
His soul is so enfettered to her love   310
That she may make, unmake, do what she list,
Even as her appetite shall play the god
With his weak function. How am I then a villain
To counsel Cassio to this parallel course,
Directly to his good? Divinity of hell!
When devils will the blackest sins put on,
They do suggest at first with heavenly shows,
As I do now. For whiles this honest fool
Plies Desdemona to repair his fortune,
And she for him pleads strongly to the Moor,   320
I'll pour this pestilence into his ear—
That she repeals him for her body's lust;
And by how much she strives to do him good,
She shall undo her credit with the Moor.
So will I turn her virtue into pitch,
And out of her own goodness make the net
That shall enmesh them all.

(Enter RODERIGO.*)*

How now, Roderigo?
RODERIGO: I do follow here in the chase, not like a hound that hunts,
but one that fills up the cry. My money is almost spent; I have been
tonight exceedingly well cudgelled; and I think the issue will be,   330
I shall have so much experience for my pains; and so, with no
money at all, and a little more wit, return again to Venice.
IAGO: How poor are they that have not patience!
What wound did ever heal but by degrees?
Thou know'st we work by wit, and not by witchcraft;
And wit depends on dilatory time.
Does't not go well? Cassio hath beaten thee,
And thou by that small hurt hast cashiered Cassio.
Though other things grow fair against the sun,

l. 313. *function:* intelligence.
l. 315. *Divinity:* theology.
l. 316. *put on:* incite.
l. 319. *Plies:* entreats.
l. 322. *repeals:* calls back.
ll. 328–329. *hound . . . fills up the cry:* not like a hound leading the
pack, but like one who only lends his bay to the chase.

Yet fruits that blossom first will first be ripe.   34
Content thyself awhile. By th' mass, 'tis morning!
Pleasure and action make the hours seem short.
Retire thee; go where thou art billeted.
Away, I say! Thou shalt know more hereafter.
Nay, get thee gone!   (*Exit* RODERIGO.)
       Two things are to be done:
My wife must move for Cassio to her mistress;
I'll set her on;
Myself a while to draw the Moor apart
And bring him jump when he may Cassio find
Soliciting his wife. Ay, that's the way!   35
Dull not device by coldness and delay.

                         (*Exit.*)

ACT III

SCENE I

(*Cyprus. Before the Castle.*)

(*Enter* CASSIO, *with* MUSICIANS.)

CASSIO: Masters, play here, I will content your pains:
    Something that's brief; and bid "Good morrow, General."
    (*They play.*)

(*Enter the* CLOWN.)

CLOWN: Why, masters, have your instruments been at Naples, that
    they speak i'th' nose thus?
MUSICIANS: How, sir, how?
CLOWN: Are these, I pray, called wind instruments?
MUSICIANS: Ay, marry, are they, sir.
CLOWN: O, thereby hangs a tail.

l. 346. *move for:* petition for.
l. 349. *jump:* at the exact moment.
l. 351. *device:* scheme.
l. 1. *content:* reward.
l. 3. *Naples:* notorious for its association with venereal disease.

MUSICIANS: Whereby hangs a tale, sir?

CLOWN: Marry, sir, by many a wind instrument that I know. But,   10
masters, here's money for you; and the General so likes your music
that he desires you, of all loves, to make no more noise with it.

MUSICIANS: Well, sir, we will not.

CLOWN: If you have any music that may not be heard, to 't again. But,
as they say, to hear music the General does not greatly care.

MUSICIANS: We have none such, sir.

CLOWN: Then put up your pipes in your bag, for I'll away. Go, vanish
into air, away!   (*Exeunt* MUSICIANS.)

CASSIO: Dost thou hear, my honest friend?

CLOWN: No, I hear not your honest friend. I hear you.   20

CASSIO: Prithee keep up thy quillets. There's a poor piece of gold for
thee. If the gentlewoman that attends the General's wife be stirring, tell her there's one Cassio entreats her a little favor of speech.
Wilt thou do this?

CLOWN: She is stirring, sir. If she will stir hither, I shall seem to notify
unto her.

CASSIO: Do, good my friend.   (*Exit* CLOWN.)

(*Enter* IAGO.)

In happy time, Iago.

IAGO: You have not been abed then?

CASSIO: Why, no. The day had broke
Before we parted. I have made bold, Iago,   30
To send in to your wife. My suit to her
Is that she will to virtuous Desdemona
Procure me some access.

IAGO: I'll send her to you presently;
And I'll devise a mean to draw the Moor
Out of the way, that your converse and business
May be more free.

CASSIO: I humbly thank you for't.   (*Exit* IAGO.)
                              I never knew
A Florentine more kind and honest.

(*Enter* EMILIA.)

l. 21. *keep . . . quillets:* put away your puns.
l. 27. *In happy time:* well met.
ll. 37–38. *I never . . . honest:* Cassio means that even one from his own
home, Florence, couldn't have been kinder than the Venetian Iago.

EMILIA: Good morrow, good Lieutenant. I am sorry
For your displeasure; but all will sure be well.   4
The General and his wife are talking of it,
And she speaks for you stoutly. The Moor replies
That he you hurt is of great fame in Cyprus
And great affinity, and that in wholesome wisdom
He might not but refuse you. But he protests he loves you,
And needs no other suitor but his likings
To take the safest occasion by the front
To bring you in again.

CASSIO: Yet I beseech you,
If you think fit, or that it may be done,
Give me advantage of some brief discourse   5
With Desdemona alone.

EMILIA: Pray you come in.
I will bestow you where you shall have time
To speak your bosom freely.

CASSIO: I am much bound to you.

                                              (*Exeunt.*)

SCENE II

(*Cyprus. Within the Castle.*)

                    (*Enter* OTHELLO, IAGO, *and* GENTLEMEN.)

OTHELLO: These letters give, Iago, to the pilot
And by him do my duties to the senate.
That done, I will be walking on the works.
Repair there to me.

IAGO: Well, my good lord, I'll do't.

OTHELLO: This fortification, gentlemen, shall we see't?

GENTLEMEN: We'll wait upon your lordship.

                                              (*Exeunt.*)

l. 40. *For your displeasure:* that you are held in displeasure.
l. 44. *affinity:* family connections.
l. 45. *might not but:* must.
l. 47. *front:* forelock.
l. 3. *works:* fortifications.

SCENE III

(Cyprus. The garden of the Castle.)

(Enter DESDEMONA, CASSIO, *and* EMILIA.*)*

DESDEMONA: Be thou assured, good Cassio, I will do
    All my abilities in thy behalf.
EMILIA: Good madam, do. I warrant it grieves my husband
    As if the cause were his.
DESDEMONA: O, that's an honest fellow. Do not doubt, Cassio,
    But I will have my lord and you again
    As friendly as you were.
CASSIO: Bounteous madam,
    Whatever shall become of Michael Cassio,
    He's never anything but your true servant.
DESDEMONA: I know't; I thank you. You do love my lord;   10
    You have known him long; and be you well assured
    He shall in strangeness stand no farther off
    Than in a politic distance.
CASSIO: Ay, but, lady,
    That policy may either last so long,
    Or feed upon such nice and waterish diet,
    Or breed itself so out of circumstance,
    That, I being absent, and my place supplied,
    My general will forget my love and service.
DESDEMONA: Do not doubt that. Before Emilia here
    I give thee warrant of thy place. Assure thee,   20
    If I do vow a friendship, I'll perform it
    To the last article. My lord shall never rest;
    I'll watch him tame and talk him out of patience;
    His bed shall seem a school, his board a shrift;
    I'll intermingle everything he does
    With Cassio's suit. Therefore be merry, Cassio,

l. 13. *politic distance:* as policy requires.
ll. 14–17. *That policy . . . supplied:* Othello's dismissal of Cassio may go
on so long or be so encouraged or taken for granted that he will grow used to
Cassio's replacement and forget his Lieutenant's former value.
l. 23. *watch him tame:* a reference to falconry; wild hawks are kept awake
for long periods so that they may be made tame.
l. 24. *shrift:* confessional.

For thy solicitor shall rather die
Than give thy cause away.

(*Enter* OTHELLO *and* IAGO.)

EMILIA: Madam, here comes my lord.
CASSIO: Madam, I'll take my leave.
DESDEMONA: Why, stay, and hear me speak.
CASSIO: Madam, not now. I am very ill at ease,
   Unfit for mine own purposes.
DESDEMONA: Well, do your discretion.   (*Exit* CASSIO.)
IAGO: Ha! I like not that.
OTHELLO: What dost thou say?
IAGO: Nothing, my lord; or if—I know not what.
OTHELLO: Was not that Cassio parted from my wife?
IAGO: Cassio, my lord? No, sure, I cannot think it,
   That he would steal away so guilty-like,
   Seeing you coming.
OTHELLO: I do believe 'twas he.
DESDEMONA: How now, my lord?
   I have been talking with a suitor here,
   A man that languishes in your displeasure.
OTHELLO: Who is't you mean?
DESDEMONA: Why, your lieutenant, Cassio. Good my lord,
   If I have any grace or power to move you,
   His present reconciliation take;
   For if he be not one that truly loves you,
   That errs in ignorance, and not in cunning,
   I have no judgment in an honest face.
   I prithee call him back.
OTHELLO: Went he hence now?
DESDEMONA: Yes, faith; so humbled
   That he hath left part of his grief with me
   To suffer with him. Good love, call him back.
OTHELLO: Not now, sweet Desdemon; some other time.
DESDEMONA: But shall't be shortly?
OTHELLO: The sooner, sweet, for you.
DESDEMONA: Shall't be tonight at supper?
OTHELLO: No, not tonight.
DESDEMONA: Tomorrow dinner then?
OTHELLO: I shall not dine at home.

   l. 49. *in ignorance . . . cunning:* from ignorance rather than by design.

I meet the captains at the citadel.
DESDEMONA: Why then, tomorrow night, or Tuesday morn,   60
    Or Tuesday noon or night, or Wednesday morn.
    I prithee name the time, but let it not
    Exceed three days. I' faith, he's penitent;
    And yet his trespass, in our common reason
    (Save that, they say, the wars must make examples
    Out of their best) is not almost a fault
    T' incur a private check. When shall he come?
    Tell me, Othello. I wonder in my soul
    What you could ask me that I should deny
    Or stand so mamm'ring on. What? Michael Cassio,   70
    That came a-wooing with you, and so many a time,
    When I have spoke of you dispraisingly,
    Hath ta'en your part—to have so much to do
    To bring him in? Trust me, I could do much—
OTHELLO: Prithee no more. Let him come when he will!
    I will deny thee nothing.
DESDEMONA: Why, this is not a boon;
    'Tis as I should entreat you wear your gloves,
    Or feed on nourishing dishes, or keep you warm,
    Or sue to you to do a peculiar profit
    To your own person. Nay, when I have a suit   80
    Wherein I mean to touch your love indeed,
    It shall be full of poise and difficult weight,
    And fearful to be granted.
OTHELLO: I will deny thee nothing!
    Whereon I do beseech thee grant me this,
    To leave me but a little to myself.
DESDEMONA: Shall I deny you? No. Farewell, my lord.
OTHELLO: Farewell, my Desdemon. I'll come to thee straight.
DESDEMONA: Emilia, come.—Be as your fancies teach you.
    Whate'er you be, I am obedient.
                    (*Exeunt* DESDEMONA *and* EMILIA.)
OTHELLO: Excellent wretch! Perdition catch my soul   90
    But I do love thee! and when I love thee not,
    Chaos is come again.
IAGO: My noble lord—
OTHELLO: What dost thou say, Iago?

l. 70. *mamm'ring:* hesitating.
l. 90. *wretch:* a word of endearment.

IAGO: Did Michael Cassio, when you wooed my lady,
   Know of your love?

OTHELLO: He did, from first to last. Why dost thou ask?

IAGO: But for a satisfaction of my thought;
   No further harm.

OTHELLO: Why of thy thought, Iago?

IAGO: I did not think he had been acquainted with her.

OTHELLO: O, yes, and went between us very oft.   10

IAGO: Indeed?

OTHELLO: Indeed? Ay, indeed! Discern'st thou aught in that?
   Is he not honest?

IAGO: Honest, my lord?

OTHELLO: Honest? Ay, honest.

IAGO: My lord, for aught I know.

OTHELLO: What dost thou think?

IAGO: Think, my lord?

OTHELLO: Think, my lord?
   By heaven, he echoes me,
   As if there were some monster in his thought
   Too hideous to be shown. Thou dost mean something.
   I heard thee say even now, thou lik'st not that,
   When Cassio left my wife. What didst not like?   11
   And when I told thee he was of my counsel
   In my whole course of wooing, thou criedst "Indeed?"
   And didst contract and purse thy brow together,
   As if thou then hadst shut up in thy brain
   Some horrible conceit. If thou dost love me,
   Show me thy thought.

IAGO: My lord, you know I love you.

OTHELLO: I think thou dost;
   And, for I know thou'rt full of love and honesty
   And weigh'st thy words before thou giv'st them breath,
   Therefore these stops of thine fright me the more;   12
   For such things in a false disloyal knave
   Are tricks of custom; but in a man that's just
   They are close dilations, working from the heart
   That passion cannot rule.

IAGO: For Michael Cassio,
   I dare be sworn I think that he is honest.

l. 115. *conceit:* thought.
l. 123. *close dilations:* signs of emotion.

OTHELLO: I think so too.

IAGO: Men should be what they seem;
   Or those that be not, would they might seem none!

OTHELLO: Certain, men should be what they seem.

IAGO: Why then, I think Cassio's an honest man.

OTHELLO: Nay, yet there's more in this.   130
   I prithee speak to me, as to thy thinkings,
   As thou dost ruminate, and give thy worst of thoughts
   The worst of words.

IAGO: Good my lord, pardon me.
   Though I am bound to every act of duty,
   I am not bound to that all slaves are free to.
   Utter my thoughts? Why, say they are vile and false,
   As where's that palace whereinto foul things
   Sometimes intrude not? Who has a breast so pure
   But some uncleanly apprehensions
   Keep leets and law days, and in session sit   140
   With meditations lawful?

OTHELLO: Thou dost conspire against thy friend, Iago,
   If thou but think'st him wronged, and mak'st his ear
   A stranger to thy thoughts.

IAGO: I do beseech you—
   Though I perchance am vicious in my guess
   (As I confess it is my nature's plague
   To spy into abuses, and oft my jealousy
   Shapes faults that are not)—that your wisdom
   From one that so imperfectly conceits
   Would take no notice, nor build yourself a trouble   150
   Out of his scattering and unsure observance.
   It were not for your quiet nor your good,
   Nor for my manhood, honesty, or wisdom,
   To let you know my thoughts.

OTHELLO: What dost thou mean?

IAGO: Good name in man and woman, dear my lord,
   Is the immediate jewel of their souls.
   Who steals my purse steals trash; 'tis something, nothing;
   'Twas mine, 'tis his, and has been slave to thousands;
   But he that filches from me my good name
   Robs me of that which not enriches him   160

l. 140. *Keep leets:* court sessions.
l. 156. *immediate:* closest, most precious.

And makes me poor indeed.

OTHELLO: By heaven, I'll know thy thoughts!

IAGO: You cannot, if my heart were in your hand;
   Nor shall not whilst 'tis in my custody.

OTHELLO: Ha!

IAGO: O, beware, my lord, of jealousy!
   It is the green-eyed monster, which doth mock
   The meat it feeds on. That cuckold lives in bliss
   Who, certain of his fate, loves not his wronger;
   But O, what damned minutes tells he o'er
   Who dotes, yet doubts; suspects, yet strongly loves!   17

OTHELLO: O misery!

IAGO: Poor and content is rich, and rich enough;
   But riches fineless is as poor as winter
   To him that ever fears he shall be poor.
   Good heaven, the souls of all my tribe defend
   From jealousy!

OTHELLO: Why, why is this?
   Think'st thou I'd make a life of jealousy,
   To follow still the changes of the moon
   With fresh suspicions? No! To be once in doubt
   Is once to be resolved. Exchange me for a goat   18(
   When I shall turn the business of my soul
   To such exsufflicate and blown surmises,
   Matching thy inference. 'Tis not to make me jealous
   To say my wife is fair, feeds well, loves company,
   Is free of speech, sings, plays, and dances well.
   Where virtue is, these are more virtuous.
   Nor from mine own weak merits will I draw
   The smallest fear or doubt of her revolt,
   For she had eyes, and chose me. No, Iago;
   I'll see before I doubt; when I doubt, prove;   19(
   And on the proof there is no more but this—
   Away at once with love or jealousy!

IAGO: I am glad of it; for now I shall have reason
   To show the love and duty that I bear you
   With franker spirit. Therefore, as I am bound,
   Receive it from me. I speak not yet of proof.

l. 173. *fineless:* unlimited.
l. 182. *exsufflicate:* contemptible.

Look to your wife; observe her well with Cassio;
Wear your eye thus, not jealous nor secure.
I would not have your free and noble nature,
Out of self-bounty, be abused. Look to't.   200
I know our country disposition well:
In Venice they do let heaven see the pranks
They dare not show their husbands; their best conscience
Is not to leave't undone, but keep't unknown.

OTHELLO: Dost thou say so?

IAGO: She did deceive her father, marrying you;
And when she seemed to shake and fear your looks,
She loved them most.

OTHELLO: And so she did.

IAGO: Why, go to then!
She that, so young, could give out such a seeming
To seel her father's eyes up close as oak—   210
He thought 'twas witchcraft—but I am much to blame.
I humbly do beseech you of your pardon
For too much loving you.

OTHELLO: I am bound to thee for ever.

IAGO: I see this hath a little dashed your spirits.

OTHELLO: Not a jot, not a jot.

IAGO: I' faith, I fear it has.
I hope you will consider what is spoke
Comes from my love. But I do see y'are moved.
I am to pray you not to strain my speech
To grosser issues nor to larger reach
Than to suspicion.   220

OTHELLO: I will not.

IAGO: Should you do so, my lord,
My speech should fall into such vile success
As my thoughts aim not at. Cassio's my worthy friend—
My lord, I see y'are moved.

OTHELLO: No, not much moved.
I do not think but Desdemona's honest.

IAGO: Long live she so! and long live you to think so!

OTHELLO: And yet, how nature erring from itself—

IAGO: Ay, there's the point! as (to be bold with you)

---

l. 200. *self-bounty:* generosity.

Not to affect many proposed matches
Of her own clime, complexion, and degree,   23
Whereto we see in all things nature tends—
Foh! one may smell in such a will most rank,
Foul disproportion, thoughts unnatural—
But pardon me—I do not in position
Distinctly speak of her; though I may fear
Her will, recoiling to her better judgment,
May fall to match you with her country forms,
And happily repent.
OTHELLO: Farewell, farewell!
   If more thou dost perceive, let me know more.
   Set on thy wife to observe. Leave me, Iago.   24
IAGO: My lord, I take my leave.
   (*Walks away.*)
OTHELLO: Why did I marry? This honest creature doubtless
   Sees and knows more, much more, than he unfolds.
IAGO (*returns*): My lord, I would I might entreat your Honor
   To scan this thing no further. Leave it to time.
   Although 'tis fit that Cassio have his place,
   For sure he fills it up with great ability,
   Yet, if you please to hold him off awhile,
   You shall by that perceive him and his means.
   Note if your lady strain his entertainment   25
   With any strong or vehement importunity.
   Much will be seen in that. In the mean time
   Let me be thought too busy in my fears
   (As worthy cause I have to fear I am)
   And hold her free, I do beseech your Honor.
OTHELLO: Fear not my government.
IAGO: I once more take my leave.   (*Exit.*)
OTHELLO: This fellow's of exceeding honesty,
   And knows all qualities, with a learned spirit

---

ll. 229–231. *Not to affect . . . tends:* Iago is reminding Othello of Desdemona's lack of interest in the many proposals of marriage she had received
from men of her own country, color, and rank and insinuates that it signifies
something perverse in her.
   ll. 237–238. *May fall . . . repent:* may begin to compare you with her
countrymen and perhaps (*happily:* haply) regret her marriage.
   l. 250. *strain his entertainment:* urge you to entertain.
   l. 256. *government:* self-control.

Of human dealings. If I do prove her haggard,   260
Though that her jesses were my dear heartstrings,
I'd whistle her off and let her down the wind
To prey at fortune. Haply, for I am black
And have not those soft parts of conversation
That chamberers have, or for I am declined
Into the vale of years (yet that's not much),
She's gone. I am abused, and my relief
Must be to loathe her. O curse of marriage,
That we can call these delicate creatures ours,
And not their appetites! I had rather be a toad   270
And live upon the vapor of a dungeon
Than keep a corner in the thing I love
For others' uses. Yet 'tis the plague of great ones;
Prerogatived are they less than the base.
'Tis destiny unshunnable, like death:
Even then this forked plague is fated to us
When we do quicken. Desdemona comes.

(*Enter* DESDEMONA *and* EMILIA.)

If she be false, O, then heaven mocks itself!
I'll not believe't.
DESDEMONA: How now, my dear Othello?
Your dinner, and the generous islanders   280
By you invited, do attend your presence.
OTHELLO: I am to blame.
DESDEMONA: Why do you speak so faintly?
Are you not well?
OTHELLO: I have a pain upon my forehead, here.
DESDEMONA: Faith, that's with watching; 'twill away again.
Let me but bind it hard, within this hour

ll. 260–263. *If I do prove . . . fortune:* The metaphor is from falconry.
The *haggard* was a mature hawk which could sometimes be trained, sometimes not. *Jesses* were the leather thongs the falconer attached to the hawk's
legs. Othello says that if Desdemona cannot be tamed, he will call her to him
and loose her to the wild state again.
l. 265. *chamberers:* courtiers who lounge around rather than going off into
battle.
l. 274. *Prerogatived:* exempted.
l. 276. *forked plague:* the horns of the cuckold.
l. 277. *quicken:* first stir in the womb.
l. 285. *watching:* staying awake too long.

It will be well.

OTHELLO: Your napkin is too little.

(*He pushes it away and it drops.*)

Let it alone. Come, I'll go in with you.

DESDEMONA: I am very sorry that you are not well.

(*Exeunt* OTHELLO *and* DESDEMONA.)

EMILIA: I am glad I have found this napkin.   29

This was her first remembrance from the Moor.

My wayward husband hath a hundred times

Wooed me to steal it; but she so loves the token

(For he conjured her she should ever keep it)

That she reserves it evermore about her

To kiss and talk to. I'll have the work ta'en out

And give't Iago.

What he will do with it heaven knows, not I;

I nothing but to please his fantasy.

(*Enter* IAGO.)

IAGO: How now? What do you here alone?   30

EMILIA: Do not you chide; I have a thing for you.

IAGO: A thing for me? It is a common thing—

EMILIA: Ha?

IAGO: To have a foolish wife.

EMILIA: O, is that all? What will you give me now

For that same handkerchief?

IAGO: What handkerchief?

EMILIA: What handkerchief?

Why, that the Moor first gave to Desdemona;

That which so often you did bid me steal.

IAGO: Hast stol'n it from her?   31

EMILIA: No, faith; she let it drop by negligence,

And to th' advantage, I, being here, took't up.

Look, here it is.

IAGO: A good wench! Give it me.

EMILIA: What will you do with't, that you have been so earnest

To have me filch it?

IAGO: Why, what's that to you?

(*Snatches it.*)

l. 287. *napkin:* handkerchief.

l. 292. *wayward:* unfathomable; unaccountable.

l. 294. *conjured her:* made her promise.

l. 296. *work ta'en out:* pattern copied.

EMILIA: If it be not for some purpose of import,
    Give't me again. Poor lady, she'll run mad
    When she shall lack it.
IAGO: Be not you acknown on't; I have use for it.
    Go, leave me.   (*Exit* EMILIA.) 320
    I will in Cassio's lodging lose this napkin
    And let him find it. Trifles light as air
    Are to the jealous confirmations strong
    As proofs of holy writ. This may do something.
    The Moor already changes with my poison.
    Dangerous conceits are in their natures poisons
    Which at the first are scarce found to distaste,
    But with a little act upon the blood
    Burn like the mines of sulphur.

                (*Enter* OTHELLO.)

                      I did say so.
    Look where he comes! Not poppy nor mandragora, 330
    Nor all the drowsy syrups of the world,
    Shall ever medicine thee to that sweet sleep
    Which thou ow'dst yesterday.
OTHELLO: Ha! ha! false to me?
IAGO: Why, how now, General? No more of that!
OTHELLO: Avaunt! be gone! Thou hast set me on the rack.
    I swear 'tis better to be much abused
    Than but to know't a little.
IAGO: How now, my lord?
OTHELLO: What sense had I of her stol'n hours of lust?
    I saw't not, thought it not, it harmed not me.
    I slept the next night well, was free and merry; 340
    I found not Cassio's kisses on her lips.
    He that is robbed, not wanting what is stol'n,
    Let him not know't, and he's not robbed at all.
IAGO: I am sorry to hear this.
OTHELLO: I had been happy if the general camp,
    Pioners and all, had tasted her sweet body,
    So I had nothing known. O, now for ever
    Farewell the tranquil mind! farewell content!

l. 316. *purpose of import:* important purpose.
l. 319. *Be not you acknown on't:* show no knowledge of it.
l. 328. *with a little:* soon.
l. 330. *mandragora:* a sedative.
l. 333. *ow'dst:* owned.
l. 346. *Pioners:* lowest-ranking soldiers.

Farewell the plumed troop, and the big wars
That make ambition virtue! O, farewell!   350
Farewell the neighing steed and the shrill trump,
The spirit-stirring drum, th' ear-piercing fife,
The royal banner, and all quality,
Pride, pomp, and circumstance of glorious war!
And O ye mortal engines whose rude throats
Th' immortal Jove's dread clamors counterfeit,
Farewell! Othello's occupation's gone!

IAGO: Is't possible, my lord?

OTHELLO: Villain, be sure thou prove my love a whore!
Be sure of it; give me the ocular proof;   360
Or, by the worth of man's eternal soul,
Thou hadst been better have been born a dog
Than answer my waked wrath!

IAGO: Is't come to this?

OTHELLO: Make me to see't; or at the least so prove it
That the probation bear no hinge nor loop
To hang a doubt on—or woe upon thy life!

IAGO: My noble lord—

OTHELLO: If thou dost slander her and torture me,
Never pray more; abandon all remorse;
On horror's head horrors accumulate;   370
Do deeds to make heaven weep, all earth amazed;
For nothing canst thou to damnation add
Greater than that.

IAGO: O grace! O heaven forgive me!
Are you a man? Have you a soul or sense?—
God b' wi' you! take mine office. O wretched fool,
That liv'st to make thine honesty a vice!
O monstrous world! Take note, take note, O world,
To be direct and honest is not safe.
I thank you for this profit; and from hence
I'll love no friend, sith love breeds such offense.   380

OTHELLO: Nay, stay. Thou shouldst be honest.

IAGO: I should be wise; for honesty's a fool
And loses that it works for.

OTHELLO: By the world,
I think my wife be honest, and think she is not;
I think that thou art just, and think thou art not.

l. 365. *probation:* proof.
l. 380. *sith:* since.

I'll have some proof. Her name, that was as fresh
As Dian's visage, is now begrimed and black
As mine own face. If there be cords, or knives,
Poison, or fire, or suffocating streams,
I'll not endure it. Would I were satisfied!   390
IAGO: I see, sir, you are eaten up with passion.
   I do repent me that I put it to you.
   You would be satisfied?
OTHELLO: Would? Nay, I will.
IAGO: And may. But how? how satisfied, my lord?
   Would you, the supervisor, grossly gape on?
   Behold her topped?
OTHELLO: Death and damnation! O!
IAGO: It were a tedious difficulty, I think,
   To bring them to that prospect. Damn them then,
   If ever mortal eyes do see them bolster
   More than their own! What then? How then?   400
   What shall I say? Where's satisfaction?
   It is impossible you should see this,
   Were they as prime as goats, as hot as monkeys,
   As salt as wolves in pride, and fools as gross
   As ignorance made drunk. But yet, I say,
   If imputation and strong circumstances
   Which lead directly to the door of truth
   Will give you satisfaction, you may have't.
OTHELLO: Give me a living reason she's disloyal.
IAGO: I do not like the office.   410
   But sith I am entered in this cause so far,
   Pricked to't by foolish honesty and love,
   I will go on. I lay with Cassio lately,
   And being troubled with a raging tooth,
   I could not sleep.
   There are a kind of men so loose of soul
   That in their sleeps will mutter their affairs.
   One of this kind is Cassio.
   In sleep I heard him say, "Sweet Desdemona,
   Let us be wary, let us hide our loves!"   420

l. 387. *Dian's visage:* the face of Diana, goddess of chastity.
l. 399. *See them bolster:* sleep together (on one pillow).
l. 403. *prime:* lecherous.
l. 404. *salt:* lecherous.
       in pride: in heat.

And then, sir, would he gripe and wring my hand,
Cry "O sweet creature!" and then kiss me hard,
As if he plucked up kisses by the roots
That grew upon my lips; then laid his leg
Over my thigh, and sighed, and kissed, and then
Cried "Cursed fate that gave thee to the Moor!"

OTHELLO: O monstrous! monstrous!

IAGO: Nay, this was but his dream.

OTHELLO: But this denoted a foregone conclusion.
  'Tis a shrewd doubt, though it be but a dream.

IAGO: And this may help to thicken other proofs   430
  That do demonstrate thinly.

OTHELLO: I'll tear her all to pieces!

IAGO: Nay, but be wise. Yet we see nothing done;
  She may be honest yet. Tell me but this—
  Have you not sometimes seen a handkerchief
  Spotted with strawberries in your wife's hand?

OTHELLO: I gave her such a one; 'twas my first gift.

IAGO: I know not that; but such a handkerchief
  (I am sure it was your wife's) did I today
  See Cassio wipe his beard with.

OTHELLO: If't be that—

IAGO: If it be that, or any that was hers,   440
  It speaks against her, with the other proofs.

OTHELLO: O, that the slave had forty thousand lives!
  One is too poor, too weak for my revenge.
  Now do I see 'tis true. Look here, Iago:
  All my fond love thus do I blow to heaven.
  'Tis gone.
  Arise, black vengeance, from the hollow hell!
  Yield up, O love, thy crown and hearted throne
  To tyrannous hate! Swell, bosom, with thy fraught,
  For 'tis of aspics' tongues!

IAGO: Yet be content.   450

OTHELLO: O, blood, blood, blood!

IAGO: Patience, I say. Your mind perhaps may change.

OTHELLO: Never, Iago. Like to the Pontic sea,
  Whose icy current and compulsive course

l. 421. *gripe:* grip.
l. 449. *fraught:* burden.
l. 450. *aspics':* vipers'.

Ne'er feels retiring ebb, but keeps due on
To the Propontic and the Hellespont;
Even so my bloody thoughts, with violent pace,
Shall ne'er look back, ne'er ebb to humble love,
Till that a capable and wide revenge
Swallow them up. (*He kneels.*) Now, by yond marble heaven,   460
In the due reverence of the sacred vow
I here engage my words.

IAGO: Do not rise yet.
   (IAGO *kneels.*)
   Witness, you ever-burning lights above,
   You elements that clip us round about,
   Witness that here Iago doth give up
   The execution of his wit, hands, heart
   To wronged Othello's service! Let him command,
   And to obey shall be in me remorse,
   What bloody business ever.
   (*They rise.*)

OTHELLO: I greet thy love,
   Not with vain thanks but with acceptance bounteous,   470
   And will upon the instant put thee to't.
   Within these three days let me hear thee say
   That Cassio's not alive.

IAGO: My friend is dead; 'tis done at your request.
   But let her live.

OTHELLO: Damn her, lewd minx! O, damn her!
   Come, go with me apart. I will withdraw
   To furnish me with some swift means of death
   For the fair devil. Now art thou my lieutenant.

IAGO: I am your own for ever.

                                        (*Exeunt.*)

SCENE IV

(*Cyprus. Before the Castle.*)

(*Enter* DESDEMONA, EMILIA *and* CLOWN.)

DESDEMONA: Do you know, sirrah, where Lieutenant Cassio lies?
CLOWN: I dare not say he lies anywhere.

   l. 456. *Propontic . . . Hellespont:* seas.

DESDEMONA: Why man?

CLOWN: He's a soldier; and for one to say a soldier lies is stabbing.

DESDEMONA: Go to. Where lodges he?

CLOWN: To tell you where he lodges is to tell you where I lie.

DESDEMONA: Can anything be made of this?

CLOWN: I know not where he lodges; and for me to devise a lodging, and say he lies here or he lies there, were to lie in mine own throat.

DESDEMONA: Can you enquire him out, and be edified by report?   1(

CLOWN: I will catechize the world for him; that is, make questions, and by them answer.

DESDEMONA: Seek him, bid him come hither. Tell him I have moved my lord on his behalf and hope all will be well.

CLOWN: To do this is within the compass of man's wit, and therefore I'll attempt the doing it.   (*Exit.*)

DESDEMONA: Where should I lose that handkerchief, Emilia?

EMILIA: I know not, madam.

DESDEMONA: Believe me, I had rather have lost my purse
    Full of crusadoes; and but my noble Moor   2(
    Is true of mind, and made of no such baseness
    As jealous creatures are, it were enough
    To put him to ill thinking.

EMILIA: ·   Is he not jealous?

DESDEMONA: Who? he? I think the sun where he was born
    Drew all such humors from him.

(*Enter* OTHELLO.)

EMILIA: Look where he comes.

DESDEMONA: I will not leave him now till Cassio
    Be called to him.—How is't with you, my lord?

OTHELLO: Well, my good lady. (*Aside*) O, hardness to dissemble!—
    How do you, Desdemona?

DESDEMONA: Well, my good lord.

OTHELLO: Give me your hand. This hand is moist, my lady.   3(

DESDEMONA: It yet hath felt no age nor known no sorrow.

OTHELLO: This argues fruitfulness and liberal heart.
    Hot, hot, and moist. This hand of yours requires
    A sequester from liberty, fasting and prayer,

---

l. 20. *crusadoes:* gold coins.

l. 25. *humors:* The primary emotions once were thought to be brought on by the juices of the body—blood, phlegm, yellow bile, and black bile.

l. 34. *sequester:* withdrawal.

Much castigation, exercise devout;
For here's a young and sweating devil here
That commonly rebels. 'Tis a good hand,
A frank one.

DESDEMONA: You may, indeed, say so;
For 'twas that hand that gave away my heart.

OTHELLO: A liberal hand! The hearts of old gave hands;   40
But our new heraldry is hands, not hearts.

DESDEMONA: I cannot speak of this. Come now, your promise!

OTHELLO: What promise, chuck?

DESDEMONA: I have sent to bid Cassio come speak with you.

OTHELLO: I have a salt and sorry rheum offends me.
Lend me thy handkerchief.

DESDEMONA: Here, my lord.

OTHELLO: That which I gave you.

DESDEMONA: I have it not about me.

OTHELLO: Not?

DESDEMONA: No indeed, my lord.

OTHELLO: That is a fault.
That handkerchief
Did an Egyptian to my mother give.   50
She was a charmer, and could almost read
The thoughts of people. She told her, while she kept it,
'Twould make her amiable and subdue my father
Entirely to her love; but if she lost it
Or made a gift of it, my father's eye
Should hold her loathed, and his spirits should hunt
After new fancies. She, dying, gave it me,
And bid me, when my fate would have me wive,
To give it her. I did so; and take heed on't;
Make it a darling like your precious eye.   60
To lose't or give't away were such perdition
As nothing else could match.

DESDEMONA: Is't possible?

OTHELLO: 'Tis true. There's magic in the web of it.
A sibyl that had numb'red in the world
The sun to course two hundred compasses,
In her prophetic fury sewed the work;
The worms were hallowed that did breed the silk;

l. 45. *rheum:* head cold.
l. 65. *two hundred compasses:* two hundred years.

And it was dyed in mummy which the skilful
Conserved of maidens' hearts.

DESDEMONA: I' faith? It's true?

OTHELLO: Most veritable. Therefore look to't well.

DESDEMONA: Then would to God that I had never seen't!

OTHELLO: Ha! Wherefore?

DESDEMONA: Why do you speak so startingly and rash?

OTHELLO: Is't lost? Is't gone? Speak, is it out o' th' way?

DESDEMONA: Heaven bless us!

OTHELLO: Say you?

DESDEMONA: It is not lost. But what an' if it were?

OTHELLO: How?

DESDEMONA: I say it is not lost.

OTHELLO: Fetch't, let me see't!

DESDEMONA: Why, so I can, sir; but I will not now.
This is a trick to put me from my suit.
Pray you let Cassio be received again.

OTHELLO: Fetch me the handkerchief! My mind misgives.

DESDEMONA: Come, come!
You'll never meet a more sufficient man.

OTHELLO: The handkerchief!

DESDEMONA: I pray talk me of Cassio.

OTHELLO: The handkerchief!

DESDEMONA: A man that all his time
Hath founded his good fortunes on your love,
Shared dangers with you—

OTHELLO: The handkerchief!

DESDEMONA: In sooth, you are to blame.

OTHELLO: Away!   (*Exit.*)

EMILIA: Is not this man jealous?

DESDEMONA: I ne'er saw this before.
Sure there's some wonder in this handkerchief.
I am most unhappy in the loss of it.

EMILIA: 'Tis not a year or two shows us a man.
They are all but stomachs, and we all but food;
They eat us hungerly, and when they are full,
They belch us.

(*Enter* IAGO *and* CASSIO.)

---

l. 68. *mummy:* a drug, supposed to have magic powers, made from mummified corpses.

Look you—Cassio and my husband!

IAGO: There is no other way; 'tis she must do't.
    And lo the happiness! Go and importune her.

DESDEMONA: How now, good Cassio? What's the news with you?

CASSIO: Madam, my former suit. I do beseech you
    That by your virtuous means I may again
    Exist, and be a member of his love
    Whom I with all the office of my heart
    Entirely honor. I would not be delayed.
    If my offense be of such mortal kind
    That neither service past, nor present sorrows,   110
    Nor purposed merit in futurity,
    Can ransom me into his love again,
    But to know so must be my benefit.
    So shall I clothe me in a forced content,
    And shut myself up in some other course,
    To fortune's alms.

DESDEMONA: Alas, thrice-gentle Cassio!
    My advocation is not now in tune.
    My lord is not my lord; nor should I know him,
    Were he in favor as in humor altered.
    So help me every spirit sanctified   120
    As I have spoken for you all my best
    And stood within the blank of his displeasure
    For my free speech! You must awhile be patient.
    What I can do I will; and more I will
    Than for myself I dare. Let that suffice you.

IAGO: Is my lord angry?

EMILIA: He went hence but now,
    And certainly in strange unquietness.

IAGO: Can he be angry? I have seen the cannon
    When it hath blown his ranks into the air
    And, like the devil, from his very arm   130
    Puffed his own brother—and can he be angry?
    Something of moment then. I will go meet him.
    There's matter in't indeed if he be angry.

DESDEMONA: I prithee do so.   *(Exit IAGO.)*
          Something sure of state,

ll. 114–116. *So shall . . . alms:* I shall make the best of it and try my
fortune elsewhere.
    l. 122. *blank:* target.

Either from Venice or some unhatched practice
Made demonstrable here in Cyprus to him,
Hath puddled his clear spirit; and in such cases
Men's natures wrangle with inferior things,
Though great ones are their object. 'Tis even so.
For let our finger ache, and it endues   140
Our other healthful members even to that sense
Of pain. Nay, we must think men are not gods,
Nor of them look for such observancy
As fits the bridal. Beshrew me much, Emilia,
I was (unhandsome warrior as I am!)
Arraigning his unkindness with my soul;
But now I find I had suborned the witness,
And he's indicted falsely.

EMILIA: Pray heaven it be state matters, as you think,
And no conception nor no jealous toy   150
Concerning you.

DESDEMONA: Alas the day! I never gave him cause.

EMILIA: But jealous souls will not be answered so.
They are not ever jealous for the cause,
But jealous for they are jealous. 'Tis a monster
Begot upon itself, born on itself.

DESDEMONA: Heaven keep that monster from Othello's mind!

EMILIA: Lady, amen.

DESDEMONA: I will go seek him. Cassio, walk here about.
If I do find him fit, I'll move your suit   160
And seek to effect it to my uttermost.

CASSIO: I humbly thank your ladyship.

(*Exeunt* DESDEMONA *and* EMILIA.)

(*Enter* BIANCA.)

BIANCA: Save you, friend Cassio!

CASSIO: What make you from home?
How is it with you, my most fair Bianca?
I' faith, sweet love, I was coming to your house.

BIANCA: And I was going to your lodging, Cassio.
What, keep a week away? seven days and nights?

ll. 135–137. *unhatched practice . . . Hath puddled:* Some political plot,
revealed to him here, has disturbed his spirit.
l. 155. *for:* because.

Eightscore eight hours? and lovers' absent hours,
More tedious than the dial eightscore times?
O weary reck'ning!
CASSIO: Pardon me, Bianca.   170
I have this while with leaden thoughts been pressed;
But I shall in a more convenient time
Strike off this score of absence. Sweet Bianca,
(*Gives her Desdemona's handkerchief.*)
Take me this work out.
BIANCA: O Cassio, whence came this?
This is some token from a newer friend.
To the felt absence now I feel a cause.
Is't come to this? Well, well.
CASSIO: Go to, woman!
Throw your vile guesses in the devil's teeth,
From whence you have them. You are jealous now
That this is from some mistress, some remembrance.   180
No, by my faith, Bianca.
BIANCA: Why, whose is it?
CASSIO: I know not, sweet. I found it in my chamber.
I like the work well. Ere it be demanded,
As like enough it will, I would have it copied.
Take it and do't, and leave me for this time.
BIANCA: Leave you? Wherefore?
CASSIO: I do attend here on the General
And think it no addition, nor my wish,
To have him see me womaned.
BIANCA: Why, I pray you?
CASSIO: Not that I love you not.
BIANCA: But that you do not love me!   190
I pray you bring me on the way a little,
And say if I shall see you soon at night.
CASSIO: 'Tis but a little way that I can bring you,
For I attend here; but I'll see you soon.
BIANCA: 'Tis very good. I must be circumstanced.
                                        (*Exeunt.*)

---

l. 174. *this work out:* copy the embroidery.
l. 188. *addition:* advantage.
l. 189. *womaned:* accompanied by a woman.
l. 195. *circumstanced:* accept circumstances.

ACT IV

SCENE I

(*Cyprus. Before the Castle.*)

(*Enter* OTHELLO *and* IAGO.)

IAGO: Will you think so?

OTHELLO: Think so, Iago?

IAGO: What,
　To kiss in private?

OTHELLO: An unauthorized kiss.

IAGO: Or to be naked with her friend in bed
　An hour, or more, not meaning any harm?

OTHELLO: Naked in bed, Iago, and not mean harm?
　It is hypocrisy against the devil.
　They that mean virtuously, and yet do so,
　The devil their virtue tempts, and they tempt heaven.

IAGO: So they do nothing, 'tis a venial slip.
　But if I give my wife a handkerchief—   1

OTHELLO: What then?

IAGO: Why, then 'tis hers, my lord; and being hers,
　She may, I think, bestow't on any man.

OTHELLO: She is protectress of her honor too.
　May she give that?

IAGO: Her honor is an essence that's not seen;
　They have it very oft that have it not.
　But for the handkerchief—

OTHELLO: By heaven, I would most gladly have forgot it!
　Thou said'st (O, it comes o'er my memory   2
　As doth the raven o'er the infected house,
　Boding to all!) he had my handkerchief.

IAGO: Ay, what of that?

OTHELLO: That's not so good now.

IAGO: What
　If I had said I had seen him do you wrong?

ll. 21–22. *As doth* . . . *Boding to all!*: like a raven or vulture waiting for
the death of the sick.

Or heard him say—as knaves be such abroad
Who having, by their own importunate suit,
Or voluntary dotage of some mistress,
Convinced or supplied them, cannot choose
But they must blab—
OTHELLO: Hath he said anything?
IAGO: He hath, my lord; but be you well assured,   30
   No more than he'll unswear.
OTHELLO: What hath he said?
IAGO: Faith, that he did—I know not what he did.
OTHELLO: What? what?
IAGO: Lie—
OTHELLO: With her?
IAGO: With her, on her; what you will.
OTHELLO: Lie with her? lie on her?—We say lie on her when they
   belie her.—Lie with her! 'Zounds, that's fulsome.—Handkerchief
   —confessions—handkerchief!—To confess, and be hanged for his
   labor—first to be hanged, and then to confess! I tremble at it.
   Nature would not invest herself in such shadowing passion without
   some instruction. It is not words that shakes me thus.—Pish! Noses,   40
   ears, and lips? Is't possible?—Confess?—handkerchief?—O devil!
   (*Falls in a trance.*)
IAGO: Work on,
   My medicine, work! Thus credulous fools are caught,
   And many worthy and chaste dames even thus,
   All guiltless, meet reproach.—What, ho! my lord!
   My lord, I say! Othello!

(*Enter* CASSIO.)

                    How now, Cassio?
CASSIO: What's the matter?
IAGO: My lord is fall'n into an epilepsy.
   This is his second fit; he had one yesterday.
CASSIO: Rub him about the temples.
IAGO: No, forbear.   50
   The lethargy must have his quiet course.
   If not, he foams at mouth, and by-and-by
   Breaks out to savage madness. Look, he stirs.
   Do you withdraw yourself a little while.

l. 36. *fulsome:* disgusting.
l. 51. *lethargy . . . course:* the coma must be allowed to work itself off.

He will recover straight. When he is gone,
I would on great occasion speak with you.

(*Exit* CASSIO.)

How is it, General? Have you not hurt your head?
OTHELLO: Dost thou mock me?
IAGO: I mock you? No, by heaven.
Would you would bear your fortune like a man!
OTHELLO: A horned man's a monster and a beast.   60
IAGO: There's many a beast then in a populous city,
And many a civil monster.
OTHELLO: Did he confess it?
IAGO: Good sir, be a man.
Think every bearded fellow that's but yoked
May draw with you. There's millions now alive
That nightly lie in those unproper beds
Which they dare swear peculiar. Your case is better.
O, 'tis the spite of hell, the fiend's arch-mock,
To lip a wanton in a secure couch,
And to suppose her chaste! No, let me know;   70
And knowing what I am, I know what she shall be.
OTHELLO: O, thou art wise! 'Tis certain.
IAGO: Stand you awhile apart;
Confine yourself but in a patient list.
Whilst you were here, o'erwhelmed with your grief
(A passion most unfitting such a man),
Cassio came hither. I shifted him away
And laid good 'scuse upon your ecstasy;
Bade him anon return, and here speak with me;
The which he promised. Do but encave yourself
And mark the fleers, the gibes, and notable scorns   80
That dwell in every region of his face;
For I will make him tell the tale anew—
Where, how, how oft; how long ago, and when
He hath, and is again to cope your wife.

l. 57. *Have . . . head?:* Iago is hinting at the pain of the cuckold's horns.
ll. 64–65. *yoked/May draw with you:* married, may be in the same situation.
ll. 66–67. *unproper beds . . . peculiar:* the beds they believe are exclusive to them, but which are not.
l. 77. *ecstasy:* fit.
l. 80. *fleers:* sneers.
l. 84. *cope:* top, copulate with.

I say, but mark his gesture. Marry, patience!
Or I shall say you are all in all in spleen,
And nothing of a man.
OTHELLO:　　　　　　　　Dost thou hear, Iago?
I will be found most cunning in my patience;
But (dost thou hear?) most bloody.
IAGO:　　　　　　　　　　That's not amiss;
But yet keep time in all. Will you withdraw?　　　　90

　　　　　　　　　(OTHELLO *retires.*)

Now will I question Cassio of Bianca,
A huswife that by selling her desires
Buys herself bread and clothes. It is a creature
That dotes on Cassio, as 'tis the strumpet's plague
To beguile many and be beguiled by one.
He, when he hears of her, cannot refrain
From the excess of laughter. Here he comes.

　　　　　　　　(*Enter* CASSIO.)

As he shall smile, Othello shall go mad;
And his unbookish jealousy must conster
Poor Cassio's smiles, gestures, and light behavior　　100
Quite in the wrong. How do you now, Lieutenant?
CASSIO: The worser that you give me the addition
Whose want even kills me.
IAGO: Ply Desdemona well, and you are sure on't.
Now, if this suit lay in Bianca's power,
How quickly should you speed!
CASSIO:　　　　　　　　Alas, poor caitiff!
OTHELLO: Look how he laughs already!
IAGO: I never knew woman love man so.
CASSIO: Alas, poor rogue! I think, i' faith, she loves me.
OTHELLO: Now he denies it faintly, and laughs it out.　　110
IAGO: Do you hear, Cassio?
OTHELLO:　　　　　　　Now he importunes him
To tell it o'er. Go to! Well said, well said!
IAGO: She gives it out that you shall marry her.

l. 92. *huswife*: hussy.
l. 99. *unbookish*: ignorant.
　　　conster: construe, interpret.
l. 102. *addition*: the title of Lieutenant.
l. 106. *caitiff*: wretch.

Do you intend it?

CASSIO: Ha, ha, ha!

OTHELLO: Do you triumph, Roman? Do you triumph?

CASSIO: I marry her? What, a customer? Prithee bear some charity to my wit; do not think it so unwholesome. Ha, ha, ha!

OTHELLO: So, so, so, so! Laugh that wins!

IAGO: Faith, the cry goes that you shall marry her.   120

CASSIO: Prithee say true.

IAGO: I am a very villain else.

OTHELLO: Have you scored me? Well.

CASSIO: This is the monkey's own giving out. She is persuaded I will marry her out of her own love and flattery, not out of my promise.

OTHELLO: Iago beckons me. Now he begins the story.

CASSIO: She was here even now; she haunts me in every place. I was t'other day talking on the sea bank with certain Venetians, and thither comes the bauble, and, by this hand, she falls me thus about my neck—   130

OTHELLO: Crying "O dear Cassio!" as it were. His gesture imports it.

CASSIO: So hangs, and lolls, and weeps upon me; so hales and pulls me! Ha, ha, ha!

OTHELLO: Now he tells how she plucked him to my chamber. O, I see that nose of yours, but not that dog I shall throw't to.

CASSIO: Well, I must leave her company.

(Enter BIANCA.*)*

IAGO: Before me! Look where she comes.

CASSIO: 'Tis such another fitchew! marry, a perfumed one. What do you mean by this haunting of me?

BIANCA: Let the devil and his dam haunt you! What did you mean by   140
that same handkerchief you gave me even now? I was a fine fool to take it. I must take out the work? A likely piece of work that you should find it in your chamber and know not who left it there! This is some minx's token, and I must take out the work? There! give it your hobbyhorse. Wheresoever you had it, I'll take out no work on't.

l. 116. *Roman:* conqueror.
l. 117. *customer:* prostitute.
l. 123. *scored:* marked by lashes.
l. 137. *Before me:* a mild exclamation or oath.
l. 138. *fitchew:* whore.
l. 140. *dam:* mother.
l. 145. *hobbyhorse:* harlot.

CASSIO: How now, my sweet Bianca? How now? how now?

OTHELLO: By heaven, that should be my handkerchief!

BIANCA: An you'll come to supper tonight, you may; an you will not, come when you are next prepared for.   (*Exit.*)   150

IAGO: After her, after her!

CASSIO: Faith, I must; she'll rail i' the street else.

IAGO: Will you sup there?

CASSIO: Yes, I intend so.

IAGO: Well, I may chance to see you; for I would very fain speak with you.

CASSIO: Prithee come. Will you?

IAGO: Go to! say no more.   (*Exit* CASSIO.)

OTHELLO (*comes forward*): How shall I murder him, Iago?

IAGO: Did you perceive how he laughed at his vice?   160

OTHELLO: O Iago!

IAGO: And did you see the handkerchief?

OTHELLO: Was that mine?

IAGO: Yours, by this hand! And to see how he prizes the foolish woman your wife! She gave it him, and he hath giv'n it his whore.

OTHELLO: I would have him nine years a-killing!—A fine woman! a fair woman! a sweet woman!

IAGO: Nay, you must forget that.

OTHELLO: Ay, let her rot, and perish, and be damned tonight, for she shall not live. No, my heart is turned to stone: I strike it, and it   170 hurts my hand. O, the world hath not a sweeter creature! She might lie by an emperor's side and command him tasks.

IAGO: Nay, that's not your way.

OTHELLO: Hang her! I do but say what she is. So delicate with her needle! an admirable musician! O, she will sing the savageness out of a bear! Of so high and plenteous wit and invention!

IAGO: She's the worse for all this.

OTHELLO: O, a thousand thousand times! And then, of so gentle a condition!

IAGO: Ay, too gentle.   180

OTHELLO: Nay, that's certain. But yet the pity of it, Iago! O Iago, the pity of it, Iago!

IAGO: If you are so fond over her iniquity, give her patent to offend; for if it touch not you, it comes near nobody.

OTHELLO: I will chop her into messes! Cuckold me!

l. 183. *patent:* the right.

IAGO: O, 'tis foul in her.

OTHELLO: With mine officer!

IAGO: That's fouler.

OTHELLO: Get me some poison, Iago, this night. I'll not expostulate with her, lest her body and beauty unprovide my mind again. This night, Iago!

IAGO: Do it not with poison. Strangle her in her bed, even the bed she hath contaminated.

OTHELLO: Good, good! The justice of it pleases. Very good!

IAGO: And for Cassio, let me be his undertaker. You shall hear more by midnight.

OTHELLO: Excellent good!

(*A trumpet.*)

What trumpet is that same?

IAGO: Something from Venice, sure.

(*Enter* LODOVICO, DESDEMONA, *and* ATTENDANTS.)

'Tis Lodovico,

Come from the Duke; and see, your wife is with him.

LODOVICO: God save you, worthy General!

OTHELLO: With all my heart, sir.

LODOVICO: The Duke and Senators of Venice greet you.

(*Gives him a letter.*)

OTHELLO: I kiss the instrument of their pleasures.

(*Opens the letter and reads.*)

DESDEMONA: And what's the news, good cousin Lodovico?

IAGO: I am very glad to see you, signior.

Welcome to Cyprus.

LODOVICO: I thank you. How does Lieutenant Cassio?

IAGO: Lives, sir.

DESDEMONA: Cousin, there's fall'n between him and my lord

An unkind breach; but you shall make all well.

OTHELLO: Are you sure of that?

DESDEMONA: My lord?

OTHELLO (*reads*): "This fail you not to do, as you will—"

LODOVICO: He did not call; he's busy in the paper.

Is there division 'twixt thy lord and Cassio?

DESDEMONA: A most unhappy one. I would do much

T' atone them, for the love I bear to Cassio.

OTHELLO: Fire and brimstone!

l. 195. *let me . . . undertaker:* let me take care of the business of Cassio.
l. 215. *atone:* reconcile.

DESDEMONA: My lord?

OTHELLO: Are you wise?

DESDEMONA: What, is he angry?

LODOVICO: May be the letter moved him;
    For, as I think, they do command him home,
    Deputing Cassio in his government.

DESDEMONA: By my troth, I am glad on't.

OTHELLO: Indeed?

DESDEMONA: My lord   220

OTHELLO: I am glad to see you mad.

DESDEMONA: ·   Why, sweet Othello!

OTHELLO: Devil!
    (*Strikes her.*)

DESDEMONA: I have not deserved this.

LODOVICO: My lord, this would not be believed in Venice,
    Though I should swear I saw't. 'Tis very much.
    Make her amends; she weeps.

OTHELLO: O devil, devil!
    If that the earth could teem with woman's tears,
    Each drop she falls would prove a crocodile.
    Out of my sight!

DESDEMONA: I will not stay to offend you.
    (*Going.*)

LODOVICO: Truly, an obedient lady.   230
    I do beseech your lordship call her back.

OTHELLO: Mistress!

DESDEMONA: My lord?

OTHELLO: What would you with her, sir?

LODOVICO: Who? I, my lord?

OTHELLO: Ay! You did wish that I would make her turn.
    Sir, she can turn, and turn, and yet go on,
    And turn again; and she can weep, sir, weep;
    And she's obedient; as you say, obedient,
    Very obedient.—Proceed you in your tears.—
    Concerning this, sir (O well-painted passion!),
    I am commanded home.—Get you away;   240
    I'll send for you anon.—Sir, I obey the mandate
    And will return to Venice.—Hence, avaunt!

                         (*Exit* DESDEMONA.)

l. 219. *in his government*: as governor in his place.
ll. 238–242. *Proceed . . . avaunt!*: Othello is talking to both Lodovico
and Desdemona in these lines; the commands are to Desdemona.

Cassio shall have my place. And, sir, tonight
I do entreat that we may sup together.
You are welcome, sir, to Cyprus.—Goats and monkeys!

(*Exit.*)

LODOVICO: Is this the noble Moor whom our full senate
Call all in all sufficient? Is this the nature
Whom passion could not shake? whose solid virtue
The shot of accident nor dart of chance
Could neither graze nor pierce?
IAGO: He is much changed.   25
LODOVICO: Are his wits safe? Is he not light of brain?
IAGO: He's that he is. I may not breathe my censure.
What he might be—if what he might he is not—
I would to heaven he were!
LODOVICO: What, strike his wife?
IAGO: Faith, that was not so well; yet would I knew
That stroke would prove the worst!
LODOVICO: Is it his use?
Or did the letters work upon his blood
And new-create this fault?
IAGO: Alas, alas!
It is not honesty in me to speak
What I have seen and known. You shall observe him,   26
And his own courses will denote him so
That I may save my speech. Do but go after
And mark how he continues.
LODOVICO: I am sorry that I am deceived in him.

(*Exeunt.*)

SCENE II

(*Cyprus. Within the Castle.*)

(*Enter* OTHELLO *and* EMILIA.)

OTHELLO: You have seen nothing then?
EMILIA: Nor ever heard, nor ever did suspect.
OTHELLO: Yes, you have seen Cassio and she together.
EMILIA: But then I saw no harm, and then I heard

---

l. 256. *Is it his use?*: Does he usually behave this way, i.e., strike his wife?

Each syllable that breath made up between them.

OTHELLO: What, did they never whisper?

EMILIA: Never, my lord.

OTHELLO: Nor send you out o' the way?

EMILIA: Never.

OTHELLO: To fetch her fan, her gloves, her mask, nor nothing?

EMILIA: Never, my lord.   10

OTHELLO: That's strange.

EMILIA: I durst, my lord, to wager she is honest,
  Lay down my soul at stake. If you think other,
  Remove your thought; it doth abuse your bosom.
  If any wretch have put this in your head,
  Let heaven requite it with the serpent's curse!
  For if she be not honest, chaste, and true,
  There's no man happy; the purest of their wives
  Is foul as slander.

OTHELLO: Bid her come hither. Go.

                                            (*Exit* EMILIA.)

  She says enough; yet she's a simple bawd   20
  That cannot say as much. This is a subtle whore,
  A closet lock and key of villainous secrets;
  And yet she'll kneel and pray; I have seen her do't.

              (*Enter* DESDEMONA *and* EMILIA.)

DESDEMONA: My lord, what is your will?

OTHELLO: Pray, chuck, come hither.

DESDEMONA: What is your pleasure?

OTHELLO: Let me see your eyes.
  Look in my face.

DESDEMONA: What horrible fancy's this?

OTHELLO (*to* EMILIA): Some of your function, mistress.
  Leave procreants alone and shut the door;
  Cough or cry hem if anybody come.
  Your mystery, your mystery! Nay, dispatch!   30

                                            (*Exit* EMILIA.)

DESDEMONA: Upon my knees, what doth your speech import?
  I understand a fury in your words,
  But not the words.

l. 20. *bawd:* brothel keeper.
ll. 27–30. *Some . . . dispatch!:* Othello is pretending that Emilia's function is that of brothel-keeper and, thus, that Desdemona is a whore.

OTHELLO: Why, what art thou?

DESDEMONA: Your wife, my lord; your true
  And loyal wife.

OTHELLO: Come, swear it, damn thyself;
  Lest, being like one of heaven, the devils themselves
  Should fear to seize thee. Therefore be double-damned—
  Swear thou art honest.

DESDEMONA: Heaven doth truly know it.

OTHELLO: Heaven truly knows that thou art false as hell.

DESDEMONA: To whom, my lord? With whom? How am I false?

OTHELLO: Ah, Desdemon! away! away! away!

DESDEMONA: Alas the heavy day! Why do you weep?
  Am I the motive of these tears, my lord?
  If haply you my father do suspect
  An instrument of this your calling back,
  Lay not your blame on me. If you have lost him,
  Why, I have lost him too.

OTHELLO: Had it pleased heaven
  To try me with affliction, had they rained
  All kinds of sores and shames on my bare head,
  Steeped me in poverty to the very lips,
  Given to captivity me and my utmost hopes,
  I should have found in some place of my soul
  A drop of patience. But, alas, to make me
  A fixed figure for the time of scorn
  To point his slow and moving finger at!
  Yet could I bear that too; well, very well.
  But there where I have garnered up my heart,
  Where either I must live or bear no life,
  The fountain from the which my current runs
  Or else dries up—to be discarded thence,
  Or keep it as a cistern for foul toads
  To knot and gender in—turn thy complexion there,
  Patience, thou young and rose-lipped cherubin!
  I here look grim as hell!

DESDEMONA: I hope my noble lord esteems me honest.

OTHELLO: O, ay! as summer flies are in the shambles,

  ll. 54–55. *time of scorn . . . finger at!:* a scornful world to deride him
forever.
  l. 57. *garnered . . . heart:* stored my love.

That quicken even with blowing. O thou weed,
Who art so lovely fair, and smell'st so sweet,
That the sense aches at thee, would thou hadst ne'er been born!
DESDEMONA: Alas, what ignorant sin have I committed?   70
OTHELLO: Was this fair paper, this most goodly book,
Made to write "whore" upon? What committed?
Committed? O thou public commoner!
I should make very forges of my cheeks
That would to cinders burn up modesty,
Did I but speak thy deeds. What committed?
Heaven stops the nose at it, and the moon winks;
The bawdy wind, that kisses all it meets,
Is hushed within the hollow mine of earth
And will not hear it. What committed?   80
Impudent strumpet!
DESDEMONA: By heaven, you do me wrong!
OTHELLO: Are not you a strumpet?
DESDEMONA: No, as I am a Christian!
If to preserve this vessel for my lord
From any other foul unlawful touch
Be not to be a strumpet, I am none.
OTHELLO: What, not a whore?
DESDEMONA: No, as I shall be saved!
OTHELLO: Is't possible?
DESDEMONA: O, heaven forgive us!
OTHELLO: I cry you mercy then.
I took you for that cunning whore of Venice
That married with Othello.—You, mistress,   90
That have the office opposite to Saint Peter
And keep the gate of hell!

(*Enter* EMILIA.)

                                You, you, ay, you!
We have done our course. There's money for your pains.
I pray you turn the key, and keep our counsel.   (*Exit.*)
EMILIA: Alas, what does this gentleman conceive?
How do you, madam? How do you, my good lady?

ll. 66–67. *as summer flies . . . blowing:* like blowflies which lay their
eggs in the slaughterhouse (*shambles*).
l. 73. *commoner:* whore.
l. 91. *office . . . Peter:* St. Peter's office was to keep the gates of Heaven.

DESDEMONA: Faith, half asleep.

EMILIA: Good madam, what's the matter with my lord?

DESDEMONA: With who?

EMILIA: Why, with my lord, madam.   10

DESDEMONA: Who is thy lord?

EMILIA: He that is yours, sweet lady.

DESDEMONA: I have none. Do not talk to me, Emilia.
　　I cannot weep; nor answer have I none
　　But what should go by water. Prithee tonight
　　Lay on my bed my wedding sheets, remember;
　　And call thy husband hither.

EMILIA: Here's a change indeed!   (*Exit.*)

DESDEMONA: 'Tis meet I should be used so, very meet.
　　How have I been behaved, that he might stick
　　The small'st opinion on my least misuse?

(*Enter* IAGO *and* EMILIA.)

IAGO: What is your pleasure, madam? How is't with you?   11

DESDEMONA: I cannot tell. Those that do teach young babes
　　Do it with gentle means and easy tasks.
　　He might have chid me so; for, in good faith,
　　I am a child to chiding.

IAGO: What is the matter, lady?

EMILIA: Alas, Iago, my lord hath so bewhored her,
　　Thrown such despite and heavy terms upon her
　　As true hearts cannot bear.

DESDEMONA: Am I that name, Iago?

IAGO: What name, fair lady?

DESDEMONA: Such as she says my lord did say I was.

EMILIA: He called her whore. A beggar in his drink   12
　　Could not have laid such terms upon his callet.

IAGO: Why did he so?

DESDEMONA: I do not know. I am sure I am none such.

IAGO: Do not weep, do not weep. Alas the day!

EMILIA: Hath she forsook so many noble matches,
　　Her father and her country, all her friends,
　　To be called whore? Would it not make one weep?

---

l. 104. *go by water:* be expressed by tears.

ll. 108–109. *How have I been behaved . . . my least misuse?:* What have
I done that he could have the slightest cause to be suspicious?

l. 121. *callet:* prostitute.

DESDEMONA: It is my wretched fortune.

IAGO: Beshrew him for't!
How comes this trick upon him?

DESDEMONA: Nay, heaven doth know.

EMILIA: I will be hanged if some eternal villain,   130
Some busy and insinuating rogue,
Some cogging, cozening slave, to get some office,
Have not devised this slander. I'll be hanged else.

IAGO: Fie, there is no such man! It is impossible.

DESDEMONA: If any such there be, heaven pardon him!

EMILIA: A halter pardon him! and hell gnaw his bones!
Why should he call her whore? Who keeps her company?
What place? what time? what form? what likelihood?
The Moor's abused by some most villainous knave,
Some base notorious knave, some scurvy fellow.   140
O heaven, that such companions thou'dst unfold,
And put in every honest hand a whip
To lash the rascals naked through the world
Even from the East to the West!

IAGO: Speak within door.

EMILIA: O, fie upon them! Some such squire he was
That turned your wit the seamy side without
And made you to suspect me with the Moor.

IAGO: You are a fool. Go to.

DESDEMONA: O good Iago,
What shall I do to win my lord again?
Good friend, go to him; for, by this light of heaven,   150
I know not how I lost him. Here I kneel.
If e'er my will did trespass 'gainst his love
Either in discourse of thought or actual deed,
Or that mine eyes, mine ears, or any sense
Delighted them in any other form,
Or that I do not yet, and ever did,
And ever will (though he do shake me off
To beggarly divorcement) love him dearly,

l. 132. *cogging, cozening*: cheating, lying.
l. 141. *O heaven . . . unfold*: Oh, that heaven would reveal such creatures.
l. 144. *Speak within door*: watch your tongue.
ll. 145–147. *Some such squire . . . Moor*: It was just such a fine gentleman who filled your head with suspicion about me and Othello.

Comfort forswear me! Unkindness may do much;
And his unkindness may defeat my life,
But never taint my love. I cannot say "whore."
It doth abhor me now I speak the word;
To do the act that might th' addition earn
Not the world's mass of vanity could make me.

IAGO: I pray you be content. 'Tis but his humor.
The business of the state does him offense,
And he does chide with you.

DESDEMONA: If 'twere no other—

IAGO: 'Tis but so, I warrant.

(*Trumpets within*)
Hark how these instruments summon you to supper.
The messengers of Venice stay the meat.
Go in, and weep not. All things shall be well.

                    (*Exeunt* DESDEMONA *and* EMILIA.)

           (*Enter* RODERIGO.)

How now, Roderigo?

RODERIGO: I do not find that thou deal'st justly with me.

IAGO: What in the contrary?

RODERIGO: Every day thou daff'st me with some device, Iago, and rather, as it seems to me now, keep'st from me all conveniency then suppliest me with the least advantage of hope. I will indeed no longer endure it; nor am I yet persuaded to put up in peace what already I have foolishly suffered.

IAGO: Will you hear me, Roderigo?

RODERIGO: Faith, I have heard too much; for your words and performances are no kin together.

IAGO: You charge me most unjustly.

RODERIGO: With naught but truth. I have wasted myself out of means. The jewels you have had from me to deliver to Desdemona would half have corrupted a votarist. You have told me she hath received them, and returned me expectations and comforts of sudden respect and acquaintance; but I find none.

IAGO: Well, go to; very well.

ll. 163–164. *To do . . . me:* Not for all the riches in the world could I do the act that would earn me that title.
l. 170. *stay the meat:* are waiting to eat.
l. 175. *daff'st:* put me off.
l. 176. *conveniency:* opportunity.
l. 186. *votarist:* a nun.

RODERIGO: Very well! go to! I cannot go to, man; nor 'tis not very well.   190
   Nay, I think it is scurvy, and begin to find myself fopped in it.
IAGO: Very well.
RODERIGO: I tell you 'tis not very well. I will make myself known to
   Desdemona. If she will return me my jewels, I will give over my
   suit and repent my unlawful solicitation. If not, assure yourself I
   will seek satisfaction of you.
IAGO: You have said now.
RODERIGO: Ay, and said nothing but what I protest intendment of
   doing.
IAGO: Why, now I see there's mettle in thee; and even from this in-   200
   stant do build on thee a better opinion than ever before. Give me
   thy hand, Roderigo. Thou hast taken against me a most just exception; but yet I protest I have dealt most directly in thy affair.
RODERIGO: It hath not appeared.
IAGO: I grant indeed it hath not appeared; and your suspicion is not
   without wit and judgment. But, Roderigo, if thou hast that in thee
   indeed which I have greater reason to believe now than ever (I
   mean purpose, courage, and valor), this night show it. If thou the
   next night following enjoy not Desdemona, take me from this
   world with treachery and devise engines for my life.   210
RODERIGO: Well, what is it? Is it within reason and compass?
IAGO: Sir, there is especial commission come from Venice to depute
   Cassio in Othello's place.
RODERIGO: Is that true? Why, then Othello and Desdemona return
   again to Venice.
IAGO: O, no. He goes into Mauritania and takes away with him the
   fair Desdemona, unless his abode be lingered here by some acci-
   dent; wherein none can be so determinate as the removing of
   Cassio.
RODERIGO: How do you mean removing of him?   220
IAGO: Why, by making him uncapable of Othello's place—knocking
   out his brains.
RODERIGO: And that you would have me to do?
IAGO: Ay, if you dare do yourself a profit and a right. He sups tonight
   with a harlotry, and thither will I go to him. He knows not yet of

l. 191. *fopped:* fooled.
l. 197. *You . . . now:* A contemptuous expression meaning, approxi-
mately, "All right, you've said your little speech."
l. 202. *just exception:* fair grievance.
l. 210. *engines:* instruments of torture.
l. 225. *with a harlotry:* in a house of prostitution.

his honorable fortune. If you will watch his going thence, which I will fashion to fall out between twelve and one, you may take him at your pleasure. I will be near to second your attempt, and he shall fall between us. Come, stand not amazed at it, but go along with me. I will show you such a necessity in his death that you shall think yourself bound to put it on him. It is now high supper time, and the night grows to waste. About it!

RODERIGO: I will hear further reason for this.

IAGO: And you shall be satisfied.   (*Exeunt.*)

SCENE III

(*Cyprus. Another room in the Castle.*)

(*Enter* OTHELLO, LODOVICO, DESDEMONA, EMILIA,
and ATTENDANTS.)

LODOVICO: I do beseech you, sir, trouble yourself no further.

OTHELLO: O, pardon me; 'twill do me good to walk.

LODOVICO: Madam, good night. I humbly thank your ladyship.

DESDEMONA: Your Honor is most welcome.

OTHELLO: Will you walk, sir?
   O, Desdemona—

DESDEMONA: My lord?

OTHELLO: Get you to bed on th' instant. I will be returned forthwith.
   Dismiss your attendant there. Look 't be done.

DESDEMONA: I will, my lord.
                    (*Exeunt* OTHELLO, LODOVICO, *and* ATTENDANTS.)

EMILIA: How goes it now? He looks gentler than he did.

DESDEMONA: He says he will return incontinent.
   He hath commanded me to go to bed,
   And bid me to dismiss you.

EMILIA: Dismiss me?

DESDEMONA: It was his bidding. Therefore, good Emilia,
   Give me my nightly wearing, and adieu.
   We must not now displease him.

EMILIA: I would you had never seen him!

DESDEMONA: So would not I. My love doth so approve him
   That even his stubbornness, his checks, his frowns
   (Prithee unpin me) have grace and favor in them.

l. 11. *incontinent:* at once.

EMILIA: I have laid those sheets you bade me on the bed.

DESDEMONA: All's one. Good faith, how foolish are our minds!
If I do die before thee, prithee shroud me
In one of those same sheets.

EMILIA: Come, come! You talk.

DESDEMONA: My mother had a maid called Barbary.
She was in love; and he she loved proved mad
And did forsake her. She had a song of "Willow."
An old thing 'twas; but it expressed her fortune,
And she died singing it. That song tonight
Will not go from my mind. I have much to do   30
But to go hang my head all at one side
And sing it like poor Barbary. Prithee dispatch.

EMILIA: Shall I go fetch your nightgown?

DESDEMONA: No, unpin me here.
This Lodovico is a proper man.

EMILIA: A very handsome man.

DESDEMONA: He speaks well.

EMILIA: I know a lady in Venice would have walked barefoot to Pal-
estine for a touch of his nether lip.

DESDEMONA (*sings*):

       The poor soul sat sighing by a sycamore tree,
         Sing all a green willow: 40
       Her hand on her bosom, her head on her knee,
         Sing willow, willow, willow.
       The fresh streams ran by her and murmured her moans;
         Sing willow, willow, willow;
       Her salt tears fell from her, and soft'ned the stones.
         Sing willow—
       Lay by these.

       willow, willow;

Prithee hie thee; he'll come anon.

       Sing all a green willow must be my garland.   50
       Let nobody blame him; his scorn I approve—

Nay, that's not next. Hark! who is't that knocks?

EMILIA: It is the wind.

l. 22. *All's one:* It doesn't matter.
l. 38. *nether:* lower.

DESDEMONA:

> I called my love false love; but what said he then?
>   Sing willow, willow, willow:
> If I court mo women, you'll couch with mo men.
> So, get thee gone; good night. Mine eyes do itch.
> Doth that bode weeping?

EMILIA: 'Tis neither here nor there.

DESDEMONA: I have heard it said so. O, these men, these men!
> Dost thou in conscience think—tell me, Emilia—
> That there be women do abuse their husbands
> In such gross kind?

EMILIA: There be some such, no question.

DESDEMONA: Wouldst thou do such a deed for all the world?

EMILIA: Why, would not you?

DESDEMONA: No, by this heavenly light!

EMILIA: Nor I neither by this heavenly light.
> I might do't as well i' the dark.

DESDEMONA: Wouldst thou do such a deed for all the world?

EMILIA: The world's a huge thing. It is a great price for a small vice.

DESDEMONA: In troth, I think thou wouldst not.

EMILIA: In troth, I think I should; and undo't when I had done it.
Marry, I would not do such a thing for a joint-ring, nor for measures of lawn, nor for gowns, petti-coats, nor caps, nor any petty exhibition; but, for all the whole world—'Ud's pity! who would not make her husband a cuckold to make him a monarch? I should venture purgatory for't.

DESDEMONA: Beshrew me if I would do such a wrong
> For the whole world.

EMILIA: Why, the wrong is but a wrong i' the world; and having the world for your labor, 'tis a wrong in your own world, and you might quickly make it right.

DESDEMONA: I do not think there is any such woman.

EMILIA: Yes, a dozen; and as many to the vantage as would store the world they played for.
> But I do think it is their husbands' faults
> If wives do fall. Say that they slack their duties
> And pour our treasures into foreign laps;
> Or else break out in peevish jealousies,

l. 56. *mo . . . mo*: more.
ll. 71–72. *joint-ring . . . lawn*: a lover's ring made in two pieces . . . a measure of fine cloth.
l. 82. *as many . . . vantage*: more than enough.

Throwing restraint upon us; or say they strike us,
Or scant our former having in despite—
Why, we have galls; and though we have some grace, 90
Yet have we some revenge. Let husbands know
Their wives have sense like them. They see, and smell,
And have their palates both for sweet and sour,
As husbands have. What is it that they do
When they change us for others? Is it sport?
I think it is. And doth affection breed it?
I think it doth. Is't frailty that thus errs?
It is so too. And have not we affections,
Desires for sport, and frailty, as men have?
Then let them use us well; else let them know, 100
The ills we do, their ills instruct us so.

DESDEMONA: Good night, good night. Heaven me such uses send,
Not to pick bad from bad, but by bad mend!

　　　　　　　　　　　　　　　　　　　(*Exeunt.*)

ACT V

SCENE I

(*Cyprus. A street.*)

(*Enter* IAGO *and* RODERIGO.)

IAGO: Here, stand behind this bulk; straight will he come.
Wear thy good rapier bare, and put it home.
Quick, quick! Fear nothing; I'll be at thy elbow.
It makes us, or it mars us—think on that,
And fix most firm thy resolution.

RODERIGO: Be near at hand. I may miscarry in't.

IAGO: Here, at thy hand. Be bold, and take thy stand.
　　(*Stands aside.*)

RODERIGO: I have no great devotion to the deed,

l. 89. *Or scant . . . despite:* cut down on their favors to us out of spite.
l. 90. *galls:* cause for distress; literally, sores or irritations of the skin
brought on by rubbing.
l. 1. *bulk:* stall.

And yet he hath given me satisfying reasons.
'Tis but a man gone. Forth my sword! He dies!

IAGO: I have rubbed this young quat almost to the sense,
And he grows angry. Now whether he kill Cassio,
Or Cassio him, or each do kill the other,
Every way makes my gain. Live Roderigo,
He calls me to a restitution large
Of gold and jewels that I bobbed from him
As gifts to Desdemona.
It must not be. If Cassio do remain,
He hath a daily beauty in his life
That makes me ugly; and besides, the Moor
May unfold me to him; there stand I in much peril.
No, he must die. But so! I hear him coming.

(*Enter* CASSIO.)

RODERIGO: I know his gait. 'Tis he. Villain, thou diest!
(*Makes a pass at* CASSIO.)

CASSIO: That thrust had been mine enemy indeed
But that my coat is better than thou know'st.
I will make proof of thine.
(*Draws, and wounds* RODERIGO.)

RODERIGO: O, I am slain!
(IAGO *comes forward, wounds* CASSIO *from behind, and exits.*)

CASSIO: I am maimed for ever. Help, ho! Murder! murder!
(*Falls.*)

(*Enter* OTHELLO.)

OTHELLO: The voice of Cassio. Iago keeps his word.

RODERIGO: O, villain that I am!

OTHELLO: It is even so.

CASSIO: O, help, ho! light! a surgeon!

OTHELLO: 'Tis he. O brave Iago, honest and just,
That hast such noble sense of thy friend's wrong!
Thou teachest me. Minion, your dear lies dead,
And your unblest fate hies. Strumpet, I come.

---

l. 11. *quat:* a word of contempt; literally, a pimple or boil.
     almost to the sense: i.e., nearly to the quick where it really hurts.
l. 16. *bobbed:* tricked him out of.
ll. 33–34. *Minion . . . hies:* Darling (in a contemptuous sense), your death without the blessing of the priest draws near.

Forth of my heart those charms, thine eyes, are blotted.
Thy bed, lust-stained, shall with lust's blood be spotted.

(*Exit.*)

(*Enter* LODOVICO *and* GRATIANO.)

CASSIO: What, ho? No watch? No passage? Murder! murder!
GRATIANO: 'Tis some mischance. The cry is very direful.
CASSIO: O, help!
LODOVICO: Hark!   40
RODERIGO: O wretched villain!
LODOVICO: Two or three groan. It is a heavy night.
    These may be counterfeits. Let's think't unsafe
    To come in to the cry without more help.
RODERIGO: Nobody come? Then shall I bleed to death.
LODOVICO: Hark!

(*Enter* IAGO.)

GRATIANO: Here's one comes in his shirt, with light and weapons.
IAGO: Who's there? Whose noise is this that cries on murder?
LODOVICO: We do not know.
IAGO: Did not you hear a cry?
CASSIO: Here, here! For heaven's sake, help me!
IAGO: What's the matter?   50
GRATIANO: This is Othello's ancient, as I take it.
LODOVICO: The same indeed, a very valiant fellow.
IAGO: What are you here that cry so grievously?
CASSIO: Iago? O, I am spoiled, undone by villains!
    Give me some help.
IAGO: O me, Lieutenant! What villains have done this?
CASSIO: I think that one of them is hereabout
    And cannot make away.
IAGO: O treacherous villains!
    What are you there? Come in, and give some help.
    (*To* LODOVICO *and* GRATIANO)
RODERIGO: O, help me here!   60
CASSIO: That's one of them.
IAGO: O murd'rous slave! O villain!
    (*Stabs* RODERIGO.)
RODERIGO: O damned Iago! O inhuman dog!

l. 35. *Forth . . . heart*: henceforth out of my heart.
l. 37. *No passage?*: No passersby?
l. 43. *counterfeits*: fake.

IAGO: Kill men i' the dark? Where be these bloody thieves?
　　How silent is this town! Ho! murder! murder!
　　What may you be? Are you of good or evil?
LODOVICO: As you shall prove us, praise us.
IAGO: Signior Lodovico?
LODOVICO: He, sir.
IAGO: I cry you mercy. Here's Cassio hurt by villains.
GRATIANO: Cassio?　　　　　　　　　　　　　　　　　　7〇
IAGO: How is it, brother?
CASSIO: My leg is cut in two.
IAGO:　　　　　　　　　　　Marry, heaven forbid!
　　Light, gentlemen. I'll bind it with my shirt.

(*Enter* BIANCA.)

BIANCA: What is the matter, ho? Who is't that cried?
IAGO: Who is't that cried?
BIANCA: O my dear Cassio! my sweet Cassio!
　　O Cassio, Cassio, Cassio!
IAGO: O notable strumpet!—Cassio, may you suspect
　　Who they should be that thus have mangled you?
CASSIO: No.　　　　　　　　　　　　　　　　　　　8〇
GRATIANO: I am sorry to find you thus. I have been to seek you.
IAGO: Lend me a garter. So. O for a chair
　　To bear him easily hence!
BIANCA: Alas, he faints! O Cassio, Cassio, Cassio!
IAGO: Gentlemen all, I do suspect this trash
　　To be a party in this injury.—
　　Patience awhile, good Cassio.—Come, come!
　　Lend me a light. Know we this face or no?
　　Alas, my friend and my dear countryman
　　Roderigo? No. Yes, sure. O heaven! Roderigo.　　9〇
GRATIANO: What, of Venice?
IAGO: Even he, sir. Did you know him?
GRATIANO:　　　　　　　　　　　　　　　Know him? Ay.
IAGO: Signior Gratiano? I cry you gentle pardon.
　　These bloody accidents must excuse my manners
　　That so neglected you.
GRATIANO:　　　　　　　　　　I am glad to see you.
IAGO: How do you, Cassio?—O, a chair, a chair!
GRATIANO: Roderigo?
IAGO: He, he, 'tis he!

(A chair brought in)
                    O, that's well said! the chair.
Some good man bear him carefully from hence.
I'll fetch the General's surgeon.
(To BIANCA*)*
                                   For you, mistress,   100
Save you your labor.—He that lies slain here, Cassio,
Was my dear friend. What malice was between you?
CASSIO: None in the world; nor do I know the man.
IAGO *(to* BIANCA*)*: What, look you pale?—O, bear him out o' th' air.
*(*CASSIO *and* RODERIGO *are borne off.)*
Stay you, good gentlemen.—Look you pale, mistress?—
Do you perceive the gastness of her eye?—
Nay, an you stare, we shall hear more anon.
Behold her well; I pray you look upon her.
Do you see, gentlemen? Nay, guiltiness will speak,
Though tongues were out of use.   110

(Enter EMILIA.*)*

EMILIA: 'Las, what's the matter? What's the matter, husband?
IAGO: Cassio hath here been set on in the dark
    By Roderigo, and fellows that are 'scaped.
    He's almost slain, and Roderigo dead.
EMILIA: Alas, good gentleman! alas, good Cassio!
IAGO: This is the fruit of whoring. Prithee, Emilia,
    Go know of Cassio where he supped tonight.
    (To BIANCA*)*
    What, do you shake at that?
BIANCA: He supped at my house; but I therefore shake not.
IAGO: O, did he so? I charge you go with me.   120
EMILIA: Fie, fie upon thee, strumpet!
BIANCA: I am no strumpet, but of life as honest
    As you that thus abuse me.
EMILIA: As I? Foh! fie upon thee!
IAGO: Kind gentlemen, let's go see poor Cassio dressed.
    (To BIANCA*)*
    Come, mistress, you must tell's another tale.—
    Emilia, run you to the citadel
    And tell my lord and lady what hath happed.—

l. 106. *gastness:* terror.
l. 124. *dressed:* i.e., his wounds dressed.

Will you go on afore?
(*Aside*)

                      This is the night
That either makes me or fordoes me quite.

                                  (*Exeunt.*)

SCENE II

(*Cyprus. A bedchamber in the Castle.*)

    (DESDEMONA *in her bed. Enter* OTHELLO *with a light.*)

OTHELLO: It is the cause, it is the cause, my soul.
Let me not name it to you, you chaste stars!
It is the cause. Yet I'll not shed her blood,
Nor scar that whiter skin of hers than snow,
And smooth as monumental alabaster.
Yet she must die, else she'll betray more men.
Put out the light, and then put out the light.
If I quench thee, thou flaming minister,
I can again thy former light restore,
Should I repent me; but once put out thy light,   10
Thou cunning'st pattern of excelling nature,
I know not where is that Promethean heat
That can thy light relume. When I have plucked the rose,
I cannot give it vital growth again;
It needs must wither. I'll smell it on the tree.
(*He kisses her.*)
O balmy breath, that dost almost persuade
Justice to break her sword! One more, one more!
Be thus when thou art dead, and I will kill thee,
And love thee after. One more, and this the last!
So sweet was ne'er so fatal. I must weep,   20
But they are cruel tears. This sorrow's heavenly,
It strikes where it doth love. She wakes.
DESDEMONA: Who's there? Othello?
OTHELLO: Ay, Desdemona.
DESDEMONA: Will you come to bed, my lord?

l. 129. *fordoes:* does for me, i.e., ruins me.
l. 12. *Promethean heat:* fire from heaven.
l. 13. *relume:* reillumine.

OTHELLO: Have you prayed tonight, Desdemon?

DESDEMONA: Ay, my lord.

OTHELLO: If you bethink yourself of any crime
   Unreconciled as yet to heaven and grace,
   Solicit for it straight.

DESDEMONA: Alack, my lord, what may you mean by that?

OTHELLO: Well, do it, and be brief; I will walk by.   30
   I would not kill thy unprepared spirit.
   No, heaven forfend! I would not kill thy soul.

DESDEMONA: Talk you of killing?

OTHELLO: Ay, I do.

DESDEMONA: Then heaven
   Have mercy on me!

OTHELLO: Amen, with all my heart!

DESDEMONA: If you say so, I hope you will not kill me.

OTHELLO: Humh!

DESDEMONA: And yet I fear you; for you are fatal then
   When your eyes roll so. Why I should fear I know not,
   Since guiltiness I know not; but yet I feel I fear.

OTHELLO: Think on thy sins.

DESDEMONA: They are loves I bear to you.   40

OTHELLO: Ay, and for that thou diest.

DESDEMONA: That death's unnatural that kills for loving.
   Alas, why gnaw you so your nether lip?
   Some bloody passion shakes your very frame.
   These are portents; but yet I hope, I hope,
   They do not point on me.

OTHELLO: Peace and be still!

DESDEMONA: I will so. What's the matter?

OTHELLO: That handkerchief which I so loved and gave thee
   Thou gav'st to Cassio.

DESDEMONA: No, by my life and soul!
   Send for the man and ask him.

OTHELLO: Sweet soul, take heed,   50
   Take heed of perjury; thou art on thy deathbed.

DESDEMONA: Ay, but not yet to die.

OTHELLO: Yes, presently.
   Therefore confess thee freely of thy sin;
   For to deny each article with oath
   Cannot remove nor choke the strong conception
   That I do groan withal. Thou art to die.

DESDEMONA: Then Lord have mercy on me!

OTHELLO: I say amen.

DESDEMONA: And have you mercy too! I never did
    Offend you in my life; never loved Cassio
    But with such general warranty of heaven   60
    As I might love. I never gave him token.

OTHELLO: By heaven, I saw my handkerchief in's hand!
    O perjured woman! thou dost stone my heart,
    And mak'st me call what I intend to do
    A murder, which I thought a sacrifice.
    I saw the handkerchief.

DESDEMONA: He found it then.
    I never gave it him. Send for him hither.
    Let him confess a truth.

OTHELLO: He hath confessed.

DESDEMONA: What, my lord?

OTHELLO: That he hath used thee.

DESDEMONA: How? unlawfully?

OTHELLO: Ay.   70

DESDEMONA: He will not say so.

OTHELLO: No, his mouth is stopped.
    Honest Iago hath ta'en order for't.

DESDEMONA: O, my fear interprets. What, is he dead?

OTHELLO: Had all his hairs been lives, my great revenge
    Had stomach for them all.

DESDEMONA: Alas, he is betrayed, and I undone!

OTHELLO: Out, strumpet! Weep'st thou for him to my face?

DESDEMONA: O, banish me, my lord, but kill me not!

OTHELLO: Down, strumpet!

DESDEMONA: Kill me tomorrow; let me live tonight!   80

OTHELLO: Nay, an you strive—

DESDEMONA: But half an hour!

OTHELLO: Being done, there is no pause.

DESDEMONA: But while I say one prayer!

OTHELLO: It is too late.

    (*He smothers her.*)

    (EMILIA *calls within, at the door.*)

EMILIA: My lord, my lord! What, ho, my lord, my lord!

OTHELLO: What noise is this? Not dead? not yet quite dead?

    l. 60. *warranty*: permission.
    l. 63. *stone*: turn to stone.

I that am cruel am yet merciful;
I would not have thee linger in thy pain.
So, so.

EMILIA (*within*):
      What, ho! my lord, my lord!
OTHELLO: Who's there?
EMILIA (*within*): O, good my lord, I would speak a word with you!
OTHELLO: Yes.—'Tis Emilia.—By-and-by.—She's dead.—   90
  'Tis like she comes to speak of Cassio's death:
  The noise was high. Ha! no more moving?
  Still as the grave.—Shall she come in? Were't good?—
  I think she stirs again. No.—What's best to do?
  If she come in, she'll sure speak to my wife.
  My wife! my wife! what wife? I have no wife.
  O, insupportable! O heavy hour!
  Methinks it should be now a huge eclipse
  Of sun and moon, and that th' affrighted globe
  Should yawn at alteration.
EMILIA (*within*):   I do beseech you   100
  That I may speak with you, O good my lord!
OTHELLO: I had forgot thee. O, come in, Emilia.
  Soft, by-and-by.—Let me the curtains draw.—
  Where art thou?
  (*Opens the door.*)

               (*Enter* EMILIA.)

            What's the matter with thee now?
EMILIA: O my good lord, yonder's foul murder done!
OTHELLO: What? Now?
EMILIA: But now, my lord.
OTHELLO: It is the very error of the moon.
  She comes more near the earth than she was wont
  And makes men mad.   110
EMILIA: Cassio, my lord, hath killed a young Venetian
  Called Roderigo.
OTHELLO: Roderigo killed?
  And Cassio killed?
EMILIA: No, Cassio is not killed.
OTHELLO: Not Cassio killed? Then murder's out of tune,

l. 100. *yawn at alteration:* break open as a result of the terrible change.

And sweet revenge grows harsh.

DESDEMONA: O, falsely, falsely murdered!

EMILIA: O Lord! what cry is that?

OTHELLO: That? What?

EMILIA: Out and alas! that was my lady's voice.
　　Help! help, ho! help! O lady, speak again!
　　Sweet Desdemona! O sweet mistress, speak!   120

DESDEMONA: A guiltless death I die.

EMILIA: O, who hath done this deed?

DESDEMONA: Nobody—I myself. Farewell.
　　Commend me to my kind lord. O, farewell!
　　(*She dies.*)

OTHELLO: Why, how should she be murd'red?

EMILIA: Alas, who knows?

OTHELLO: You heard her say herself, it was not I.

EMILIA: She said so. I must needs report a truth.

OTHELLO: She's like a liar gone to burning hell!
　　'Twas I that killed her.

EMILIA: O, the more angel she,
　　And you the blacker devil!   130

OTHELLO: She turned to folly, and she was a whore.

EMILIA: Thou dost belie her, and thou art a devil.

OTHELLO: She was false as water.

EMILIA: Thou art rash as fire to say
　　That she was false. O, she was heavenly true!

OTHELLO: Cassio did top her. Ask thy husband else.
　　O, I were damned beneath all depth in hell
　　But that I did proceed upon just grounds
　　To this extremity. Thy husband knew it all.

EMILIA: My husband?

OTHELLO: Thy husband.   140

EMILIA: That she was false to wedlock?

OTHELLO: Ay, with Cassio. Nay, had she been true,
　　If heaven would make me such another world
　　Of one entire and perfect chrysolite,
　　I'd not have sold her for it.

EMILIA: My husband?

OTHELLO: Ay, 'twas he that told me first.
　　An honest man he is, and hates the slime

---

l. 144. *chrysolite:* a semiprecious stone.

That sticks on filthy deeds.

EMILIA: My husband?

OTHELLO: What needs this iterance, woman? I say, thy husband.

EMILIA: O mistress, villainy hath made mocks with love!   150
My husband say that she was false?

OTHELLO: He, woman.
I say, thy husband. Dost understand the word?
My friend, thy husband; honest, honest Iago.

EMILIA: If he say so, may his pernicious soul
Rot half a grain a day! he lies to the heart.
She was too fond of her most filthy bargain.

OTHELLO: Ha!

EMILIA: Do thy worst.
This deed of thine is no more worthy heaven
Than thou wast worthy her.

OTHELLO: Peace, you were best.   160

EMILIA: Thou hast not half the power to do me harm
As I have to be hurt. O gull! O dolt!
As ignorant as dirt! thou hast done a deed—
I care not for thy sword; I'll make thee known,
Though I lost twenty lives. Help! help, ho! help!
The Moor hath killed my mistress! Murder! murder!

(*Enter* MONTANO, GRATIANO, IAGO, *and others.*)

MONTANO: What is the matter? How now, General?

EMILIA: O, are you come, Iago? You have done well,
That men must lay their murders on your neck.

GRATIANO: What is the matter?   170

EMILIA: Disprove this villain, if thou be'st a man:
He says thou told'st him that his wife was false.
I know thou didst not; thou'rt not such a villain.
Speak, for my heart is full.

IAGO: I told him what I thought, and told no more
Than what he found himself was apt and true.

EMILIA: But did you ever tell him she was false?

IAGO: I did.

EMILIA: You told a lie, an odious damned lie!
Upon my soul, a lie! a wicked lie!   180
She false with Cassio? Did you say with Cassio?

l. 149. *iterance:* repetition.

IAGO: With Cassio, mistress. Go to, charm your tongue.

EMILIA: I will not charm my tongue; I am bound to speak:
My mistress here lies murdered in her bed—

ALL: O heavens forfend!

EMILIA: And your reports have set the murder on.

OTHELLO: Nay, stare not, masters. It is true indeed.

GRATIANO: 'Tis a strange truth.

MONTANO: O monstrous act!

EMILIA: Villainy, villainy, villainy!
I think upon't, I think! I smell't! O villainy!   190
I thought so then. I'll kill myself for grief.
O villainy, villainy!

IAGO: What, are you mad? I charge you get you home.

EMILIA: Good gentlemen, let me have leave to speak.
'Tis proper I obey him, but not now.
Perchance, Iago, I will ne'er go home.

OTHELLO: O! O! O!
(*Falls on the bed.*)

EMILIA: Nay, lay thee down and roar!
For thou hast killed the sweetest innocent
That e'er did lift up eye.

OTHELLO: O, she was foul!
(*Rises.*)
I scarce did know you, uncle. There lies your niece,   200
Whose breath, indeed, these hands have newly stopped.
I know this act shows horrible and grim.

GRATIANO: Poor Desdemon! I am glad thy father's dead.
Thy match was mortal to him, and pure grief
Shore his old thread in twain. Did he live now,
This sight would make him do a desperate turn;
Yea, curse his better angel from his side,
And fall to reprobance.

OTHELLO: 'Tis pitiful; but yet Iago knows
That she with Cassio hath the act of shame   210
A thousand times committed. Cassio confessed it;
And she did gratify his amorous works
With that recognizance and pledge of love
Which I first gave her; I saw it in his hand:

ll. 204–205. *Thy match . . . in twain:* Your marriage was the death of
him and grief cut the thread of his life in two.
l. 208. *reprobance:* reprobation.

It was a handkerchief, an antique token
My father gave my mother.

EMILIA: O God! O heavenly pow'rs!

IAGO: 'Zounds, hold your peace!

EMILIA: 'Twill out, 'twill out! I peace?
No, I will speak as liberal as the North.
Let heaven and men and devils, let them all,   220
All, all, cry shame against me, yet I'll speak.

IAGO: Be wise, and get you home.

EMILIA: I will not.

(IAGO *draws and threatens* EMILIA.)

GRATIANO: Fie!
Your sword upon a woman?

EMILIA: O thou dull Moor, that handkerchief thou speak'st of
I found by fortune, and did give my husband;
For often with a solemn earnestness
(More than indeed belonged to such a trifle)
He begged of me to steal't.

IAGO: Villainous whore!

EMILIA: She give it Cassio? No, alas, I found it,
And I did give't my husband.

IAGO: Filth, thou liest!   230

EMILIA: By heaven, I do not, I do not, gentlemen.
O murd'rous coxcomb! what should such a fool
Do with so good a wife?

OTHELLO: Are there no stones in heaven
But what serves for the thunder? Precious villain!

(The MOOR *runs at* IAGO, *but is disarmed by* MONTANO.)
(IAGO *kills his wife.*)

GRATIANO: The woman falls. Sure he hath killed his wife.

EMILIA: Ay, ay. O, lay me by my mistress' side.

                                              (Exit IAGO.)

GRATIANO: He's gone, but his wife's killed.

MONTANO: 'Tis a notorious villain. Take you this weapon,
Which I have here recovered from the Moor.
Come, guard the door without. Let him not pass,   240
But kill him rather. I'll after that same villain,
For 'tis a damned slave.

        (Exeunt MONTANO *and* GRATIANO *with* OTHELLO *and* EMILIA.)

l. 219. *as liberal as the North:* as freely as the North wind.

OTHELLO: I am not valiant neither;
But every puny whipster gets my sword.
But why should honor outlive honesty?
Let it go all.

EMILIA: What did thy song bode, lady?
Hark, canst thou hear me? I will play the swan,
And die in music. [*Sings*] "Willow, willow, willow."
Moor, she was chaste; she loved thee, cruel Moor.
So come my soul to bliss as I speak true.
So speaking as I think, I die, I die.
(*She dies.*)   250

OTHELLO: I have another weapon in this chamber;
It is a sword of Spain, the ice-brook's temper.
O, here it is.—Uncle, I must come forth.

GRATIANO (*within*): If thou attempt it, it will cost thee dear.
Thou hast no weapon, and perforce must suffer.

OTHELLO: Look in upon me then and speak with me,
Or, naked as I am, I will assault thee.

(*Enter* GRATIANO.)

GRATIANO: What is the matter?

OTHELLO: Behold, I have a weapon.
A better never did itself sustain
Upon a soldier's thigh. I have seen the day   260
That with this little arm and this good sword
I have made my way through more impediments
Than twenty times your stop. But O vain boast!
Who can control his fate? 'Tis not so now.
Be not afraid, though you do see me weaponed.
Here is my journey's end, here is my butt,
And very seamark of my utmost sail.
Do you go back dismayed? 'Tis a lost fear.
Man but a rush against Othello's breast,
And he retires. Where should Othello go?—   270
Now, how dost thou look now? O ill-starred wench!
Pale as thy smock! When we shall meet at compt,
This look of thine will hurl my soul from heaven,
And fiends will snatch at it. Cold, cold, my girl?

l. 243. *whipster:* contemptible person.
l. 252. *ice-brook's temper:* the sword was tempered in ice-cold water.
l. 272. *compt:* reckoning, i.e., Judgment Day.

Even like thy chastity.—O cursed slave!
Whip me, ye devils,
From the possession of this heavenly sight!
Blow me about in winds! roast me in sulphur!
Wash me in steep-down gulfs of liquid fire!
O Desdemona, Desdemona! dead!   280
O! O! O!

(*Enter* LODOVICO, CASSIO, MONTANO, *and* IAGO, *with* OFFICERS.)

LODOVICO: Where is this rash and most unfortunate man?
OTHELLO: That's he that was Othello. Here I am.
LODOVICO: Where is that viper? Bring the villain forth.
OTHELLO: I look down towards his feet—but that's a fable.
    If that thou be'st a devil, I cannot kill thee.
    (*Wounds* IAGO.)
LODOVICO: Wrench his sword from him.
    (OTHELLO *is disarmed.*)
IAGO: I bleed, sir, but not killed.
OTHELLO: I am not sorry neither. I'd have thee live;
    For in my sense, 'tis happiness to die.
LODOVICO: O thou Othello that wert once so good,   290
    Fall'n in the practice of a damned slave,
    What shall be said to thee?
OTHELLO: Why, anything:
    An honorable murderer, if you will;
    For naught did I in hate, but all in honor.
LODOVICO: This wretch hath part confessed his villainy.
    Did you and he consent in Cassio's death?
OTHELLO: Ay.
CASSIO: Dear General, I never gave you cause.
OTHELLO: I do believe it, and I ask your pardon.
    Will you, I pray, demand that demi-devil   300
    Why he hath thus ensnared my soul and body?
IAGO: Demand me nothing. What you know, you know.
    From this time forth I never will speak word.
LODOVICO: What, not to pray?
GRATIANO: Torments will ope your lips.
OTHELLO: Well, thou dost best.

    l. 285. *I look down towards his feet:* i.e., he looks for a devil's cloven
hooves.
    l. 291. *Fall'n . . . practice:* destroyed by the work.

LODOVICO: Sir, you shall understand what hath befall'n,
    Which, as I think, you know not. Here is a letter
    Found in the pocket of the slain Roderigo;
    And here another. The one of them imports
    The death of Cassio to be undertook   31
    By Roderigo.
OTHELLO: O villain!
CASSIO: Most heathenish and most gross!
LODOVICO: Now here's another discontented paper
    Found in his pocket too; and this, it seems,
    Roderigo meant t' have sent this damned villain;
    But that, belike, Iago in the interim
    Came in and satisfied him.
OTHELLO: O thou pernicious caitiff!—
    How came you, Cassio, by that handkerchief
    That was my wife's?
CASSIO: I found it in my chamber;
    And he himself confessed but even now   32
    That there he dropped it for a special purpose
    Which wrought to his desire.
OTHELLO: O fool! fool! fool!
CASSIO: There is besides in Roderigo's letter,
    How he upbraids Iago that he made him
    Brave me upon the watch; whereon it came
    That I was cast; and even but now he spake,
    After long seeming dead—Iago hurt him,
    Iago set him on.
LODOVICO: You must forsake this room and go with us.
    Your power and your command is taken off,   33
    And Cassio rules in Cyprus. For this slave,
    If there be any cunning cruelty
    That can torment him much and hold him long,
    It shall be his. You shall close prisoner rest
    Till that the nature of your fault be known
    To the Venetian state. Come, bring away.
OTHELLO: Soft you! a word or two before you go.
    I have done the state some service, and they know't—
    No more of that. I pray you, in your letters,

l. 317. *satisfied:* killed.
l. 325. *Brave:* challenge.
ll. 325–326. *Whereon . . . cast:* as a result of which I was cashiered.

When you shall these unlucky deeds relate,   340
Speak of me as I am. Nothing extenuate,
Nor set down aught in malice. Then must you speak
Of one that loved not wisely, but too well;
Of one not easily jealous, but, being wrought,
Perplexed in the extreme; of one whose hand
(Like the base Indian) threw a pearl away
Richer than all his tribe; of one whose subdued eyes,
Albeit unused to the melting mood,
Drop tears as fast as the Arabian trees
Their med'cinable gum. Set you down this;   350
And say besides that in Aleppo once,
Where a malignant and a turbaned Turk
Beat a Venetian and traduced the state,
I took by the throat the circumcised dog
And smote him—thus.
(*He stabs himself.*)
LODOVICO: O bloody period!
GRATIANO: All that's spoke is marred.
OTHELLO: I kissed thee ere I killed thee. No way but this—
Killing myself, to die upon a kiss.
(*He falls across* DESDEMONA *and dies.*)
CASSIO: This did I fear, but thought he had no weapon;
For he was great of heart.
LODOVICO: O Spartan dog,   370
More fell than anguish, hunger, or the sea!
Look on the tragic loading of this bed.
This is thy work. The object poisons sight;
Let it be hid. Gratiano, keep the house,
And seize upon the fortunes of the Moor,
For they succeed on you. To you, Lord Governor,
Remains the censure of this hellish villain.
The time, the place, the torture—O, enforce it!
Myself will straight aboard, and to the state
This heavy act with heavy heart relate.   370
                                        (*Exeunt.*)

l. 360. *Spartan dog:* known for its fierceness.
l. 361. *fell:* cruel.

Molière

In 1622, six years after the death of England's greatest playwright, Shakespeare, France's greatest dramatist, Jean-Baptiste Poquelin, was born. This child of a Parisian upholsterer and furniture-maker was given an excellent education at the Collège de Clermont, the foremost school in the French capital. The Jesuit teachers conducted all courses in Latin and the students were expected to converse and write in the classical tongue. When he completed his studies at the Collège, Jean-Baptiste read law at Orléans.

The elder Poquelin, who was attached to the royal court as a *valet de chambre tapissier* (one who cared for the king's furniture and household furnishings), made his eldest son heir to this royal position. However, though Jean-Baptiste was to be closely connected to the court of Louis XIV, it was not in the role of upholsterer. In 1643 he ceded his right to inherit his father's royal position and founded with Madeleine Béjart, an actress five years his senior, an acting company called L'Illustre Théâtre. This upstart theatrical group, with its headquarters in a converted, enclosed tennis court, had to compete against the established companies that had the patronage of the king. Financial difficulties ensued, and Jean-Baptiste, who had adopted the name Molière, once spent a week in jail for debt before being rescued by his father. Undaunted, the troupe left Paris to tour the provinces. By 1650, Molière was not only the leading actor of the company but had become its director. After nearly six years of traveling from town to town, the company settled in Lyons, under the patronage of Prince

Conti. With an established base and release from the ordeals of an itinerant life, Molière had time to try his hand at writing. His first work, a light situation comedy, *L'Étourdi* (*The Blunderer*), was enacted by his company in 1655. Prince Conti withdrew his support, but a second comedy by Molière, *Le Dépit Amoureux* (*The Amorous Quarrel*), enhanced the reputation of the company and brought it the patronage of the younger brother of Louis XIV, the Duc D'Anjou.

This connection with the royal family brought Molière and his company to Paris. On October 24, 1658, at the invitation of Louis XIV, the company performed for the king. The tragedy that was presented drew only mild applause from the royal audience. Quick-witted and clever, Molière addressed the audience and requested permission to present *Le Dépit Amoureux,* the play for which his company had been widely applauded in the provinces. The king granted permission and was so delighted with the comedy that he promptly installed Molière's company in the Théâtre du Petit Bourbon, one of the two royal theaters in Paris. Molière's group had to share the theater with a company led by the famous Scaramouche, performing on alternate days. The following year, however, Louis gave Molière a theater to himself, the Palais Royal, which is the ancestor of the present Comédie Française.

During the fifteen years that remained of his life, Molière led a busy existence that was rewarded by a growing reputation as actor and writer. He managed the company, directed its productions, remained one of its chief actors, and at the same time wrote and produced twenty-eight plays. These comedies included farces, comedy-ballets, and the great dramas, known as high comedy. Many of these works were composed rapidly at the direct request of the king, who desired new plays for his lavish entertainments at the Louvre, his Parisian palace, and at Versailles. Some of Molière's minor works betray the speed with which they were composed, but the great comedies were carefully structured by a master craftsman and artist. Molière's growing popularity with Parisian audiences during this period is perhaps best attested by the bitter attacks to which he was subjected. One priest went so far as to write a pamphlet urging that the author of *Tartuffe* be burned alive. Molière did suffer some setbacks (such as the banning of *Tartuffe*) because of such attacks, but generally the patronage of the king protected him, and Parisians acclaimed him for his talents as actor and playwright.

In his private life, however, Molière suffered much personal disappointment and distress. In the provinces and in Paris he had for many years enjoyed a liaison with Madeleine Béjart and amorous adventures with other women in the company. At forty, however, he fell in love with a twenty-year-old actress, Armande Béjart, who was said to be the sister of the forty-five-year-old Madeleine, but who may very well have been her daughter. Molière's marriage to Armande set the tongues of Parisian scandalmongers to wagging with the suggestion that Molière was not only Armande's husband, but probably her father. Such scandal was disturbing but Molière was far more distressed by his young wife's avid need for admiration and her penchant for flirtation. The trials of such a marriage were compounded by the death of a son less than a year after his birth. A daughter survived, but a second son, born in the final year of Molière's life, lived only a few weeks. During his final five or six years, the playwright was plagued by ill health, and perhaps the low point of these years of public triumph and private anguish came in 1669 when his father and Madeleine, then his companion of nearly thirty years, died.

Despite these personal misfortunes, Molière, during these years, wrote and produced the greatest of his high comedies: *Le Misanthrope* (*The Misanthrope*) and *Le Médecin malgré lui* (*The Doctor in Spite of Himself*) in 1666; *L'Avare* (*The Miser*) and *Amphitryon* in 1668, the third and final version of *Tartuffe* (*The Hypocrite*) in 1669; *Le Bourgeois gentil-homme* (*The Would-Be Gentleman*) in 1670; *Les Fourberies de Scapin* (*Scapin's Sharp Tricks*) in 1671; and the very fine *Les Femmes Savantes* (*The Learned Ladies*) in 1672. Molière never relinquished any of his activities. He continued to write and direct and act, and it was during a performance of *Le Malade imaginaire* (*The Imaginary Invalid*) in 1673 that he became fatally ill. That same night he died. The local parish priest refused the rites of burial until the king, to prevent a scandal, intervened. When he died at the age of fifty-one, Molière was known as the favorite actor of Louis XIV, and Parisian theatergoers applauded his dramas. However, literary recognition as one of the greatest dramatists of the world was bestowed on him, as it was with Shakespeare, only by posterity.

Like the English playwright, Molière was a working member of a stock company, in which the actors worked together and shared in the profits of the theater. Before he began to write, he spent ten years acting and then managing the company; thus, his craft, like Shakespeare's, was grounded on a thorough knowledge of the stage, of audience response, and of the particular abilities of the actors in the company. Though Molière was born a writer of comedy, his art underwent a process of development that began with farce and progressed to that comedy of character with a theme which is called "high comedy."

His first work *L'Etourdi* is a very clever work that utilizes some of the stock characters of ancient comedy: the bumbling hero, for instance, and the clever, scheming servant. This initial work reveals that Molière, like Rabelais, began with a natural sense for sheer fun, and an ability to wring humor from extravagance and caricature. Perhaps the most influential force in Molière's artistic development was the *commedia del arte,* which had been developed by Italian actors. From the old Roman comedies the Italian actors took a number of humorous characters—the soldier who brags of his courage but who is really a coward (Shakespeare's Falstaff is a lineal descendant of this type), the shrewish wife, the fop, the bumpkin, the miser. Such characters were generally identified, in the *commedia del arte,* by masks, and an actor usually acted the same character throughout his career. In the *commedia,* a story would be devised or chosen, but for the most part, the drama was one of improvisation. With merely a sketch outline of the plot to guide them, the actors allowed situations to develop out of the jokes and comical responses they improvised on stage. Much buffoonery and earthy joking characterized these spontaneous performances whose sole aim was to make people laugh.

Though Molière refined this comedy of masks, his farces have the same stock characters and are marked by a similar quality of spontaneous fun; the story is generally contrived to permit incessant activity and buffoonery. In such plays the situations create the humor. As he developed his art, however, Molière shifted from the comedy of situation to the comedy of character. In a high comedy, such as *Tartuffe,* the situations and the story derive from the characters of Orgon and Tartuffe. Some of the devices of farce, such as having Orgon beneath the table while Tartuffe attempts to seduce Orgon's wife, are retained, but the major emphasis is upon character and the laughter provoked is thoughtful laughter. The writer of high comedy wants to make his audience laugh, but he wants them to think as they laugh. He wants them to become aware as they laugh of the flatulence, the silly pretensions, and the foibles of themselves and their fellow men.

Tragedy exalts the outstanding individualist, and it appeals primarily to emotions. Comedy assumes that social norms are to be respected; individualists—the overpious, the pompous, the mannered, and the precious—who exceed these norms are subject to ridicule. The appeal of comedy is to the intellect. Tragedy requires audience empathy with the tragic hero, but comedy demands sufficient detachment to permit the audience to view the characters objectively and to laugh at them. "Humor," James Thurber once said, "is a serious thing." And perhaps his point is best illustrated by the impact of a famous ancient comedy upon the philosopher it subjected to ridicule. Aristophanes' *The Clouds* contributed to the eventual trial of Socrates and his death sentence.

The writer of comedy is a keen observer of the world in which he lives, and his satiric thrusts are aimed not only at the manners and customs of daily life, the hallowed traditions and mores, the respected ideas and ideals of his society, but also at the silly and grotesque poses of his fellow men. Human beings are capable of an infinite variety of follies in their pursuit of ego satisfaction. People very readily become pompous or excessively mannered or hypocritical in their anxious struggle to dignify their individual sense of self and to see themselves as better than others. Comedy makes us aware of such excesses by exposing us to scorn and restoring us to a healthy balance. The writer with a gift for making people laugh who feels impelled to expose human folly has the essential talent for comedy. If, like Molière, he can also create characters on stage, write brilliant, witty dialogue, and can expertly structure a play, he can produce high comedy.

Perhaps what made Molière so great a writer of high comedy was the unique combination of much stage experience, genius, and his own personality, which embodied so many of the characteristics of his age and his nation. Molière was an easy-going, generous, kindly, unpretentious, fun-loving man. Like most Frenchmen of his age, he was not given to moral introspection and to morbid philosophizing. He accepted life for what it was, and though he exposed the foibles of his fellow men, he did so without bitterness and without any idealistic belief that he could change human nature. He saw much life and had much opportunity to study human character during his many years of traveling from town to town. By nature, he tended to laugh rather than cry at the conditions of existence and the antics of human beings. Like Montaigne and later the French thinkers of the seventeenth century, Molière respected order, proportion, and man's power to reason, and he measured the reality of men's lives against these concepts. Molière was no revolutionary attacking the status quo. He was, in fact, an upholder of the established social, political, and religious institutions. In *Tartuffe,* for example, Orgon's submission to the hypocrite, Tartuffe, threatens the institution of the family, and the comedy ends with the restoration of order. Molière's conformity to the rules of the Catholic Church may have been minimal, but he never attacked the Church as a religious institution. His targets were always pretension, affectation, and hypocrisy in whatever guises or professions he found them.

Molière's dramatic art also reflects his respect for logic, order, and proportion. With his contemporaries he shared a profound admiration for the social and artistic concepts of Greek civilization, and his plays adhere to the Aristotelian rules of drama. His stories are simple; they are developed lucidly and logically, and unities of time and place are respected. Perhaps of most importance, his characters are presented as universal types, though they are convincingly real and sufficiently individualized.

Tartuffe has endured as the very essence of hypocrisy, but when Molière first introduced him on stage, many Parisians recognized him as a member of contemporary society. The portrait evoked so much opposition that Louis XIV considered it politically expedient to forbid Molière to present the drama. The attack on *Tartuffe* was led by The Society of the Holy Sacrament, a group which had been formed in 1627 to serve as the moral conscience of Parisian society. Its avowed aims were to do good works, reform morals, protect the honor of women, and expose adulterers and free thinkers. One of the methods adopted to achieve these goals was to introduce lay members of the organization into the households of wealthy families. These do-gooders, without revealing their purpose, would ingratiate themselves with the family and then serve as moral advisors. The Society of the Holy Sacrament had the sanction of the Queen Mother and also of the Archbishop of Paris, and though the king apparently enjoyed Molière's comedy, he deemed it wise to forbid its performance.

Molière was incensed by the outcry and the ban, and he fought it for five years. The original version, which was performed before the king on May 12, 1664, was a three-act play. Three years later, he presented a five-act version of the same play, toning down the satire and trying to make clear that he was attacking hypocrisy and not the priests. This second version was also banned. Molière's faith in his drama did not falter, and once again he revised. Finally, on February 5, 1669, his company enacted the third and final version of *Tartuffe* at the Palais Royal. This time Louis XIV licensed the drama and it was regularly presented by the repertory company. Most scholars believe that Molière expanded the original version without fundamentally altering its theme, and that it was not the revisions but the changing political climate that made the 1669 version acceptable.

In a preface which he wrote for the published edition of this final version, Molière defended himself against the attacks that had been leveled at him. He was addressing himself, he said, "to the truly devout people everywhere." If the play were carefully studied, he argued, it would be perfectly clear to any unbiased reader that the playwright's "intentions were innocent throughout, that it in no wise tends to hold up to ridicule things to which reverence is due and that I have handled it all with the delicacy which the subject demands and used all my skill and taken every possible precaution to distinguish the hypocrite from the truly devout man."

To the modern reader, it is certainly obvious that Molière is attacking hypocrisy rather than piety. The playwright, for instance, ignored the fact that members of The Society of the Holy Sacrament kept their identity and purpose secret from members of the family they chose to advise. Tartuffe makes no attempt to disguise himself; in the very first scene it is clear to everyone in the entire family, except Orgon and Madame Pernelle, that Tartuffe is a hypocrite. As Molière pointed out in his preface, Tartuffe does not make his appearance until the third act, and "the audience is never for a moment in doubt about him; he is recognizable at once by the distinguishing marks I have given him and from first to last he never utters a word or performs one single action which does not clearly indicate to the audience that he is a scoundrel. . . ."

It is probably indicative of the validity of Molière's portrait that contemporary Parisian audiences viewed the play as an exposure of hypocrisy rather than an exposure of paternal tyranny. Orgon, rather than Tartuffe, is really the central character of the drama. Though he appears to be the dupe of Tartuffe, in reality he is using the hypocrite to justify his tyranny. The restoration of order by the king in the final scene dramatizes the father of society, the king, using his power wisely and justly to restore the order that Orgon has foolishly disrupted.

As Molière, in the same preface, wrote, "If the purpose of comedy be to chastise human weaknesses I see no reason why any class of people should be exempt. . . . The finest passages of a serious moral treatise are all too often less effective than those of a satire and for the majority of people there is no better form of reproof than depicting their faults to them: the most effective way of attacking vice is to expose it to public ridicule. People can put up with rebukes but they cannot bear being laughed at: they are prepared to be wicked but they dislike appearing ridiculous."

Though three hundred years have passed since Molière wrote

those words, they continue to be true, and his comedies therefore have endured.

≈≈

BIBLIOGRAPHY

Fernandez, Ramon. *Molière: The Man Seen Through the Plays,* trans. Wilson Follett. New York: Hill and Wang, 1958.

Gossman, Lionel. *Men and Masks: A Study of Molière.* Baltimore: The Johns Hopkins Press, 1963.

Guicharnaud, Jacques (ed.). *Molière: A Collection of Critical Essays.* Englewood Cliffs, N.J.: Prentice-Hall, 1964.

Hubert, Judd. *Molière and the Comedy of Intellect.* Berkeley: University of California Press, 1962.

Lewis, Wyndham. *Molière: The Comic Mask.* London: Eyre & Spottiswood, 1959.

Matthews, Brander. *Molière: His Life and His Works.* New York: Scribner's, 1916.

Tartuffe

Translated by Morris Bishop

CHARACTERS

MADAME PERNELLE	*mother of Orgon*
ORGON	
ELMIRE	*Orgon's wife*
DAMIS	*son of Orgon, stepson of Elmire*
MARIANE	*daughter of Orgon and stepdaughter of Elmire*
VALÈRE	
CLÉANTE	*brother-in-law of Orgon, brother of Elmire*
TARTUFFE	
DORINE	*companion of Mariane*
MONSIEUR LOYAL	*bailiff*
A POLICE OFFICER	
FLIPOTE	*Madame Pernelle's servant*

The setting throughout is the salon of Orgon's house, in Paris. The furnishings are those of a well-to-do bourgeois.

ACT I

(MADAME PERNELLE, FLIPOTE, ELMIRE, MARIANE, DORINE, DAMIS, CLÉANTE.)

MME. PERNELLE: Come on, Flipote, come on; I've had enough.

ELMIRE: Mother, you walk so fast I can't keep up.

MME. PERNELLE: Don't try to keep up, then. Ha! Daughter-in-law!
Little I care if you're polite with me.

ELMIRE: I want to be so with my husband's mother.
Why must you go? I hope you're not offended.

MME. PERNELLE: Why? I can't stand the way that things are going!
In my son's house they pay no heed to me.
I am not edified; not edified.
I give you good advice. Who pays attention?
Everyone speaks his mind, none shows respect.
This place is Bedlam; everyone is king here.

DORINE: If—

MME. PERNELLE: You, my dear, you're just a paid companion,
A forward hussy, who talks a lot too much.
You have to give your views on everything.

DAMIS: But—

MME. PERNELLE: You are a fool. F-O-O-L spells fool.
Your grandmother, she ought to know a fool.
And I have told your father a hundred times
You're impudent, your character is bad;
And what he'll get from you, my boy, is trouble.

MARIANE: I think—

MME. PERNELLE: You think! The fool's little sister thinks!
Butter won't melt in that prim mouth of yours.
Still waters, they are deep—and dangerous.
And something hides behind that mousy manner.

ELMIRE: But, Mother—

MME. PERNELLE: Dear Elmire, I will be frank.
I find your attitude unfortunate.
Your task should be to set a good example.
Their own dead mother did so, better than you.
I disapprove of your extravagance;
You get yourself all rigged up like a princess.

A wife, my dear, needs no such finery,
If she would please her husband's eyes alone.

CLÉANTE: But, madame, after all—

MME. PERNELLE: You are her brother.
You have my reverence, esteem, and love.
But if I were my son, her happy husband,
I'd beg of you never to call again.
The principles I hear you recommend
Are not the sort that decent folk observe.
I'm speaking frankly; that's the way I am;
And when I feel a thing, I cannot hide it.

DAMIS: There's nothing wrong about Monsieur Tartuffe?

MME. PERNELLE: He is a worthy man with principles;
And I admit that I am irritated
To hear him criticized by fools like you.

DAMIS: You want me to permit a canting critic
To come and play the tyrant in our home?
We can't indulge in innocent amusement
Unless that gentleman gives his consent?

DORINE: If one believes him and his principles,
Everything that we do becomes a crime.
He checks on everything, he's so sincere.

MME. PERNELLE: And what he checks on is most properly checked.
He wants to lead you on the road to heaven.
My son is well inspired to make you love him.

DAMIS: Grandmother, look; Father can do his utmost;
Nothing on earth can make me love the fellow.
Anything else I'd say would be a lie.
I simply cannot stand him and his actions.
I can see trouble coming; I can see
I'll have a set-to with that holy fraud.

DORINE: It seems to me perfectly scandalous
That this outsider should take over things.
He came to us a beggar, with no shoes,
And all his clothes were worth about a dollar.
But that's forgotten, now he's found his place;
He has the final veto; he's the boss.

MME. PERNELLE: Mercy upon us! Things would be much better
If all his pious rules were put in force.

DORINE: He is a saint in your imagination.
In fact, he's nothing but a hypocrite.

MME. PERNELLE: What silly talk is this!

DORINE: I wouldn't trust him
   Out of my sight; his servant Laurent either.

MME. PERNELLE: The servant I don't know; but for the master,
   I guarantee that he's a man of virtue.
   And you dislike him, you cold-shoulder him
   Merely because he tells the truth about you.
   The one thing that he really hates is sin,
   And heaven's advantage is his only motive.

DORINE: Yes, but why is it that for some time now
   He won't allow us any visitors?
   What is so shocking in a friendly call,
   That he should make a frightful fuss about it?
   And shall I tell you what I really think?
   I think that he is jealous of Madame.

(*She indicates* ELMIRE.)

MME. PERNELLE: Be quiet, you! Be careful what you say!
   He's not the only one who blames these visits.
   All the commotion that these callers make,
   Their carriages forever at the door,
   The noisy gangs of lackeys, hanging around,
   Have caused a lot of comment from the neighbors.
   Oh, I will grant that nothing serious happens,
   But people talk, and people shouldn't talk.

CLÉANTE: You want to put a stop to conversation?
   Wouldn't it be somewhat regrettable
   If we should have to give up our best friends,
   Just because fools may say some foolish things?
   Even supposing we should bar the door,
   Do you think people then would cease to talk?
   There is no wall so high it shuts out slander.
   So let's not give a thought to silly gossip,
   And let us try to live in innocence,
   And let the talkers talk just as they please.

DORINE: Our neighbor Daphne and her little husband
   Are doubtless those who speak so ill of us.
   Those whose behavior is ridiculous
   Always are first to see the faults of others.
   They never fail to catch the faintest hint
   That mutual attachments may exist.
   And then how glad they are to spread the news,

Suggesting—oh, what horrors they suggest!
And others' acts, colored to suit their tastes,
They put to use to authorize their own.
They think that some resemblance will appear
To mask their own intrigues with innocence;
They hope thus to confuse the public censure
And make it fall on good and ill alike.

MME. PERNELLE: All these fine words do not affect the case.
Orante, for instance, leads a model life.
She works for heaven alone; and people say
That she condemns the customs of this house.

DORINE: There is a fine example! That good woman!
She lives austerely now, that's true enough;
But age has put this ardor in her soul,
And makes her play the prude, despite herself.
As long as men would pay their court to her,
She made her graces work for her advantage.
But her allurements ceasing to allure,
She quits society, which quitted her,
And with a veil of virtue tries to hide
The dimming of her antiquated charms.
That is the classic fate of old coquettes;
They hate to see their gallants disappear.
Unhappy and abandoned, they can see
No other recourse than the trade of prude.
And these good women with severity
Make universal censure, pardon nothing.
Loudly they blame the lives of everyone,
Not out of charity, but out of envy,
Which can't endure that any woman share
In pleasures time has thieved away from them.

MME. PERNELLE (*to* ELMIRE): That is the kind of nonsense that you
    like;
Thus in your house we have to hold our tongues
So that my lady here can hold the floor.
But I've a little speech to make myself,
And here it is: My son did very wisely
In welcoming that pious gentleman;
And heaven sent him here advisedly
To guide your spirits, strayed from the true path.
And you should heed him, for your souls' salvation.

What he reproves has needed his reproof.
These parties and these balls, these conversations,
Are all inventions of the Evil One.
There one may hear no edifying speeches,
But only idle words and songs and chatter,
Often at some poor fellow man's expense.
There you find masters in the art of slander.
Even the man of sense may be upset
By the loose talk one hears in such assemblies,
All a great buzz of gossip and of rumor.
As a great preacher said the other day,
These gatherings are towers of Babylon,
For people merely babble on, he said.
And then in illustration of his point—
(*Points to* CLÉANTE.)
And now Monsieur is snickering already!
Go join the funny men who make you laugh!
My dear Elmire, good-by; I've said enough.
This household has come down in my opinion.
'Twill be a blue moon ere I come again.
(*Giving* FLIPOTE *a box on the ear.*)
Wake up, woolgatherer! Wake up, rattlehead!
God's mercy! I will beat those brains of yours!
On your way, trollop!

                    (*Exit all except* CLÉANTE *and* DORINE.)
CLÉANTE: I wouldn't see her out
For fear I'd get another dressing-down.
For really, that good woman—
DORINE: It's too bad
The lady didn't hear you call her good.
She'd tell you you are kind to term her good,
But she's not old enough yet to be good.
CLÉANTE: Didn't she get excited about nothing!
And isn't she crazy about her Tartuffe!
DORINE: In fact, that son of hers is twice as bad.
If you could see him, you'd be really shocked.
He played a fine part in the civil wars,
Was faithful to the King through thick and thin;
But now he acts as if he'd lost his wits,
Since he has been bewitched by his Tartuffe.
He calls him brother, actually loves him

More than his mother, son, daughter, and wife,
Confides his secrets to Tartuffe alone,
And makes him sole director of his actions;
Hugs him and pats him tenderly; he couldn't
Show more affection for a darling bride;
Gives him the place of honor at his table,
And beams to see him eat enough for six.
He saves the best bits for Tartuffe alone,
And cries "God bless you!" when the fellow belches.
He's mad about the man, his pet, his hero,
And quotes him, apropos of everything,
And makes a miracle of every action,
An oracle of every slightest word.
And Tartuffe knows a good thing when he sees it,
Puts on an act, the better to fool his dupe;
His holy manner pays him off in cash,
While he makes bold to criticize us all.
Even that boy who serves him as a lackey
Takes it upon himself to give us lessons,
And lectures us with angry, popping eyes,
And throws away our ribbons, rouge, and patches.
The rascal tore to bits a neckerchief
We'd put to press in some big holy book,
Saying we made a criminal connection
Between the devil's toys and holiness!

(*Enter* ELMIRE, MARIANE, DAMIS.)

ELMIRE: Lucky for you you didn't come and hear
The speech she made us, standing in the doorway.
I saw my husband, but he didn't see me.
I think I'll wait for him in the upstairs parlor.
(*Exit* ELMIRE *and* MARIANE.)
CLÉANTE: Not to waste time, I'll wait to see him here.
I merely want to greet him and be gone.
DAMIS: Bring up the question of my sister's marriage.
I've an idea Tartuffe is against it.
He's swaying Father, making difficulties.
You know I'm personally interested.
As Valère and my sister are in love,
I'm more than fond myself of Valère's sister.
And if I had to—

DORINE: He's coming.

(*Exit* DAMIS. *Enter* ORGON.)

ORGON: Good morning, brother.
CLÉANTE: I was just leaving. I'm glad to see you back.
    And did you find the country all in bloom?
ORGON: Dorine . . . Just wait a minute, please, Cléante,
    Until I have a chance to inform myself
    About the household news during my absence.
(*To* DORINE)
    Everything's been all right, the past few days?
    How's everyone? What has been going on?
DORINE: Two days ago, your lady had a fever,
    And a bad headache, really terrible.
ORGON: And Tartuffe?
DORINE: Tartuffe? Oh, he's doing fine,
    So fat and red-faced, such a healthy color.
ORGON: Poor fellow!
DORINE: She had some nausea in the evening,
    And couldn't touch a single thing at supper.
    Her headache still was a real torture to her.
ORGON: And Tartuffe?
DORINE: Ate his supper in her presence,
    And piously devoured two partridges,
    Also a hash of half a leg of mutton.
ORGON: Poor fellow!
DORINE: During all the following night
    She did not shut her eyes a single moment.
    It was so very warm she could not sleep;
    We had to sit beside her until morning.
ORGON: And Tartuffe?
DORINE: Oh, Tartuffe was sleepy enough.
    He went right after dinner to his room,
    Immediately he got in his warm bed,
    And peacefully slept until the following day.
ORGON: Poor fellow!
DORINE: She listened to our arguments,
    And had the doctor give her a good bleeding,
    And after that she felt a great deal better.
ORGON: And Tartuffe?
DORINE: Why, he cheered up very nicely.

To fortify his spirit against trouble
And to make up for Madame's loss of blood,
He took at lunch four glasses full of wine.

ORGON: Poor fellow!

DORINE: Now both are doing very well.
I'll tell Madame the sympathetic interest
You've taken in the news of her recovery.

(*Exit* DORINE.)

CLÉANTE: She's laughing in your face, my dear Orgon;
And while I wouldn't want to make you angry,
I'm frank to say she has good reason to.
I can't conceive such an infatuation.
This fellow must cast some uncanny spell
Which paralyzes all your common sense.
After you've rescued him from poverty,
To think you've gone so far—

ORGON: Enough, Cléante.
You do not know the man you're talking of.

CLÉANTE: Well, I don't know him personally, it's true,
But I know well what kind of man he is.

ORGON: Brother-in-law, you would be charmed to know him.
You would be simply overwhelmed with pleasure.
He's a man who . . . a man who . . . well, he's a man!
Follow his teachings, you gain peace of mind,
You learn to see the world as so much filth.
My talks with him have changed me utterly;
He's taught me to despise worldly attachments,
He frees my soul from earthly love and friendship;
If brother and children, mother and wife should die,
It wouldn't bother me as much as that!

(*Snaps his fingers.*)

CLÉANTE: These sentiments are what I call humane.

ORGON: If you'd been present when we made acquaintance,
You'd have become his friend, the same as I.
He used to come to our church every day,
And kneel near me, with such a gentle air!
And everyone in church would notice him
Because of the fervent way in which he prayed.
He sighed so deep, he made such cries of transport!
And every now and then he'd kiss the floor!
When I was going out, he'd run ahead

To offer me holy water at the door.
His servant lad, no less devout than he,
Told me about his life, his poverty.
I made him presents; but with modesty,
He always tried to give me back a part.
"This is too much!" he'd tell me. "Twice too much!
I don't deserve to have you pity me!"
And when I would refuse to take them back,
He'd give them to the poor! I saw him do it!
'Twas heaven that made me bring him to my house;
And since that time, everything prospers here.
He censures everything, and for my honor
He takes an active interest in my wife,
Warns me when people look too kindly at her—
He's twice as jealous of her as I could be.
You can't imagine his religious scruples!
The merest trifle is a sin to him;
Nothing's too insignificant to shock him.
Why, he accused himself the other day
Of capturing a flea while he was praying,
And pinching it to death with too much anger!

CLÉANTE: Good Lord, my dear Orgon, I think you're crazy!
Or are you trying to make a fool of me?
What do you think that all this nonsense means?

ORGON: Cléante, this sounds to me like irreligion!
You've had some tendency to that already;
And as I've warned you a good dozen times,
You'll get yourself in trouble some fine day.

CLÉANTE: I've heard that kind of talk from others like you.
They want to make the whole world blind like them.
It's irreligion just to have open eyes!
If you're not taken in by mummery,
They say you've no respect for sacred things.
You cannot scare me with that sort of language.
I know what I say, and heaven can see my heart.
We aren't befooled by such performances;
There's false devotion like false bravery.
And as you see upon the field of honor
The really brave are not the noisiest ones,
The truly pious, whom we should imitate,
Are not the ones who show off their devotion.

Isn't there some distinction to be made
Between hypocrisy and piety?
It seems you want to treat them both alike,
Honor the mask as much as the true face,
Make artifice equal sincerity,
Confuse the outward semblance with the truth,
Esteem the phantom equally with the person,
Take counterfeit money on a par with gold.
Really, humanity is most peculiar!
Men won't remain in the mean middle way;
The boundaries of reason are too narrow.
They force their character beyond its limits,
And often spoil even most noble aims
By exaggeration, carrying things too far.
All this, Orgon, is only said in passing.

ORGON: Cléante, you are no doubt a reverend doctor.
All of man's wisdom has been lodged in you.
You are the world's one wise, enlightened sage,
The oracle, the Cato of our times,
And all mankind, compared with you, are fools.

CLÉANTE: No, Orgon, I am not a reverend doctor,
And the world's wisdom is not lodged in me.
But there is one thing that I do well know:
To tell the difference between true and false.
And as I see no kind of character
More honorable than true devotion is,
Nothing more noble and more beautiful
Than fervent, genuine, holy piety,
So I find nothing on earth more odious
Than the false show of whited sepulchres,
These charlatans, these public pietists
Whose sacrilegious and perfidious manners
Deliberately betray and parody
All that men hold most hallowed and most sacred.
These are the people who for mean advantage
Make piety their trade and merchandise,
And try to buy credit and offices,
Rolling their eyes and mouthing holy words.
Their pilgrim's progress takes the road to heaven
As a short, easy way to worldly fortune.
We see them pray with one hand out for alms;

They preach of solitude, but stay at court.
And with their holy zeal they keep their vices;
They're vengeful, faithless, treacherous, and tricky,
And to destroy an enemy, they cover
Their savage hate with heaven's interest.
And when they hate, they're the more dangerous,
Because they take up weapons we revere,
Because their fury, to general applause,
Takes an anointed sword to stab our backs.
The type that I describe is all too common.
But the true pietists can be recognized.
Take Ariston, for instance, Périandre,
Oronte, Alcidamas, or Polydore.
No one's suspicious of their genuineness.
Such people don't go trumpeting their virtue,
They don't put on a nauseating show,
For their devotion's human, reasonable.
They do not censure all the acts of men—
There's too much pride in taking on that role.
They leave the high talk to their imitators,
And by their actions set us an example.
They don't see evil everywhere abounding;
Indeed, they're lenient toward their fellow men.
They don't form pressure groups to push intrigues;
To lead a good life is their only aim.
They don't pursue the sinner with their hate;
The sin and not the sinner is their target.
They don't espouse the interests of heaven
With greater zeal than heaven does itself.
That is the kind of people I admire;
They are the models we should imitate;
And, to be frank, your man's not one of them.
Although I know you praise him in good faith,
I think you're taken in by false appearance.

ORGON: Cléante, you've now entirely finished?
CLÉANTE: Yes.
ORGON: I am your humble servant.
(*Starts to leave.*)
CLÉANTE: Just a moment.
    Let's deal with something else. You have consented
    That young Valère should have your daughter's hand.

ORGON: Yes.
CLÉANTE: And what's more, you'd even set the day.
ORGON: That is correct.
CLÉANTE: Then why is it postponed?
ORGON: I don't know why.
CLÉANTE: You have another idea?
ORGON: Perhaps.
CLÉANTE: You hint you'd go back on your word.
ORGON: I won't say that.
CLÉANTE: There is some obstacle
   To keep you from fulfilling your engagement?
ORGON: Maybe.
CLÉANTE: Why must you beat around the bush?
   Valère has asked me to inquire about it.
ORGON: How fortunate!
CLÉANTE: What shall I tell him, then?
ORGON: Whatever you like.
CLÉANTE: But it is necessary
   To know your plans. So what are they?
ORGON: To follow
   The will of heaven.
CLÉANTE: I want to get this clear.
   You've given Valère your word. You'll keep your word?
ORGON: Good-by.
                                    (*Exit* ORGON.)

CLÉANTE: I fear that courtship's in for trouble;
   And I must tell Valère the look of things.

❦❦

ACT II

(ORGON, MARIANE.)

ORGON: Mariane!
MARIANE: Father?
ORGON: Come here. I want to speak
   In confidence.
(*He peers into a cupboard.*)
MARIANE: What are you looking for?

ORGON: I want to see if there's an eavesdropper there,
　　For that's the kind of place they choose to hide in.
　　No, it's all right. Now, Mariane, my dear,
　　You've always had a gentle character,
　　And I have always been most fond of you.
MARIANE: I have been very grateful for your love.
ORGON: Excellent, daughter. To deserve my affection
　　You should be ready to accept my judgments.
MARIANE: I've always done so, and I'm proud of it.
ORGON: Splendid. Now tell me, what do you think of Tartuffe?
MARIANE: What do I think?
ORGON:　　　　　　　　　　　Yes. Don't speak hastily.
MARIANE: Dear me! I think whatever you think I should.

(DORINE *enters unnoticed.*)

ORGON: Well said. Now this is what you ought to think.
　　He is a man of most unusual merit;
　　He moves your heart, and you'd be overjoyed
　　To have me pick him out to be your husband.
　　Eh?
(MARIANE *starts back in surprise.*)
MARIANE:　　Eh?
ORGON:　　　　　　What?
MARIANE:　　　　　　　　　　　What did you say?
ORGON:　　　　　　　　　　　　　　　　　What?
MARIANE:　　　　　　　　　　　　　　　Did I hear rightly?
ORGON: What's this?
MARIANE:　　　　　　　Who is it you say that moves my heart?
　　Who is it that it would make me overjoyed
　　To have you fix upon to be my husband?
ORGON: Tartuffe.
MARIANE:　　　　　　Oh, no, no, no, it's impossible.
　　Why do you want to make me say what's false?
ORGON: I say it because I want to make it true.
　　I have decided on it, that's enough.
MARIANE: Father, you really mean—
ORGON:　　　　　　　　　　　　Yes, it's my purpose
　　To make Tartuffe a member of our family.
　　He'll be your husband, I'm resolved on that.
　　And your desires—
(*He turns, and perceives* DORINE.)

What are you doing here?
Your curiosity is certainly excessive
To make you listen to our private talk.

DORINE: I'd heard the story—I suppose it started
  Out of pure guesswork or some chance remark—
  That this peculiar marriage was afoot;
  But I've been saying it's all poppycock.

ORGON: You mean you find it unbelievable?

DORINE: So much so that I don't believe you now.

ORGON: I know how I can bring you to believe it.

DORINE: Yes, you're just being funny. I know *you*.

ORGON: I'm telling you exactly what will happen.

DORINE: Rubbish!

ORGON: My good girl, it's not rubbish at all.

DORINE (*to* MARIANE): Do not believe a word your father says.
  He's joking.

ORGON: I tell you—

DORINE: No, whatever you do,
  Nobody can believe it.

ORGON: I can't hold in—

DORINE: All right, then, I'll believe you, if I must.
  But how a sensible-looking man like you,
  With a big beard in the middle of his face,
  Can be so simple-minded—

ORGON: Listen to me.
  You have been taking certain liberties here
  Which I don't like at all, I tell you frankly.

DORINE: Now, let's not get excited, sir, I beg you.
  Is your idea just to look absurd?
  A bigot has no business with your daughter;
  He has a lot of other things to think of.
  What good does such a marriage do to you?
  How comes it that you, with your property,
  Should choose a beggar son-in-law—

ORGON: Be quiet!
  That's just the reason why we should revere him!
  His poverty's a worthy poverty,
  Which properly sets him above rank and wealth.
  He's let his worldly goods all slip away,
  Because he'd no concern for temporal things,
  Because he loved eternal goods alone.

But my financial aid will help him rise
Out of his troubles, regain his property,
Estates well known in his home territory.
He is a landed squire, a gentleman.
DORINE: Yes, so he says. His vanity about it
Is unbecoming with his piety.
When you take up a holy, innocent life,
You shouldn't boast about your name and rank.
Devotion should imply humility,
Which doesn't fit with smugness and ambition.
Why be so proud? . . . But you don't like this talk.
Let's treat his person, not his noble blood.
Doesn't it trouble you that a man like him
Should be possessor of a girl like her?
Shouldn't you think about the decencies,
Foresee the consequence of such a union?
You're putting a girl's virtue to the test
By forcing her to a distasteful marriage;
And her desire to be a faithful wife
Depends upon the qualities of the husband.
The men who wear the horns are just the ones
Who force their wives to be—what they become.
It's hard indeed for a woman to be faithful
To certain husbands cast in a certain mold.
A father who gives a girl to a man she hates
Must be responsible for her missteps.
So think how dangerous your project is!
ORGON: And so you want to teach me about life!
DORINE: You could do worse than follow my advice.
ORGON: Daughter, we'll waste no time with all this nonsense.
I know what's best for you; I am your father.
It's true that I had pledged you to Valère,
But now I hear that he plays cards for money;
Further, I fear he's somewhat a freethinker.
I do not see him frequently in church.
DORINE: You think he ought to go there just when you do,
Like those who only want to catch your attention?
ORGON: I didn't ask your views upon the matter.
(*To* MARIANE)
The other man has made his peace with heaven,
And that's the greatest wealth a man can have.

This marriage will be rich in every blessing,
And filled with pleasures and with satisfactions.
You will be faithful, in your mutual joys,
Just like a pair of little turtle doves.
There'll never be an argument between you;
You'll make of him whatever you want to make.

DORINE: All that she'll make of him is a horned monster.

ORGON: What talk is this?

DORINE: I say he has the build for it.
The stars have doomed him, and his natural fate
Will be more powerful than your daughter's virtue.

ORGON: Stop interrupting me, and hold your tongue,
And don't go meddling in what's none of your business.

DORINE: I'm only speaking, sir, for your own good.

(*She interrupts* ORGON *whenever he turns to speak to his daughter.*)

ORGON: That's all too kind of you; and so, be silent.

DORINE: If I didn't love you—

ORGON: I don't want to be loved.

DORINE: I want to love you, sir, in spite of yourself.

ORGON: Ha!

DORINE: Cherishing your honor, I can't bear
The mockeries you'd lay yourself open to.

ORGON: You won't shut up?

DORINE: My conscientious duty
Is not to permit you to make such an alliance.

ORGON: Will you shut up, you snake! Your impudence—

DORINE: Why, you're so holy, and you fly in a rage!

ORGON: You drive me crazy with your balderdash,
And so I order you to keep your mouth shut.

DORINE: All right. But even when silent, I can think.

ORGON: Think if you like; but take good care you don't
Utter a word, or else—

(*Threatens* DORINE *with a gesture. Turns to* MARIANE.)

As a sensible man,
I've thought the matter out.

DORINE: It drives me mad
Not to be able to speak.

(ORGON *turns to her; she falls silent.*)

ORGON: Although no dandy,
Tartuffe has looks—

DORINE: All right, if you like them hard.

ORGON: And even if you had no sympathy
　　For his other gifts—
DORINE:　　　　　　　　　　Oh, what a lucky girl!
　　If I were she, I would make sure no man
　　Would marry me by force and escape scot-free;
　　And I would prove, soon after the ceremony,
　　That a woman always has her vengeance ready.
ORGON (*to* DORINE): So, you won't pay attention to my orders?
DORINE: What's your objection? I'm not talking to you.
ORGON: Then what are you doing?
DORINE:　　　　　　　　　　Talking to myself.
ORGON: Excellent. So, to punish her insolence,
　　I'll have to give her a good slap in the face.
(*Raises his hand and poises it for a blow, but whenever he looks at*
DORINE, *she stands still and mute.*)
　　Daughter, you ought to think well of my project . . .
　　Believe the husband . . . whom I've chosen for you . . .
(*To* DORINE)
　　Why don't you talk to yourself?
DORINE:　　　　　　　　　　I've nothing to say.
ORGON: Just say one little word!
DORINE:　　　　　　　　　　I don't feel like it.
ORGON: I was all ready for you.
DORINE:　　　　　　　　　　I'm not so dumb.
ORGON (*turns to* MARIANE): In short, Mariane, you owe obedience,
　　And you must show respect for my opinion.
DORINE (*fleeing*): You'd never make me agree to such a husband.
(ORGON *tries to slap her; she escapes, and exits.*)
ORGON: That forward girl of yours, Mariane, is a pest,
　　And she provokes me to the sin of anger.
　　I'm in no state to carry on our talk;
　　Her insolent speech has got me all excited,
　　And I must take a walk to calm myself.

　　　　　　(*Exit* ORGON. DORINE *re-enters cautiously.*)

DORINE: What, Mariane, you've lost your power of speech?
　　And do I have to play your part for you?
　　You'll let him make this asinine proposal,
　　And not combat it with a single word?
MARIANE: What can I do against his absolute power?
DORINE: Anything, in the face of such a threat.

MARIANE: And what?

DORINE: Tell him a heart can't love by proxy;
    The marriage is for your sake, not for his;
    And since you are the person who's concerned,
    The husband ought to please you and not him;
    And since he finds Tartuffe so fascinating,
    He is the one who ought to marry him.

MARIANE: I know; but Father is so masterful
    I've never had the courage to oppose him.

DORINE: Look here; Valère has made his formal suit;
    Now let me ask you: Do you love him, or don't you?

MARIANE: Oh, you're unjust, Dorine! You know I love him!
    You have no reason even to ask the question!
    Haven't I poured it out a hundred times,
    And don't you know the greatness of my love?

DORINE: I never know if one is quite sincere,
    If your great love is really genuine.

MARIANE: You do me a great wrong in doubting it.
    I thought my feelings were sufficiently clear.

DORINE: In short, you love him?

MARIANE: Yes, and passionately.

DORINE: And it would seem that he loves you no less?

MARIANE: I think so.

DORINE: And you both are equally eager
    To be united in marriage?

MARIANE: Certainly.

DORINE: About this other proposal, what's your plan?

MARIANE: To kill myself, if I am driven to it.

DORINE: Splendid! I hadn't thought of that way out.
    To escape from trouble, you only have to die.
    A marvelous remedy . . . It makes me furious,
    Whenever I listen to that kind of talk.

MARIANE: Good heavens, what a temper you get into!
    You don't much sympathize with others' sorrows.

DORINE: I don't much sympathize with those who drivel,
    And then go limp, like you, when the test comes.

MARIANE: What can I do? I'm naturally timid—

DORINE: But love demands a firm, courageous heart.

MARIANE: I have been constant, answering Valère's love.
    But he must ask, and gain, Father's consent.

DORINE: But if your father is a perfect crank,

Who's so infatuated with Tartuffe
He disavows the marriage he agreed to,
Is that a thing to blame your suitor for?

MARIANE: If I refuse Tartuffe with open scorn,
Won't I reveal how deeply I'm in love?
Brilliant though Valère is, shall I abandon
For him my modesty, my daughterly duty?
Do you want me to display my love to the world?

DORINE: No, I want nothing at all. I see you wish
To be Madame Tartuffe; and now I think of it,
I'm wrong in weaning you from this alliance.
Why should I argue against your inclinations?
The match would seem an advantageous one.
Monsieur Tartuffe! He's not a nobody!
Monsieur Tartuffe is not the kind who needs
To stand on his head to get applause and money.
One would be lucky indeed to be his wife.
Why, everyone is glorifying him!
He's noble—in his own home town! And handsome!
His ears are rosy red, like his complexion!
You will be all too happy with such a husband.

MARIANE: Yes, but—

DORINE: What ecstasy will fill your soul,
When you are wife to that good-looking man!

MARIANE: Stop, if you please, this agonizing talk,
And give me counsel how to escape the marriage.
I've made my mind up; I'll do anything.

DORINE: No, a good daughter should obey her father,
Though he should choose a monkey for her mate.
You've a fine future; what are you grumbling for?
You'll have a coach to perambulate his city,
Which you'll find rich in uncles, aunts, and cousins
Whom you will be delighted to entertain.
You'll be received in high society,
You'll call upon the Lord High Mayoress,
And on the Lord High Tax-Collectoress,
Who'll seat you honorably on a kitchen chair.
And you can hope for a ball at carnival time,
An orchestra consisting of two bagpipes,
And sometimes a marionette show—with a monkey!
However, if your husband—

MARIANE: You're killing me!
   Stop it, and help me with some good advice.
DORINE: You must excuse me.
MARIANE: Oh, dear Dorine, please!
DORINE: To punish you, the marriage must go through.
MARIANE: Dorine!
DORINE: No!
MARIANE: If I state my opposition—
DORINE: Tartuffe's your man. You must put up with him.
MARIANE: I have confided everything to you.
   So now—
DORINE: No. You will be tartufficated.
MARIANE: Since my unhappy destiny can't move you,
   I must surrender now to my despair.
   And from despair my heart will take advice.
   I know the infallible remedy for my woes.
DORINE: Here, here, come back. I'll put aside my anger.
   I must take pity upon you after all.
MARIANE: If they insist on making a martyr of me,
   I tell you, Dorine, that I shall simply die.
DORINE: Don't worry. If we're clever enough, we can
   Prevent it . . . But here's your lover, your Valère.

   (*Enter* VALÈRE. *He speaks at first jestingly.*)

VALÈRE: Mademoiselle, a story's going round
   That's new to me. Very fine news, no doubt.
MARIANE: What's that?
VALÈRE: That you're to marry Tartuffe.
MARIANE: Truly,
   My father has this idea in his head.
VALÈRE: Your father, mademoiselle—
MARIANE: Has changed his purpose.
   And he has just been making this proposal.
VALÈRE: Seriously?
MARIANE: Yes, seriously indeed.
   He has come out in favor of this marriage.
VALÈRE: And what is your opinion on the matter,
   Mademoiselle?
MARIANE: I don't know.
VALÈRE: Frank, at least.
   You don't know?

MARIANE: No.

VALÈRE: No?

MARIANE: What is your advice?

VALÈRE: Why, my advice is to accept this husband.

MARIANE: That's your advice?

VALÈRE: Yes.

MARIANE: Really?

VALÈRE: Certainly.
     It is an opportunity not to be scorned.

MARIANE: Well, I am very glad to have your counsel.

VALÈRE: I think you'll follow it without much trouble.

MARIANE: With no more trouble than you had in giving it.

VALÈRE: I gave the advice only to give you pleasure.

MARIANE: And I shall follow it to give *you* pleasure.

DORINE (*aside*): We'll soon find out how this is going to end.

VALÈRE: So this is how you love me? You deceived me
     When you—

MARIANE: I beg you not to talk of that.
     You told me outright that I ought to accept
     The man who is designated for my husband;
     And I say that's what I intend to do,
     Since now you give me that excellent advice.

VALÈRE: Don't try to excuse yourself by quoting me;
     You had already formed your resolution,
     And now you're seizing on a frivolous pretext
     To authorize yourself to break your word.

MARIANE: Well said; it's true.

VALÈRE: Certainly. And your heart
     Has never felt any real love for me.

MARIANE: Oh, dear! Why, you may think so, if you wish.

VALÈRE: Yes, if I wish! You think you've wounded me,
     But maybe I have other plans in mind.
     I know where I can get a better welcome.

MARIANE: I don't doubt that. Anyone would admire
     Your character.

VALÈRE: Let's leave my character out.
     It's not so wonderful; indeed, you prove it.
     But there's another girl who may be kinder;
     She won't be ashamed to take me on the rebound,
     And gladly she'll console me for losing you.

MARIANE: The loss is not so great. The consolation

Ought to come easily in this shift of partners.

VALÈRE: I'll do my very best, you may be sure.
Nobody likes to know he's been forgotten.
In such a case, the best is to forget,
And if you can't forget, pretend to do so.
It is unpardonably weak, I think,
To display love for one who abandons us.

MARIANE: That is a very lofty sentiment.

VALÈRE: You're right. It should be generally approved.
What! You would like to have me keep forever
My love for you unchanging in my heart,
See you go happily to another's arms,
And seek no solace for my cast-off love?

MARIANE: Why, not at all! That's just what I desire!
I wish that it were all arranged already!

VALÈRE: You'd like that?

MARIANE: Yes.

VALÈRE: I've borne insults enough!
I'll try immediately to satisfy you.
(*Starts to leave and returns, as in succeeding speeches.*)

MARIANE: Good.

VALÈRE: Remember at least that you're the one
Who is driving me to this expedient.

MARIANE: Yes.

VALÈRE: And remember that my purpose is
To follow your example.

MARIANE: If you like.

VALÈRE: Enough. Your wishes will be carried out.

MARIANE: Fine!

VALÈRE: So this is the last time that you'll see me.

MARIANE: Excellent!

VALÈRE (*starts to exit; at the door, turns*):
                    Uh?

MARIANE: What?

VALÈRE: Did I hear you call me?

MARIANE: You must be dreaming.

VALÈRE: Well, I'm on my way.
I bid you farewell.

MARIANE: Adieu, sir.

DORINE: As for me,
I think you both are addled in the brain.

I've let you squabble to your heart's content
To find out where you'd land yourselves at last.
Monsieur Valère!

(DORINE *tries to take* VALÈRE *by the arm, but he makes a show of resistance.*)

VALÈRE: What do you want, Dorine?

DORINE: Come here!

VALÈRE: No, no, she's put me in a fury.
I'm doing what she wanted, don't restrain me.

DORINE: Stop!

VALÈRE: No, the matter's settled, you can see.

DORINE: Aha!

MARIANE: My presence seems to irritate him;
The best thing is for me to leave him alone.

(DORINE *leaves* VALÈRE *and runs to* MARIANE.)

DORINE: Where are you going?

MARIANE: Let me alone!

DORINE: Come back!

MARIANE: There's no use trying to hold me back, Dorine.

VALÈRE: Clearly it tortures her to look at me.
I'd better free her from that painful sight.

DORINE (*leaving* MARIANE *and running to* VALÈRE): What the deuce!
You'll do nothing of the sort!
Stop all this nonsense! Both of you come here!

(*She pulls at them, one with each hand.*)

VALÈRE: What's your idea?

MARIANE: What do you want to do?

DORINE: Make peace between you and get you out of trouble.

(*To* VALÈRE)
You must be crazy to get in such a quarrel.

VALÈRE: Didn't you hear the way she talked to me?

DORINE (*to* MARIANE): You must be crazy too, to get so angry.

MARIANE: Didn't you see the way he treated me?

DORINE (*to* VALÈRE): You're crazy, both of you. I can bear witness
The only thing she wants is to be yours.

(*To* MARIANE)
He loves you only, and his one desire
Is marriage with you, I'll stake my life on that.

MARIANE (*to* VALÈRE): Then why did you give me your horrible advice?

VALÈRE (*to* MARIANE): And why ask my advice on such a subject?

DORINE: I said you were both crazy. Give me your hands.
(*To* VALÈRE)
　Yours, now.
VALÈRE (*giving* DORINE *his hand*): Why give you my hand?
DORINE (*to* MARIANE): Now give me yours.
MARIANE (*giving* DORINE *her hand*): What is the sense of this?
DORINE: Come on, step forward.
　You're both in love more than you realize.
VALÈRE (*to* MARIANE): Yes, but don't do things so reluctantly,
　And give a man at least a friendly look.
(MARIANE *looks at* VALÈRE, *and smiles feebly.*)
DORINE: The fact is, lovers are extremely crazy!
VALÈRE (*to* MARIANE): Haven't I reason to complain of you?
　Tell me sincerely, wasn't it unkind
　To amuse yourself by hurting me so much?
MARIANE: But you yourself, aren't you the most ungrateful—
DORINE: Let's leave this argument to another time,
　And think of fending off that fatal marriage.
MARIANE: But have you any idea how to do so?
DORINE: There are a lot of things that we can do.
　Your father's talking nonsense, he's not serious.
　But the best thing for you is to pretend
　To gently yield to his fantasticality
　So that, in case of crisis, you can easily
　Keep on postponing the wedding ceremony.
　You can cure many things by gaining time.
　First you will take as your excuse some illness,
　Which will strike suddenly and cause delays;
　And then you'll meet an omen of misfortune.
　You'll pass, perhaps, a funeral in the street,
　Or break a mirror, or dream of muddy water.
　The great thing is that nobody can bind you
　To anyone without your saying yes.
　But out of prudence, it would be advisable
　That you two shouldn't be caught talking together.
(*To* VALÈRE)
　Now go, and use the influence of your friends
　To help you get the girl who was promised you.
　And we shall make her brother work for us;
　And her stepmother, she'll be on our side.
　Good-by.

VALÈRE (*to* MARIANE): Though we'll all do the most we can,
 My greatest hope and confidence lie in you.
MARIANE: I can't be sure what Father may decide,
 But I shall never be anyone's bride but yours.
VALÈRE: You make me very happy! In spite of all—
DORINE: Lovers are never tired; they talk forever.
 Come on; get going.
VALÈRE (*takes a step toward exit, and returns*): Finally—
DORINE: Talk, talk, talk!
(*Pushes each of them by the shoulder.*)
 You go out this way; you go out the other.

ACT III

(DAMIS, DORINE.)

DAMIS: Now let a bolt of lightning strike me dead,
 Call me a scoundrel, anything you please,
 If any talk of duty will hold me back,
 If I don't take some action to settle things.
DORINE: Just take it easy, calm yourself a little.
 Your father has merely talked about the matter.
 People don't execute all they propose;
 There's many a slip between the cup and the lip.
DAMIS: I've got to stop that swine's conspiracies;
 I've got to tell him a few simple facts.
DORINE: I tell you, take it easy; let your stepmother
 Handle the fellow, as she does your father.
 She has some influence on Tartuffe's mind.
 He acts in a very obliging way to her;
 Maybe he has a kind of weakness for her.
 Lord knows I hope so! That would be convenient!
 For your sake she will have to interview him,
 Learn what his feelings are, point out to him
 What dreadful troubles he will bring about
 If he encourages Orgon in his purpose.
 His valet says he's praying; I couldn't see him.
 But he'll be coming down in a moment or two.

So go out, please; let me arrange the matter.
DAMIS: I can be present during the interview.
DORINE: No, they must be alone.
DAMIS: I will keep quiet.
DORINE: Nonsense! I know how you can get excited,
    And that's the way to ruin everything.
    Go on!
DAMIS: I want to see, and I won't get angry.
DORINE: Oh, what a nuisance you are! He's coming! Get out!
(DORINE *pushes* DAMIS *out. Enter* TARTUFFE. *He observes* DORINE *and calls off-stage.*)
TARTUFFE: Put my hair shirt away and my flagellator,
    Laurent; and pray for heaven's continual grace.
    If anyone wants me, say I'm off to the prison
    To give away the charity given me.
DORINE (*aside*): Eyewash and affectation, if you ask me!
TARTUFFE: What do you want?
DORINE: To tell you—
TARTUFFE (*drawing out a handkerchief*):   Oh, dear heaven!
    Before you speak, please take this handkerchief.
DORINE: What?
TARTUFFE: Cover that bosom which I must not see.
    Such sights as that are hurtful to the spirit,
    And they may well awaken guilty thoughts.
DORINE: You must be very sensitive to temptation.
    Flesh makes a great impression on your senses!
    Of course, I don't know how you're stimulated,
    But I am not so readily aroused.
    If I should see you naked from head to foot,
    I wouldn't be tempted by all the skin you've got.
TARTUFFE: Please be a little modest in your speech,
    Or I must leave the room immediately.
DORINE: No, no, it's I who will go and leave you in peace.
    But there is something that I have to tell you.
    Madame Elmire is coming to the parlor,
    And she would like to have a word with you.
TARTUFFE: Oh, very gladly.
DORINE (*aside*):   How he softens down!
    Bless me, I think that I was right about him.
TARTFUFE: She's coming soon?
DORINE: I think I hear her now.

Yes, here she is. I'll leave you two together.

(*Exit* DORINE. *Enter* ELMIRE.)

TARTUFFE: May heaven, by its high, omnipotent mercy,
Forever grant you health of soul and body,
And bless your days according to the desire
Of one who is humblest of heaven's worshipers!
ELMIRE: I'm deeply grateful for your pious wish.
Let us sit down, to be more comfortable.
TARTUFFE: I hope you have recovered from your illness?
ELMIRE: It's better, thank you; the fever left me soon.
TARTUFFE: My prayers are all too insignificant
To have brought this grace upon you from on high;
But every supplication I have made
Has had as object your recovery.
ELMIRE: Your pious zeal took all too much upon it.
TARTUFFE: Your precious health concerned me very deeply,
And to restore it gladly I'd give my own.
ELMIRE: You're carrying Christian charity too far;
But I'm indebted to you for your kindness.
TARTUFFE: What I have done is less than you deserve.

(*Enter* DAMIS *cautiously, behind backs of* TARTUFFE *and*
ELMIRE; *he hides in the cupboard previously mentioned.*)

ELMIRE: I wanted to speak privately to you.
I'm glad we have this chance to be unobserved.
TARTUFFE: I am glad too. It's very sweet to me,
Madame, to find myself alone with you.
It is an opportunity I've prayed for
Without success, until this happy moment.
ELMIRE: I too have wished a chance for intimate talk,
When you might speak from the heart, without disguise.
TARTUFFE: And what I wish is, as a singular grace,
To lay my soul utterly bare before you,
And vow to you that all of my objections
To the visitors who come to pay you homage
Do not arise from any hostility,
But rather from the extravagance of my zeal,
From my emotion—
ELMIRE: I gladly take it so.
I'm sure my welfare gives you this concern.

TARTUFFE (*squeezing her fingertips*): Indeed, madame, indeed; such
    is my ardor—
ELMIRE: Ouch! You are hurting me!
TARTUFFE: Excess of zeal!
    I'd no idea of hurting you at all.
    I'd rather . . .
(*Puts his hand on her knee.*)
ELMIRE: Your hand—what, pray, is it doing there?
TARTUFFE: Just feeling the material; so soft!
ELMIRE: Well, please stop feeling it. I'm very ticklish.
(*She pushes her chair aside;* TARTUFFE *brings his chair close.*)
TARTUFFE: Really, this lace is marvelously done!
    The modern needlework is truly astounding.
    There's never before been anything to match it.
ELMIRE: Quite so. But let us talk about our business.
    I hear my husband wants to break his word
    And marry to you his daughter. Is that true?
TARTUFFE: He's hinted at it. But to tell the truth,
    That's not the happiness I languish for.
    It's elsewhere that I see the alluring charms
    Of the felicity that I desire.
ELMIRE: I see; you do not love the things of earth.
TARTUFFE: The heart in my bosom is not made of stone.
ELMIRE: I think that all your longings turn to heaven,
    That nothing upon this earth tempts your desires.
TARTUFFE: The love which draws us to eternal beauty
    Does not exclude the love of temporal things.
    And easily our senses may be charmed
    By the perfect vessels heaven has fabricated.
    Its glory is reflected in such creatures
    As you, who show its rarest marvels forth.
    Upon your face are heavenly beauties lavished
    To dazzle the eyes, to fill the heart with transport.
    O perfect beauty! I could not look upon you
    Without admiring in you Nature's author,
    And without feeling ardent love in my heart
    For this fair portrait of divinity!
    At first I trembled, lest my secret flame
    Should be a stratagem of the Evil One;
    Even, I was resolved to flee your presence,
    A possible obstacle to my salvation.

But finally I realized, my fair one,
That there need be no guilt in such a passion,
That I can make it chime with modesty;
And so I let my heart follow its bent.
I know it is a great audacity
For me to dare to offer you this heart;
But my affection seeks all from your bounty,
And nothing from my own weak enterprise.
In you is all my hope, my good, my peace;
On you depends my punishment or my bliss;
By your decree alone may I be happy,
If you are willing; unhappy, if that's your will.

ELMIRE: This is a gallant declaration indeed,
But I must say I find it rather surprising.
I think you should have steeled your emotions better,
Considering what such a purpose means.
A pious man like you, so widely known—

TARTUFFE: Ah, pious though I be, I'm still a man.
And when one glimpses your celestial beauties,
The heart is captured, and it cannot argue.
I know such words from me may seem surprising,
But after all, madame, I'm not an angel.
If you condemn the avowal I make to you,
You must accuse your own bewitching charms.
Since I first saw their more than earthly splendor,
You were the sovereign of my secret soul,
And the ineffable sweetness of your glance
Broke the resistance of my struggling heart.
You conquered all, my fasting, prayers, and tears;
And all my vows were made to you alone.
My eyes have told you this, so have my sighs;
And now, for greater clarity, my words.
And if you look with a compassionate spirit
Upon the woes of your unworthy slave,
If you consent to bring me consolation,
To condescend to my unworthiness,
I'll vow to you, O lovely miracle,
Immeasurable worship and devotion.
And in my hands your honor runs no risk,
Nor need it fear any disgrace or scandal.
These young court gallants women dote upon

Are careless in their acts and vain of speech.
They like to boast about their amorous triumphs;
There are no favors that they don't divulge;
Their inconsiderate tongues betray their trust,
Dishonoring the altar where they worship.
Men of my stamp, however, are discreet;
With us one is always sure of secrecy.
The care we take of our own reputations
Is a guarantee to the person we adore.
She who accepts our heart acquires in us
Love without scandal, pleasure without fear.

ELMIRE: I'm fascinated; and your rhetoric
    Explains itself in very lucid terms.
    Aren't you afraid that I may be in the mood
    To tell my husband about your gallant longings,
    And that this information may disturb
    The warm affection that he holds for you?

TARTUFFE: I know that you are far too merciful,
    That you will pardon my temerity;
    Pity for human weakness will excuse
    The violence of a love which may offend you.
    Look in your mirror, you will recognize
    A man's not blind, he's only flesh and blood.

ELMIRE: Another woman might take it otherwise,
    But I will show that I can be discreet.
    I'll not repeat the matter to my husband,
    But in return I want one thing of you:
    That's to urge openly, with no quibbling talk,
    The marriage of Valère and Mariane,
    And to renounce the unreasonable claim
    By which you'd win her who is pledged to another.
    And—

DAMIS (*emerging from the cupboard*): No, madame, no! This news
    must be reported!
    I was concealed there, I could hear everything!
    And heaven's favor must have led me there
    To confound the pride of a treacherous evildoer,
    To open a way for me to avenge myself
    On his hypocrisy and insolence,
    To undeceive my father, and lay bare
    The soul of a scoundrel who talks to you of love!

ELMIRE: No, Damis; it's enough if he mends his ways,
    Deserving the pardon which I offer him.
    I've promised it; don't make me break my word.
    It's not my character to make a scene.
    A woman laughs at such absurdities,
    And doesn't trouble her husband's ears about them.
DAMIS: You have your reasons to take matters thus,
    And I've my reasons to do otherwise.
    It is ridiculous to try to spare him.
    His sanctimonious impudence too long
    Has got the better of my just resentment;
    Too long he's roused up trouble in our home;
    And far too long the rogue has ruled my father,
    And blocked my courtship as he has Valère's.
    It's time that Father should be told the truth,
    And heaven has given me the means to do so.
    To heaven I owe this opportunity;
    It's far too favorable to be neglected.
    Why, I'd deserve to have it snatched away,
    If I held it in my hand and didn't use it.
ELMIRE: Damis—
DAMIS: Please, I must do what I think best.
    I've never been so happy as I am now!
    There's no use trying to force me to surrender
    The pleasure of holding vengeance in my hand!
    I'm going to settle things immediately—
    And here's my opportunity in person.

               (*Enter* ORGON.)

    Father, we're going to celebrate your coming
    With a tasty bit of news which will surprise you.
    You are well paid for all your kindnesses!
    Monsieur has a special form of gratitude.
    He's just revealed his zeal for your well-being,
    Which aims at nothing less than your dishonor.
    I have surprised him making to Madame
    The insulting avowal of a guilty love.
    Her character is gentle; generously
    She earnestly desired to keep it secret.
    But I cannot condone such impudence.
    To keep you in the dark would be an outrage.

ELMIRE: I think a wife ought never to disturb
   A husband's peace with silly tales like these;
   They have no application to her honor,
   And it's enough that we defend ourselves.
   That's what I think. Damis, you'd have said nothing,
   If I had had some influence over you.

                                    (*Exit* ELMIRE.)

ORGON: Oh, heavens, is this strange story credible?
TARTUFFE: Yes, brother; I am a wicked, guilty man,
   A wretched sinner full of iniquity,
   The greatest scoundrel who has ever lived.
   Each moment of my life has been polluted,
   It is a mass of crime and filthiness.
   I see that heaven, for my punishment,
   Chooses this circumstance to mortify me.
   However great the misdeed I am charged with,
   I will not pridefully defend myself.
   Believe their words, and give your anger rein,
   And drive me from the house like a criminal.
   No matter what may be my portion of shame,
   I have deserved to suffer far, far more.
ORGON (*to* DAMIS): Traitor! And do you dare, by lying words,
   To try to tarnish his virtue's purity?
DAMIS: What! All this hypocritic blubbering
   Will make you disbelieve—
ORGON: Silence, you pest!
TARTUFFE: Ah, let him speak! How wrongly you accuse him!
   You would do better to believe his words.
   Why, in this case, be favorable to me?
   How do you know of what I am capable?
   How can you trust, dear brother, my appearance?
   Does my behavior prove me better in fact?
   No, no, you let my outward semblance cheat you.
   Alas, I am far from being what men think!
   I'm taken commonly for an upright man,
   But the truth is that I am nothing worth.
(*To* DAMIS)
   Speak, my dear boy, and call me infamous,
   Perfidious, worthless, thief and murderer,
   Load me with names still more detestable;
   I do not contradict, for I have deserved them.

(*Kneels.*)

    I long to suffer their shame upon my knees,
      As retribution for my criminal life.

ORGON (*to* TARTUFFE): Dear brother, it's too much.

(*To* DAMIS.)

                                        Your heart's not moved,
    Traitor?

DAMIS: His talk can fool you to this point?

ORGON: Silence, scoundrel!

(*To* TARTUFFE)

                        Brother, I beg you stand.

(*To* DAMIS)

    Rascal!

DAMIS: He can—

ORGON: Silence!

DAMIS: I will go mad!

ORGON: Just say a word, and I will break your head!

TARTUFFE: Be not enangered, brother, in God's name.
    For I would rather bear most grievous pain
    Than have him suffer the slightest scratch for me.

ORGON (*to* DAMIS): Ingrate!

TARTUFFE: Leave him in peace. If I must kneel
    To ask you for his pardon—

ORGON (*to* TARTUFFE):   Alas, you're joking!

(*To* DAMIS.)

    Observe his goodness!

DAMIS: Then—

ORGON: Peace!

DAMIS: What, I—

ORGON: Enough!
    I can see well the motive of your attack.
    You hate him, all of you; I see my wife,
    Children, and servants baying after him.
    You're using every impudent device
    To oust this holy person from my home.
    But the more efforts you make to banish him,
    The greater efforts I'll make to keep him here.
    And now I'll hasten to give him my daughter's hand
    To abase the pride of the entire family.

DAMIS: You think that you will force her to marry him?

ORGON: Yes, and to spite you, on this very evening.

Oh, I defy you all! And I will teach you
You'll have to obey me! I'm the master here.
Now, take your words back, ruffian! On the spot
Cast yourself at his feet to ask his pardon!

DAMIS: What! From this scoundrel, by whose trickeries—

ORGON: Ah, you resist, you knave! And you insult him!
Give me a stick, a stick!

(*To* TARTUFFE)

                      Don't hold me back!

(*To* DAMIS)

Now you get out of this house this very minute.
And never dare to enter it again!

DAMIS: All right, I'll go, but—

ORGON: Quick, get out of here!
Reptile, I'll take your name out of my will,
And for good measure you can have my curse!

                              (*Exit* DAMIS.)

Think of offending so a holy man!

TARTUFFE: May heaven pardon him the pain he gives me!

(*To* ORGON)

Ah, could you know how grievous it is to see
My character blackened in my brother's eyes—

ORGON: Alas!

TARTUFFE: The thought of this ingratitude
Makes my soul suffer such a cruel torture . . .
The horror it inspires . . . My heart is torn
So that I cannot speak! I'll die of it!

ORGON (*runs weeping to the door whence he has driven* DAMIS):
Villain! I'm sorry I withheld my hand,
And didn't knock you down upon the spot!
Brother, compose yourself; don't be distressed.

TARTUFFE: Let's have no more of these afflicting quarrels.
I see I bring dissensions to your home;
I think it best, dear brother, that I leave it.

ORGON: You're joking!

TARTUFFE: Here I'm hated, and I see
That one would bring my rectitude in question.

ORGON: What of it? Do you think I listen to them?

TARTUFFE: Ah, they'll continue surely their campaign.
These stories you repudiate today
Perhaps another time will be believed.

ORGON: Oh, never, brother, never.
TARTUFFE: Brother, a wife
   Can easily beguile a husband's mind.
ORGON: No, No!
TARTUFFE: I'll leave the house upon the instant,
   And thus remove all reason to attack me.
ORGON: No, you'll remain; my life depends upon it.
TARTUFFE: Well, I'll remain, to mortify my spirit.
   Still, if you wished it—
ORGON: Oh!
TARTUFFE: We'll say no more.
   I see how I must now conduct myself.
   Honor is delicate, and as your friend
   I'll avoid cause for gossip and suspicion,
   And flee the presence of your wife; I'll never—
ORGON: No, you'll attend her, to defy them all.
   My greatest pleasure is to spite the world.
   I want you to be seen with her constantly.
   And that's not all; the better to affront them
   I want to have no other heir than you.
   And so I'll take immediately the steps
   To make you sole inheritor of my wealth.
   A good friend, whom I make my son-in-law,
   Is dearer to me than my wife and children.
   Will you accept what I propose to you?
TARTUFFE: May heaven's will be done in everything!
ORGON: Poor fellow! Let's draw up the document,
   And let the jealous drown in their own bile!

ACT IV

(CLÉANTE, TARTUFFE.)

CLÉANTE: The matter's common talk. You may believe me,
   The scandalous tale is not to your advantage.
   And I am glad I chanced to find you, sir,
   To tell you my opinion in a word.

I won't attempt to weigh the rights and wrongs,
I will assume the unpleasant story's true.
Granted that Damis acted badly toward you,
And that his accusation was unfounded,
Should not a Christian pardon the offense,
Extinguishing thus Damis' desire for vengeance?
And should you let this quarrel be the cause
Of the exile of a son from his father's house?
Let me repeat to you, in perfect frankness,
That everybody's scandalized about it.
And if you take my advice, you will make peace
And not let things be carried to extremes;
You'll sacrifice your bitterness to God,
And bring the son back to his father's favor.

TARTUFFE: Alas, for my part, I would happily do so.
I harbor no resentment, sir, against him.
I pardon him freely, blame him not at all;
I long with all my heart to do him good.
But this is not in heaven's interest.
If he returns here, I must leave the house.
After his unimaginable action
We can't associate without disgrace.
God knows what people would conclude about it;
They would accuse me of sheer calculation.
Knowing my guilt, they'd say, I was pretending
Feelings of charity for my accuser.
They'd say I fear him and want to humor him
In order to persuade him to keep silence.

CLÉANTE: You try to give me plausible excuses,
But all your arguments are too far-fetched.
Why take heaven's interest upon yourself?
Does heaven need you to punish malefactors?
No, no; let God take care of his own vengeance;
He has prescribed forgiveness for offenses.
Don't be concerned about the world's reactions
When you are following heaven's almighty orders.
Will you let worry about what people say
Wipe out the credit of doing a good deed?
No, no; let's rather do what God commands,
And let's not trouble with other considerations.

TARTUFFE: I've told you that I pardon him in my heart;

Thus I obey God's holy ordinances.
But after the scandalous insults of today,
God does not order me to live with him.
CLÉANTE: And does God order you to lend yourself
    To the father's act, prompted by pure caprice,
    And to accept the gift of property
    To which you have no legal right at all?
TARTUFFE: No one who knows me well can have the thought
    That I am prompted by self-interest.
    All this world's goods have little charm for me,
    I am not dazzled by their deceptive glitter.
    If I decide to accept from the father's hands
    This gift of his benevolence, the reason
    Is only, I tell you truly, that I fear
    That all this wealth may fall in wicked hands,
    That its possessors may be men who make
    A criminal usage of it in the world,
    Who will not use it, as my purpose is,
    For heaven's glory and for my neighbor's good.
CLÉANTE: Your fears, my good sir, are sophistical.
    They may give rise to suits by legal heirs.
    Let Damis be inheritor of his wealth
    At his own risk, without your interference.
    Reflect, it's better that he should misuse it
    Than that you be accused of cheating him.
    I am astounded that you could have heard
    This proposition made without being shocked.
    For are there any maxims of true piety
    Which teach the robbing of legitimate heirs?
    If God has put in your heart an adamant
    Objection to your living with Damis,
    Would not the best thing be for you to leave
    Decently and with honor, and not permit
    The son of the house to be forbidden the door,
    Against all common sense, and for your sake?
    Believe me, sir, your character would look
    Extremely strange—
TARTUFFE: Sir, it is half-past three;
    And it is time for my pious exercises.
    You will excuse me if I leave you now.

                              (*Exit* TARTUFFE.)

CLÉANTE: Oh!

(*Enter* ELMIRE, MARIANE, DORINE.)

DORINE: Sir, I beg you, won't you help to save her?
  For she is suffering from a cruel grief.
  The pledge of marriage that her father has made
  Plunges her in continual despair.
  He's coming now; please, let's unite our efforts
  And try to upset, either by force or trick,
  That fatal project which undoes us all.

(*Enter* ORGON.)

ORGON: Ah! I'm delighted to see you all assembled!
(*To* MARIANE)
  There's something nice for you in this contract here!
  And certainly you know what that implies.
MARIANE (*kneeling*): Father, I call on heaven, which knows my
      grief!
  By everything that can affect your heart,
  Relax a little the rights of fatherhood,
  And set me free from this obedience.
  Do not reduce me, by your harsh command,
  To cry to heaven against my bounden duty.
  Alas, don't make a long calamity
  Of the life which you, Father, have given me.
  Though you forbid me to wed the one I love,
  In spite of all the fond hopes I had cherished,
  At least—I beg your mercy on my knees—
  Spare me the anguish of wedding one I hate,
  And do not force me to some desperate act
  By using all your powers upon my person.
ORGON (*aside*): Courage, my heart! Down with this human weakness!
MARIANE: I'm not distressed by your affection for him;
  Openly show it; give him your property;
  And if that's not enough, give him mine too.
  I'm perfectly willing; I'll hand it over to you.
  But do not give him, pray, my self, my person!
  And let me in the austerity of a convent
  Consume the unhappy days allotted me.
ORGON: Aha! You're one of those who seek a convent
  As soon as a father crosses them in love!

Get up! The more your heart recoils from him,
All the more meritorious is the yielding.
So mortify your senses by this marriage,
And let's have no more nonsense out of you!

DORINE: But what—

ORGON: Be silent! Speak when you're spoken to!
I won't allow you to utter a single word!

CLÉANTE: If you'll permit me to offer some advice—

ORGON: Cléante, your advice is perfectly marvelous,
So sensible I prize it very highly;
But it's my privilege not to follow it.

ELMIRE (*to* ORGON): Seeing what's happening, I'm almost speechless.
I am amazed by your infatuation.
You must be totally bewitched by him
To doubt our word about today's occurrence.

ORGON: My precious, I believe the evidence.
I know how fond you are of my rascal son.
Clearly you were afraid to disavow
The scheme he tried to work on that poor fellow.
You were too calm, in short, to be quite convincing.
You'd have looked otherwise if really moved.

ELMIRE: And should a woman's honor be so stirred
If someone makes an amorous proposal?
And does the mere suggestion then require
A fiery glance and fierce, abusive words?
Why, all I do is laugh at such advances,
And I don't like to bring them into notice.
I think that we should show our virtue calmly;
I don't agree with those excited prudes
Whose honor is equipped with teeth and claws,
Ready to scratch your face at the slightest word.
Heaven preserve me from such purity!
For Virtue needs no diabolic look;
I've noticed that a haughty, chilly No
As a rebuff is mightily effective.

ORGON: You needn't try to throw me off the track.

ELMIRE: Your gullibility amazes me!
I wonder if your blind faith would be shaken
If I could make you witness of the truth.

ORGON: Witness?

ELMIRE: Yes.

ORGON: Nonsense!

ELMIRE: What if I found a way
To show you the fact under your very eyes?

ORGON: Fairy tales!

ELMIRE: What a man! I wish you'd answer.
I don't suggest that you believe our words.
But let's suppose that we could hide you here
Where you could clearly see and hear everything,
Then what would you say about your worthy friend?

ORGON: I'd say in that case . . . I'd say nothing at all,
For it can't be.

ELMIRE: You've been too long in error,
And you've accused me far too long of falsehood.
Now for my satisfaction, on the spot
I'll make you witness that we tell the truth.

ORGON: I'll take you up on that. We'll see your tricks;
We'll see what you can do to keep your promise.

ELMIRE (*to* DORINE): Send him in here.

DORINE: He's clever as a fox;
Perhaps it won't be easy to decoy him.

ELMIRE: No, one is easily fooled by one's belovèd,
And self-conceit will end in self-deception.
Have him come down.

(*To* CLÉANTE *and* MARIANE)
                              And you two, please go out.
                    (*Exit* DORINE, CLÉANTE, *and* MARIANE.)

(*To* ORGON)
Pull up this table. Now get under it.

ORGON: What?

ELMIRE: You will have to be concealed, of course.

ORGON: But why beneath this table?

ELMIRE: Good heavens, don't argue!
I have my plan; you'll see how it comes out.
Under the table, I say; and when you're there,
Make sure that nobody can see or hear you.

ORGON: I'm very indulgent to you, I confess.
I want to see how you get out of this.

(*Crawls under table, which is draped with a cloth hanging nearly to floor.*)

ELMIRE: I doubt if you'll have any reproach to make.
But I am going to deal with a ticklish subject,

So please don't let yourself be scandalized.
Whatever I say must be permissible;
It's only to convince you, as I promised.
Since I am forced to it, I'll have to use
Blandishing words to tempt him to unmask,
And smile upon his impudent desires,
And let him be audacious as he likes.
As it's for your sake, and for his confusion,
That I'll pretend to yield to his appeals,
I'll stop as soon as you are quite convinced;
Things will go only so far as you may wish.
Your task will be to check his bold advances
When you think matters have gone far enough,
And you must spare your wife, and not expose her
To more than you need to disillusion you.
Your interests are concerned; you are the master—
He's coming! Keep quiet! Don't let yourself be seen!

(*Enter* TARTUFFE.)

TARTUFFE: I understand you wished to speak to me.
ELMIRE: Yes, I've a secret to reveal to you.
But first, please shut that door before I speak;
And take a look around for fear of surprise.
(TARTUFFE *shuts door and looks in cupboard.*)
We certainly don't want a repetition
Of what took place a little while ago.
That was a disagreeable surprise,
And Damis put me into a panic for you.
You saw that I did everything I could
To cross his purpose and to calm him down.
It's true that I was thrown in such confusion
It didn't occur to me to deny his words.
But heaven be praised, the result was all the better,
And everything is on a surer footing.
Your reputation is proof against all storms;
And now my husband cannot be suspicious.
In order to show a confident face to slander,
He wants us to be constantly together.
So now I'm able, without fear of blame,
To be alone with you here—and with the door shut.
And so I am at liberty to reveal

My feelings—but perhaps I go too far.

TARTUFFE: This talk is somewhat hard to understand,
   Madame. You seem to have changed considerably.

ELMIRE: Why, if you're angry that I once rebuffed you,
   Little you understand a woman's heart!
   You don't know what it's trying to convey,
   When it defends itself so languidly!
   Our modesty must always make a struggle
   Against the emotions which may rise in us.
   Even though overmastered by our feelings,
   We always find it shameful to admit them.
   At first we fight against them; but our manner
   Ought to make evident the heart's surrender.
   For honor's sake we must oppose our longings,
   And our denials promise everything.
   I am afraid I'm speaking all too frankly,
   And showing small regard for modesty;
   But since I've come into the open, tell me,
   Would I have struggled to hold Damis back?
   And would I, please, so graciously, so long,
   Have listened to the offer of your heart?
   Would I have taken the matter as I did,
   If I had not found pleasure in your offer?
   And when I tried on my own part to force you
   To refuse the marriage which had been announced,
   What was the import of my urgency,
   If not my personal interest in you,
   And my distress for fear the projected union
   Would divide a heart I wanted to keep entire?

TARTUFFE: Surely, madame, it gives me joy extreme
   To hear such words from the belovèd lips!
   Their honey pours into my senses, makes
   Undreamed-of sweetness flood through all my veins!
   My highest aim is that of pleasing you;
   My heart finds its beatitude in your love;
   And yet this heart now begs the liberty
   To dare to doubt its own felicity.
   For I could think your words a mere device
   To force me to break off a marriage arranged.
   And to explain myself with perfect clearness,
   I shall not put my trust in your sweet words,

Until the tangible favors which I long for
Will guarantee your words' sincerity,
And in my soul implant a constant faith
In the dear bounties which you would bestow.
ELMIRE (*coughs to warn her husband*): What do you mean? You
    want to go so fast
And push love to its climax all in a moment?
I've forced myself to make a fond admission;
However, that is not enough for you.
You won't be satisfied unless you gain
The final favors at the very beginning?
TARTUFFE: The less one merits, the less one dares to hope;
And talk gives little assurance to our longing.
One easily mistrusts a promise of bliss;
One has to enjoy it before one can believe it.
Knowing how little I deserve your bounty,
I doubt the happiness I dare aspire to.
And I shall not believe a word, madame,
Until you crown my ardent love with facts.
ELMIRE: Dear me! Your love is acting like a tyrant!
It puts me in an awkward situation!
It seems to set a fury in men's hearts,
With such a violence it seeks its goal!
Can I not raise my hands against your onslaught?
Will you not give me even time to breathe?
And is it decent to be so exacting,
To give no quarter when you ask surrender?
And thus, by your insistence, to abuse
The inclination a person may have for you?
TARTUFFE: If you receive my homage with compassion,
Why, pray, withhold the tangible testimony?
ELMIRE: But how can I consent, without offending
Heaven, according to your constant theme?
TARTUFFE: If it is only heaven that stands in the way,
It's easy for me to remove such obstacles,
And that need not restrain your heart's desire.
ELMIRE: And yet they frighten us so with heaven's decrees!
TARTUFFE: I can soon banish such ridiculous fear,
Madame; there is an art of removing scruples.
It's true that heaven forbids some satisfactions,
But there are possible ways to understandings.

To suit our various needs, there is a science
Of loosening the bonds of human conscience,
And rectifying the evil of an action
By means of the purity of our intention.
Madame, I shall instruct you in these secrets,
If you will put your confidence in me.
Content my longings, do not be afraid;
All the responsibility is mine . . .

(ELMIRE *coughs.*)

You have a nasty cough.

ELMIRE: It tortures me.

TARTUFFE: Perhaps you'd care to accept a licorice cough drop?

ELMIRE: It's a persistent cold, and I'm afraid
That all the cough drops in the world won't help it.

TARTUFFE: Very distressing.

ELMIRE: More than I can say.

TARTUFFE: Well, anyway, I can dispel your scruples.
You are assured that I will keep the secret.
Evil does not exist until it's published;
It's worldly scandal that creates the offense;
And sin in silence is not sin at all.

ELMIRE (*coughs*): In short, I see that I shall have to yield,
Make up my mind to grant you everything.
Otherwise, I suppose, I can't convince
One who is asking irrefutable proof.
Certainly I dislike to go so far,
I take the step against my better judgment;
But since I'm mercilessly driven to it,
Since no one listens to my arguments,
Since absolute conviction is demanded,
I must decide to satisfy all doubts.
And if there's any offense in my consenting,
The one who forces me must take the blame;
Certainly I am not responsible.

TARTUFFE: I take it on myself, madame. The matter—

ELMIRE: But first, open the door a little, please;
See if my husband isn't in the hall.

TARTUFFE: What sense is there in worrying about him?
He is the type that you can lead by the nose,
The type to glory in our intimacies.
He can see anything now and not believe it.

ELMIRE: It makes no difference. Please, I'd feel much safer
 If you would take a careful look around.
    (*Exit* TARTUFFE. ORGON *emerges from under the table.*)
ORGON: Oh, what a bad, abominable man!
 I am astounded! I just can't understand it.
ELMIRE: What, coming out so soon? Don't be absurd!
 Crawl in again, nothing has happened yet!
 Why don't you wait till the end to make quite sure,
 So you won't have to trust to mere conjectures?
ORGON: Nothing more wicked has ever come out of hell!
ELMIRE: You shouldn't be in a hurry to believe things,
 So why not let yourself be quite convinced?
 Just take your time; maybe you're still mistaken . . .
(*As* TARTUFFE *returns,* ELMIRE *makes* ORGON *crouch behind her.*)
TARTUFFE: Everything's working out, madame, for the best.
 I've had a look into the neighboring rooms.
 There's no one there. And now, to my delight—
ORGON (*springing forth*): Hold on a minute! Don't get so excited,
 And let your passions run away with you!
 Aha! You holy man, you wanted to fool me!
 How rapidly you yielded to temptation!
 Wedding my daughter and lusting for my wife!
 I've long suspected things were not aboveboard;
 I always thought that you would change your style.
 But now the proof is carried far enough.
 I'm satisfied, and this is all I need.
ELMIRE (*to* TARTUFFE): It's not my nature to have done all this,
 But I've been forced to treat you in this manner.
TARTUFFE (*to* ORGON): What, you can think—
ORGON: Come on, don't make a fuss.
 Get out of here without another word.
TARTUFFE: I only wanted—
ORGON: There's no time for talk.
 But now, this very second, leave the house!
TARTUFFE: You are the one to leave! Don't be so proud!
 I will remind you, the house belongs to me!
 I'll show you that it's useless to resort
 To such poor shifts to pick a quarrel with me!
 You're in a bad position to insult me,
 For I have means to break and punish imposture,

To avenge offended heaven, and make repent
Those who dare say that I must leave the house!

(*Exit* TARTUFFE.)

ELMIRE: What is he talking about? What can he mean?
ORGON: Faith, I am worried. It's no laughing matter.
ELMIRE: What is it?
ORGON: His talk has shown me my mistake.
    I am disturbed about that deed of gift.
ELMIRE: A deed of gift?
ORGON: Yes; it's been signed already.
    But there's another thing which bothers me.
ELMIRE: What's that?
ORGON: I'll tell you; but first I want to see
    If there's a certain strongbox still upstairs.

ACT V

(*Enter* ORGON *and* CLÉANTE.)

CLÉANTE: Where are you hurrying to?
ORGON: How do I know?
CLÉANTE: I think we ought to have a consultation
    To see what can be done about the affair.
ORGON: It is the strongbox that alarms me most,
    More than the other matters all together.
CLÉANTE: So the mysterious strongbox is important?
ORGON: My poor friend Argas gave it me in trust,
    Pledging me to the utmost secrecy.
    When he was exiled, he came first to me;
    He said his life and all his property
    May hang upon the contents of these papers.
CLÉANTE: Then why did you entrust them to another?
ORGON: My motive was to keep my conscience easy.
    I told that scoundrel all about the matter,
    And then his arguments persuaded me
    To let him keep the strongbox in his hands,
    So that, in case of any investigation,

I'd have a pretext to deny the facts,
And thus my conscience, in security,
Could take an oath contrary to the truth.

CLÉANTE: It looks to me as if you're in for it.
The deed of gift, the transfer of the strongbox—
I have to tell you frankly what I think—
Were inconsiderate, to say the least.
With these as evidence, he can involve you deeply.
Since he has such a weapon in his hands,
You were imprudent to push him to extremes;
You should have looked for some more subtle method.

ORGON: What! Under all his outward show of fervor,
To hide a treacherous heart, an evil soul!
To think I picked him up, a penniless beggar!
All right, I now renounce all worthy men.
Henceforth I'll have a terrible horror of them;
I'm going to be a devil to them all!

CLÉANTE: Now there you go again, getting excited!
You can't be moderate in anything.
You never seem to find the sensible course;
From one excess you fall into the other.
You see your error, and you recognize
That you were taken in by pious fraud;
But now, to correct yourself, what reason is there
That you should fall into a greater error,
And lump the character of all worthy men
With the character of a perfidious rascal?
Because a blackguard boldly takes you in,
Impersonating an austere believer,
You would conclude that everyone's like him,
And that no true believer now exists?
Let the freethinkers draw those false conclusions.
Distinguish virtue from its outward seeming,
Never give your esteem too hastily,
Keep to the reasonable middle way.
Try not to give your honor to impostors,
But don't insult genuine piety.
And if you must choose one extreme or the other,
Let your fault be excessive leniency.

(*Enter* DAMIS.)

DAMIS: Is it true, father, that a rogue threatens you,

Forgetting all the favors he's received,
And that he's now presumptuous enough
To use your benefits as arms against you?

ORGON: I'm deeply grieved to say, my son, it's true.

DAMIS: Give me the word, I'll go and cut his ears off!
One shouldn't waver before his insolence.
I'll undertake to set you free of him;
I'll fix him so he'll never bother us!

CLÉANTE: That's a young man's solution, certainly.
Compose yourself and don't get so excited.
Under the government we have today,
Violence is no way to settle matters.

(*Enter* MADAME PERNELLE, MARIANE, ELMIRE, DORINE.)

MME. PERNELLE: What are these goings-on I hear about?

ORGON: Strange things indeed I've seen with my own eyes,
And a strange reward for all my kindnesses!
I rescue a man out of his poverty,
Give him a home, treat him like my own brother,
And every day I load him with benefits,
I give him my daughter and all my property;
At the same time, the faithless, infamous scoundrel
Foully proposes to seduce my wife!
And still not satisfied with this base purpose,
He dares to use against me my own favors,
And tries to ruin me by using the hold
I've given him, out of my foolish kindness,
To throw me out of my own property,
And bring me down to the state in which I found him!

DORINE: Poor fellow!

MME. PERNELLE: My son, I can't believe
He could have wished to do such an evil thing.

ORGON: What!

MME. PERNELLE: Men of principle are always envied.

ORGON: Mother, please tell me exactly what you mean.

MME. PERNELLE: I mean that people here are very peculiar,
And I know well how everybody hates him.

ORGON: And what has hatred got to do with it?

MME. PERNELLE: When you were a boy, I told you a thousand times
Virtue is always unpopular in this world;
The envious, they will die, but envy won't.

ORGON: What has all that to do with the present case?

MME. PERNELLE: Surely, people have made up stories about him.

ORGON: I told you that I saw everything myself!

MME. PERNELLE: The malice of slanderers is most excessive.

ORGON: You'll make me sin through anger, Mother! I tell you
    I saw his attempt at crime with my own eyes!

MME. PERNELLE: Many a tongue is ready to spread slander,
    And nothing in this world is proof against it.

ORGON: What you are saying makes no sense at all.
    I saw him, I say, with my own eyes I saw him!
    I saw him try to do it! Now do I have to
    Yell in your ears a hundred times: "I saw him"?

MME. PERNELLE: Mercy! Appearances are often deceptive;
    You cannot always judge by what you see.

ORGON: You'll drive me crazy!

MME. PERNELLE: False suspicions are common,
    And good is often ill interpreted.

ORGON: I should interpret then as a charity
    The attempt to kiss my wife?

MME. PERNELLE: To accuse a man,
    You have to have a full and sufficient reason;
    You ought to wait until you're sure of things.

ORGON: And how the devil can I be any surer?
    I should have waited until, before my eyes,
    He'd . . . No, you pretty nearly made me say it.

MME. PERNELLE: His soul is filled with a too holy zeal.
    I simply can't conceive the possibility
    He could have attempted the things that people say.

ORGON: Good heavens, you put me into such a fury,
    I don't know what I'd say, if you weren't my mother!

DORINE: It's only fair, good sir; you wouldn't believe us,
    And now you find they won't believe you either.

CLÉANTE: We're losing precious time in idle talk.
    We ought to plan our actions, and not sleep
    In view of the threats that scoundrel has expressed.

DAMIS: What! Do you really think he'd have the nerve—

ELMIRE: Oh, I don't think that he'd take legal action,
    For his ingratitude would be all too clear.

CLÉANTE: Don't be too sure. No doubt he has devices
    To get a show of reason on his side.
    For less than this a powerful organization
    Has got men into a very nasty mess.
    And I repeat that since he holds such weapons,

You never ought to have driven him so far.
ORGON: All right, but what could I do? At his insolence
  I simply couldn't hold my anger in.
CLÉANTE: I wish with all my heart we could patch up
  Some kind of outward peace between you two.
ELMIRE: If I had known he held such trumps in hand,
  I wouldn't have given him such provocation.
(MONSIEUR LOYAL *appears at door.* DORINE *goes to meet him.*)
ORGON (*to* DORINE): What does that fellow want? Find out and tell
  me.
  I'm in no state to deal with callers now.
MONSIEUR LOYAL: How do you do, dear sister? Will you arrange
  For me to speak to the gentleman?
DORINE: He's engaged.
  I doubt if he can talk to anyone now.
MONSIEUR LOYAL: I shouldn't like to intrude upon him here,
  But I don't think my business will upset him.
  I'm sure he'll find my news most interesting.
DORINE: Your name?
MONSIEUR LOYAL: Just tell him that Monsieur Tartuffe
  Has sent me, with a most obliging message.
DORINE (*to* ORGON): He is a messenger—and quite soft-spoken—
  From our Tartuffe. He says he has some news
  That you'll be glad to hear.
CLÉANTE: You'd better see
  Who this man is and what he has to say.
ORGON: Maybe he's coming to patch the business up.
  How do you think I ought to act to him?
CLÉANTE: You mustn't show how deeply you're offended;
  And if he offers peace, you'd better heed him.
MONSIEUR LOYAL: Greetings, good sir! May heaven smite your foes,
  And shower its blessings on you in abundance!
ORGON (*to* CLÉANTE): A civil opening! As I foresaw,
  This is a hint of reconciliation.
MONSIEUR LOYAL: Your family was always dear to me,
  And frequently I served your honored father.
ORGON: I am ashamed, sir, and I ask your pardon;
  I cannot place you or recall your name.
MONSIEUR LOYAL: My name is Loyal; I'm from Normandy [1]
  And I'm a process server by profession.

_____
[1] A byword for pettifoggery.

For forty years I've had the happiness
Praise God, to hold that honorable office.
And so I come, sir, with your kind permission,
To serve upon you this judicial writ.

ORGON: What! You came here—

MONSIEUR LOYAL: Now, no excitement, please.
It's just a little notice of eviction.
You and your family must quit the house,
Remove your furniture, make place for others,
Without delay, deferment, or reprieve.

ORGON: What, leave this house!

MONSIEUR LOYAL: If you will be so good.
The house belongs, as you are well aware,
To good Monsieur Tartuffe, beyond dispute.
He is possessed of all your property
By virtue of a contract which I bear.
It's in due form, it cannot be protested.

DAMIS: I am amazed to hear such impudence!

MONSIEUR LOYAL: Young sir, I have no business here with you,
But with your father, a reasonable man,
Who knows the duties of a court officer,
And wouldn't think of contravening justice.

ORGON: But—

MONSIEUR LOYAL: Yes, I know that not for a million francs
Would you propose to defy authority,
And that, like a gentleman, you will permit
The execution of my orders here.

DAMIS: You might well get a sound and wholesome caning
On your black jacket, Monsieur Process Server.

MONSIEUR LOYAL (*to* ORGON): Sir, bid your son be silent or retire.
I should regret to put in my report
Menaces of assault and battery.

DORINE (*aside*): His name is Loyal? I should say Disloyal.

MONSIEUR LOYAL: I have a great respect for upright men,
And I agreed to serve this writ on you
Just to oblige you and to give you pleasure,
To keep the service from the hands of others
Who would not feel my admiration for you,
And would not act with my consideration.

ORGON: What could be worse than ordering a man
To quit his home?

MONSIEUR LOYAL: But I am giving you time.
  I will suspend, monsieur, until tomorrow
  The execution of the legal writ.
  I'll merely come with a dozen of my men
  To spend the night, without publicity.
  And for form's sake I'll ask you, please, to being me
  The keys of the house before you go to bed.
  We'll take care not to trouble your repose,
  Nor suffer any impropriety.
  Tomorrow morning early you'll remove
  Your personal possessions from the house.
  My men will help you; I picked sturdy ones
  To serve you in putting everything outside.
  No one, I think, could act more fairly with you.
  And as I'm treating you with great indulgence,
  I'll ask you for your kind co-operation
  In not impeding my duties' execution.

ORGON (*aside*): How happily I'd give this very moment
  My last remaining hundred golden louis
  For the pleasure of landing on that ugly snout
  The most enormous punch in history!

CLÉANTE (*aside to* ORGON): Easy, don't spoil things.

DAMIS: At his insolence
  I can't hold in; I've got an itching fist.

DORINE: That noble back of yours, Monsieur Loyal,
  Seems to demand a few good cudgel blows.

MONSIEUR LOYAL: Such words, my dear, may call for penal action.
  The law makes no distinction as to sex.

CLÉANTE: Let's have no more of this, sir. That's enough.
  Give us that paper, please, and leave the house.

MONSIEUR LOYAL: *Au revoir,* gentlemen. God keep you in joy!

ORGON: May he confound you, and the man who sent you!

                      (*Exit* MONSIEUR LOYAL.)

  Well, Mother, you see if I was right or not;
  And by this summons you can judge of the rest.

MME. PERNELLE: I'm flabbergasted, I'm struck all of a heap!

DORINE: Oh, really! Aren't you doing wrong to blame him?
  Clearly his purposes are for your good!
  He's showing how he loves his fellow man;
  He knows that often wealth corrupts the soul.
  Out of pure charity, he would remove

The slightest obstacle to your salvation.

ORGON: Shut up, shut up! How often must I say it?

CLÉANTE: Let's think about the proper course to take.

ELMIRE: Go tell the world of his audacity!
His action makes the contract null and void.
Public opinion will be so aroused
By his black treason that he can't succeed.

(*Enter* VALÈRE.)

VALÈRE: I'm sorry, sir, to bring you any distress,
But I'm obliged to by the pressing danger.
An old and excellent friend of mine, who knows
How I'm affected by all that touches you,
Out of regard for me has violated
The secrecy he owes to state affairs.
The news he sends me makes it very clear
That you can save yourself only by flight.
The scoundrel who befooled you for so long
Has made an accusation to the King,
And to support his charges has delivered
The strongbox of an outlaw of the state,
Which you, he says, have criminally hidden,
Flouting the duty of a loyal subject.
I don't know much about the crime alleged,
But orders to arrest you have been issued.
Tartuffe himself is charged to accompany
The officer who is to take you prisoner.

CLÉANTE: Thus he gets armed support, to aid his purpose
To take possession of your property.

ORGON: Oh what a wicked creature that man is!

VALÈRE: Any delay is fatal; so I've brought
My carriage to the door to whisk you off,
And a thousand louis for the emergency.
So don't lose time; this is a knock-down blow;
The only way to dodge it is to flee.
I'll guarantee you a sure hiding place,
And I'll accompany you until the end.

ORGON: Oh, I owe everything to your kindly actions!
I'll leave my thanks until a better time;
I pray that heaven may grant me the occasion
Some day, to recognize your generous service.

Good-by, my friends; be sure to—
CLÉANTE: Hurry, hurry!
   Dear brother, we will take care of everything.
(ORGON *and* VALÈRE *start to run off. Enter* POLICE OFFICER *and*
TARTUFFE.)
TARTUFFE: Here, here, good sir! Don't run away so fast!
   A lodging's ready for you close at hand.
   By the King's orders you're a prisoner!
ORGON: Scoundrel, you kept this wicked deed till last!
   And thus, you rascal, you complete my ruin!
   This is the crown of all your villainies!
TARTUFFE: I shall not be embittered by your insults.
   I have been taught by heaven to suffer all.
CLÉANTE: So this is holy moderation, is it?
DAMIS: Shameful to make of heaven his accomplice!
TARTUFFE: You cannot move me by a show of anger,
   For all I think of is to do my duty.
MARIANE: Much glory you will draw from this affair,
   And surely you'll derive much honor from it.
TARTUFFE: An action can be only glorious
   When it's commanded by the royal power.
ORGON: Have you remembered that my helping hand
   Was all that rescued you from beggary?
TARTUFFE: True, I may be beholden for some aid,
   But my first duty is to serve the King.
   This sacred, just, and all-compelling duty
   Extinguishes all gratitude in my heart.
   To its compulsion I would sacrifice
   My friends, my relatives, my wife—myself!
ELMIRE: Impostor!
DORINE: How he treacherously makes
   A cloak and shield of all that we revere!
CLÉANTE: But if this noble zeal which animates you
   Is quite as perfect as you say it is,
   How comes it that it waited to appear
   Till you were caught addressing Orgon's wife?
   And why did you denounce him only when,
   For honor's sake, he had to throw you out?
   I won't allege—though it might have held you back—
   His gift to you of all his property;
   But since you treat him now as a guilty man,

Why did you stoop to accepting all his money?

TARTUFFE (*to* POLICE OFFICER): Deliver me, sir, from all these railing words,

And execute your orders, if you please.

OFFICER: Yes, I've delayed too long in doing so.

Aptly enough, you ask for it yourself.

So here's the execution: follow me

To the prison cell that's ready for your lodging.

TARTUFFE: What, me, sir?

OFFICER: You, sir, yes.

TARTUFFE: But why to prison?

OFFICER: It's not to you I owe an explanation.

(*To* ORGON)

You've had a nasty scare; but calm yourself.

Our present King is enemy of fraud,

His eyes can penetrate his subjects' hearts;

The art of charlatans cannot delude him.

And his great spirit, wise in the ways of men,

Watches his kingdom with discerning eyes.

No one can take him easily by surprise,

And his firm reason yields to no excess.

To worthy men he gives immortal glory,

And yet his zeal for virtue is not blind.

His love for genuine faith does not eclipse

The horror one should feel for false devotion.

Tartuffe was not the sort to hoodwink him

Who has avoided many a subtler snare.

Immediately he saw in its true color

The base conniving of that evil mind.

This man, accusing you, betrayed himself;

And, by the retribution of high justice,

The King identified him as a rogue

Already famous under another name,

And with a criminal record to his credit

Lengthy enough to fill a score of volumes.

In short, His Majesty abhorred this man's

Mean and ungrateful treachery toward you.

With this crime added to the ample list,

The King commanded me to accompany him,

Only to see what impudence would dare,

And force Tartuffe to make you reparation.

College
SIOUX CITY, IOWA
51104

Christopher John Case
405-90-4465 HISTORY

EG 000988409
3/02/93

STUDENTS GRADE CARD

A – SUPERIOR
B – GOOD
C – SATISFACTORY
D – INCOMPLETE
F – FAILURE
P – PASS
W – WITHDRAWAL
X – AUDIT
N – DELAYED GRADE

TERM	YEAR	DEPT.	CRSE. NO.	DESCRIPTION	GR.	SEM. CR	GR. PT.
2	92-93	EN	0345	AMER REALISM	B+	3	10.5
2	92-93	HS	0460	SEMINAR INTELL	C	3	6.0
2	92-93	HS	191R	PREP FOR COMPS	N		

TERM AVERAGE	ACCUMULATIVE TOTAL
2.750	3.170

NOT VALID AS A TRANSCRIPT
WITHOUT SIGNATURE AND SEAL

_____
REGISTRAR

Christopher John Case
1816 Jones
Sioux City   IA 51105

Now in your presence I shall seize the papers
Of which the scoundrel has possessed himself.
The King declares the contract null and void
Which made Tartuffe a gift of all your wealth,
And finally he pardons that offense
In which the exile of a friend involved you.
Thus he rewards your past fidelity,
Which, in the civil wars, upheld his rights;
And thus he proves his heart ever remembers
To recompense a subject's worthy action.
He shows that merit's not unrecognized,
That he is mindful more of good than evil.

DORINE: May heaven be praised!

MME. PERNELLE: Now I can breathe again!

ELMIRE: All's well then!

MARIANE: Who would have dared foretell it!

ORGON (*to* TARTUFFE): So now we've got you, villian—

CLÉANTE: Brother, stop.
    Don't stoop to any unworthy exultation,
    But leave a wretched man to his wretched fate;
    You need not add to the pangs of his remorse.
    Hope rather that his heart may now be touched
    To heed the call of virtue; that he may
    Detest his vice and thus correct his life,
    And move the justice of our King to mercy;
    While you shall kneel before the royal bounty,
    And pay its due to the King's clemency.

ORGON: Well said, indeed. So let us, at his feet,
    Joyfully thank him for his heartfelt kindness.
    And after this first duty has been done,
    There is a second claiming our concern;
    So by a happy marriage we shall crown
    The noble-hearted ardor of Valère.

Henrik Ibsen

Henrik Ibsen, born in Skien, Norway in 1828, has frequently been called the greatest dramatist since Shakespeare and Molière. Since only a few decades have passed since his death in 1906, placing him among such greats may be premature, but there can be no question that Ibsen had a profound effect upon the dramatists who followed him, and that for reader or audience, many of his plays are powerful and moving experiences.

Basically a man with an intensely romantic temperament, the Norwegian playwright wrote the first, and perhaps the greatest, realistic dramas. He demanded in *Brand,* an early play, that his fellow men sacrifice everything—possessions, love, family—to achieve, without compromise or concession, their highest ideals. Some years later in *The Wild Duck,* he was able to reveal the havoc that such absolute idealism could wreak upon human life. He was a man who led a comparatively uneventful life, spending most of his time secluded in his study, but creating out of his own moods and limited experience some of the most intense and exciting dramas of modern times.

Such contradictions derive from Ibsen's remarkable sensitivity to the dynamic intellectual currents of the nineteenth century, from his unrelenting determination to become an "immortal man," from his fierce honesty, and from his fearless probing of his own inner being. In an early essay, which he wrote in preparation for college entrance examinations, he set down the principle that guided him throughout his career: "As a means to aid one in judging the characters of others and for a knowledge of mankind in general, it is necessary to have understood one's own character and manner of thinking, because only through conclusions which he draws therefrom is it possible for a man to attain fairly certain results in that direction." Upon the simple granite shaft beside Ibsen's grave is carved a miner's hammer, symbolizing the life work of the poet-dramatist who sought to expose the deepest recesses of the human personality. In an early poem entitled "The Miner," he wrote, "Deeper I must thrust and lower / Till I hear the ring of ore."

One would think that the biography of a writer who sought the key to human character within himself would be of the utmost importance in understanding his work. However, aside from a few important incidents that left their indelible mark upon Ibsen's character, external details of his life are of minor importance. His plays evolved from his inner life. "All that I have written," he said when he was nearing fifty, "I have, mentally, lived through."

Perhaps the most formative event in Ibsen's life was the business failure of his father when the boy was about ten years old. During the early years of the poet's life, Knud Ibsen was a prosperous business-man, living in one of the finest houses in Skien. He sent his children to the best school in the town, and the family associations were with the upper-class townspeople. But when Knud Ibsen went bankrupt, the family had to move to a cottage on the outskirts of town, and the sensitive, imaginative, brooding, future dramatist had to attend an inferior school and suffer the ignominy of no longer being respectable. As always when he was hurt, Ibsen retreated into himself. During these early years, he spent much time alone in an attic room, reading and brooding. He displayed a talent for painting, but there was no money for art lessons. He had little in common with his brothers and felt close to only one person in the family, his sister Hedvig. It was made clear to the boy that he would have to earn his own keep as soon as possible; before he was sixteen his father apprenticed him to an apothecary in Grimstad, a town a day's sea journey away from Skien. Ibsen remained in Grimstad for six years, the first three of which he spent almost entirely alone, working long hours in the apothecary shop for almost no pay and living in a small room in the back of the store. The effects of the loss of social stature and of poverty left deep scars upon the boy who sensed great talent in himself and feared that his circumstances would prevent him from fulfilling his potential. He read the romantic poets and dreamed of freeing himself from the bonds of poverty and becoming a great man by sacrificing himself to his highest ideals. Throughout the years of his success and prosperity, Ibsen was excessively cautious about spending money, and he sought and cherished all possible honors and decorations. He went about in formal dress and on every possible occasion he pinned to his coat all the decorations he had been awarded. He desperately wanted the applause of his fellow countrymen, and whenever they failed to appreciate his plays, he reacted with fury.

During his last three years in Grimstad, Ibsen formed friendships with two young men to whom he could speak about art and literature. He had begun to write poetry, and after his day's work he spent many hours studying Latin to qualify for admission to the university in Oslo. During this period in Grimstad, he wrote his first play, *Cataline,* based upon his Latin reading. He read the play to his two friends who were so impressed that one of them, Schulerud, undertook to have it produced or published. When the publishers and the managers of the Oslo theaters rejected the drama, Schulerud, on borrowed money, underwrote its publication.

In 1850, Ibsen went to Oslo to take the entrance examinations for the university. He passed in most of the subjects but received several conditionals. He never retook the tests. At the tutoring school which he had been attending, he had met several literary aspirants. He joined with them to publish a satirical journal and gave up his dream of becoming a medical doctor. One of his poems, written for a student benefit performance, brought him to the attention of Ole Bull, a famous violinist and nationalist who was determined to establish a Norwegian national theater. Ibsen's poem so impressed the violinist, who learned that Ibsen had written two plays, that he engaged the inexperienced young man as director and playwright of the theater he was establishing in Bergen.

Ibsen remained in Bergen for six years. A shy, nervous youth with no theatrical experience, he had much difficulty coaching his actors in their roles. But with characteristic intensity and devotion, he worked hard, long hours, drawing up elaborate sketches for each scene. Once he left Norway, Ibsen was never again to have any working relations with the theater, but during these years in Bergen he learned all he needed to know about the demands of the stage. At this period of his career, Ibsen was passionately involved with the nationalistic movement of Norway, and the plays he wrote to fulfill his Bergen theater contract were intensely nationalistic and romantic.

Before he left Bergen to be the director of a theater in Oslo, he met Susannah Thoresen. They were married in 1857 and their only child, Sigurd, was born the following year. Ibsen did not repeat in Oslo his success with the Bergen theater; at that point he entered one of the most troubled periods of his life. He was unable to write and lost confidence in his future. With his meager income, he felt oppressed by the burden of supporting a wife and child. His petition for a government stipend to support his poetic activities was rejected, and Ibsen sank into depression and even contemplated suicide. Struggling to regain mastery of himself he tried writing again and in 1862 published *Love's Comedy*. *The Pretenders* (1864), a stirring drama based upon Norwegian history, followed.

Ibsen's nationalistic fervor and that of his countrymen underwent a severe test about this time. Denmark became involved in a border dispute with Prussia. Many Norwegians, including Ibsen, urged that Norway assist its Scandinavian neighbor by sending troops. At the final moment, Norway decided not to send its soldiers, and in 1864, when Ibsen, with a grant for foreign travel, arrived in Berlin, he witnessed the triumphal return of the German soldiers who spat into the mouths of captured Danish cannons. Ibsen was not a man of action, and he characteristically avoided physical danger, but he was humiliated by the failure of his countrymen and by his own failure to fight for the ideal of Scandinavian unity he had preached for so many years. His next play, *Brand* (1866), was the story of a heroic preacher who sacrifices everything to fulfill his moral ideals.

In 1864 Ibsen traveled to Italy alone, but soon sent for his wife and child. For nearly three decades he remained in exile, living in Italy, Dresden, and Munich. The fame, prosperity, and success that he sought came to him during those years. His plays were translated and he became internationally known. But he never deviated from the strict regimen he imposed upon himself, and it is said that anyone who dared disturb him while he wrote was treated to a violent reception. With his great mane of hair, side whiskers, formal dress, and forbidding eyes, Ibsen was unapproachable, and each evening he could sit at a café with a glass of beer reading his newspaper with no fear of interruption. Every two years, with the regularity that characterized his daily routine, he published a play.

As he grew older, Ibsen began to feel once again the pull of his native country and in 1891 he returned to Norway to live the rest of his life in Oslo. His fellow countrymen had both praised him and damned him for his views and his plays, but they were greatly honored by his return from self-imposed exile. In 1900 the dramatist suffered a stroke, and though he lived for six more years, his creative powers were gone. His final words, it is said, were "On the contrary," addressed to his wife when she told him he was getting better. On his deathbed, Ibsen remained devoted to absolute truth.

Despite the secluded life he led, Henrik Ibsen was in the vanguard of all the major intellectual currents sweeping across Europe in the nineteenth century. One of the reasons that he felt more comfortable away from Norway was that he frequently was so much in the forefront that his countrymen were not yet ready to respond to the new ideas he embodied in his dramas. His 1881 play *Ghosts,* for instance, with its naturalistic emphasis upon the hereditary forces that dominate and control the lives of men was denounced as odious by Norwegian critics, and no theater manager would stage it. Such response infuriated the exile even though he knew that within a decade his audience would be prepared to accept the new ideas.

Like all great artists, Ibsen was a man of his age, incorporating into his art the new insights and attitudes of his period and finding the appropriate form to express the new thoughts. During his early years, romanticism dominated Norwegian thinking, and Ibsen's early poetry and dramas such as *Peer Gynt* (1867) are idealistic, nationalistic, mystical, and imaginative. Trolls and other legendary creatures play important roles; the romanticist's fascination with the past is apparent in Ibsen's early subjects, and his interest in the potential of individual man led him to create heroic characters who achieve or fail to achieve the highest moral ideals.

When Ibsen responded to the ideas of such thinkers as Darwin and John Stuart Mill and, later, Freud, he abandoned most of the attitudes of romanticism, though he did retain his idealism and his interest in individual man. One major theme resounds throughout his work: the individual must free himself from all the fetters that prevent him from developing fully his potential as a human being.

In *The Master Builder* (1892) Ibsen capsules his own career when he has Solness, his hero, who had devoted his genius and energy to building great cathedrals, cry out: "Hear me thou Mighty One! From this day forward I will be a free builder—I, too, in my sphere— just as Thou in Thine. I will never more build churches for Thee— only homes for human beings." About 1875 Ibsen ended the cathedral-building phase of his career. When he began to work on *The Pillars of Society* (1877), he turned from portraying the unusual creative individual fighting for ideals to presenting the ordinary lives of common men. Despite this shift to realism, Ibsen remained a crusade¯. He did not consider drama an entertainment designed to be amusing. "I for my part," he declared, "think that rejuvenating truths ought to be spoken from the stage just as well as from the pulpit or the professor's chair."

In *A Doll's House* (1879), *Ghosts* (1881), and *An Enemy of the People* (1882), he urged his fellow men to clear away the cobwebs of tradition, of antiquated social customs and laws, and boldly seek their own individualities. The pillars of society, he insisted, are not the men and women who uphold the status quo, but those who pursue liberty and truth. The heroine of *A Doll's House,* the greatest play of this group, is trapped by the binding traditions of a male-dominated society. She must act out the role that society has decreed women shall play. A crisis brings Nora to a full understanding of her position, and she determines at the end of the play to leave home, husband, and children to discover her true self. When the first actress who played Nora slammed the door as she left the stage, the noise reverberated round the world. The play was considered a plea for the emancipation of women. Essentially, it was a plea, as are all these plays, for liberty of the individual and for truth.

These dramas reflect Ibsen's response to the concepts of Darwin and the social vision of John Stuart Mill. The human being was no longer to be viewed as a finished product placed upon earth by God, but as a biological entity, the product of nature and environment. As such, he, like plants and animals, was a fit subject for scientific inquiry to discover what forces made him what he is. Darwin's view of man diminished his stature, but his concept of an evolutionary process seemed to Ibsen and others a promise that if man could know more about himself he could move forward and upward. Mill's vision of the sanctity of the human being and his insistence upon the liberty of the individual found a responsive chord in Ibsen's heart. He responded also to the writings of a fellow Scandinavian, George Brandes, who, in France, had studied the works of Hippolyte Taine and returned to his home country to fight for a return to eighteenth-century French emphasis upon the power of human reason and intellect. Amalgamating these ideas, Ibsen believed that through a combination of will power and intellect, the human being could discover the truth about himself and achieve the liberty necessary to fulfill his latent potential. He, therefore, urged men to open the windows of their homes and hearts to the fresh air of truth.

Though *A Doll's House* made Ibsen world famous, the dramatist was discouraged by the general reception of his social dramas. When

Ghosts was denied a hearing by his countrymen, he was so enraged that he broke his routine of spending two years on each play and wrote *An Enemy of the People* in six months. The hero of that play, a doctor, who warns his fellow townsmen that the spa they are opening is fed by polluted waters, arouses the fury of the town for speaking the truth. As he is being stoned, Dr. Stockman cries out, "The strongest man in the world is the man who stands most alone."

Despite this defiant statement, Ibsen apparently did a great deal of soul searching at this period and came to recognize that a study of his own character did not necessarily reveal the character of all men. Ibsen himself had fought for the freedom essential to his creative activities, and he had the determination and strength to seek the truth. Saddened by the realization that not all men are capable of spiritual independence, but aware that he had discovered a truth about human beings, Ibsen wrote *The Wild Duck* (1884), a play in which he revealed his deep sympathy for his fellow men, despite their foibles and weaknesses. This play with two others of this period, *Rosmersholm* (1886) and *Hedda Gabler* (1890), are generally considered his masterpieces. In these dramas, Ibsen probes to expose the wounds that can shape and destroy the character and lives of human beings.

Ibsen's earliest dramas are traditional in form and written in verse. They present a story chronologically, each successive scene moving toward the climax and conclusion. When he began to portray the lives of ordinary men and to expose the forces that shaped and imprisoned them, he required a new technique. The type of play that he developed is known as realistic drama. When we speak of comedy or tragedy, melodrama or farce we speak of dramatic forms in which attitude and form have been fused. But realism is not so much a form as a dramatic mode, the product of the playwright's vision of life and of man. The writer of tragedy exalts the human being; in the character of the tragic hero, man achieves sublime grandeur. The writer of comedy ridicules man because he fails to measure up to his potential. In contrast, the writer of realistic drama wants to present man as he is, a creature of nature and his environment, driven by certain basic needs, molded by external forces. He seeks to view man objectively and to discover the truth about him, reveal the basic drives that direct his actions, his inner desires, and aspirations. A realist like Ibsen refused to cater to the taboos and cherished ideas of his society. Like a scientist he sought the truth about men and their lives and presented his findings in dramatic form.

Because he sought to reveal the way in which the human being is entrapped by abstractions, by the past, by the codes and traditions of society, Ibsen developed a technique that has been called "retrospective drama." It set the pattern for most of the realistic dramas that followed. Ibsen begins his play *in medias res*. The central crisis is imminent, but before the crisis occurs the audience must be made aware, through the dialogue, of the background that produced this moment. Typically, an Ibsen drama opens upon a household that seems relatively peaceful. Then someone who has been away for a number of years enters and precipitates a crisis by resurrecting the past. Gradually, like a detective story, clues about the past relations of the characters are provided until the causes and their effects are clearly established. This process of revelation serves at the same time to move the situation forward to its climax. Somerset Maugham described, amusingly but accurately, the typical Ibsen pattern when he wrote: "A number of people are living in a closed or stuffy room, then someone comes (from the mountains or over the sea) and flings the window open; everyone gets a cold in the head and the curtain falls."

The technique of retrospective drama permitted Ibsen to stage a very compact drama that respected the unities of time and place. He also developed a number of techniques to create an atmosphere of realism. He abandoned the use of verse so that his characters would speak as real people speak in ordinary life, and he emphasized visual effects. The settings he describes for the stage are designed to create a sense of a real room in a real house. Stage properties and stage effects, such as the pistols in *The Wild Duck* or the attic room at the back of the stage are given an integral place in the story. But perhaps the greatest contribution to the atmosphere of realism was his creation of psychologically comprehensible characters. To a visitor, Ibsen once described the importance he attached to knowing each of his characters completely:

> Before I write down one word I have to have the character in mind through and through, I must penetrate into the last wrinkle of his soul. I always proceed from the individual; the stage setting, the dramatic ensemble, all of that comes naturally and does not cause me any worry, as soon as I am certain of the individual in every aspect of his humanity. But I have to have his exterior in mind also, down to the last button, how he stands and walks, how he conducts himself, what his voice sounds like. Then I do not let him go until his fate is fulfilled.

Ibsen has been frequently described, with justification, as a dramatist of ideas, but he was never guilty of violating the integrity of a character for the sake of presenting an idea. In *The Wild Duck,* for example, he has obviously set out to show the dangers of idealism. And yet, Gregers Werle who preaches the demands of the ideal, who insists that Ekdal face the truth and build a new life upon it, is the idealist he is because his character was shaped by the relationship of his father and mother. And the tragic consequence of Gregers' interference in the life of the Ekdal family is made possible only because Hjalmar is the kind of man he is. In these great dramas of Ibsen, there are no real villains. The dramatist understands and sympathizes with his characters too much to present them simply as heroes or villains. They are complex, many-sided human beings, the products of complicated emotional relationships and experiences.

Ibsen once declared that to write is to see. He was a very keen observer of human beings and of their world, and his dramas are filled with realistic details, but what he really meant by "seeing" was not simply observation of surface reality. When we say "I see" in response to someone's statement, we are close to using "seeing" as Ibsen did. He continually reviewed and analyzed the ideas he held. As a result, it is possible to pair many of his dramas. When he finished a play, he would review the ideas and attitudes he had dramatized, and then write another play, frequently from the opposite point of view. *The Wild Duck* cannot be paired with a specific play but with a lifetime of writing in which Ibsen had urged his fellow men to follow their ideals, to seek and face the truth about themselves and about their lives and then build a new life upon the truth they discovered.

≈≈

BIBLIOGRAPHY

Jorgenson, Theodore. *Henrik Ibsen: A Study in Art and Personality.* Northfield, Minn.: St. Olaf College Press, 1945.

Knight, G. Wilson. *Henrik Ibsen.* New York: Grove Press, 1963.

Northam, John. *Ibsen's Dramatic Method.* London: Faber & Faber, 1953.

Valency, Maurice. *The Flower and the Castle: An Introduction to Modern Drama.* New York: Macmillan, 1963.

Weigand, Kermann. *The Modern Ibsen: A Reconsideration.* New York: Holt, Rinehart & Winston, 1925.

The Wild Duck

Translated by Eva Le Gallienne

CHARACTERS

WERLE	*a wholesale merchant and manufacturer*
GREGERS WERLE	*his son*
OLD EKDAL	
HJALMAR EKDAL	*his son, a photographer*
GINA EKDAL	*Hjalmar's wife*
HEDVIG	*their daughter, a girl of fourteen*
MRS. SÖRBY	*Werle's housekeeper*
RELLING	*a doctor*
MOLVIK	*a former student of theology*
GRAABERG	*Werle's bookkeeper*
PETTERSEN	*Werle's servant*
JENSEN	*a hired waiter*
A FAT GENTLEMAN	
A BALD GENTLEMAN	
A NEARSIGHTED GENTLEMAN	
SIX OTHER GENTLEMEN	*guests at Werle's party*
SEVERAL HIRED WAITERS	

The first act takes place in Werle's house, the four following acts at Hjalmar Ekdal's.

ACT I

(SCENE: *In Werle's house. A study richly and comfortably furnished; bookcases and upholstered furniture; a desk covered with papers and documents stands in the center of the room; several lamps with green shades give a subdued light. In the back wall double doors stand open, with portieres drawn back. Beyond them is seen a large elegantly furnished room, brightly lighted with lamps and branched candlesticks. A small baize door down right leads to Werle's office. Down left a fireplace with a brightly burning coal fire, and above this a double door to the dining room.*

Werle's servant PETTERSEN, *in livery, and* JENSEN, *a hired waiter in black, are straightening up the room. In the large room beyond, two or three other waiters move about tidying up and lighting more candles. From the dining room comes the hum of conversation, laughter, the sound of many voices; a glass is tapped with a knife; silence follows, then a toast is proposed. Shouts of "Bravo!" and then again the buzz of conversation.*)

PETTERSEN (*as he lights a lamp on the mantlepiece and replaces the shade*): Hear that, Jensen? The old boy's on his feet again toasting Mrs. Sörby. Listen to him holding forth!

JENSEN (*pushing forward an armchair*): Is it true what people say? That he's sweet on her, I mean?

PETTERSEN: Hell! How should I know!

JENSEN: I'll bet he was quite a chaser in his day!

PETTERSEN: I shouldn't wonder.

JENSEN: He's giving this party for his son, I hear.

PETTERSEN: Yes; he got home yesterday.

JENSEN: I never even knew Werle had a son.

PETTERSEN: He has a son all right. But he spends most of his time up at the Works, in Höjdal; he hasn't been back once; not in all the years I've worked here.

A WAITER (*in the doorway of the inner room*): Pettersen! There's an old fellow out here—says he wants—

PETTERSEN (*muttering*): What is it *now!*

(OLD EKDAL *appears from the right in the inner room. He wears a threadbare overcoat with a turned-up collar; has on woollen mittens and carries a stick and an old fur cap. There is a brown paper parcel under his arm. He wears a dirty reddish-brown wig and has a small gray mustache.*)

PETTERSEN (*going toward him*): What the devil are *you* doing here?

EKDAL (*in the doorway*): Got to get into the office, Pettersen.

PETTERSEN: The office was closed an hour ago—

EKDAL: I know—the porter told me. But Graaberg's still there, isn't he? Let me slip in this way, Pettersen—there's a good fellow! (*Points to the baize door.*) Not the first time I've used this door, eh?

PETTERSEN: All right. (*Opens the door.*) But when you leave, go out the other way—don't come back through here. We have company, you know.

EKDAL: Oh, yes—I know; I know. Hm! Thanks, Pettersen. Thanks, old man. You're a good friend. (*Mutters under his breath.*) Ass! (*He goes into the office;* PETTERSEN *closes the door after him.*)

JENSEN: Does *he* belong to the office?

PETTERSEN: No! He just does a bit of copying now and then—when they're extra busy. Takes it home with him. Poor old Ekdal! Quite a swell in his day, he was.

JENSEN: He still has a way with him—

PETTERSEN: Yes, indeed! A military man he was. A lieutenant, no less.

JENSEN: A lieutenant! *Him?*

PETTERSEN: It's a fact. Then he went into business—something to do with timber, I believe. They say he once played Mr. Werle a very dirty trick. They were running the Höjdal Works together—they were partners then, you see. Oh, I know old Ekdal well. Many's the time we've drunk a bottle of ale at Mrs. Eriksen's; we've downed many a glass of bitters there together he and I.

JENSEN: Shouldn't think there was much chance of a treat from him!

PETTERSEN: Don't be a fool, Jensen! I'm the one who does the treating. It's as well to be kind to a gent like that who's come down in the world.

JENSEN: What happened? Did he go bankrupt?

PETTERSEN: Worse than that; he went to jail.

JENSEN: To jail!

PETTERSEN: Some kind of penitentiary, at any rate. (*Listens.*) Sh! They're getting up from table.

(*The dining-room door is flung open from within by a couple of waiters.* MRS. SÖRBY *comes out talking to two gentlemen.* WERLE *and the other guests follow gradually. Finally* HJALMAR EKDAL *and* GREGERS WERLE *appear.*)

MRS. SÖRBY (*in passing*): You can serve the coffee in the music room, Pettersen.

PETTERSEN: Very well, Madam. (*She and the two gentlemen go into the inner room and off right.* PETTERSEN *and* JENSEN *go out the same way.*)

FAT GENTLEMAN (*to* BALD GENTLEMAN): Phew! That was hard work! Quite a meal!

BALD GENTLEMAN: With a little good will it's quite amazing what one can put away in three hours!

FAT GENTLEMAN: Oh, my dear fellow—I'm thinking of the aftermath!

A THIRD GENTLEMAN: They say coffee and liqueurs are being served in the music room.

FAT GENTLEMAN: Splendid! Perhaps Mrs. Sörby will play a tune for us.

BALD GENTLEMAN: If we aren't careful she may play us the wrong kind of tune someday!

FAT GENTLEMAN: Don't worry about Bertha! She's not the kind to go back on old friends!

WERLE (*in a low tone, dejectedly*): I don't think anyone noticed— did they, Gregers?

GREGERS (*looks at him*): Noticed what?

WERLE: Then you didn't notice either?

GREGERS: No. What do you mean?

WERLE: We were thirteen at table.

GREGERS: Really? Were we?

WERLE (*with a glance towards* HJALMAR EKDAL): As a rule we're never more than twelve. (*To the others*) This way, gentlemen! (WERLE *and the others go out through the inner room to the right. Only* HJALMAR *and* GREGERS *remain.*)

HJALMAR (*who has overheard*): Gregers—you shouldn't have invited me.

GREGERS: Don't be absurd! Not invite my best and only friend—? The party was given for me, wasn't it?

HJALMAR: Your father didn't approve, I'm afraid. I'm never asked to the house, you know.

GREGERS: So I gather. But I had to see you and have a talk. I'll be going away again soon—We've drifted so far apart since the old days at school. Do you realize it's sixteen or seventeen years since we last met?

HJALMAR: Is it really as long as that?

GREGERS: It is indeed! Well—how have you been? You're looking well. You've put on weight, I think; you've grown quite stout.

HJALMAR: I wouldn't exactly call it stout. I'm no longer a boy—if that's what you mean. I've filled out a bit—that's only natural.

GREGERS: Yes, of course. Well—outwardly you seem in splendid shape.

HJALMAR (*in a gloomy tone*): But inwardly—that's another story! I don't have to tell you all that I've been through. You know all about *that* catastrophe!

GREGERS: Yes. What's happened to your father? What's he doing now?

HJALMAR: Don't speak of it! The poor, miserable old man! I look after him, of course; he lives with me. He has no one else to turn to. But it's too painful to talk about—Tell me about yourself. Have you been getting on well—up at the Works?

GREGERS: I've been living in splendid isolation. I've had plenty of time for contemplation, I can tell you. Let's sit here and be comfortable. (*He sits down in an armchair by the fire, and pulls* HJALMAR *down to another one beside him.*)

HJALMAR (*sentimentally*): As a matter of fact, Gregers, I'm very grateful that you asked me here today. It proves that you no longer have anything against me.

GREGERS (*surprised*): Why on earth should you think I had anything against you?

HJALMAR: You had at first, you know.

GREGERS: At first? How do you mean?

HJALMAR: Directly after the—catastrophe. It was understandable enough. It was only by a miracle that your father escaped being dragged into all that ghastly business.

GREGERS: But that's no reason why I should have had anything against *you*. What put that into your head?

HJALMAR: I happen to know you did, Gregers. Your father told me so himself.

GREGERS: *Father* did? Well! Hm—Was that why I never heard from you? Why you never wrote to me?

HJALMAR: Of course.

GREGERS: You never even told me you'd decided to take up photography.

HJALMAR: I know. Your father advised me not to write to you at all.

GREGERS (*gazes straight before him*): Well—well! Perhaps he was wise in that—But, tell me—are you happy in your work? Does it appeal to you, I mean?

HJALMAR (*with a sigh*): Yes—more or less; I really can't complain. It all seemed very strange to me at first. I found myself in such totally different circumstances, you see. Father had lost absolutely everything—he was completely ruined. And then there was all the scandal—the disgrace—

GREGERS (*moved*): Yes, yes. I understand.

HJALMAR: I naturally had to give up my studies—I was forced to leave the university. We hadn't a penny left—nothing but debts—mostly to your father, I believe.

GREGERS: Hm.

HJALMAR: I thought it best to break off all my former friendships—sever all my old connections. In fact it was your father who advised me to do so; and since he seemed to want to help me—

GREGERS: Father did?

HJALMAR: You must be aware of that. Where was *I* to get the money to learn photography, furnish a studio, and buy all the necessary equipment? It takes quite a bit of capital to make a start, you know.

GREGERS: You mean—*Father* provided that?

HJALMAR: Of course; didn't you know? I understood him to say he'd written you about it.

GREGERS: No—he never mentioned it. He must have forgotten, I suppose. Actually we've never exchanged anything but business letters. So it was *Father* who—!

HJALMAR: Yes, it was. He didn't want it generally known, he said —but it was he. He also made it possible for me to marry. Didn't you know that either?

GREGERS: No—I didn't. (*Shakes him by the arm.*) My dear Hjalmar —I can't tell you how glad I am about all this. But I feel guilty, too. I've misjudged Father all these years—in some ways, anyhow. I thought he had no heart—no feelings. This proves me wrong. It's funny—one would almost think he was trying to atone for something—

HJALMAR: Atone?

GREGERS: Yes—it's as though he were suffering from a sense of guilt; I don't know *what* to call it. But I'm certainly delighted to hear all this about him. So you're married, are you? You're a braver man than I am! How does it feel? Are you content?

HJALMAR: Yes—I'm very happy, thank you. She's a thoroughly good wife—and very capable, as well. And, after all—she's not *entirely* without education.

GREGERS (*rather surprised*): No—I don't suppose she is—

HJALMAR: Life's the best education, when you come right down to it. And, being so much with me, she— And I've a couple of very brilliant friends who drop in almost every day. She's learning— Gina's learning! You'd never recognize her.

GREGERS: Gina?

HJALMAR: Yes; Gina's her name—don't you remember?

GREGERS: *Whose* name is Gina? I don't know what you're—

HJALMAR: You must remember Gina! She worked here for a while.

GREGERS (*looks at him*): You don't mean Gina Hansen?

HJALMAR: Gina Hansen, yes—of course.

GREGERS: —who kept house for us those last few years—when Mother was so ill?

HJALMAR: Yes, that's the one. But—my dear fellow—your father wrote you all about it; I'm *positive* he did!

GREGERS (*who has risen*): He wrote and told me you were married, but not that— (*Walks about the room.*) Wait, though! On second thought—I think he may have—His letters were always so very brief. (*Sinks down on the arm of the chair.*) Tell me, Hjalmar— this is most interesting—how did you happen to meet this Gina— your wife, I mean?

HJALMAR: It was all quite simple. Gina didn't stay here long, you know. Things were very upset here at the time—what with your mother's illness; it was all too much for Gina, so she left. It was the year before your mother died, I think; or the same year, perhaps— I'm not quite sure.

GREGERS: It was the same year; I was away—up at the Works. And then what happened?

HJALMAR: Gina went home to her mother—Mrs. Hansen; an honest, hard-working woman who ran a little restaurant. They had a room to rent—a nice, comfortable room—

GREGERS: And I suppose you were lucky enough to acquire it?

HJALMAR: Yes. It was your father who recommended it. And, of course, there I got to know Gina very well.

GREGERS: And then you got engaged?

HJALMAR: Yes. It doesn't take young people long to fall in love— hm—

GREGERS (*rises and paces about*): Tell me—was it *after* you became engaged that Father—I mean—was it after that, that you took up photography?

HJALMAR: Yes; I had to work at something; I was anxious to have a home of my own, you see. Your father and I agreed that a photographer's career would be practical and easy. And Gina thought so too—especially as she'd done a bit of retouching herself and knew quite a lot about it.

GREGERS: So it worked out very neatly, didn't it?

HJALMAR (*rises, pleased*): Yes—wasn't it amazing? It really worked out very neatly!

GREGERS: No doubt of that! My father seems to have played the part of Divine Providence where you're concerned!

HJALMAR: He came to the rescue of his old friend's son. That shows what a kind heart he has!

(MRS. SÖRBY *enters arm in arm with* WERLE.)

MRS. SÖRBY: It's no use arguing, dear Mr. Werle! You mustn't stay in those bright lights another moment. It's bad for you!

WERLE (*lets go of her arm and passes his hand over his eyes*): You know—I believe you're right.

(PETTERSEN *and* JENSEN *carry round trays of refreshments*.)

MRS. SÖRBY (*to the guests in the inner room*): Do come in here, gentlemen, and have some punch.

FAT GENTLEMAN (*comes up to* MRS. SÖRBY): It can't be true! No smoking? You surely don't mean to deprive us of that precious prerogative!

MRS. SÖRBY: I'm afraid it can't be helped, Your Excellency! Smoking is not allowed in Mr. Werle's sanctum.

BALD GENTLEMAN: My dear lady! And when did you inaugurate this harsh decree?

MRS. SÖRBY: After our last dinner party, Mr. Balle. Several of our guests quite overstepped the mark.

BALD GENTLEMAN: Isn't it ever permitted to overstep the mark, dear Madam Bertha! Not even by an inch or two?

MRS. SÖRBY: Never! Under any circumstances, Mr. Balle.

(*Most of the guests are now gathered in the study; servants hand round glasses of punch*.)

WERLE (*to* HJALMAR, *who is standing apart beside a table*): What are you so engrossed in, Ekdal?

HJALMAR: I was just looking at this album, Mr. Werle.

BALD GENTLEMAN (*who is wandering about*): Ah, photographs! Of course—that's your line, isn't it?

FAT GENTLEMAN (*in an armchair*): I do hope you've brought some of your own!

HJALMAR: No, I'm afraid I haven't.

FAT GENTLEMAN: Too bad! It's good for the digestion to look at pictures after dinner.

BALD GENTLEMAN: And it provides entertainment, too.

NEARSIGHTED GENTLEMAN: All such contributions thankfully received!

MRS. SÖRBY: In other words, gentlemen, you mean a guest should sing for his supper!

FAT GENTLEMAN: Certainly, Mrs. Sörby—especially when the supper is so excellent!

BALD GENTLEMAN: Still—when it involves one's livelihood—

MRS. SÖRBY: Of course! I quite agree! (*They go on laughing and joking.*)

GREGERS (*softly*): You ought to join in the conversation, Hjalmar.

HJALMAR (*squirming*): What have I got to talk about?

FAT GENTLEMAN: Werle—I claim that Tokay is a comparatively mild wine; don't you agree?

WERLE (*by the mantelpiece*): Yes, I suppose so. I'll vouch for that Tokay you had today, at any rate. It's quite an exceptional vintage; an unusually good year—but I needn't tell *you* that!

FAT GENTLEMAN: I admit it had a most delicate bouquet.

HJALMAR (*diffidently*): Is there a difference in the years, then?

FAT GENTLEMAN (*laughing*): Come now! What a question!

WERLE (*smiles, to* HJALMAR): Fine wines are lost on you it seems!

BALD GENTLEMAN: Wines are like photographs, Mr. Ekdal—they both need sunshine. Or am I mistaken?

HJALMAR: No—light is certainly important.

MRS. SÖRBY: What about court chamberlains? I hear they thrive on sunshine too!

BALD GENTLEMAN: Such sarcasm! Is that kind?

NEARSIGHTED GENTLEMAN: Mrs. Sörby will have her joke, you know!

FAT GENTLEMAN: Yes! And at our expense! (*Wags his finger at her.*) Oh, Madam Bertha! Madam Bertha!

MRS. SÖRBY: Joking apart, however, Mr. Ekdal—wines differ greatly according to the year. Old vintages are nearly always best.

NEARSIGHTED GENTLEMAN: Am I an old vintage, Mrs. Sörby?

MRS. SÖRBY: Far from it, Excellency!

BALD GENTLEMAN: There! You see? How about me, dear Mrs. Sörby—?

FAT GENTLEMAN: And me! What would *my* vintage be?

MRS. SÖRBY: A most sweet vintage, Excellency! (*She sips her glass of punch. The men all laugh and flirt with her.*)

WERLE: Trust Mrs. Sörby to find a way out—when she wants to! Fill up your glasses, gentlemen! See to it, Pettersen—! Drink with me, Gregers, won't you? (GREGERS *doesn't move.*) And you, Ekdal—won't you join us? There was no opportunity to drink with you at dinner.

(GRAABERG, *the bookkeeper, sticks his head in at the baize door.*)

GRAABERG: Excuse me, sir. I'm afraid I can't get out—

WERLE: Have they locked you in again?

GRAABERG: I'm afraid so, sir—Flakstad went off with the keys.

WERLE: Never mind—come through this way.

GRAABERG: But—I'm not alone, sir; there are two of us, sir.

WERLE: It doesn't matter; come along! The two of you!

(GRAABERG *and* OLD EKDAL *come out of the office.*)

WERLE (*involuntarily*): Ugh!

(*The laughter and talk among the guests breaks off suddenly.* HJALMAR *starts at the sight of his father, puts down his glass and turns towards the fireplace.*)

EKDAL (*without looking up, makes little bows to right and left as he passes through, murmuring*): Excuse me. Came in the wrong way. Door was locked. Door locked. Excuse me. (*He and* GRAABERG *go into the inner room and off right.*)

WERLE (*between his teeth*): That blasted Graaberg!

GREGERS (*stares open-mouthed; to* HJALMAR): Surely—that couldn't have been—!

FAT GENTLEMAN: What's going on? Who *was* that?

GREGERS: Nobody; just the bookkeeper, and someone with him.

NEARSIGHTED GENTLEMAN (*to* HJALMAR): Who *was* that man? Did you know him?

HJALMAR: No—I don't know—I didn't notice—

FAT GENTLEMAN (*rising*): What the devil's happening? (*He joins another group, who are talking under their breath.*)

MRS. SÖRBY (*to* PETTERSEN *in a whisper*): Give him something to take home with him; something nice—you understand?

PETTERSEN (*nods*): I'll see to it. (*Goes out.*)

GREGERS (*softly, with emotion, to* HJALMAR): It really was he, then!

HJALMAR: Yes.

GREGERS: And you actually stood there and said you didn't know him!

HJALMAR (*in a vehement whisper*): But how could I—!

GREGERS: —acknowledge your own father?

HJALMAR (*miserably*): If you were in *my* place, you—

(*The conversation among the guests, which has been carried on in a low tone, now swells into forced joviality.*)

BALD GENTLEMAN (*in a friendly manner approaches* HJALMAR *and* GREGERS): Aha! Reminiscing about old days at college, eh? Don't you smoke, Mr. Ekdal? May I give you a light? Oh—but of course!—it's not allowed!

HJALMAR: Thank you—I don't think I—

FAT GENTLEMAN: How about reciting a poem for us, Mr. Ekdal? You used to be so good at it.

HJALMAR: I'm afraid I don't remember any.

FAT GENTLEMAN: What a pity! Well—what can we find to do, Balle? (*They move away and go into the other room.*)

HJALMAR (*gloomily*): I'm going, Gregers. When a man's been through what I've been through, you see— Say goodbye to your father for me.

GREGERS: Yes—of course. Do you think you'll go straight home?

HJALMAR: Yes—why do you ask?

GREGERS: I thought I might drop in a little later.

HJALMAR: No, don't do that—don't come to my place, Gregers; it's too sad and depressing there. Especially on top of all this splendour! We'll arrange to meet somewhere in town.

MRS. SÖRBY (*comes over to them and speaks in a low voice*): Are you going, Ekdal?

HJALMAR: Yes.

MRS. SÖRBY: Remember me to Gina.

HJALMAR: Thanks.

MRS. SÖRBY: Tell her I'll drop in one of these days.

HJALMAR: Thanks—I will. (*To* GREGERS) Don't come with me. I'll slip out without being seen. (*He strolls across the room, into the inner room, and out to the right.*)

MRS. SÖRBY (*in a low voice to* PETTERSEN, *who has returned*): Did you give the old man something?

PETTERSEN: A nice bottle of brandy, Madam.

MRS. SÖRBY: You might have thought of something better than that!

PETTERSEN: Oh, no, Mrs. Sörby! He'd rather have that than anything!

FAT GENTLEMAN (*in the doorway, with a sheet of music in his hand*): How about playing a duet, Mrs. Sörby?

MRS. SÖRBY: Yes! That would be delightful!

GUESTS: Bravo! Bravo! (*She joins the guests in the inner room and they all go out to the right.* GREGERS *remains standing by the fire-place.* WERLE *pretends to be looking for something on the desk and seems to want* GREGERS *to go;* GREGERS *doesn't move,* WERLE *goes toward the door.)*

GREGERS: Can you spare a moment, Father?

WERLE: Yes; what is it?

GREGERS: I'd like to talk to you.

WERLE: Can't it wait till we're alone?

GREGERS: No, it can't; we may never be alone again, you see.

WERLE *(comes toward him):* And what does *that* mean? *(During the following the sound of a piano is heard in the distance, from the music room.)*

GREGERS: Why has that family been allowed to go downhill like that?

WERLE: You're referring to the Ekdals, I presume.

GREGERS: Yes; I'm referring to the Ekdals. There was a time when you and Lieutenant Ekdal were close friends.

WERLE: Yes; too close for comfort—I've suffered for it for years. That friendship almost cost me my good name.

GREGERS: Was he the only guilty one? You're sure of that?

WERLE: What do you mean?

GREGERS: You were in that big timber deal together, weren't you?

WERLE: Ekdal was in charge of the entire transaction. He surveyed the land—he drew up the maps. How was I to know that they were fraudulent! He deliberately encroached on property belonging to the Government; he felled all that timber—acres of it!—belonging to the State. Lieutenant Ekdal acted entirely on his own responsibility. I never for a moment realized what he was up to.

GREGERS: Perhaps he didn't quite realize it himself.

WERLE: That may be. The fact remains that he was found guilty, and I was acquitted.

GREGERS: Yes; I know nothing was ever proved against you.

WERLE: An acquittal is an acquittal. But what makes you bring up that distressing business? God knows it turned my hair gray long before its time. Is that the kind of thing you've spent all these years brooding about up there? I assure you here in town it's been forgotten long ago—at least as far as *I'm* concerned.

GREGERS: But what about the Ekdals?

WERLE: What do you expect me to do for them? Ekdal came out of prison a broken man; he was beyond all help. There are certain people in this world who, given the slightest blow, dive straight to the bottom and never come up again. Believe me, Gregers, I did everything I could—short of exposing myself to suspicion and endless gossip—

GREGERS: Suspicion? Yes—I see.

WERLE: I've arranged for Ekdal to do some odd jobs for the office—copying and so forth—and I pay him ten times what the work is worth—

GREGERS (*without looking at him*): I don't doubt *that* for a moment.

WERLE: Why do you laugh? Do you think I'm not telling you the truth? I admit there's no record of it on the books; I never enter payments of that sort.

GREGERS (*with a cold smile*): You're very wise.

WERLE (*taken aback*): What do you mean?

GREGERS (*summoning up his courage*): How about the money you gave Hjalmar Ekdal to learn photography? Is *that* entered on the books?

WERLE: Entered—how? I don't—

GREGERS: I know now it was you who paid for his tuition; I also know that it was you who set him up in business.

WERLE: And you call that doing nothing for the Ekdals! Those people have cost me plenty, I assure you!

GREGERS: And are *those* expenses entered on the books?

WERLE: Why do you ask me that?

GREGERS: I have my reasons. Now, tell me: when you evinced this sudden interest in your old friend's son—it was just before his marriage, wasn't it?

WERLE: Good heavens! You don't expect me—after all, it's years ago—!

GREGERS: You wrote me a letter at that time—a business letter, naturally—and you mentioned briefly, in a postscript, that Hjalmar Ekdal had married a Miss Hansen.

WERLE: Quite right. That was her name.

GREGERS: But you omitted the fact that this Miss Hansen was *Gina* Hansen—our former housekeeper.

WERLE (*with a slightly forced laugh of derision*): It never occurred to me you were so interested in our former housekeeper.

GREGERS: You're right; I wasn't. But—(*Lowers his voice.*) I happen to know there were others in this house who were; *extremely* interested.

WERLE: What do you mean by that? (*Flaring up*) You're not referring to *me*, by any chance?

GREGERS (*softly but firmly*): But I *am* referring to you.

WERLE: How *dare* you! How dare you presume to—! I'll teach that photographer fellow—ungrateful wretch! Spreading lies about me—!

GREGERS: Hjalmar hasn't said a single word about it. I'm certain he hasn't the faintest suspicion of such a thing.

WERLE: Then where did you get it from? Who put such ideas into your head?

GREGERS: It was poor Mother; it was she who told me about it; the very last time I ever saw her.

WERLE: Your mother! Yes—of course. I might have known. You and she—! You always held together. She turned you against me from the start.

GREGERS: That's not true; it was because of all she suffered—all she had to bear; till she broke down and went utterly to pieces.

WERLE: Nonsense! She had no more to bear, and she suffered no more, than the majority of women. But it's impossible to deal with sickly, hysterical people—I've learned that to my cost!—How could you harbor these suspicions—how could you bring yourself to rake up all these malicious rumors against your own father, Gregers? I don't understand it. I should think at your age you could apply yourself to something more constructive.

GREGERS: It's about time, isn't it?

WERLE: It would do you good; I'm sure you'd feel much happier. What do you expect to accomplish up there at the Works, slaving away year after year at a routine office job? Refusing to accept a penny above the regular wages? It's sheer madness!

GREGERS: Yes; well—I'm not so sure of that.

WERLE: I understand your reasons well enough; you don't want to owe me anything; you want to be completely independent—Now, it so happens, an excellent opportunity has opened up; one that would give you complete independence—full authority.

GREGERS: Indeed? What kind of opportunity?

WERLE: In my last letter—when I said it was essential for you to come back home at once—

GREGERS: Yes; what had you in mind? I've been waiting all day for you to tell me.

WERLE: What I had in mind was this: I propose to offer you a partnership.

GREGERS: In *your* firm? A partnership with *you?*

WERLE: It needn't be too *close* a partnership; we wouldn't necessarily

have to work *together*. You could handle the business here, and I
would move up to the Works.

GREGERS: To the Works? *You?*

WERLE: Yes; I no longer have the strength I used to have. It's time I
started to let down a bit, you see. And I have to be careful of my
eyes—they've been bad lately; I've had a lot of trouble with
them.

GREGERS: That's nothing new; they've always troubled you.

WERLE: But not as they do now. There are other circumstances, too,
that make it advisable for me to move up there—for a while, at
any rate.

GREGERS: I certainly never expected anything like this.

WERLE: We've never been close—I know that, Gregers; but, after all,
we *are* father and son. There must be some way we can come to an
understanding.

GREGERS: In the eyes of the world, I suppose you mean.

WERLE: Well—at least that would be something, wouldn't it? Think
it over, Gregers. I'm sure we can manage it. Don't you agree?

GREGERS (*looks at him coldly*): What's your real motive in all this?

WERLE: My motive?

GREGERS: You're depending on me for something. You plan to make
use of me somehow.

WERLE: It's only natural for a father to depend upon his son.

GREGERS: Yes—so they say.

WERLE: I'm most anxious that you should stay home with me a little
while. I'm very lonely, Gregers. All my life I've been a lonely man
—and one feels it more as one gets older. I need someone near me
—someone who—

GREGERS: You have Mrs. Sörby, haven't you?

WERLE: That's true—I have; and I don't know what I'd do without
her. She's good-natured and intelligent; and she's so cheerful too—
that means a lot to me.

GREGERS: Then what more do you want?

WERLE: But it's an awkward situation—for her, I mean. I'm afraid it
can't go on much longer. It puts her in a false position—there
might be talk. And that kind of thing doesn't do a man any good
either.

GREGERS: I think you can afford to risk it! As long as you go on giving
the dinner parties you can give.

WERLE: But what about *her*, Gregers? I'm afraid she may find it impossible to accept the situation any longer. And even if her affection for me prompted her to stay—at the risk of talk and scandal and all the rest of it—would I be justified in—? You, with your high sense of integrity, tell me—?

GREGERS: You're thinking of marrying her, aren't you? Why not say so?

WERLE: And supposing I were? What then?

GREGERS: What then? Exactly!

WERLE: Would you be unalterably opposed to it?

GREGERS: By no means. Not at all.

WERLE: I wasn't sure. I thought perhaps—devotion to your mother's memory—

GREGERS: I'm not hysterical, you know.

WERLE: Well—whatever you may or may not be—you've taken a great weight off my mind. I'm delighted to know I can depend on your support.

GREGERS (*looks at him intently*): Of course! *That's* how you plan to use me!

WERLE: Use you, indeed! What an expression!

GREGERS: Don't let's be fussy in our choice of words—not when we're alone, at any rate. (*With a short laugh*) Yes! Now I see! That's why it was so absolutely essential for me to come back here. We are to play the "Happy Family" in Mrs. Sörby's honor! The devoted father and the loving son! A touching picture! A new experience, indeed!

WERLE: Don't take that tone with me!

GREGERS: When was there ever a "Happy Family" in this house I'd like to know? Never—so far as *I* remember! But your plans require something of the sort. It'll make such a good impression—won't it? The beloved son rushing home to attend his dear old father's wedding! And what of all those ugly rumors about the miseries and torments the first wife had to bear? It'd be the end of them, wouldn't it? They'd be wiped out once and for all—and by her own son too!

WERLE: I don't think there's a man living you hate as much as you hate me.

GREGERS (*softly*): I've seen you at close range.

WERLE: You've seen me through your mother's eyes. (*Lowers his voice a little.*) You should remember that those eyes were—shall we say "clouded," now and then?

GREGERS (*trembling*): I know what you're implying. But who was responsible for mother's tragic weakness? It was you, and all your —! The last of them being that woman you palmed off on Hjalmar Ekdal when you no longer—! Pah!

WERLE (*shrugs his shoulders*): I hear your mother in every word you say.

GREGERS (*takes no notice of him*): Yes! And he's there now—with that noble, trusting, childlike mind of his—living under the same roof with that degraded creature—quite unaware that what he calls his home is built on nothing but a lie! (*Comes a step nearer.*) When I look back on all the wicked things you've done, I feel as though I were gazing at some ghastly battlefield—strewn with shattered corpses!

WERLE: I'm afraid the gulf between us is too wide to bridge.

GREGERS (*bowing stiffly*): I share that opinion; so I shall take my hat and go.

WERLE: Go? Leave the house, you mean?

GREGERS: Yes. My purpose in life is clear to me at last.

WERLE: What purpose, may I ask?

GREGERS: You'd only laugh if I told you.

WERLE: I don't know, Gregers; a lonely man doesn't laugh so easily.

GREGERS (*points toward the inner room*): Look, Father! Your distinguished guests are playing blindman's buff with Mrs. Sörby—Good night and goodbye.

(*He goes out by the back to the right. Sounds of laughter and gay conversation from the guests, who are now seen in the inner room.*)

WERLE (*mutters contemptuously*): Ha—! He's not hysterical, eh? Poor fellow!

CURTAIN

ACT II

(SCENE: *Hjalmar Ekdal's studio. It is a good-sized room evidently on the top floor of the building. On the right a large studio window is let into the sloping roof; it is half covered by a blue curtain. In the right-hand corner at the back is the hall door. Farther downstage on the same side is a door leading to the sitting room. Two doors on the opposite side and between them an iron stove. At the back a wide double door with sliding panels. The studio is plainly but comfortably fitted out and furnished. Between the doors on the right, standing out a little from the wall, a sofa with a table and some chairs; on the table a lighted lamp with a shade; beside the stove an old armchair. Photographic instruments and equipment of different kinds lying about the room. Against the back wall, to the left of the double door, stands a bookcase containing a few books, boxes and bottles of chemicals, instruments, tools and other objects. Photographs and small articles such as camel's hair brushes, paper and so forth, lie on the table.*

GINA EKDAL *sits on a chair by the table sewing.* HEDVIG *is sitting on the sofa, with her hands shading her eyes and her thumbs in her ears, reading a book.)*

GINA *(glances at her a couple of times as if in secret anxiety)*: Hedvig!

*(*HEDVIG *doesn't hear her.)*

GINA *(louder)*: Hedvig!

HEDVIG *(takes away her hands and looks up)*: Yes, Mother?

GINA: You mustn't go on reading any longer, Hedvig dear.

HEDVIG: Oh, just a *little* longer, Mother! A *tiny* bit longer—please!

GINA: No; put your book down now—there's a good girl. Your father'd be angry. He never reads of an evening, you know.

HEDVIG *(closes the book)*: But Father doesn't care much for reading.

GINA *(lays aside her sewing and takes up a pencil and a little account book from the table)*: How much was the butter today—do you remember?

HEDVIG: One sixty-five.

GINA: That's right. *(Marks it down.)* We certainly use enough butter in this house! Then there was the sausage, and the cheese—let's see—*(Puts it down.)*—and then the ham—*(Adding up)* that comes to nearly—

HEDVIG: And don't forget the beer—

GINA: Oh, yes—of course. *(Puts it down.)* It mounts up all right! Well—it can't be helped!

HEDVIG: But since Father was out to dinner, we saved a bit on that.

GINA: Yes, that's true. And I took in eight fifty for those photographs.

HEDVIG: Did you? As much as that!

GINA: Yes; eight fifty exactly.

(*A pause.* GINA *picks up her sewing again.* HEDVIG *takes a pencil and a piece of paper and starts to draw, shading her eyes with her left hand.*)

HEDVIG: It's fun to think of Father at Mr. Werle's; at that grand dinner party—isn't it?

GINA: But it wasn't really Mr. Werle who invited him—it was his son. (*After a pause*) We don't have nothing to do with Mr. Werle.

HEDVIG: I do hope Father'll come home soon; I'm looking forward to it. He promised he'd ask Mrs. Sörby to give him something nice for me.

GINA: They've plenty of good things to spare in *that* house!

HEDVIG (*goes on drawing*): I'm beginning to be a bit hungry, too.

(OLD EKDAL *comes in by the hall door. He has a paper parcel under his arm, and another parcel in his coat pocket.*)

GINA: Why Grandfather! How late you are today!

EKDAL: They'd locked the office. Had to wait in Graaberg's room. Then had to go through—hm.

HEDVIG: Grandfather—did they give you some more copying to do?

EKDAL: All of this—look!

GINA: Good!

HEDVIG: And you've got a parcel in your pocket, too.

EKDAL: Never mind that! That's nothing. (*Puts his stick away in a corner.*) This'll keep me busy quite a while, Gina—eh? (*Opens one of the sliding panels in the back wall a little.*) Hush! (*Peeps inside the opening for a moment and slides the panel closed again.*) He-he! They've all gone to sleep together. And she's gone into her basket of her own accord. He-he!

HEDVIG: You're sure she's not cold in that basket, Grandfather?

EKDAL: What nonsense! Cold? In all that straw? (*He goes toward the farthest door on the left.*) Are there any matches in there?

GINA: On the chest of drawers.

(EKDAL *goes into his room.*)

HEDVIG: I'm glad Grandfather got all that copying to do.

GINA: Yes, poor old Grandfather. At least it'll mean a little pocket money for him.

HEDVIG: And it'll keep him from hanging round that horrid bar at Mrs. Eriksen's.

GINA: That's true, too.

HEDVIG: Do you suppose they're still sitting at the dinner table, Mother?

GINA: Lord knows; I shouldn't wonder.

HEDVIG: I expect Father's having some lovely things to eat! He'll be in an awfully jolly mood when he gets home. Don't you think so, Mother?

GINA: Yes. But I wish we could tell him that room was rented.

HEDVIG: Oh, we shan't need that this evening.

GINA: It'd be a real help, you know. And we don't use it.

HEDVIG: No—I meant we won't need it this evening, because he'll be in a good mood anyway. The news about the room'll come in handy another time.

GINA (*looks up at her*): You like having a bit of good news to tell your father, don't you?

HEDVIG: It makes things pleasanter.

GINA (*thinks this over*): There's something in that.

(OLD EKDAL *comes in again and starts towards the door down left.*)

GINA (*half turning in her chair*): Do you want anything in the kitchen, Grandfather?

EKDAL: I just want— No! Don't get up! (*Goes out.*)

GINA: I hope he won't go messing about the stove. (*Waits a moment.*) Better go and see what he's up to, Hedvig.

(EKDAL *comes in again carrying a small jug of steaming hot water.*)

HEDVIG: Did you go to get hot water, Grandfather?

EKDAL: I did—yes. Need it for something. Got to do some writing; ink's as thick as porridge—hm.

GINA: But you'll eat your supper first—won't you, Grandfather? It's in there ready for you.

EKDAL: Can't be bothered with supper, Gina. Busy, I tell you. Don't want anyone coming in my room—not anyone—hm. (*He goes into his room.* GINA *and* HEDVIG *look at each other.*)

GINA (*softly*): Wonder where he got the money.

HEDVIG: From Graaberg, I suppose.

GINA: No! Graaberg always sends *me* his money.

HEDVIG: Then he got it on credit, I expect.

GINA: Poor Grandfather, who'd give *him* credit?

(HJALMAR EKDAL, *wearing an overcoat and a gray felt hat, comes in from the hall door.*)

GINA (*throws down her sewing and rises*): Why, Hjalmar! Are you back so soon?

HEDVIG (*jumps up at the same time*): Fancy your being back already, Father!

HJALMAR (*taking off his hat*): Most of the guests were leaving.

HEDVIG: So early?

HJALMAR: Well—it was an early dinner, after all. (*Starts to take off his overcoat.*)

GINA: Let me help you.

HEDVIG: Me too!

(*They help him off with his coat;* GINA *hangs it up on a hook on the back wall.*)

HEDVIG: Were there a lot of people, Father?

HJALMAR: No, not many; about twelve or fourteen, I should think.

GINA: I suppose you had a chance to talk to all of them?

HJALMAR: Yes, of course. Though I must say Gregers took up most of my time.

GINA: Is he just as plain as ever?

HJALMAR: I can't say he's particularly handsome—Isn't the old man home yet?

HEDVIG: Yes; Grandfather's in his room. He's busy writing.

HJALMAR: Did he say anything?

GINA: What about?

HJALMAR: Then he didn't mention—? I heard something about his being with Graaberg, you see. I'll just look in on him a minute.

GINA: No—I don't think I'd do that—

HJALMAR: Why not? Did he say he didn't want to see me?

GINA: He doesn't want to see *anyone* this evening—

HEDVIG (*signaling*): Hm—hm!

GINA (*not noticing*): He fetched himself some hot water from the kitchen.

HJALMAR: You mean he's—?

GINA: Yes—I suppose so.

HJALMAR: Ah, well! Poor old man! My poor old father! Let him be— If it makes him a little happier—!

(OLD EKDAL, *in a dressing gown and smoking a pipe, comes in from his room.*)

EKDAL: Home, are you? Thought I heard your voice.

HJALMAR: I just got back.

EKDAL: You didn't see me, did you?

HJALMAR: No; but someone told me you'd passed through—; so I thought I'd come on after you.

EKDAL: Hm. Nice of you, Hjalmar— Who were all those people?

HJALMAR: Oh, I don't know—just people. There was Court Chamberlain Balle; and then there was Flor—and Kaspersen—they're court chamberlains too—honorary, of course. I don't remember all the others—but I know most of them had titles of some sort.

EKDAL: Titled people, eh? D'you hear that, Gina?

GINA: Yes. They're very grand over there these days.

HEDVIG: What did all these titled people do, Father? Did they sing— or give recitations?

HJALMAR: No; they just talked a lot of rubbish. They tried to persuade me to recite something—but, of course, I wouldn't hear of that.

EKDAL: Wouldn't hear of that, eh?

GINA: Oh—perhaps you should have, Hjalmar.

HJALMAR: Certainly not. One shouldn't cater to every Tom, Dick and Harry. (*Paces about the room.*) I don't intend to, anyhow.

EKDAL: No; Hjalmar's not that kind.

HJALMAR: I see no reason why I should be expected to entertain the guests, on the rare occasions when I go into Society. That's up to those other fellows; they spend their lives going from one dinner table to another, gorging and guzzling day in and day out. It's only right they should do something to earn all that good food they eat.

GINA: I hope you didn't tell them that!

HJALMAR (*humming*): Hm-hm-hm— I think I made my position clear.

EKDAL: To all those titled people, eh?

HJALMAR: Why not? (*Casually*) We also had a slight argument about Tokay.

EKDAL: Tokay! There's a fine wine!

HJALMAR: Yes—it *can* be. It's all according to the year, of course; vintages differ. It depends on the amount of sunshine the grapes have.

GINA: Hjalmar—I believe there's nothing you don't know!

EKDAL: They surely didn't dispute that?

HJALMAR: Oh—they tried to; but they were reminded that there was a difference in the vintage of court chamberlains too; their quality also varies according to the year—so they were told.

GINA: The things you think up, Hjalmar!

EKDAL: He-he! You really gave it to them, eh?

HJALMAR: Straight in their silly faces!

EKDAL: Hear that, Gina? All those titled people! Straight in their silly faces!

GINA: Straight in their silly faces! Fancy!

HJALMAR: I wouldn't want this to go any further, mind you. It's not right to repeat things like that; and it was all perfectly amicable, of course. They're nice friendly fellows; I wouldn't want to hurt their feelings.

EKDAL: But—straight in their silly faces, eh?

HEDVIG (*ingratiatingly*): It's nice to see you in a dinner jacket, Father. It's so becoming to you!

HJALMAR: It is, isn't it? This one fits beautifully—almost as if it had been made for me— A little tight in the armholes, perhaps. Here— help me, Hedvig. (*Takes off the dinner jacket.*) I'll put on my old house coat. Where is it, Gina?

GINA: Here it is. (*Brings him the coat and helps him on with it.*)

HJALMAR: There we are! See that Molvik gets his jacket back first thing in the morning.

GINA (*laying it away*): I'll see to it.

HJALMAR (*stretching himself*): Ah! That feels more comfortable! And, you know—I really think a loose, casual coat like this suits my figure even better. What do *you* think, Hedvig?

HEDVIG: Yes, Father—I believe you're right!

HJALMAR: Now—I'll tie my necktie in a loose knot, with flowing ends— There! See?

HEDVIG: That looks lovely with your mustache, and your long curly hair!

HJALMAR: I don't think I'd call it *curly*; wavy, perhaps.

HEDVIG: Yes. They're too big for curls.

HJALMAR: *Wavy*—definitely.

HEDVIG (*after a pause, tugs at his coat*): Father!

HJALMAR: Well—what is it?

HEDVIG: Oh! *You* know what it is!

HJALMAR: No, I don't—

HEDVIG (*half laughing, half whimpering*): Father—please don't tease me any longer!

HJALMAR: I don't know what you mean.

HEDVIG (*shaking him*): Of course you do! Oh, please, Father! Aren't you going to give them to me? All those nice things you promised to bring home?

HJALMAR: Good Lord!—I forgot about them!

HEDVIG: You're only teasing me! It's mean of you! Where are they?

HJALMAR: No, honestly—I really *did* forget. But, wait! I've brought you something else. (*He goes and looks in the pockets of the dinner jacket.*)

HEDVIG (*jumps up and down, clapping her hands*): Oh, Mother, Mother!

GINA: You see; if you're just patient—

HJALMAR (*with a piece of paper*): Look—here it is.

HEDVIG: This? But it's just a piece of paper.

HJALMAR: It's the bill of fare, that's what it is—the entire bill of fare. Do you see—it says here: menu? That means bill of fare.

HEDVIG: Is that really all you brought?

HJALMAR: I told you—I forgot. But you just take it from me—all these fancy dishes are greatly overrated. Now you sit at the table and study the bill of fare, and I'll tell you what all the dishes taste like. Won't that be fun?

HEDVIG (*gulping down her tears*): Thanks.

(*She sits down, but doesn't read the menu.* GINA *signals to her;* HJALMAR *sees her.*)

HJALMAR (*pacing up and down the room*): The head of the family is expected to think of everything—it's quite amazing! If by chance he forgets the slightest thing, he's immediately surrounded by glum faces. Well—one has to get used to it, I suppose. (*Stops by the stove near the old man.*) Have you taken a look in there this evening, Father?

EKDAL: You bet I have! She's in her basket!

HJALMAR: No! Is she really? Then she's beginning to get used to it.

EKDAL: Told you she would, didn't I? But there are still a couple of little things—

HJALMAR: A few improvements—yes.

EKDAL: They *must* be done, you know.

HJALMAR: Yes—let's just go over them. We'll sit here on the sofa.

EKDAL: All right. Hm. First I'll fill my pipe. Got to clean it, too. Hm. (*Goes into his room.*)

GINA (*smiles, to* HJALMAR): His pipe, indeed!

HJALMAR: Leave him alone, Gina—never mind! Poor wretched old man!— About those improvements—yes. I think I'll have a go at them tomorrow.

GINA: You won't have time tomorrow, Hjalmar.

HEDVIG: Oh yes he will, Mother!

GINA: Those prints have got to be retouched; they've sent for them several times, you know.

HJALMAR: Oh do stop nagging me about those prints! I'll get them done. Anything happen today? Any new orders?

GINA: No; I'm afraid not. I have those two sittings for tomorrow, though.

HJALMAR: And that's all, eh? Of course—if no one makes the smallest effort—

GINA: But what more can I do? I've advertised in several papers—all we could afford.

HJALMAR: Advertising! A lot of good *that* does! And what about the room? I suppose nothing's happened about that either?

GINA: Not yet, no.

HJALMAR: What else can one expect? Rooms don't rent themselves! Everything requires a little effort, Gina!

HEDVIG (*going toward him*): Would you like me to fetch your flute, Father?

HJALMAR: No thanks. No flute for me; no pleasures of any sort for me. (*Pacing about*) All I have to look forward to is *work*. As long as my strength holds out, I suppose I'll have to keep on working—!

GINA: Hjalmar dear—I didn't mean—

HEDVIG: Let me get you a nice bottle of beer, Father.

HJALMAR: No; not for me. I require nothing—(*Stops*) Beer?—Beer did you say?

HEDVIG (*cheerfully*): Yes, Father. Nice, cool beer.

HJALMAR: Oh, very well—if you insist; you might bring in a bottle.

GINA: Yes, do. That would be very nice.

(HEDVIG *runs toward the kitchen door.*)

HJALMAR (*by the stove, stops her, puts his arm round her and draws her to him*): Hedvig! Hedvig!

HEDVIG (*with tears of joy*): Dear, *darling* Father!

HJALMAR: No—don't call me that. I sat there at the rich man's table —stuffing myself at that festive board—and I couldn't even—!

GINA (*sitting at the table*): Oh, don't talk nonsense, Hjalmar!

HJALMAR: No—it's not nonsense! But don't be too hard on me. You know how much I love you—

HEDVIG (*throws her arms round him*): And we love you too, Father! More than we can ever say!

HJALMAR: And remember—if I'm difficult at times—it's because I have so many problems—so many cares. There, there! (*Dries his eyes.*) No! No beer at a time like this—give me my flute. (HEDVIG *runs to the bookshelf and fetches it.*) Thanks! There! That's right —my flute in my hand, and you two at my side—!

(HEDVIG *sits at the table near* GINA; HJALMAR *walks up and down and starts to play with gusto; it is a Bohemian peasant dance; his tempo is slow and plaintive and his attack highly sentimental. He breaks off in the middle of the tune, gives his left hand to* GINA *and says emotionally*) Our rooms may be poor and humble, Gina —but they're home all the same. And I can say from the bottom of my heart: it's good to be here!

(*He starts to play again; soon after there is a knock at the hall door.*)

GINA (*rises*): Just a minute, Hjalmar. I think there's someone at the door.

HJALMAR (*puts the flute back on the shelf*): What can it be? How tiresome!

(GINA *goes and opens the door.*)

GREGERS: Excuse me—

GINA (*takes a step back*): Oh!

GREGERS: Does Mr. Ekdal, the photographer, live here?

GINA: Yes, he does.

HJALMAR (*going toward the door*): Gregers! So you came after all. Well—come in then.

GREGERS (*coming in*): I said I'd come to see you.

HJALMAR: Yes, but this evening—? Did you leave the party?

GREGERS: Both the party and my father's house— Good evening; do you recognize me, Mrs. Ekdal?

GINA: It's not hard to recognize young Mr. Werle.

GREGERS: That's true—I'm very like my mother; you remember her, I expect?

HJALMAR: Left your father's house you say?

GREGERS: Yes; I've gone to a hotel.

HJALMAR: Have you really? Well—since you're here, sit down; take off your things.

GREGERS: Thanks. (*He takes off his overcoat. He has changed his clothes and now wears a plain tweed suit.*)

HJALMAR: Here—sit on the sofa. Make yourself at home.

(GREGERS *sits on the sofa,* HJALMAR *on a chair by the table.*)

GREGERS (*looking round*): So this is your home, Hjalmar. This is where you live.

HJALMAR: Yes; this is the studio, of course—

GINA: But it's such a nice large room—we nearly always sit here.

HJALMAR: We had a better place before; but this has great advantages; there's a lot of extra space—

GINA: And there's another room we can rent out—just down the passage.

GREGERS: Oh—you have lodgers then?

HJALMAR: Well—not just now. They're not so easy to find, you know; you have to keep your wits about you. (*To* HEDVIG) We might have that beer now. (HEDVIG *nods and goes out to the kitchen.*)

GREGERS: Is that your daughter?

HJALMAR: That's Hedvig, yes.

GREGERS: Is she your only child?

HJALMAR: Yes; she's the only one. She's our greatest joy, and— (*Lowers his voice.*) our greatest sorrow too.

GREGERS: How do you mean?

HJALMAR: She's in danger of losing her eyesight, you see.

GREGERS: Of going blind!

HJALMAR: Yes; so far her eyes are not too seriously affected, and they may continue to be all right for a while; but eventually, the doctor says, it's bound to come.

GREGERS: What a dreadful thing! Has he any idea what caused it?

HJALMAR (*sighs*): It may be hereditary, he thinks.

GREGERS (*with a slight start*): Hereditary?

GINA: Hjalmar's mother's eyes were bad, you see.

HJALMAR: So Father says; I don't remember her.

GREGERS: Poor child!—How does she take it?

HJALMAR: We naturally haven't told her anything about it; she suspects nothing. She's like a gay, carefree little bird, twittering away as it flutters toward the inevitable darkness. (*Overcome*) It's a terrible grief for me; it's heartbreaking to think of, Gregers. (HEDVIG *brings in a tray with beer and glasses and puts it on the table.*)

HJALMAR (*stroking her hair*): Thank you, Hedvig, thank you! (HEDVIG *puts her arm round his neck and whispers in his ear.*)

HJALMAR: No—no sandwiches now. (*Looks at* GREGERS.) Unless you'd like one, Gregers?

GREGERS (*with a gesture of refusal*): No—no thank you.

HJALMAR (*still melancholy*): You might bring a few anyway—especially if there's a nice crusty piece of bread. And don't spare the butter, will you? (HEDVIG *nods gaily and goes out to the kitchen.*)

GREGERS (*who has been following her with his eyes*): She seems so strong and healthy otherwise.

GINA: There's nothing wrong with her apart from that, thank goodness.

GREGERS: She'll grow up to look like you—don't you think so, Mrs. Ekdal? How old is she now?

GINA: Nearly fourteen; her birthday's the day after tomorrow.

GREGERS: Tall for her age, isn't she?

GINA: She's shot up very fast in the past year.

GREGERS: It makes one feel old to see the youngsters growing up. How long is it now since you were married?

GINA: Let's see—we've been married nearly fifteen years.

GREGERS: Really! Is it as long as that?

GINA (*becoming attentive; looks at him*): It is indeed.

HJALMAR: That's right. Fifteen years—all but a few months. (*Changing the subject*) They must have been long years for you, Gregers—up there at the Works.

GREGERS: They seemed long at the time; yet in looking back at them, they went by very quickly.

(OLD EKDAL *comes in from his room, without his pipe, but wearing his old military cap; his walk is a bit unsteady.*)

EKDAL: All right, Hjalmar my boy—I'm ready now to talk about those—hm. What was it we were supposed to talk about?

HJALMAR (*goes to him*): Father—we have a visitor; Gregers Werle —I don't know if you remember him—

EKDAL (*looks at* GREGERS, *who has risen*): Werle? The son is it? What does he want with me?

HJALMAR: Nothing; he came to see me, Father.

EKDAL: Oh. Then there's nothing wrong?

HJALMAR: Of course not.

EKDAL (*waves his arms*): Not that I'm afraid, you know—but—

GREGERS (*goes over to him*): I bring you greetings from your old hunting grounds, Lieutenant Ekdal.

EKDAL: Hunting grounds?

GREGERS: Yes—up by the Höjdal Works; remember?

EKDAL: Oh, up there. I was well known in those parts once.

GREGERS: You were a mighty hunter in those days.

EKDAL: I was; that's true enough! You're looking at my cap, I see. I ask no one's permission to wear it in the house. As long as I don't walk about the streets in it—

(HEDVIG *brings in a plate of sandwiches and sets it on the table.*)

HJALMAR: Sit down, Father; have a glass of beer. Help yourself, Gregers.

(EKDAL *mutters something and stumbles over to the sofa,* GREGERS *sits on the chair nearest to him, and* HJALMAR *on the other side of*

GREGERS. GINA *sits slightly away from the table with her sewing;*
HEDVIG *stands by her father.*)

GREGERS: Do you remember, Lieutenant Ekdal, how Hjalmar and I
used to come up and visit you—in the summer, and at Christmas?

EKDAL: Did you? No—I don't remember that. Yes—I was a mighty
hunter in my day. Shot bears too. Nine of them.

GREGERS (*looks at him sympathetically*): I suppose you don't go
hunting any more.

EKDAL: I wouldn't say that, my friend. I still get a bit of hunting now
and then. Not *that* kind, of course. For the forest, you see—the
forest—! (*Drinks.*) Is the forest up there just as fine as ever?

GREGERS: Not as fine as it was in your time. It's been thinned out
quite a bit.

EKDAL: Thinned out, eh? (*Softly, as though afraid*) That's a dangerous business. That brings trouble. The forest takes revenge, you
see.

HJALMAR (*filling his glass*): Have a little more, Father.

GREGERS: It must be hard on a man like you—a man used to the open
—to live in a stuffy town, cooped up in a little room—

EKDAL (*laughs and glances at* HJALMAR): Oh, it's really not so bad
here. No. Not bad at all.

GREGERS: But don't you miss the open spaces—the cool sweep of the
wind through the trees—and all the animals and birds—?

EKDAL (*smiles*): Let's show it to him, Hjalmar.

HJALMAR (*hastily, with some embarrassment*): No—not this evening, Father.

GREGERS: What is it he wants to show me?

HJALMAR: Oh, nothing—you can see it some other time.

GREGERS (*goes on talking to the old man*): Do you know what I was
thinking, Lieutenant Ekdal? Why don't you come up to the
Works with me? I expect to be going back there soon. They'll have
plenty of copying for you to do up there, I'm sure. This is no place
for you. You've nothing here to cheer you up—or keep you
interested.

EKDAL (*looks at him in amazement*): Nothing here to keep me—!

GREGERS: You have Hjalmar here I know; but he has his own work to
attend to. And a man like you—accustomed to an active outdoor
life—

EKDAL (*thumps the table*): Hjalmar—he's *got* to see it!

HJALMAR: This is a bad time, Father: It's dark, remember—

EKDAL: Nonsense! There's the moonlight, isn't there? (*Rises.*) I tell you he *must* see it! Let me get by. Hjalmar—come and help me!

HEDVIG: Yes—*do,* Father!

HJALMAR (*rising*): Oh—very well.

GREGERS (*to* GINA): What can it be?

GINA: It's nothing very wonderful—!

(EKDAL *and* HJALMAR *have gone to the back wall and each opens his side of the sliding door.* HEDVIG *helps the old man;* GREGERS *remains standing by the sofa;* GINA *continues sewing undisturbed. Through the opening one sees a large, deep, irregularly shaped attic, filled with nooks and corners; a couple of stovepipes run through it from the rooms below. There are skylights through which the moon shines brightly on parts of the big room—while other parts are in deep shadow.*)

EKDAL (*to* GREGERS): Come closer, if you like.

GREGERS (*going over to them*): What is it I'm supposed to see?

EKDAL: Take a good look now! Hm.

HJALMAR (*somewhat embarrassed*): All this belongs to Father—you realize that, of course.

GREGERS (*at the opening peers into the attic*): Oh! I *see,* Lieutenant Ekdal—you keep poultry!

EKDAL: I should say we *do* keep poultry! They've gone to roost now—but you should see our hens by daylight!

HEDVIG: And then there's—

EKDAL: Sh! Not a word about that yet!

GREGERS: And I see doves there, too.

EKDAL: Yes! There are doves there right enough! Their nesting boxes are up under the eaves. Doves like to roost high, you know.

HJALMAR: They're not a common variety, by any means; at least not all of them.

EKDAL: Common! No indeed! We have tumblers—and a pair of pouters too. And now—look here! You see that hutch over by the wall?

GREGERS: What's that used for?

EKDAL: That, Sir, is where the rabbits sleep at night.

GREGERS: Then you have rabbits, too?

EKDAL: I should damn well say we *do* have rabbits! He wants to know if we have rabbits, Hjalmar! Hm. But just you wait! We're coming to the *real* thing now! Out of the way, Hedvig! Now you stand here—that's it. And look down there— Do you see a basket there with straw in it?

GREGERS: Yes—and isn't there a bird there, too?

EKDAL: Hm. "A bird," he says—!

GREGERS: It's a duck, isn't it?

EKDAL (*annoyed*): Yes—it's a duck; that's clear!

HJALMAR: But what *kind* of a duck do you think?

HEDVIG: It's not just an *ordinary* duck, you know—

EKDAL: Sh!

GREGERS: And it doesn't look like a Muscovy duck, either.

EKDAL: No—it's no Muscovy duck, dear Mr. Werle. It happens to be a *wild* duck, you see.

GREGERS: A wild duck! Is it really?

EKDAL: That's what it is! That "bird," as you called it, that is the wild duck. It's our wild duck, Sir.

HEDVIG: *My* wild duck. It belongs to me.

GREGERS: How does it manage in there? Is it all right?

EKDAL: It has its own trough of water, of course, to splash about in.

HJALMAR: And we change the water every other day.

GINA (*turning toward* HJALMAR): It's getting to be freezing in here, Hjalmar dear.

HJALMAR: Let's close her up, then. Anyway—they don't like to be disturbed at night. Go on, Hedvig—close her up!

(HJALMAR *and* HEDVIG *close the sliding doors.*)

EKDAL: You'll be able to see her better some other time. (*Sits in the armchair by the stove.*) Remarkable creatures those wild ducks, I can tell you!

GREGERS: How did you manage to catch it, Lieutenant Ekdal?

EKDAL: I didn't catch it myself. There's a certain man here in town, you see—we have him to thank for that.

GREGERS (*with a slight start*): That man wasn't my father, by any chance?

EKDAL: Your father—that's it; he's the man. Hm.

HJALMAR: Strange that you should guess that, Gregers!

GREGERS: You were telling me how much you owed to Father—in many different ways, you said; so I thought, perhaps—

GINA: But Mr. Werle didn't actually give us the duck himself—

EKDAL: Still, Gina—Haakon Werle is the man we have to thank for her. (*To* GREGERS) He was out shooting in a boat. He fired at her and brought her down. But his sight isn't too good now, you see— and so he only winged her. Hm.

GREGERS: But she was wounded, I suppose?

HJALMAR: Oh yes—she had some shot in her.

HEDVIG: Her wing was broken, poor thing; she couldn't fly.

GREGERS: Did she dive to the bottom then?

EKDAL (*sleepily, with thickened speech*): Course she did! Always do that—wild ducks do. Make straight for the bottom—as far as they can go. Then they get trapped down there among the slimy roots and tangled reeds—and they never come up again.

GREGERS: But *your* wild duck came up again, Lieutenant Ekdal.

EKDAL: Had an amazingly clever dog, your father had. That dog—he dived down after her and brought her back.

GREGERS (*turning to* HJALMAR): And then they gave her to you?

HJALMAR: No; not at once. First they took her to your father's house; but she started to pine away—so Pettersen was told to put an end to her—

EKDAL (*half asleep*): That ass Pettersen—hm—

HJALMAR (*lowers his voice*): And that's how we happened to get hold of her. Father knows Pettersen quite well, so when he heard about the wild duck he persuaded him to let *us* have her.

GREGERS: And the attic seems to agree with her, does it? She's doing well in there?

HJALMAR: Remarkably well—amazing, isn't it? She's grown quite plump, and she doesn't seem to miss her freedom. She's been there some time now, and I suppose she's forgotten all about it; that's what counts, you know.

GREGERS: I expect you're right; as long as she's kept away from the sky and the water—and has nothing to remind her— But I must be going now. Your father's gone to sleep, I think.

HJALMAR: Don't go on that account—

GREGERS: Oh, by the way—did you say you had an extra room? A room to rent, I mean?

HJALMAR: Yes, we have. Do you know anyone who—?

GREGERS: Would you let me have it?

HJALMAR: You?

GINA: Oh no, Mr. Werle, you—

GREGERS: If so, I'll move in first thing tomorrow morning.

HJALMAR: We'd be delighted!

GINA: But, Mr. Werle—it's not *your* kind of room—*really* it's not!

HJALMAR: What are you talking about, Gina?

GINA: I mean—it wouldn't be big enough, or light enough—

GREGERS: That doesn't matter, Mrs. Ekdal.

HJALMAR: It seems like a very nice room to me! And not badly furnished either.

GINA: How about those two fellows underneath?

GREGERS: What fellows?

GINA: There's one that says he's been a tutor—

HJALMAR: That's Molvik—Mr. Molvik—a B.A.

GINA: And the other one calls himself a doctor; his name's Relling.

GREGERS: Relling? I think I know him slightly. He had a practice up at Höjdal for a while.

GINA: Well—they're a no-good, rowdy lot! Out till all hours every night—drinking themselves silly—

GREGERS: I shan't mind them; I'll soon get used to it. I'll try to be as adaptable as the wild duck—

GINA: All the same—you'd better sleep on it.

GREGERS: You don't seem very anxious to have me as a lodger, Mrs. Ekdal.

GINA: Who, *me*? Why do you say that?

HJALMAR: I must say, Gina—you're being very odd about it. (*To* GREGERS) You plan to stay in town then—for the present?

GREGERS: That's what I've decided, yes.

HJALMAR: Not at your father's house, though? What do you plan to do?

GREGERS: I only wish I knew. When one has the misfortune to bear the name of "Gregers," followed by the name of "Werle"—a pretty hideous combination, don't you think?

HJALMAR: I don't think so at all.

GREGERS: Pah! I'd feel like spitting on a man with a name like that! But since I'm doomed to go on being Gregers Werle in this world—

HJALMAR (*laughs*): Ha! Ha! Well—if you weren't Gregers Werle, what would you choose to be?

GREGERS: I think I'd choose to be a clever dog.

GINA: A dog!

HEDVIG (*involuntarily*): Oh, no!

GREGERS: Yes, a very clever dog; the kind that plunges after wild ducks when they dive to the bottom, and get trapped down in the mud.

HJALMAR: That's beyond me, Gregers! What *are* you driving at?

GREGERS: Just nonsense; never mind. I'll move in early tomorrow morning then. (*To* GINA) I won't be any trouble; I'm used to doing things myself. (*To* HJALMAR) We'll discuss details to-morrow— Good night, Mrs. Ekdal. (*Nods to* HEDVIG.) Good night!

GINA: Good night, Mr. Werle.

HEDVIG: Good night.

HJALMAR (*who has lighted a candle*): Wait; I'll see you out. The stairs are rather dark.

(GREGERS *and* HJALMAR *go out by the hall door.*)

GINA (*sits with her sewing in her lap gazing before her*): What a queer thing to say—that he'd like to be a dog.

HEDVIG: You know, Mother—I think he really meant something quite different.

GINA: What else *could* he have meant?

HEDVIG: I don't know; but it's almost as though everything he said *really* meant something different.

GINA: Do you think so? Well—it seems very queer to me.

HJALMAR (*comes back*): The lamp down in the hall was still alight. (*Blows out the candle and puts it down.*) Ah! Now, perhaps we can have a bite to eat! (*Starts to eat the sandwiches.*) You see, Gina, what happens when you keep your wits about you—?

GINA: What do you mean—"wits about you"?

HJALMAR: We rented the room, didn't we? And to an old friend like Gregers, too.

GINA: I don't know what to think of that.

HEDVIG: It'll be fun, Mother—you'll see!

HJALMAR: You really are amazing! I thought you were so hipped on renting it—and now you behave as if you didn't want to.

GINA: If it had only been to someone else— What will Mr. Werle say I wonder.

HJALMAR: Old Werle? It's no business of his.

GINA: I expect they've been quarreling again; otherwise young Werle would never have left home. You know they've never been able to get on together.

HJALMAR: That may be, but still—

GINA: You never know; Mr. Werle may think it's all your doing.

HJALMAR: Well—let him! Mr. Werle's done a lot for me—God knows I'm the first one to admit it—but he can't expect me to go on kowtowing to him for ever!

GINA: But—Hjalmar dear—he might take it out on Grandfather; he might tell Graaberg not to give him any more copying to do.

HJALMAR: I could almost say: I wish he would! You don't seem to understand how humiliating it is for a man like me to see his old father treated like a servant. But some day the pendulum will swing the other way; it won't be long now—I feel it! (*Takes another sandwich.*) I have a sacred duty in life, and I intend to perform it to the full!

HEDVIG: You will, Father! I know you will!

GINA: Hush! Don't wake him!

HJALMAR (*lowers his voice*): To the *full*, I say! There'll come a day when— That's another reason why I'm glad we've rented the room, you see. It'll make me a bit more independent. A man needs independence if he's to face the task I have to face. (*By the armchair; with emotion*) Poor white-haired old man!—Don't you be afraid—lean on your Hjalmar; his shoulders are broad. They're strong, at any rate. One of these fine days you'll wake up to see— (*To* GINA) Don't you believe me?

GINA (*rising*): Yes, of course I do. But let's get him to bed.

HJALMAR: Yes—very well.

(*They lift up the old man carefully.*)

CURTAIN

❧

ACT III

(SCENE: *Hjalmar Ekdal's studio. It is morning; daylight streams through the large window in the slanting roof, and the curtain is drawn back.* HJALMAR *sits at the table busy retouching a photograph; several others lie before him. After a few moments* GINA *comes in through the hall door, wearing a hat and coat and with a basket on her arm.*)

HJALMAR: Back already, Gina?

GINA: Yes; I've no time for dawdling.

HJALMAR: Did you look in at Gregers?

GINA: I certainly did! You should just see the mess in there! He's made a good start, he has!

HJALMAR: Why? What's he done?

GINA: Used to doing things for himself, says he! So he lights the stove, but leaves the damper shut: the whole room's filled with smoke. The smell in there's enough to—

HJALMAR: Oh, dear!

GINA: But that isn't the worst of it: he decides to put the fire *out* again; so what does he do but take the pitcher from his washstand and empty every blessed drop of water right into the stove! The floor's a mess!

HJALMAR: What a nuisance.

GINA: I got the porter's wife to come and clean it up for him—the pig! But it'll be afternoon before the place is fit to live in.

HJALMAR: What's Gregers doing now?

GINA: He went out for a bit.

HJALMAR: While you were gone, I stopped in to see him too.

GINA: I know; you've asked him to lunch, I hear.

HJALMAR: Not *lunch* exactly—more of a snack, you know. After all, it's his first day here—I didn't know what else to do. You must have something in the house.

GINA: I'll have to try and find something, I suppose.

HJALMAR: Don't be *too* skimpy, though. Relling and Molvik are coming too, I think. I ran into Relling on the stairs, and I couldn't very well—

GINA: Oh dear! Do we have to have *them* too?

HJALMAR: Good heavens—one more or less—what difference does it make?

EKDAL (*opens his door and looks in*): Look here, Hjalmar—(*Sees* GINA.) Oh.

GINA: Anything you want, Grandfather?

EKDAL: No, no. It doesn't matter. Hm! (*Goes into his room again.*)

GINA (*picking up her basket*): Don't let him go out will you? Keep an eye on him.

HJALMAR: All right, all right—I will. Oh, Gina; some herring salad might be just the thing: Relling and Molvik were on a bit of a spree last night.

GINA: Just so long as they don't get here before I'm ready.

HJALMAR: Of course they won't. Just take your time.

GINA: Very well; meanwhile you can get a bit of work done.

HJALMAR: Work! I *am* working, aren't I? What more can I do?

GINA: I just meant—the sooner you get it done, the sooner it'll be over with. (*She takes the basket and goes out to the kitchen.* HJALMAR *sits for a few moments working reluctantly on the photograph.*)

EKDAL (*peeps in, looks round the studio, and says softly*): Are you busy, Hjalmar?

HJALMAR: Slaving away at these blasted pictures—!

EKDAL: Well—never mind; as long as you're busy—Hm! (*He goes into his room again but leaves the door open.*)

HJALMAR (*goes on working for some time in silence, then lays down his brush and goes over to the open door*): Are *you* busy, Father?

EKDAL (*in a low growl, from his room*): If *you're* busy then *I'm* busy too. Hm.

HJALMAR: Yes; very well. (*Goes back to his work*).

EKDAL (*presently, coming to the door again*): Hm. Hjalmar, I'm not as busy as all *that*, you know.

HJALMAR: I thought you were writing.

EKDAL: To hell with it! It's not a matter of life and death, after all. It won't hurt Graaberg to wait a day or two.

HJALMAR: No; and you're not his slave, either.

EKDAL: There's that job in there, you see—

HJALMAR: Just what *I* was thinking of. Would you like to go in? I'll open up for you.

EKDAL: It mightn't be a bad idea.

HJALMAR (*rises*): Then we'd have it all done, wouldn't we?

EKDAL: And we've got to finish it before tomorrow morning. It *is* tomorrow, isn't it? Hm?

HJALMAR: Of course it's tomorrow.

(HJALMAR *and* EKDAL *each pull open a side of the sliding door. Inside the attic the morning sun pours through the skylights; some doves are flying about, others sit cooing on their perches; the clucking of hens can be heard farther back in the attic.*)

HJALMAR: There! Now you can get to work, Father.

EKDAL (*goes into the attic*): Aren't you coming too?

HJALMAR: Well, you know—Yes! I believe I— (*Sees* GINA *at the kitchen door.*) No, no! I can't—haven't time! Too much work to do! How about our new invention, though? (*He pulls a cord and a curtain drops inside the opening; the lower part consists of an old piece of sailcloth, the upper part of a piece of fishing net. The floor of the attic is now concealed.*) There! Now perhaps I can have a little peace!

GINA: Must he go messing about in there again?

HJALMAR: Would you rather he'd run off to Mrs. Eriksen's? (*Sits down.*) What is it you want? I thought you said—

GINA: I wanted to ask—will it be all right to lay the table for lunch in here?

HJALMAR: Why not? There aren't any appointments, are there?

GINA: Just that engaged couple; you know—the two that want to be photographed together.

HJALMAR: Why the devil can't they be photographed together some *other* day?

GINA: It's all right, Hjalmar dear. I told them to come in the late afternoon; you'll be taking your nap by then.

HJALMAR: That's good; we'll eat in here then.

GINA: Very well; but there's no hurry—you can go on using the table for a good while yet.

HJALMAR: I'm using it—don't worry! I'm using it for all I'm worth!

GINA: Then, later on—you'll be free, you see. (*She goes into the kitchen. A short pause.*)

EKDAL (*in the doorway of the attic, behind the net*): Hjalmar!

HJALMAR: Well?

EKDAL: Afraid we'll have to move that water trough—

HJALMAR: I said so all along.

EKDAL: Hm-hm-hm. (*Goes away from the door again.* HJALMAR *goes on working a little, then glances toward the attic and starts to rise.* HEDVIG *comes in from the kitchen.*)

HJALMAR (*sits down again hurriedly*): What do you want?

HEDVIG: Just to be with you, Father.

HJALMAR: What are you snooping about in here for? Were you told to keep an eye on me?

HEDVIG: Of course not.

HJALMAR: What's your mother up to now?

HEDVIG: She's busy making the herring salad. (*Goes over to the table.*) Father—isn't there anything I can do to help?

HJALMAR: No, no. I'll carry on alone as long as my strength holds out. Never you fear, Hedvig; while your father keeps his health—

HEDVIG: Father! I won't have you say such awful things! (*She wanders about the room a little, stops by the doorway, and looks into the attic.*)

HJALMAR: What's he doing? Can you see?

HEDVIG: Making a new runway to the water trough, I think.

HJALMAR: He'll never manage that alone! And here I have to sit—*chained* to this—!

HEDVIG (*goes to him*): Give me the brush, Father. I do it quite well, you know.

HJALMAR: Nonsense! You'd only hurt your eyes.

HEDVIG: No, I wouldn't—really! Please give me the brush.

HJALMAR (*rises*): It'll only take a minute—

HEDVIG: What's the harm, then? (*Takes the brush.*) There! (*Sits down.*) I'll use this one as a model.

HJALMAR: Don't strain your eyes, do you hear? And remember, I'm not responsible; you're doing this on your own responsibility you understand!

HEDVIG (*starts retouching*): Of course.

HJALMAR: You're very good at it. I'll only be a minute. (*He slips through the side of the curtain into the attic.* HEDVIG *sits at her work.* HJALMAR *and* EKDAL *are heard arguing.*)

HJALMAR (*appears behind the net*): Hedvig—would you hand me those pincers on the shelf; and the chisel, too. (*Turning back to the attic*) You'll see, Father— Now just let me show you what I mean! (HEDVIG *has fetched the tools from the shelf and hands them in to him.*) Thanks. It's a good thing I got here when I did! (*Goes away from the opening; they can be heard carpentering and talking inside.* HEDVIG *stands watching them. A moment later there's a knock at the hall door; she doesn't hear it.*)

GREGERS (*bareheaded and without an overcoat comes in and stops near the door*): Hm—!

HEDVIG (*turns and goes toward him*): Good morning. Do come in.

GREGERS: Thanks. (*Looks toward the attic.*) Have you workmen in the house?

HEDVIG: No; it's only Father and Grandfather. I'll call them.

GREGERS: No, don't. I'd rather wait a little. (*Sits down on the sofa.*)

HEDVIG: It's so untidy here— (*Starts clearing away the photographs.*)

GREGERS: Never mind—don't bother! Are those the prints that need retouching?

HEDVIG: Yes; I was just helping Father with them.

GREGERS: Don't let me disturb you.

HEDVIG: No—you won't. (*She gathers the things together and sits down to work;* GREGERS *watches her in silence.*)

GREGERS: Did the wild duck sleep well last night?

HEDVIG: Yes, thank you; I think so.

GREGERS (*turning and looking toward the attic*): How different it looks by day; quite different than by moonlight.

HEDVIG: Yes—it changes all the time. In the morning it's not a bit the same as it is in the afternoon; and it looks quite different on rainy days from the way it looks when the sun shines.

GREGERS: You've noticed that, have you?

HEDVIG: Of course; how could I help it?

GREGERS: Do you spend much time in there with the wild duck?

HEDVIG: I go in whenever I can manage it—

GREGERS: I expect you're pretty busy. You go to school, I suppose?

HEDVIG: No—not any more; Father's afraid I'll hurt my eyes.

GREGERS: Does he give you lessons himself then?

HEDVIG: He promised to; but so far he hasn't had time.

GREGERS: Is there nobody else who could help you with your studies?

HEDVIG: There's Mr. Molvik; but he's not always—

GREGERS: Sober, you mean?

HEDVIG: Yes—I suppose that's it.

GREGERS: Then you've a good deal of spare time, haven't you? I should think it must be a world all to itself in there.

HEDVIG: Oh, it is! And it's full of the most wonderful things too!

GREGERS: Is it really?

HEDVIG: Yes. There are great big cupboards filled with books; and lots of them have pictures in them.

GREGERS: Aha!

HEDVIG: And there's an old desk with drawers and pigeon-holes; and a great big clock with figures that used to pop in and out. But the clock's stopped—so they don't work any more.

GREGERS: Time has ceased to exist in the wild duck's world.

HEDVIG: And there's an old paintbox too—and lots of other things; and all the books, of course.

GREGERS: And you read the books, I suppose?

HEDVIG: Whenever I can I do. But most of them are in English, and I don't understand English, you see. Still—I look at the pictures. There's one very large book—*Harrison's History of London* it's called—it must be a hundred years old, I should think. That has lots of pictures in it. On the front page there's a picture of death holding an hourglass—and he has a lady with him. That one's horrid, I think. But there are heaps of others; pictures of churches, and castles, and streets, and great ships sailing on the sea.

GREGERS: Where did all these wonderful things come from?

HEDVIG: An old sea captain lived here once, and he must have brought them home with him. They used to call him "The Flying Dutchman"; and that was funny, because he wasn't Dutch at all, you know.

GREGERS: Wasn't he?

HEDVIG: No. Then he went away, and never came back—and the things just stayed here.

GREGERS: Tell me—when you sit in there looking at those pictures—

don't you ever long to travel, and see something of the world yourself?

HEDVIG: Oh, no! I want to stay home always and help Father and Mother.

GREGERS: To retouch photographs?

HEDVIG: No—not only that. Do you know what I'd *really* like to do? I'd like to learn engraving; then I could make pictures like the ones in all those books.

GREGERS: Hm. What does your father say to that?

HEDVIG: He doesn't like the idea at all; Father's funny in some ways. He keeps talking about my learning basket weaving and wickerwork! I don't think that'd be much fun, do you?

GREGERS: No—I shouldn't think so.

HEDVIG: Still—in a way he's right; he says if I'd learned basketwork I could have made the wild duck its new basket.

GREGERS: That's true enough; you'd have been the logical one to do it, after all.

HEDVIG: Yes—because it's *my* wild duck, you see.

GREGERS: Of course it is.

HEDVIG: Yes, it belongs to me. But when Father and Grandfather want it, I don't mind lending it to them, you know.

GREGERS: What do they do with it?

HEDVIG: Oh, they look after it, and build things for it; all that sort of thing.

GREGERS: I'm not surprised; she's the most important creature in there!

HEDVIG: Indeed she is! After all, she's a *real* wild bird. And it must be so sad for her to be there all by herself.

GREGERS: She has no family, like the rabbits—

HEDVIG: No. And the hens, too; lots of them were hatched at the same time and were little chicks together. But she has no one belonging to her, poor thing. She's a complete stranger; no one knows where she came from—no one knows anything about her.

GREGERS: And then, too—she was rescued from the boundless deep, remember!

HEDVIG (*glances at him swiftly and represses a smile*): What makes you call it the boundless deep?

GREGERS: What would you have me call it?

HEDVIG: Most people would say "from under the water" or "from the bottom of the sea."

GREGERS: But *I* prefer the boundless deep.

HEDVIG: It sounds funny to hear somebody else say that.

GREGERS: Why? What do you mean?

HEDVIG: Nothing. You'd only laugh at me.

GREGERS: Of course I wouldn't. Tell me—what made you smile? Go on!

HEDVIG: It's just that whenever I think of that place in there—suddenly—unexpectedly, you know—I think of it as the boundless deep. It *feels* like that, somehow. You must think me awfully silly!

GREGERS: No—don't say that!

HEDVIG: After all—it's only an old attic.

GREGERS (*looks at her intently*): Are you so sure?

HEDVIG (*astonished*): That it's an attic?

GREGERS: Yes. How can you be so certain?

   (HEDVIG *is silent and looks at him open-mouthed.* GINA *comes in from the kitchen with a tablecloth.*)

GREGERS (*rising*): I'm afraid I came too early.

GINA: You have to be somewhere, I suppose. We're nearly ready now. Clear off the table, Hedvig.

   (HEDVIG *obeys; she and* GINA *lay the table during the following.* GREGERS *sits in the armchair looking through a photograph album.*)

GREGERS: I hear you've done quite a bit of retouching, Mrs. Ekdal.

GINA (*with a sidelong glance*): Yes, I have.

GREGERS: A lucky coincidence, wasn't it?

GINA: Why lucky?

GREGERS: Since Hjalmar's a photographer, I mean.

HEDVIG: And Mother can take pictures too.

GINA: I more or less *had* to take it up.

GREGERS: Then I suppose it's you who really runs the business?

GINA: When Hjalmar has too many other things to do, I—

GREGERS: I dare say his father takes up a good deal of his time.

GINA: Yes; and this is no fit job for Hjalmar anyway—wasting his time taking pictures of a lot of silly people!

GREGERS: I quite agree; but once having chosen it as his profession—

GINA: He's no *ordinary* photographer, mind you! I'm sure you understand that, Mr. Werle.

GREGERS: Yes, of course, but still—

   (*A shot is heard from the attic.*)

GREGERS (*starting up*): What's that?

GINA: There they go—at that shooting again!

GREGERS: Do you mean to say they shoot in there?

HEDVIG: They're out hunting, you see.

GREGERS: What! (*Goes to the door of the attic.*) Are you out hunting, Hjalmar?

HJALMAR (*from inside the net*): Oh, you've come. I didn't know. I was so taken up with—(*To* HEDVIG) Why didn't you call us? (*Comes into the studio.*)

GREGERS: Do you mean to tell me you go shooting in the attic?

HJALMAR (*showing a double-barreled pistol*): Only with this old thing.

GINA: You and Grandfather'll get into trouble one of these days— fooling with that gun.

HJALMAR (*irritably*): How often have I told you—this weapon is a *pistol*.

GINA: I don't see that that makes it any better.

GREGERS: Well, Hjalmar—so you've become a hunter too!

HJALMAR: We do a little rabbit shooting now and then. It pleases the old man, you know.

GINA: Men are a queer lot! Must have their divergence!

HJALMAR (*angrily*): Diversion—I suppose you mean!

GINA: That's what I said, isn't it?

HJALMAR: Well—! Hm. (*To* GREGERS) It works out very well; the attic's so high up, no one can hear the shooting. (*Lays the pistol on the top shelf of the bookcase.*) Mind you don't touch the pistol, Hedvig. One of the barrels is still loaded; remember that.

GREGERS (*peering through the net*): You have a rifle too, I see.

HJALMAR: It's an old gun of father's. But there's something wrong with the lock—it won't fire any more. It's fun to have it, though; we take it apart, grease it, give it a good cleaning—and then put it together again. That is—*Father* does; he likes puttering about with things like that.

HEDVIG (*beside* GREGERS): Look! You can see the wild duck clearly now.

GREGERS: Yes—I was just looking at her. She seems to drag her wing a bit.

HJALMAR: That's not strange; that's the broken wing, you see.

GREGERS: And she's lame in one foot, isn't she?

HJALMAR: Yes—perhaps a little.

HEDVIG: That's the foot the dog caught hold of.

HJALMAR: But she's all right otherwise; it's quite amazing—considering she had a charge of shot in her, and the dog grabbed her with his teeth—

GREGERS (*with a glance at* HEDVIG): —and she was down in the boundless deep, as well.

HEDVIG (*smiling*): Yes.

GINA (*goes on laying the table*): That blessed wild duck! She gets enough fuss made over her!

HJALMAR: Hm— Will lunch be ready soon?

GINA: Yes, in a minute. Now, Hedvig—come and help me. (GINA *and* HEDVIG *go out into the kitchen.*)

HJALMAR (*in a low voice*): I wouldn't stand there watching Father; he doesn't like it. (GREGERS *moves away from the attic door.*) I'd better close up before the others come. (*Claps his hands to drive the birds back.*) Shoo! Get back there! (*Draws up the net and pulls the door panels together.*) These contraptions are all my own invention. It's rather fun to fiddle about with things like that. Gina doesn't like the hens and rabbits to get into the studio, so it's important to keep all this in running order.

GREGERS: Yes, I see—It's your wife who really runs the business then?

HJALMAR: I leave the routine part of it to her. It gives me a chance to work on more important things; I use the sitting room, you see.

GREGERS: What kind of things?

HJALMAR: I'm surprised you haven't asked me that before. But you haven't heard about the invention, I suppose?

GREGERS: Invention? No.

HJALMAR: You haven't, eh? Of course—I know you've been living in the wilds—

GREGERS: Have you invented something?

HJALMAR: I haven't quite solved it yet; but I'm working on it constantly. I didn't become a photographer in order to spend my life taking commonplace pictures of commonplace people—I need hardly tell you that.

GREGERS: Just what your wife was saying.

HJALMAR: When I chose the photographic medium, I swore to myself that I would raise it to the level of a science and an art combined; so I set to work on this invention.

GREGERS: What kind of an invention is it? What does it consist of?

HJALMAR: My dear fellow, you mustn't try to pin me down to details yet; these things take time, you know. And, believe me, it's not a question of self-glorification—I'm not working on it for my own sake, I assure you! I have a fixed purpose in life—a sacred duty; and I consider this work part of it.

GREGERS: What is this "purpose of life" you speak of?

HJALMAR: Are you forgetting that white-haired old man in there?

GREGERS: Your poor father—yes. What exactly do you plan to do for him?

HJALMAR: I plan to give him back his self-respect by restoring the name of Ekdal to its former dignity and honor.

GREGERS: I see.

HJALMAR: Yes—I shall rescue him! Poor, broken old man! Do you know that from the moment the trouble started—from the very beginning—he went all to pieces, and he seemed unable to recover. In those terrible days—all during the trial—he was so changed, I hardly knew him— That pistol over there—the one we use to shoot rabbits with—that played its part in the Ekdal tragedy too!

GREGERS: The pistol! Really?

HJALMAR: Oh, yes! When he was found guilty, and they sentenced him to prison—he stood with that pistol in his hand—

GREGERS: You mean—he was going to—?

HJALMAR: Yes. But his courage failed him; he dared not use it. That shows you how broken and demoralized he was. Imagine! He, a soldier! A great hunter with nine bears to his credit. A man directly descended from two Lieutenant Colonels—in successive generations, naturally—and yet his courage failed him! Can you understand that, Gregers?

GREGERS: Yes; I understand that very well.

HJALMAR: I don't. But that pistol was to turn up again in the Ekdal Saga. When I thought of him in his prison clothes—under lock and key—in that gloomy prison cell—! Those were agonizing days for me! I kept all the shades down in my room. I'd look out now and then, and I couldn't understand how the sun could still be shining. I couldn't understand how people could still be walking through the streets—laughing and chatting about trivial things. It seemed to me as though the world had come to a standstill—as though life itself were under an eclipse.

GREGERS: I felt like that when Mother died.

HJALMAR: And there came a moment when Hjalmar Ekdal seized that pistol and aimed it at his own breast.

GREGERS: You, too, thought of—!

HJALMAR: Yes.

GREGERS: But you didn't fire?

HJALMAR: No—I didn't fire. By a supreme effort I conquered the temptation—and I went on living. It takes courage to choose life under such circumstances, I can tell you.

GREGERS: That depends on how you look at it.

HJALMAR: No, my dear fellow—it's indisputable. And I'm glad I managed to find the necessary strength, for now I shall be able to finish my invention. And when it's ready, Dr. Relling thinks—and I agree with him—that Father may get permission to wear his uniform again. I shall demand that as my sole reward.

GREGERS: Does that mean so much to him—?

HJALMAR: It's his dearest wish. Oh, Gregers—my heart bleeds for him! Whenever we have a little family celebration—Gina's and my wedding anniversary, whatever it may be—in comes the old man wearing the lieutenant's uniform he wore in happier days. But if there's a knock at the door, or if he hears someone in the hall—back he runs to his room as fast as his poor old legs will carry him; for he dare not be caught wearing it in public. It breaks my heart to see him!

GREGERS: When do you expect to finish the invention?

HJALMAR: Good heavens—that's impossible to say! An invention is not a matter of routine, you know. It depends on inspiration—on a sudden intuition—on factors beyond one's immediate control.

GREGERS: But you're making progress with it?

HJALMAR: Of course I'm making progress! I wrestle with it every day —my mind is full of it. Every afternoon, as soon as I've had lunch, I lock myself in the sitting room in there, where I can work in peace. But it's no use *hounding* me about it; as Relling says, that does more harm than good!

GREGERS: What about all this business in the attic? Don't you find that distracting? Doesn't it waste a great deal of your time?

HJALMAR: On the contrary! You mustn't think that for a moment! I must have *some* relaxation, after all; something to relieve the strain of incessant concentration. And, anyhow, inspiration is quite unpredictable; when it comes it comes—that's all!

GREGERS: You know, Hjalmar—I think you and the wild duck have quite a lot in common.

HJALMAR: The wild duck! What on earth do you mean?

GREGERS: You dived to the bottom too, and got yourself trapped down there.

HJALMAR: You mean that I was wounded too—by the blow that almost killed my father?

GREGERS: No, not exactly. It's not that you're wounded, Hjalmar; but you've lost your way in a poisonous swamp. You've become infected with an insidious disease, and you've sunk to the bottom to die in the dark.

HJALMAR: Die in the dark? I? Really, Gregers—how can you talk such nonsense!

GREGERS: But don't worry—I'll bring you back. I have a purpose in life too, you see. One I discovered yesterday.

HJALMAR: That's all very well—but kindly leave *me* out of it! I assure you that—apart from a perfectly justifiable melancholy— I'm as content and happy as any man could be.

GREGERS: That's part of the illness, you see. It's all part of the poison.

HJALMAR: My dear Gregers—please don't go on about illnesses and poisons any more! I dislike that kind of talk. In my house no one ever speaks to me about unpleasant things.

GREGERS: That I can well believe.

HJALMAR: I dislike it and it's bad for me—And I don't care what you say—there are no swamps or poisons here! My surroundings may be modest—my home may be humble; but I'm an inventor and the breadwinner of a family, and I assure you this exalts me above any petty material concerns—Ah! Here comes lunch!

(GINA *and* HEDVIG *enter bringing bottles of beer, a decanter of brandy, glasses, etc. At the same time* RELLING *and* MOLVIK *enter from the hall, both without hats or overcoats;* MOLVIK *is dressed in black.*)

GINA (*placing dishes on the table*): You're just in time!

RELLING: Molvik got a whiff of herring salad and there was no holding him!

HJALMAR: I'd like you to meet Mr. Molvik, Gregers; and doctor—oh, but you know Dr. Relling, don't you?

GREGERS: Slightly, yes.

RELLING: Mr. Werle Junior, of course. We had a few little skirmishes up at the Höjdal Works. Did you just move in?

GREGERS: This morning.

RELLING: Molvik and I live just below you; so if you should happen to need a doctor or a clergyman, you won't have far to go.

GREGERS: I might have to take you up on that: we were thirteen at table yesterday.

HJALMAR: I do wish you'd stop talking about unpleasant things!

RELLING: Your time hasn't come yet, Hjalmar! No need to worry!

HJALMAR: For the sake of my family I hope you're right. But let's sit down now—and eat, drink and be merry!

GREGERS: Shouldn't we wait for your father?

HJALMAR: No; he'll have lunch in his own room presently. Come on! (*The men seat themselves at table and start eating and drinking.* GINA *and* HEDVIG *go in and out waiting on them.*)

RELLING: Molvik was drunk as a Lord yesterday, Mrs. Ekdal.

GINA: Was he? Again?

RELLING: Didn't you hear him when I brought him home last night?

GINA: Can't say I did.

RELLING: Just as well; last night he was downright disgusting.

GINA: Is that true, Molvik?

MOLVIK: Let us draw a veil over last night's proceedings; they have no connection with my better self.

RELLING: He becomes like one possessed; then he insists on dragging me out with him. He's daemonic—that's what it is.

GREGERS: Daemonic?

RELLING: Yes; Molvik is daemonic.

GREGERS: Hm.

RELLING: And people with daemonic natures can't be expected to go through life on an even keel, you know. They're obliged to run amok now and then—they *have* to— Are you still slaving away at those horrible grimy Works?

GREGERS: I have been until now.

RELLING: Did you ever get anyone to honor that claim you made such a fuss about up there?

GREGERS: Claim? (*Understands him.*) Oh, I see.

HJALMAR: Claim? What sort of a claim, Gregers?

GREGERS: Nothing. A lot of nonsense.

RELLING: Not at all! He carried on a regular crusade! He went from house to house preaching about something—what was it you called it?—the Claim of the Ideal?

GREGERS: I was young then.

RELLING: Yes! You were young all right! But did you ever get anyone to honor it? You hadn't while I was there, as I remember.

GREGERS: And not since, either.

RELLING: Have you perhaps learned to compromise a little?

GREGERS: Compromise? Never in dealing with a man who really *is* a man.

HJALMAR: No! I should hope not!— More butter, Gina.

RELLING: And a bit of pork for Molvik.

MOLVIK: Ugh! Not *pork!*

(*There's a knock at the attic door.*)

HJALMAR: Father wants to come out; open up for him, Hedvig. (HEDVIG *goes and slides the door open a little way;* EKDAL *comes in carrying a fresh rabbit skin;* HEDVIG *closes the door after him.*)

EKDAL: Good morning, gentlemen! Good hunting today! Shot a big one!

HJALMAR: And you skinned it without waiting for me—!

EKDAL: Salted it, too. Good *tender* meat, is rabbit meat. And sweet; tastes like sugar. Enjoy your lunch, gentlemen! (*Goes into his room.*)

MOLVIK (*getting up*): Excuse me—I can't—I must get downstairs at once—

RELLING: Take some soda water, man!

MOLVIK: Ugh—Ugh! (*Hurries out by the hall door.*)

RELLING (*to* HJALMAR): Let's drink a toast to the old hunter.

HJALMAR (*clinks glasses with him*): To the gallant old sportsman on the brink of the grave.

RELLING: To the old gray-haired—(*Drinks.*) By the way, is his hair gray or white?

HJALMAR: A little of both, I think. As a matter of fact, he hasn't much hair left.

RELLING: Well—you can get on just as well in a wig! You know— you really are a lucky man, Hjalmar; you have a definite purpose in life to strive for—

HJALMAR: And, believe me, I *am* striving for it—!

RELLING: And there's your good, capable wife—padding about so quietly in her old felt slippers, making everything cozy and comfortable for you—

HJALMAR: Yes, Gina—(*Nods to her.*) You're a good companion on life's journey, Gina dear.

GINA: Don't go making a fool of me!

RELLING: And then, there's your Hedvig, Hjalmar—

HJALMAR (*moved*): Yes—best of all, my child! My Hedvig! Come here to me, my darling! (*Strokes her hair.*) What day is it tomorrow, eh?

HEDVIG (*shakes him*): Don't say anything about that, Father.

HJALMAR: It cuts me to the heart to think how meager it will be; just a little ceremony in the attic—

HEDVIG: But I like that best of all!

RELLING: Just you wait till the invention's finished, Hedvig!

HJALMAR: Yes!— *Then* you'll see! Your future will be taken care of; you shall live in comfort all your life—I shall make sure of that! I shall demand—well—something or other on your behalf. It will be the poor inventor's sole request.

HEDVIG (*in a whisper, her arms round his neck*): Dear, darling Father!

RELLING (*to* GREGERS): Isn't it pleasant for a change to sit here with this happy family—eating delicious food at a well-spread table?

HJALMAR: It's a joy to share a meal with such good friends!

GREGERS: Personally—I don't like the smell of poison.

RELLING: Poison?

HJALMAR: Oh, don't start *that* again!

GINA: I'd have you know, Mr. Werle, there's no smell of poison here; I air this room out every single day!

GREGERS: No amount of airing can ever get rid of the stench I mean.

HJALMAR: Stench!

GINA: Well—I must say—!

RELLING: Perhaps you brought the stench with *you,* from those mines of yours up there!

GREGERS: You *would* call what I have to bring a stench! That would be like you, Dr. Relling.

RELLING: Now listen, Mr. Werle Junior—! Unless I'm very much mistaken you're still obsessed by that blasted *Claim of the Ideal* of yours. I'll bet you have a copy on you now—hidden in some pocket.

GREGERS: You're wrong. I have it hidden in my heart.

RELLING: Well—wherever it is don't produce it here! Not while I'm around at any rate.

GREGERS: And what if I produce it all the same?

RELLING: Then I give you fair warning, I shall kick you downstairs head first.

HJALMAR (*rising*): Why, Relling!

GREGERS: All right! Why don't you try it—!

GINA (*coming between them*): Dr. Relling! Please! That's enough of that—! But I'd like to tell *you* something, Mr. Werle. After that filthy mess you made with your stove in there, you've no business to come talking about stenches and poisons to *me!*

(*There's a knock at the hall door.*)

HEDVIG: Mother, there's someone at the door.

HJALMAR: What *is* this! Now we're to be overrun with visitors, I suppose!

GINA: Never mind—I'll go. (*She goes and opens the door, starts and draws back.*) Ah!—Oh, no!

(WERLE, *wearing a fur coat, steps into the room.*)

WERLE: I beg your pardon; I'm told my son is living here.

GINA (*with a gasp*): Why—yes.

HJALMAR (*goes toward him*): Won't you do us the honor, Mr. Werle—

WERLE: Thank you; I merely wish to see my son.

GREGERS: I'm here; what is it?

WERLE: May we go to your room?

GREGERS: My room? Yes—very well—

GINA: Oh! But it's in no fit state—!

WERLE: Out here in the hall will do; but I'd like to speak to you alone.

HJALMAR: You can have this room to yourselves, Mr. Werle. Come, Relling—we'll go in here. (HJALMAR *and* RELLING *go into the sitting room*; GINA *takes* HEDVIG *with her into the kitchen.*)

GREGERS (*after a short pause*): Well? Now that we're alone, what is it?

WERLE: I gather from something you said last night—and your moving here to the Ekdals seems to confirm it—that you're bent on causing me some mischief.

GREGERS: I intend to open Hjalmar Ekdal's eyes; he must be made to see his position in its true light.

WERLE: I suppose this is the "purpose in life" you spoke of yesterday?

GREGERS: You've left me no other.

WERLE: Why hold *me* responsible for your warped mind, Gregers?

GREGERS: I hold you responsible for the fact that my whole *life* has been warped. I'm not referring now to what happened to my mother— But I have you to thank for the burden of guilt that weighs on my conscience.

WERLE: So it's your conscience that torments you, is it?

GREGERS: I knew you were laying a trap for old Lieutenant Ekdal, and I should have been man enough to face you with it. I should at least have warned him. I guessed what you were up to.

WERLE: Then why didn't you speak out?

GREGERS: I was too much of a coward; I didn't dare. At that time I was so dreadfully afraid of you. I went on being afraid of you for years.

WERLE: But you're no longer afraid now, it seems.

GREGERS: No—thank God. I know the wrong done to old Ekdal—by me and others—can never be undone. But I can at least save Hjalmar. I can prevent his life from being ruined by a mass of lies.

WERLE: What good do you think that would do? You don't imagine you'd be doing him a service?

GREGERS: I know I would.

WERLE: And Hjalmar Ekdal will agree with you, you think? You actually believe he's man enough to *thank* you for it?

GREGERS: I know he is.

WERLE: Hm—we'll see.

GREGERS: Besides—if I'm to go on living—I must try to find a cure for my sick conscience.

WERLE: You'll never find a cure; your conscience has been sick, as you choose to call it, ever since you were a little child. That's a legacy from your mother, Gregers; that's all she had to leave you.

GREGERS (*with a scornful smile*): You haven't got over it yet, have you? You expected her to bring you a fortune when you married her—you've never recovered from the shock of having been mistaken!

WERLE: Let's stick to the point, shall we? You still insist on guiding young Ekdal back to, what is in your opinion, the right path?

GREGERS: That is my intention.

WERLE: Then I might have spared myself this visit; for I suppose it's no good asking whether you'll change your mind and come back home again?

GREGERS: No.

WERLE: And you won't consider joining the firm either?

GREGERS: No.

WERLE: Very well. But, since I'm marrying again, I'll arrange to have your part of the estate transferred to you at once.

GREGERS: No—I don't want it.

WERLE: You don't want it?

GREGERS: My conscience won't allow me to accept it.

WERLE (*after a pause*): Are you going up to the Works again?

GREGERS: No; I've resigned from your employ.

WERLE: What do you plan to do?

GREGERS: I only want to fulfill my purpose in life—that's all.

WERLE: But what do you propose to live on?

GREGERS: I've saved up a little money from my wages.

WERLE: How long will *that* last!

GREGERS: Long enough for me, I expect.

WERLE: What does that mean?

GREGERS: I'll answer no more questions.

WERLE: Very well then, Gregers. Goodbye.

GREGERS: Goodbye.

(WERLE *goes out by the hall door.*)

HJALMAR (*sticks his head round the sitting-room door*): Has he gone?

GREGERS: Yes.

(HJALMAR *and* RELLING *come in.* GINA *and* HEDVIG *come from the kitchen.*)

RELLING: That certainly put an end to the lunch party, didn't it!

GREGERS: Put on your things, Hjalmar. I want you to come for a long walk with me.

HJALMAR: All right, I'd be glad to. What did your father want? Was it anything to do with me?

GREGERS: Come along. We've got to have a talk. I'll go and get my coat. (*Goes out by the hall door.*)

GINA (*to* HJALMAR): I wouldn't go with him if I were you.

RELLING: No, don't! Stay where you are.

HJALMAR (*getting his hat and overcoat*): What! When an old friend wants to pour out his heart to me in private—!

RELLING: But, damn it! Can't you see the fellow's mad? He's a crackpot—a lunatic!

GINA: You hear that, Hjalmar? His mother was a bit queer too at times.

HJALMAR: All the more reason his friend should keep a watchful eye on him. (*To* GINA) Be sure to have dinner ready in good time. Goodbye for the present. (*He goes out by the hall door.*)

RELLING: Too bad that fellow didn't fall right into Hell down one of the Höjdal mine shafts!

GINA: Good gracious! What makes you say that?

RELLING (*mutters*): I have my reasons.

GINA: Do you think young Werle's really mad?

RELLING: No, worse luck; I don't suppose he's any madder than most people. But he's a sick man all the same.

GINA: What do you think's the matter with him?

RELLING: Well—I'll tell you, Mrs. Ekdal: I'd say he had integrity-fever—a particularly bad case of it.

GINA: Integrity-fever?

HEDVIG: Is that a kind of illness?

RELLING: Yes; it's a national disease, but it only breaks out sporadically. (*Nods to* GINA.) Thanks for lunch. (*He goes out by the hall door.*)

GINA (*placing restlessly up and down*): Ugh! That Gregers Werle! He's always been a troublemaker.

HEDVIG (*stands by the table, gives her mother a searching look*): Mother; this all seems very strange.

CURTAIN

❦

ACT IV

SCENE: *Hjalmar Ekdal's studio. A photograph has just been taken; a camera covered with its cloth, a pedestal, two chairs and a console table stand forward in the room. It is late afternoon, the sun is setting; during the act dusk falls.* GINA *stands at the hall door with a slide and a wet photographic plate in her hand; she is talking to somebody outside.*

GINA: Without fail! Don't worry, I never break a promise. I'll have the first dozen ready for you Monday—Good afternoon. (*Someone is heard going down the stairs.* GINA *closes the door, slips the plate into the slide and puts it into the camera.*)

HEDVIG (*comes in from the kitchen*): Have they gone?

GINA (*tidying up*): Yes, thank God I got rid of them at last.

HEDVIG: It's funny Father isn't back yet.

GINA: You're sure he's not in Relling's room?

HEDVIG: No, he's not there; I just ran down the back stairs to see.

GINA: And his dinner's getting cold too.

HEDVIG: It's funny—Father's never late for dinner.

GINA: He'll be here soon—you'll see.

HEDVIG: I wish he'd come: things seem so queer today.

GINA (*calls out*): Here he is now!

(HJALMAR EKDAL *comes in by the hall door.*)

HEDVIG (*runs to him*): We thought you'd *never* come back, Father!

GINA (*gives him a sidelong look*): You were out a long time, Hjalmar.

HJALMAR (*doesn't look at her*): A fairly long time, yes.

GINA: Did you have something to eat with Werle?

HJALMAR (*hanging up his coat*): No.

GINA (*going toward the kitchen*): I'll bring your dinner at once, then.

HJALMAR: Never mind about dinner. I don't want anything to eat.

HEDVIG (*goes nearer to him*): Don't you feel well, Father?

HJALMAR: Well? Yes—well enough. We had a very tiring walk, Gregers and I.

GINA: You shouldn't have gone with him, Hjalmar. You know you're not used to long walks.

HJALMAR: There are many things one has to get used to in this world. (*He wanders about the room.*) Has anyone been here while I was out?

GINA: Only that engaged couple.

HJALMAR: No new orders, I suppose?

GINA: No, not today.

HEDVIG: But tomorrow there are sure to be some, Father!

HJALMAR: Let's hope so. For tomorrow I mean to set to work in earnest.

HEDVIG: Tomorrow! Have you forgotten what day it is tomorrow, Father?

HJALMAR: Ah, yes—of course. The day after tomorrow, then. I intend to take personal charge of everything. From now on I shall do all the work myself.

GINA: Why should you bother to do that, Hjalmar? You know it only makes you miserable. I can take the pictures well enough; and that sets you free to work on your invention.

HEDVIG: And then there's the wild duck, Father—and all the hens and rabbits—

HJALMAR: I won't hear another word about that childish nonsense! From tomorrow on I shall never set foot in there again.

HEDVIG: But, Father, tomorrow you promised we'd have our celebration—

HJALMAR: Hm. Yes, that's true. From the day *after* tomorrow, then. As for that wild duck, I'd like to wring its neck!

HEDVIG (*cries out*): The wild duck!

GINA: I never heard of such a thing!

HEDVIG (*shakes him*): But, Father! It's *my* wild duck! You can't—!

HJALMAR: That's the only thing that stops me. I haven't the heart to do it, Hedvig—for your sake. But I ought to do it, I'm convinced of that. No creature that has been in that man's hands should be allowed to stay under my roof.

GINA: Good Lord—what if Grandfather did get it from poor old Pettersen—

HJALMAR: One has certain moral obligations; there are laws—one might call them the laws of the Ideal. A man may jeopardize his soul by failing to obey them.

HEDVIG: But the poor wild duck, Father! Think of the wild duck!

HJALMAR: I told you—I intend to spare it for your sake. Not a hair of its head—I mean—it shall be spared. I've other things to deal with—far more important things than that. Now that it's dusk, Hedvig, you'd better run along and take your walk as usual.

HEDVIG: Must I, Father? I don't much feel like going out.

HJALMAR: I think you'd better go. You seem to be blinking your eyes a lot—it's this foul air in here. It's bad for you.

HEDVIG: Very well. I'll go by the back stairs. My hat and coat—? They must be in my room. But, Father—promise me you won't hurt the wild duck while I'm gone?

HJALMAR: Not a feather on it shall be harmed, I promise you. (*Clasps her to him.*) You and I, Hedvig—we two—! Run along now.

(HEDVIG *nods to her parents and goes out through the kitchen.*)

HJALMAR (*walks about the room with downcast eyes*): Gina.

GINA: Yes?

HJALMAR: From tomorrow on—from the day *after* tomorrow, rather —I wish to take charge of the household accounts myself.

GINA: You want to look after the accounts as well?

HJALMAR: I intend to check all the receipts at any rate.

GINA: Lord knows *that* won't take you very long.

HJALMAR: I wonder. It seems to me our money stretches a surprisingly long way. (*Stops and looks at her.*) How do you manage it?

GINA: It's because Hedvig and I use so very little, I suppose.

HJALMAR: What about Father's work for Mr. Werle? Is it true that he gets very generously paid for it?

GINA: I don't know how generous it is. I don't know what other people get, you see.

HJALMAR: Well—how much *do* they pay him? Tell me!

GINA: It varies; he gets enough to cover his expenses here, and maybe a little pocket money besides.

HJALMAR: Enough to cover his expenses! Why have you never told me this?

GINA: I didn't like to; I knew it made you happy to think he owed everything to you.

HJALMAR: And instead he owes it all to Mr. Werle!

GINA: Well, God knows, Mr. Werle can afford it.

HJALMAR: Light the lamp!

GINA (*lighting the lamp*): Anyway—how do we know it *does* come from Mr. Werle? It might be Graaberg who—

HJALMAR: Don't try to evade matters by dragging Graaberg into this!

GINA: Well, I mean—I only thought—

HJALMAR: Hm!

GINA: I didn't get Grandfather that copying to do: it was Bertha—in the days when she still used to come and see us—

HJALMAR: Why is your voice trembling?

GINA (*putting on the lamp shade*): My voice—?

HJALMAR: Yes; and your hands are shaking too. Don't tell me I'm mistaken!

GINA (*firmly*): What's he been saying about me, Hjalmar? You might just as well come out with it.

HJALMAR: Is it true—*can* it be true, that—that there was something between you and Werle, while you were in service there?

GINA: No. It wasn't true then, at any rate. Mr. Werle wouldn't leave me alone, *that's* true enough. His wife got suspicious, and fussed and fumed and made a lot of scenes; made my life miserable, she did. And then I gave my notice.

HJALMAR: And after that?

GINA: Then I went home, and Mother—well, she wasn't the kind of woman you took her for, Hjalmar; she kept on at me all the time— you see Mr. Werle had become a widower by then.

HJALMAR: Well?

GINA: I suppose I'd better tell you; he gave me no peace until I let him have his way.

HJALMAR (*clasps his hands together*): So this is the mother of my child! How could you hide this from me!

GINA: It was wrong of me, I know; I should have told you long ago.

HJALMAR: You should have told me at the very start; then I'd have known what kind of woman I was dealing with.

GINA: But if you'd known—would you have married me?

HJALMAR: What do you think? Of course not!

GINA: That's why I couldn't bring myself to tell you. I'd grown so fond of you, you see. I'd have been so miserable—I couldn't bear the thought of it.

HJALMAR (*paces about*): So this is my Hedvig's mother! And to think that I owe all I possess—(*Kicks a chair.*) my home and everything that's in it, to a man who was your former lover! To that damned scoundrel Werle!

GINA: Hjalmar, do you regret these years we've been together?

HJALMAR (*stands in front of her*): Tell me! Haven't your days been filled with remorse at the thought of the web of deceit you've spun around me? Answer me! Hasn't it been a constant source of agony and shame to you?

GINA: Hjalmar dear—I've had so much to do. My days have been so full—what with the house and all—

HJALMAR: So you've never even given a moment's thought to your past life!

GINA: It's a long time ago—to tell you the truth I'd almost forgotten the whole stupid business.

HJALMAR: It's this crude, sluggish content that I find so shocking—so revolting! Not a twinge of remorse—incredible!

GINA: I'd like you to tell *me* something, Hjalmar; what would have become of you if you hadn't found a wife like me?

HJALMAR: Like you—!

GINA: Yes. You know I was always more practical and more efficient than you were; I suppose that's only natural—I'm a couple of years older, after all.

HJALMAR: What would have become of *me!*

GINA: You were getting into some pretty wild habits when you first met me. You can't deny that, can you?

HJALMAR: Wild habits! That's what you call them, do you? But how could *you* understand what a man goes through when he's on the brink of despair, as I was! Especially a man with my ardent, sensitive nature.

GINA: Maybe that's true. Anyway—I don't hold it against you; you made a real good husband once we got married and settled down— And things were beginning to be so cozy and comfortable here. Hedvig and I were thinking we might even start spending a bit more on ourselves—get ourselves a few clothes, perhaps—and a little extra food.

HJALMAR: In this swamp of deceit, you could actually think of things like that!

GINA: Oh, God! I wish that awful man had never set foot inside this house!

HJALMAR: I was happy here too; I loved my home. But it was all a delusion! How I shall ever find the necessary inspiration now to bring my invention to fruition, heaven knows! It will die with me,

I expect. And it will be your fault—it will be your past, Gina, that will have killed it.

GINA (*on the verge of tears*): You mustn't say that, Hjalmar! Please don't say things like that! All I've ever wanted was to serve you—to do the best I could for you. You must know that!

HJALMAR: What's become of the poor breadwinner's dream now! As I lay in there on the sofa, incessantly brooding over my invention, I realized only too well that the effort of creation was fast sapping my strength. I had a premonition: I knew that the day when I finally held the patent in my hand—I knew that day would be my last! I saw you in my dream—the proud widow of the inventor—sad, but prosperous and grateful.

GINA (*drying her tears*): Hjalmar, you *mustn't* say such things! God forbid that I should ever be a widow.

HJALMAR: It makes no difference now one way or the other. The dream is over now—all over!

(GREGERS WERLE *opens the hall door cautiously and looks in.*)

GREGERS: May I come in?

HJALMAR: Yes; come in.

GREGERS (*comes forward, his face beaming with joy, and holds out both his hands to them*): Well, my dear friends—! (*Looks from one to the other and says to* HJALMAR *in a whisper.*) Perhaps you haven't had your talk yet?

HJALMAR (*loudly*): Yes—we have.

GREGERS: You *have*?

HJALMAR: I've just been through the bitterest moments of my life.

GREGERS: But, surely, the most uplifting too?

HJALMAR: Anyway—we've got it over with; at least for the time being.

GREGERS (*in great surprise*): But—I don't understand—

HJALMAR: What don't you understand?

GREGERS: This crisis was to have been a turning point; the basis for a whole new way of life. No more falsehood and deception, but a union based on confidence and truth—

HJALMAR: Yes, I know; I know all that.

GREGERS: I expected to find you both radiant—transfigured. But you seem sad and gloomy—

GINA: Yes—well. (*Takes off the lamp shade.*)

GREGERS: I don't expect you to understand me, Mrs. Ekdal. It's only natural that you should need time to— But *you*, Hjalmar? You must feel like a man newly dedicated to higher things.

HJALMAR: Yes, of course I do. To some extent—that is.

GREGERS: Surely there can be no greater joy than to forgive a poor erring creature; to rehabilitate her through love and understanding.

HJALMAR: It's not so easy to recover from the bitter experience I've just lived through!

GREGERS: Perhaps not for an *ordinary* man; but for a man like *you*—

HJALMAR: Yes—I realize that. But don't *hound* me about it, Gregers. These things take time, you know.

GREGERS: There's a lot of the wild duck in you, Hjalmar.

(RELLING *enters through the hall door.*)

RELLING: Well, well! So we're on the subject of the wild duck again!

HJALMAR: Yes: Mr. Werle's poor wounded victim—

GREGERS: Mr. Werle? Were you talking about *him*?

HJALMAR: Him—and *us*; yes.

RELLING (*to* GREGERS *in an undertone*): You damned interfering fool!

HJALMAR: What did you say?

RELLING: Nothing. I was just expressing my feelings about this quack here. (*To* GREGERS) Why don't you get out before you ruin both their lives?

GREGERS: Their lives won't be ruined, I assure you, Dr. Relling. I needn't speak of Hjalmar—we know him. But I feel sure that, fundamentally, she too possesses the necessary qualities of decency and loyalty—

GINA (*almost in tears*): Then why couldn't you have let me be?

RELLING: May I ask you, Mr. Werle Junior, what you think you're doing in this house?

GREGERS: Laying the foundations of a true marriage.

RELLING: I see; so you think the Ekdals' marriage wasn't good enough?

GREGERS: I suppose it was as good as the majority of marriages—unfortunately! But it certainly was never based on truth.

HJALMAR (*to* RELLING): I'm afraid you've never given much thought to the Ideal.

RELLING: Rubbish, my friend! Tell me, Mr. Werle—roughly speaking—how many true marriages have you encountered in your life?

GREGERS: Hardly any—now I come to think of it.

RELLING: Neither have I.

GREGERS: But I've seen all too many of the other kind. And I know only too well how harmful such marriages can be to both people concerned.

HJALMAR: A man's spiritual integrity can be totally destroyed—that's the appalling part of it!

RELLING: I've never actually been married—so perhaps I'm not competent to judge. But one thing I *do* know: the child is part of the marriage too; and I advise you to leave the child alone.

HJALMAR: Hedvig!—My poor Hedvig!

RELLING: Yes; you'd better damn well leave Hedvig out of this! You two are grown-up people; if you want to make a mess of your lives, that's up to you. But I warn you to be careful about Hedvig. You might cause her irreparable harm.

HJALMAR: Harm?

RELLING: Yes. Or she might try to harm herself—and others too.

GINA: What makes you think that, Relling?

HJALMAR: You mean—? There's no immediate danger to her eyesight, is there?

RELLING: I'm not talking about her eyesight! Hedvig's at a difficult age. Heaven knows *what* she might get into her head.

GINA: You're right—she's had some queer ideas of late. She's taken to messing about with the kitchen stove, for instance. Playing at house-on-fire" she calls it. I've been afraid she might really set fire to the place one of these days.

RELLING: There, you see! I knew it.

GREGERS (*to* RELLING): But how do you explain that kind of thing?

RELLING (*curtly*): Adolescence—Mr. Werle Junior.

HJALMAR: As long as she has her father—! As long as I'm this side of the grave—!

(*There's a knock at the door.*)

GINA: Hush, Hjalmar; there's someone in the hall. (*Calls out.*) Come in!

(MRS. SÖRBY *enters; she wears a hat and a warm coat.*)

MRS. SÖRBY: Good evening!

GINA (*goes toward her*): Why, Bertha! Is it you?

MRS. SÖRBY: Yes. I hope I'm not disturbing you?

HJALMAR: Good heavens, no! How could an emissary from *that* house—!

MRS. SÖRBY (*to* GINA): Actually—I'd hoped to find you alone, at this time of day. I just ran over to have a little chat with you, and say good-bye.

GINA: Good-bye? Are you going away?

MRS. SÖRBY: Early tomorrow morning—up to Höjdal. Mr. Werle left this afternoon. (*To* GREGERS, *casually*) He told me to say goodbye to you for him.

GINA: Well—fancy!

HJALMAR: So Mr. Werle's gone, has he? And you're going after him?

MRS. SÖRBY: Yes. What do you say to that, Ekdal?

HJALMAR: I say: be careful!

GREGERS: Let me explain; my father is going to marry Mrs. Sörby.

HJALMAR: Marry her!

GINA: Oh, Bertha! So it's really happened at last!

RELLING (*with a slight quiver in his voice*): This surely can't be true?

MRS. SÖRBY: Yes, dear Dr. Relling, it's true enough.

RELLING: You're really going to marry again?

MRS. SÖRBY: It looks like it! Mr. Werle got a special license, and we're to have a very quiet wedding, up at the Works.

GREGERS: Then let me be a dutiful stepson, and wish you happiness.

MRS. SÖRBY: Thanks very much—if you really mean it. I hope it will bring happiness to both of us.

RELLING: I don't see why it shouldn't. Mr. Werle never gets drunk, as far as I know—and, unlike the late-lamented horse doctor, he's not in the habit of beating his wives either.

MRS. SÖRBY: Oh, let poor Sörby rest in peace. He had his good points too.

RELLING: But I expect Mr. Werle has even better ones.

MRS. SÖRBY: At least he hasn't wasted all that was best in him; when a man does that, he must face the consequences.

RELLING: Tonight I shall go out with Molvik.

MRS. SÖRBY: Don't do that, Relling. Please—for my sake!

RELLING: What else is there to do? (*To* HJALMAR) If you feel like joining us, Hjalmar—come along!

GINA: No, thank you. Hjalmar doesn't go to places of *that* sort!

HJALMAR (*in an angry undertone*): Oh, do be quiet!

RELLING: Goodbye Mrs.—Werle. (*Goes out by the hall door.*)

GREGERS (*to* MRS. SÖRBY): You seem to be on very intimate terms with Dr. Relling.

MRS. SÖRBY: We've known each other for many years. At one time it looked as though something might have come of it.

GREGERS: It's just as well for you it didn't.

MRS. SÖRBY: Yes, you're right. But then, I've never been one to act on impulse. A woman can't afford to throw herself away.

GREGERS: Aren't you afraid I might say something to my father about this former friendship?

MRS. SÖRBY: I've naturally told him all about it.

GREGERS: Oh?

MRS. SÖRBY: Yes; I've told him everything that anyone could possibly find to say against me. The moment I realized what was in his mind, I made a point of doing so.

GREGERS: Then you're more than usually frank, it seems to me.

MRS. SÖRBY: I've always been frank. I think for a woman it's the best policy.

HJALMAR: What do you say to that, Gina?

GINA: We can't all be alike. Some women are one way, and some another.

MRS. SÖRBY: You know, Gina—I believe my way is best. And Mr. Werle has no secrets from me either. He can sit and talk to me quite openly—just like a child. It's the first time he's ever been able to do that. It's all wrong that a man of his type—full of health and vigor—should have had to spend the best years of his life listening to interminable lectures on his sins! And mostly imaginary sins too—as far as I can make out.

GINA: Lord knows *that's* true enough!

GREGERS: If you ladies intend to pursue this topic, I think I'd better go.

MRS. SÖRBY: No—you needn't go; I shan't say any more. I just wanted you to know that my dealings have been honorable and aboveboard from the start. I dare say many people will envy me and think me very lucky—and in a way I am. But I shall give as good as I get, I promise you. I shall never fail him. And now that he'll soon be helpless, I'll be able to repay him by serving him and caring for him always. I can do that better than anyone else, I think.

HJALMAR: What do you mean—helpless?

GREGERS (*to* MRS. SÖRBY): Don't say anything about that here.

MRS. SÖRBY: It's no use trying to hide it any longer; he's going blind.

HJALMAR (*with a start*): Blind? He's going blind you say? That's very strange.

GINA: Lots of people do, unfortunately.

MRS. SÖRBY: You can imagine what that means to a man in his position. I shall simply have to use my eyes for both of us, and do the best I can— But I really can't stay any longer—I have so much to do— By the way, I was to give you a message, Mr. Ekdal: If there's anything Werle can ever do for you, just mention it to Graaberg.

GREGERS: An offer that Hjalmar Ekdal will most certainly refuse.

MRS. SÖRBY: Really? He didn't used to be so—

GINA: No, Bertha. Hjalmar doesn't need anything from Mr. Werle now.

HJALMAR (*slowly and forcefully*): Be so good as to give my regards to your future husband, and tell him I intend to call on Mr. Graaberg very shortly—

GREGERS: What! You don't mean you—?

HJALMAR: —call on Mr. Graaberg, I say, and demand a full accounting of the money I owe to his employer. I intend to pay this debt of honor—ha-ha-ha! debt of honor is a good name for it!—but no more of that—I intend to pay it in full with interest at 5 per cent.

GINA: But, Hjalmar dear—where will we ever get the money?

HJALMAR: You may tell your fiancé that I am forging ahead with my invention. Tell him that I am sustained in this laborious task by the desire to rid myself once and for all of this painful debt. That is my chief motive in pursuing the work on my invention so relentlessly. I plan to devote the profits to freeing myself from all obligation to your future husband.

MRS. SÖRBY: What has been happening here?

HJALMAR: You may well ask!

MRS. SÖRBY: Well—I'll say good-bye. There were a couple of other things I wanted to talk to you about, Gina—but they must wait till some other time—Goodbye.

(HJALMAR *and* GREGERS *bow silently;* GINA *takes* MRS. SÖRBY *to the door.*)

HJALMAR: Not beyond the threshold, Gina!

(MRS. SÖRBY *goes out;* GINA *closes the door after her.*)

HJALMAR: There, Gregers! That burden of debt is off my mind!

GREGERS: It soon will be, at any rate.

HJALMAR: I think my behavior might be described as suitably correct?

GREGERS: Your behavior was admirable, as I knew it would be.

HJALMAR: There are times when one cannot possibly disregard the claim of the Ideal. But it will be a long hard struggle. It's not easy for a man without a penny to his name, and with a family to support, to pay off a long-standing debt of this sort—on which, one might say, the dust of oblivion has settled. But it must be faced; my integrity as a human being demands it.

GREGERS (*puts his hands on* HJALMAR's *shoulders*): My dear Hjalmar—wasn't it a good thing that I came?

HJALMAR: Ye-es.

GREGERS: Don't you feel happier, now that you see your position clearly?

HJALMAR (*somewhat impatiently*): Yes—of course I do. But there's one thing that offends my sense of justice.

GREGERS: What thing?

HJALMAR: It's just that—but perhaps I shouldn't speak of your father in this way—

GREGERS: Say anything you like as far as I'm concerned.

HJALMAR: It shocks me to think that he has succeeded where I have failed. His marriage will be a *true* marriage, you see.

GREGERS: How can you say a thing like that!

HJALMAR: But it's so, isn't it? Your father's marriage to Mrs. Sörby is based on truth and mutual confidence. They've kept nothing back; they hold no secrets from each other. They've reached a complete agreement. It's as though they'd each confessed their sins and given each other absolution.

GREGERS: Well—what then?

HJALMAR: That's the whole point—don't you see? You said yourself that no true marriage could exist unless these problems had been faced and cleared away.

GREGERS: But this is quite different, Hjalmar. You surely don't compare yourself—or Gina here—with *those* two—? You know quite well what I mean.

HJALMAR: All the same—there's something about this that offends my sense of justice. If things like this are allowed to happen, there's obviously no such thing as a Divine Power ruling the Universe!

GINA: Hjalmar! For God's sake don't say such things!

GREGERS: Hm. Don't let's embark on that subject.

HJALMAR: Yet—now I come to think of it—it's possible to see the hand of Destiny at work in this: He's going blind.

GINA: But perhaps that isn't true.

HJALMAR: I'm positive it's true; if there *is* such a thing as Divine Justice it *must* be true. Look at all the unsuspecting people he's hoodwinked in his time—!

GREGERS: A great many, unfortunately.

HJALMAR: And now he's being made to pay for it by going blind himself: it's retribution.

GINA: You frighten me when you say such dreadful things.

HJALMAR: It's sometimes salutary to examine the darker sides of life.

(HEDVIG, *in her hat and coat, comes in by the hall door.*
She is breathless and excited.)

GINA: Back already?

HEDVIG: Yes; I didn't want to stay out any longer. And it was just as well, because I met someone at the front door as I came in—

HJALMAR: That Mrs. Sörby, I suppose.

HEDVIG: That's right.

HJALMAR (*pacing up and down*): I hope that's the last time you'll ever lay eyes on *her.*

(*A pause.* HEDVIG *glances from one to the other as if trying to gauge their mood.*)

HEDVIG (*coaxingly, going up to* HJALMAR): Father.

HJALMAR: Well—what is it?

HEDVIG: Mrs. Sörby brought me something.

HJALMAR: Something for you?

HEDVIG: Yes—it's something for tomorrow.

GINA: Bertha always has some little present for you on your birthday.

HJALMAR: What is it?

HEDVIG: Oh, we're not supposed to see it yet. Mother's to bring it in to me early tomorrow morning.

HJALMAR: What *is* this? A conspiracy behind my back?

HEDVIG (*rapidly*): No, of course not! You can see it if you like! Look —it's this great big letter. (*She takes it out of her coat pocket.*)

HJALMAR: So there's a letter too.

HEDVIG: That's all she gave me; the rest'll come later, I suppose. But, just think—a letter! It's the first one I've ever had. And there's "Miss" written on the envelope. (*Reads.*) "Miss Hedvig Ekdal." Just think of it—that's *me!*

HJALMAR: Let me see that letter.

HEDVIG (*hands it to him*): There you are.

HJALMAR: This is Mr. Werle's handwriting.

GINA: Are you sure, Hjalmar?

HJALMAR: Look for yourself.

GINA: I don't know about such things.

HJALMAR: May I open it, and read it, Hedvig?

HEDVIG: Of course, Father, if you want to.

GINA: Not this evening, Hjalmar; we're supposed to save it till tomorrow.

HEDVIG (*softly*): Oh, let him read it, Mother. I'm sure it's something nice. Father will be pleased and things will be all right again.

HJALMAR: I may open it then?

HEDVIG: Yes, Father, do! It'll be such fun to see what's in it!

HJALMAR: Very well. (*He opens the envelope, takes out a paper, reads it through, and seems bewildered.*) What does this mean—?

GINA: What does it say?

HEDVIG: Do tell us, Father dear!

HJALMAR: Be quiet. (*Reads it through again; he turns pale but speaks with self-control.*) It's a deed of gift.

HEDVIG: Really? What do I get?

HJALMAR: Here—read it yourself. (HEDVIG *takes it and goes over to the lamp to read it.*)

HJALMAR (*in an undertone, clenching his hands*): The eyes! The eyes—and now, *this!*

HEDVIG: But—isn't this for Grandfather?

HJALMAR (*takes the paper from her*): Gina—what do you make of it?

GINA: I wouldn't understand anything about it. Just tell me what it is.

HJALMAR: It's a letter to Hedvig from Mr. Werle, informing her that in the future her grandfather need trouble himself no further with any copying work; but, instead—he may draw on Mr. Werle's office for a hundred crowns a month.

GREGERS: Aha!

HEDVIG: A hundred crowns, Mother! That's what I thought it said!

GINA: That's nice for Grandfather.

HJALMAR: —a hundred crowns a month as long as he may need it; which means as long as he lives, of course.

GINA: Poor old man—so he's provided for at least.

HJALMAR: Wait. There's more to come. You probably didn't read this, Hedvig. Afterwards the gift reverts to you.

HEDVIG: To me! All that money to *me!*

HJALMAR: For the rest of your life you will receive a hundred crowns a month, he writes. Do you hear that, Gina?

GINA: Yes, I hear it.

HEDVIG: All that money, Father! Think of it! (*Shakes him.*) Father, Father—aren't you glad?

HJALMAR (*shakes her off*): Glad! (*Paces up and down.*) God! What perspectives—what vistas all this opens up to me! So—it's Hedvig! Why should he shower gifts on her!

GINA: Well, I suppose—it's Hedvig's birthday after all—

HEDVIG: But it will all belong to you, Father! You know I'll give it all to you and Mother!

HJALMAR: To your mother, yes! Of course—that's as it should be!

GREGERS: Hjalmar—this is a trap he's laid for you.

HJALMAR: Another one of his traps, you think?

GREGERS: He said to me only this morning: Hjalmar Ekdal is not the man you take him for.

HJALMAR: Not the man—!

GREGERS: You'll soon find out, he said.

HJALMAR: So he wants to show you he can bribe me—

HEDVIG: Mother, what does all this mean?

GINA: Go and take off your things.

(HEDVIG *goes out through the kitchen, on the verge of tears.*)

GREGERS: Well, Hjalmar—? Was *he* right about you, or am I?

HJALMAR (*slowly tears the paper in two and lays the pieces on the table*): There is my answer.

GREGERS: Just what I expected.

HJALMAR (*goes over to* GINA *who is standing by the stove and says in a low voice*): I want no more lies, I warn you, Gina. If things were really over between you and Werle when you became "fond of me"—as you choose to put it—why did he make it possible for us to marry?

GINA: He perhaps thought he'd be able to come and go as he liked, here in our house.

HJALMAR: Was that all? Mightn't he have been afraid? Wasn't it something to do with your condition at the time?

GINA: I don't know what you mean.

HJALMAR: I must know—Has your child the right to live under my roof?

GINA (*draws herself up; her eyes flash*): You ask *me* that!

HJALMAR: Answer me! Does Hedvig belong to me—or—? Well?

GINA (*looks at him coldly and defiantly*): I don't know.

HJALMAR (*trembling slightly*): You don't know?

GINA: No. How should I? A creature like *me*—?

HJALMAR (*quietly, turning away from her*): Then I have nothing more to do in this house.

GREGERS: Consider what you're doing, Hjalmar!

HJALMAR (*putting on his overcoat*): What is there to consider? For a man like me there can be no alternative.

GREGERS: There are many things to be considered. You three must stay together. How else can you start afresh in a spirit of forgiveness and self-sacrifice?

HJALMAR: I don't want to. Never, never! My hat! (*Takes his hat.*) My home is nothing but a mass of ruins! (*Bursts into tears.*) Gregers! I have no child!

HEDVIG (*who has opened the kitchen door*): Father! What are you saying! (*Runs to him.*) Father!

GINA: There, you see!

HJALMAR: Don't touch me, Hedvig! Keep away from me—I can't bear to look at you! Oh! Those eyes—! Good-bye. (*Starts towards the door.*)

HEDVIG (*clings to him, screaming*): No! No! Don't leave me!

GINA (*cries out*): The poor child, Hjalmar! Look at the child!

HJALMAR: I won't! I can't! I must get out of here—away from this! (*He tears himself away from* HEDVIG *and goes out through the hall door.*)

HEDVIG (*her eyes full of despair*): He's going away from us, Mother! He's going away! He'll never come back—never!

GINA: Don't cry, Hedvig. Father will come back—you'll see.

HEDVIG (*flings herself down on the sofa sobbing*): No he won't! He won't! He'll never come home to us any more!

GREGERS: I meant it all for the best, Mrs. Ekdal. You do believe that, don't you?

GINA: Yes—I suppose so. But God forgive you all the same.

HEDVIG: I shall die if he doesn't come back, Mother—I shall die! What have I done to him? Go and find him, Mother, and bring him home again!

GINA: Yes, darling—yes! Try and be calm now. I'll go and look for him. (*Puts on her outdoor things.*) Perhaps he's down at Relling's. Don't cry any more—promise!

HEDVIG (*sobbing convulsively*): I won't—I won't! I promise! If only he'll come back!

GREGERS: You don't think it would be better to let him fight it out alone?

GINA: Let him do that later! We must get the child quieted down first. (*Goes out by the hall door.*)

HEDVIG (*sits up and dries her tears*): Please! What is it all about? You've got to tell me! Why doesn't Father want me any more?

GREGERS: You must wait till you're grown-up before asking about that.

HEDVIG: But I can't wait till I'm grown-up and go on being miserable like this!—I think I know what it's all about—Perhaps I'm not really Father's child.

GREGERS (*uneasily*): How could *that* be?

HEDVIG: Mother may have picked me up somewhere; and Father's just discovered it. I've read about things like that.

GREGERS: But even if that were so—

HEDVIG: I don't see why he should stop being fond of me on that account; I should think he'd love me even more. The wild duck came to us as a present too—and I love it very dearly all the same.

GREGERS (*switches the conversation*): The wild duck—yes! Let's talk about the wild duck for a while.

HEDVIG: Poor wild duck. He can't bear to look at her either any more. Just think—he said he'd like to wring her neck!

GREGERS: But I'm sure he'd never do it!

HEDVIG: He said he'd like to! I thought it was horrid of him. I say a prayer for the wild duck every night. I ask God to protect it from death and everything that's evil.

GREGERS (*looking at her*): Do you say your prayers every night?

HEDVIG: Yes, I do.

GREGERS: Who taught you to do that?

HEDVIG: I taught myself. Father was terribly ill once—they had to put leeches on his chest. He kept saying death was staring him in the face.

GREGERS: Well?

HEDVIG: So that night when I went to bed, I said a prayer for him. And I've kept on with it ever since.

GREGERS: And now you pray for the wild duck too?

HEDVIG: Yes, I thought I'd better; she was so very weak at first, you know.

GREGERS: Do you say your prayers in the morning too?

HEDVIG: No—of course not!

GREGERS: Why not? Aren't morning prayers any good?

HEDVIG: Well—in the morning it's light, you see; there's nothing to be afraid of then.

GREGERS: And this wild duck you're so fond of— You say your father wanted to wring its neck?

HEDVIG: He said he'd *like* to—but that he'd spare her for my sake. That was kind of him, I thought.

GREGERS (*coming a little nearer*): What if you were to offer up the wild duck as a sacrifice? For *his* sake?

HEDVIG (*rises*): The wild duck!

GREGERS: Yes. Supposing you were to sacrifice to him the thing you love most dearly in the world?

HEDVIG: Would that do any good—do you think?

GREGERS: Try it, Hedvig.

HEDVIG (*softly, with shining eyes*): Very well—I *will*.

GREGERS: Do you think you'll really have the courage?

HEDVIG: The wild duck! I'll ask Grandfather to shoot it for me.

GREGERS: Yes, do that. But don't say a word to your mother about it.

HEDVIG: Why not?

GREGERS: She doesn't understand us.

HEDVIG: The wild duck! I'll try and do it the first thing in the morning.

(GINA *comes in from the hall door.*)

HEDVIG (*goes to her*): Did you find him, Mother?

GINA: No. But he went to fetch Relling, and they went out together.

GREGERS: Are you sure?

GINA: The porter's wife told me—she saw them. Molvik was with them too, she said.

GREGERS: That's strange! I should have thought he'd want to fight things out alone—!

GINA (*taking off her things*): Men are queer creatures! God knows *where* Relling's dragged him off to. I ran over to Mrs. Eriksen's—but they weren't there.

HEDVIG (*fighting back her tears*): What if he *never* comes back to us, Mother!

GREGERS: He'll come back. I'll send him word tomorrow. You'll see—he'll come. Go to sleep now, Hedvig—and don't worry. Good night. (*He goes out by the hall door.*)

HEDVIG (*sobbing, throws herself into her mother's arms*): Mother! Mother!

GINA (*pats her shoulder and sighs*): Ah, yes! Relling was right. That's what happens when people come around with all this crazy talk of claims and idols!

CURTAIN

ACT V

SCENE: *Hjalmar Ekdal's studio. Cold gray morning light; patches of snow lie on the large panes of the studio window.*

GINA enters from the kitchen wearing an apron with a bib and carrying a broom and a duster; she goes toward the sitting-room door. At the same moment HEDVIG comes in quickly from the hall.

GINA (*stops*): Well?

HEDVIG: Mother—you know, I think he's down at Relling's—

GINA: There, you see!

HEDVIG: —Because the porter's wife says there were two people with Relling when he came home last night.

GINA: Just what I thought.

HEDVIG: But what good does it do, if he won't come up to us?

GINA: At least I can go down and have a talk with him.

(*OLD EKDAL in his slippers and a dressing gown, and smoking his pipe, appears at the door of his room.*)

EKDAL: Oh, Hjalmar— Isn't Hjalmar home?

GINA: No, he's gone out.

EKDAL: What—so early? And in all this snow? Well—never mind. I'll take my morning walk alone.

(*He slides open the attic door; HEDVIG helps him; he goes in; she closes it after him.*)

HEDVIG: Mother—what will poor Grandfather do, when he hears that Father's going to leave us?

GINA: Nonsense! Grandfather mustn't know anything about it. Thank God he was out yesterday—during all the rumpus.

HEDVIG: Yes, but—

(*GREGERS comes in from the hall.*)

GREGERS: Well? Any news of him?

GINA: They say he's down at Relling's.

GREGERS: Relling's! Did he *really* go out with those two?

GINA: It looks like it.

GREGERS: How could he! When it was so important for him to be alone—to collect his thoughts in solitude!

GINA: Yes. That's what he should have done.

(*RELLING comes in from the hall.*)

HEDVIG (*going to him*): Is Father down with you?

GINA (*simultaneously*): Is he down there?

RELLING: Yes, of course he is.

HEDVIG: You might have let us know!

RELLING: Yes—I'm a swine, I know. But I had that other swine on my hands—our daemonic friend, I mean. And I got so tired, I fell into a stupor—

GINA: What has Hjalmar got to say today?

RELLING: Nothing whatever.

HEDVIG: Hasn't he said anything at all?

RELLING: Not a blessed word.

GREGERS: Well—that's understandable enough.

GINA: Then what's he doing?

RELLING: Lying on the sofa snoring.

GINA: Is he? He's a great one for snoring, Hjalmar is.

GREGERS: You mean—he's actually *asleep*?

RELLING: He certainly appears to be.

GREGERS: I expect it's only natural; after the spiritual crisis he's been through—

GINA: And then, he's not used to gadding about at night.

HEDVIG: It'll do him good to get some sleep, Mother.

GINA: That's what I think. We'd better not wake him up too early. Thanks, Relling. I'll see about getting the house cleaned up a bit —come and help me, Hedvig.

(GINA *and* HEDVIG *go into the sitting room.*)

GREGERS (*turning to* RELLING): How would you explain this spiritual upheaval that Hjalmar Ekdal's going through?

RELLING: Damned if I saw anything resembling a spiritual upheaval—!

GREGERS: Come now! At a turning point like this? When he's about to start on a whole new way of life—? You must realize that a man of Hjalmar's character—

RELLING: Did you say *character*? Hjalmar? If he ever possessed a vestige of that rare attribute, it was crushed in him, I assure you— thoroughly extirpated—while he was still a child.

GREGERS: That seems hardly likely—considering the loving care with which he was brought up.

RELLING: By those doting, hysterical maiden aunts of his, you mean?

GREGERS: Let me tell you they were women who never lost sight of the Ideal—now, I suppose, you'll start jeering again!

RELLING: No—I'm in no mood for that. I happen to know a lot about these ladies; he's often waxed eloquent on the subject of his two "soul-mothers"—as he calls them! Hjalmar has had the great misfortune of always being looked on as a shining light in his own particular circle—

GREGERS: And don't you think he is? Deep down—I mean?

RELLING: I've certainly never noticed it. That his father should have thought so—that's understandable enough; the old lieutenant's always been somewhat of an ass.

GREGERS: He's a man who has never lost his childlike nature—that's what you fail to understand.

RELLING: All right—have it your own way! Then, when our dear sweet Hjalmar went to college, his fellow students looked on him as the great hope of the Future, too. He was handsome enough— the scoundrel! Pink and white—the kind the girls all go for. And then he had a facile mind, and a romantic voice which he used to good effect declaiming other people's poetry, and other people's thoughts—

GREGERS (*indignantly*): It can't be Hjalmar Ekdal you're talking about like this—?

RELLING: Yes—with your permission. This is the truth about that idol of yours to whom you bow the knee.

GREGERS: It never occurred to me I could be quite *that* blind.

RELLING: You are though—pretty nearly. You're a sick man too, you see.

GREGERS: You're right about that, at least.

RELLING: Yes. Yours is a complicated case. First you've got that blasted Integrity-Fever to contend with; then—what's worse—you live in a constant delirium of hero worship; it's absolutely necessary for you to look up to and adore something outside yourself.

GREGERS: It would inevitably have to be something outside myself.

RELLING: But you make such ridiculous mistakes about these imaginary paragons of yours! Why do you persist in presenting your Claim of the Ideal to people who are totally insolvent?

GREGERS: Why do you spend so much time with Hjalmar Ekdal, if this is your opinion of him?

RELLING: I'm a doctor of sorts, you know—God help me! I feel obliged to look after the sick people who live under the same roof with me.

GREGERS: So you think Hjalmar Ekdal is sick too?

RELLING: Most people are sick, unfortunately.

GREGERS: May I ask what cure you're using in Hjalmar's case?

RELLING: My usual one. I try to discover the Basic Lie—the pet illusion—that makes life possible; and then I foster it.

GREGERS: The basic lie? Surely—I misunderstood—?

RELLING: No, no; that's what I said: the Basic Lie that makes life possible.

GREGERS: And what "basic lie" do you suppose Hjalmar to be suffering from?

RELLING: I don't betray secrets like that to quacks. You've made enough mess of the case for me already. But my method is infallible; I've used it on Molvik too; I've convinced him he's daemonic —that did the trick for him.

GREGERS: You mean—he's *not* daemonic?

RELLING: What the Hell does it mean: to be daemonic? It's a lot of nonsense I invented to make life possible for him. Without that the poor harmless wretch would have gone under years ago—in an agony of despair and self-contempt. And what about the old lieutenant? But that's different: he discovered the cure for himself, you see.

GREGERS: Lieutenant Ekdal? What do you mean?

RELLING: Just think of it! The mighty bear hunter shooting rabbits in the attic. And there's no happier hunter in the world than that old man fooling about in there in all that rubbish. He's saved four or five withered old Christmas trees, and to him they're just as beautiful and green and fresh as the whole of the great Höjdal forest. To him the rooster and the hens are wild birds in the treetops; and the rabbits that lope about the attic floor are the bears he used to grapple with out in the wilds, when he was young and vigorous.

GREGERS: Poor old Lieutenant Ekdal; he's gone a long way from the ideals of his youth.

RELLING: While I think of it, Mr. Werle Junior—I wish you'd stop using that foreign word: ideals. We have a perfectly good one of our own: lies.

GREGERS: You seem to think the two things are related!

RELLING: They are: they're as alike as typhoid and malignant fever.

GREGERS: I shall never give up until I've rescued Hjalmar from your clutches, Dr. Relling.

RELLING: So much the worse for *him*. Rob the average man of his basic lie and you rob him of his happiness as well. (*To* HEDVIG *who comes in from the sitting room*) And now, little wild-duck mother, I'll just run down and see how your father's getting on; I expect he's lying there meditating on that wonderful invention. (*He goes out through the hall door.*)

GREGERS (*going up to* HEDVIG): You haven't done it yet, have you? I can see it in your face.

HEDVIG: What? Oh, you mean—about the wild duck? No.

GREGERS: When it actually came to the point, I suppose your courage failed you.

HEDVIG: No—it wasn't that. But when I woke up this morning and remembered what we'd talked about, it seemed queer to me somehow.

GREGERS: Queer?

HEDVIG: Yes; I don't know— Last night, right at the time, I thought it was a very beautiful idea; but I didn't think so much of it—after I'd slept on it, you see.

GREGERS: I see that growing up in the atmosphere of this house has unfortunately had its effect on you.

HEDVIG: I don't care about that—if only Father would come back to us—

GREGERS: If only your eyes had been opened to the true values in life; if you only had the joyous, courageous spirit of self-sacrifice, you'd see how quickly your father would come back to you— But I still have faith in you, Hedvig—don't forget that. (*He goes out into the hall.*)

(HEDVIG *paces about the room; she is about to go into the kitchen when a knock is heard at the attic door;* HEDVIG *goes over and opens it a little way;* OLD EKDAL *comes out. She slides the door closed again.*)

EKDAL: Hm. Not much fun going for your morning walk alone.

HEDVIG: Didn't you feel like going hunting, Grandfather?

EKDAL: Weather's not right for hunting; it's so dark you can hardly see.

HEDVIG: Do you ever feel like shooting anything besides the rabbits?

EKDAL: Why? Aren't the rabbits good enough?

HEDVIG: Yes, of course; but, what about the wild duck?

EKDAL: Ho-ho! You're afraid I'll shoot your wild duck, are you? I'd never do that. Never.

HEDVIG: No. I don't suppose you could, could you? It's very difficult to shoot wild ducks, they say.

EKDAL: What do you mean I *could*n't? I should rather think I *could!*

HEDVIG: How would you go about it, Grandfather?—Not with *my* wild duck, of course; I mean with others?

EKDAL: I'd shoot at the breast, you see; that's the surest place. And then you must always shoot *against* the feathers, you understand— not *with* them.

HEDVIG: And then do they die, Grandfather?

EKDAL: They die all right—if you shoot properly. I'll go in and brush up a bit. Hm—you see—hm. (*Goes into his room.*)

(HEDVIG *waits a moment or two, glances towards the sitting room door, goes over to the bookcase, stands on tiptoe, takes the double-barreled pistol down from the shelf and looks at it.* GINA *carrying her broom and duster comes in from the sitting room.* HEDVIG *puts down the pistol hastily without being seen.*)

GINA: Don't stand there messing about with your father's things, Hedvig.

HEDVIG (*going away from the bookcase*): I was just trying to tidy up a bit.

GINA: You'd better go in the kitchen and see if the coffee's keeping hot. I'll take a tray down to him when I go.

(HEDVIG *goes out;* GINA *begins sweeping and cleaning up the studio. After a while the hall door opens cautiously and* HJALMAR EKDAL *looks in; he wears his overcoat but no hat; he is unwashed and his hair is dishevelled and unkempt. His eyes are dull and heavy.*)

GINA (*stands with the broom in her hand and looks at him*): Well now, Hjalmar—you came back after all.

HJALMAR (*comes in and answers in a gloomy voice*): I've come back —but only to go away again immediately.

GINA: Yes—I suppose so. But, my goodness! What a state you're in!

HJALMAR: A state?

GINA: And it's your good overcoat too! That's done for, I'm afraid!

HEDVIG (*at the kitchen door*): Mother, shall I—? (*Sees* HJALMAR, *gives a cry of joy and runs toward him.*) Father, Father!

HJALMAR (*turns away with a gesture of repulsion*): Keep away from me! (*To* GINA) Keep her away, I tell you!

GINA (*in an undertone*): Go into the sitting room, Hedvig. (HEDVIG *silently obeys.*)

HJALMAR (*making a show of being busy opens the table drawer*): I want my books—I'll need them with me. Where are my books?

GINA: What books?

HJALMAR: My scientific books, of course— All those technical periodicals I need for my invention.

GINA (*looking in the bookcase*): Are they these things—without a binding?

HJALMAR: Yes—naturally.

GINA (*lays a pile of magazines on the table*): Don't you want Hedvig to cut the pages for you?

HJALMAR: I want no pages cut for me.

(*A short pause.*)

GINA: So you still intend to leave us, Hjalmar?

HJALMAR (*rummaging among the books*): I should think that was obvious.

GINA: Well, well!

HJALMAR: I don't intend to stay here to be stabbed through the heart each hour of the day!

GINA: God forgive you for believing all those dreadful things about me!

HJALMAR: Then prove—!

GINA: I think you're the one who ought to prove!

HJALMAR: After a past like yours? There are certain claims—I'm tempted to call them claims of the Ideal—

GINA: What about Grandfather? What's going to happen to him— poor old man?

HJALMAR: I know my duty. The poor helpless old man shall go with me. I'll go out presently and make arrangements—Hm. (*Hesitating*) Did anyone find my hat on the stairs?

GINA: No. Have you lost your hat?

HJALMAR: I naturally had it on when I came in last night; there's no doubt about that. But this morning I couldn't find it.

GINA: Dear Lord! Where on earth did you go with those two good-for-nothings?

HJALMAR: Don't bother me with trifles. I'm in no mood to remember details.

GINA: I do hope you haven't caught cold, Hjalmar! (*Goes out into the kitchen.*)

HJALMAR (*mutters to himself in a low angry tone as he empties the table drawer*): You're a scoundrel, Relling; an infamous, treacherous scoundrel! I wish to God someone would wring your neck! (*He lays aside some old letters, catches sight of the torn document from the day before, picks it up and examines the two pieces; puts it down hurriedly as* GINA *enters.*)

GINA (*puts a tray with coffee, etc. down on the table*): You might like a drop of something hot. And there's some bread and butter and a bit of that smoked tongue.

HJALMAR (*glancing at the tray*): Smoked tongue, you say? No! Nothing under this roof! I haven't eaten a morsel of food for nearly twenty-four hours, that's true enough—but never mind! My notes! And the preliminary chapters of my autobiography! What has become of my diary—and all my important papers? (*Opens the door to the sitting room but draws back.*) There she is again!

GINA: The poor child has to be somewhere!

HJALMAR: Come out. (*He stands aside.* HEDVIG, *terrified, comes into the studio.* HJALMAR, *his hand on the door knob, says to* GINA.) During these last few moments in my former home I wish to be spared all contact with intruders— (*Goes into the sitting room.*)

HEDVIG (*runs to her mother and says softly in a trembling voice*): Does he mean me?

GINA: Stay in the kitchen, Hedvig; or, no—perhaps you'd better go to your own room. (*Speaks to* HJALMAR *as she goes in to him.*) Wait a minute, Hjalmar. Don't rummage about in all the drawers; I know where everything is.

HEDVIG (*stands motionless for a moment, confused and terrified; she bites her lips to prevent herself from crying. Then she clenches her hands convulsively and says softly*): The wild duck!
(*She steals over and takes the pistol from the shelf, slides open the attic door a little way, creeps in, and draws the door closed after her.* HJALMAR *and* GINA *begin to argue in the sitting room.*)

HJALMAR (*comes in with some notebooks and old loose sheets of paper and lays them on the table*): What's the good of that portmanteau! That won't hold anything—I've *hundreds* of things to take with me!

GINA (*follows him carrying the portmanteau*): Why not leave everything here for the time being, and just take a clean shirt and a pair of extra underdrawers?

HJALMAR: Phew! These exhausting preparations—! (*He pulls off his overcoat and throws it on the sofa.*)

GINA: Look! Your coffee's getting cold!

HJALMAR: Hm. (*Drinks a gulp without thinking and then another.*)

GINA (*dusting the backs of the chairs*): You'll have a hard time finding a big enough place for all those rabbits.

HJALMAR: Good God! You don't expect me to drag all those rabbits with me!

GINA: Grandfather could never get along without his rabbits.

HJALMAR: He'll just have to get used to it. After all *I'm* sacrificing far more important things than rabbits!

GINA (*dusting the bookcase*): I'd better pack your flute, hadn't I?

HJALMAR: No. No flute for me. But I shall need my pistol.

GINA: Are you going to take that gun along?

HJALMAR: My loaded pistol—yes.

GINA (*looks for it*): It isn't here. He must have taken it in there with him.

HJALMAR: Is he in the attic?

GINA: Of course he is.

HJALMAR: Hm. Poor lonely old man. (*He takes some bread and butter and smoked tongue, eats it, and finishes his cup of coffee.*)

GINA: If we hadn't rented that room, you could have moved in there.

HJALMAR: And go on living under the same roof as—! Never! Never!

GINA: I suppose you couldn't manage in the sitting room for a day or two? You could have it all to yourself; I'd see to that.

HJALMAR: No! I can't breathe inside these walls!

GINA: Why not down with Relling and Molvik, then?

HJALMAR: Never mention their names to me again! The very thought of them is enough to take away my appetite—No—I shall simply have to go out into the storm; go from house to house, seeking shelter for my old father and myself.

GINA: But you have no hat, Hjalmar! You've gone and lost it, you know.

HJALMAR: Those two scoundrels! Vicious, infamous brutes! I'll have to pick up a hat somewhere on the way. (*Takes some more bread and tongue.*) Something'll have to be done about it; I've no desire to risk my life. (*Looks for something on the tray.*)

GINA: What are you looking for?

HJALMAR: Butter.

GINA: I'll get you some at once. (*She goes out into the kitchen.*)

HJALMAR (*shouting after her*): Oh, never mind; dry bread is good enough for me.

GINA (*bringing in a dish of butter*): There you are; it's freshly churned.

(*She pours him a fresh cup of coffee; he sits on the sofa, spreads more butter on the already-buttered bread, and eats and drinks for a while in silence.*)

HJALMAR: Would it be possible for me, without being annoyed by anyone—anyone at all—to stay in the sitting room in there, just for a day or two?

GINA: Why, of course. I only wish you would.

HJALMAR: I don't see how I can possibly get Father moved in such a hurry.

GINA: No. And then, you ought to prepare him too. Tell him you don't want to live here with us any more.

HJALMAR (*pushing away his coffee cup*): Yes, there is that. It's awful to think of having to broach this difficult subject with him. I must have a breathing spell—a chance to think things out. I can't cope with all these problems in a single day!

GINA: Of course not; and it's such awful weather too.

HJALMAR (*touching* WERLE's *letter*): I see that paper is still hanging about.

GINA: Yes. I haven't touched it.

HJALMAR: Well—it's no concern of mine—

GINA: I certainly never thought of using it.

HJALMAR: Still—there's no sense in throwing it away; in all the commotion of my moving, it might easily—

GINA: I'll take good care of it, Hjalmar.

HJALMAR: In the first place, the gift was made to Father; it's really up to him to decide whether he'll make use of it or not.

GINA (*sighs*): Yes—poor old Father—

HJALMAR: Just as a matter of precaution, I think—have you any paste?

GINA (*goes to the bookcase*): There's a pot of paste right here.

HJALMAR: And a brush?

GINA: Here's a brush too. (*Brings him the things.*)

HJALMAR (*takes a pair of scissors*): Just a strip of paper on the back —Far be it from me to lay hands on other people's property— especially when it belongs to a penniless old man. And to—that other one as well. There! Leave it there for now, and when it's dry, put it away. I never want to lay eyes on that document again. Never!

(GREGERS WERLE *comes in from the hall.*)

GREGERS (*somewhat surprised*): Oh—you're sitting in here, are you?

HJALMAR (*rises hurriedly*): I just sat down for a moment; out of sheer exhaustion.

GREGERS: You seem to have had breakfast too.

HJALMAR: The body has its claims too, you know—occasionally.

GREGERS: Well—what have you decided?

HJALMAR: For a man like me there can be only one possible decision. I was busy gathering a few of my most important things together; but it's bound to take a little time.

GINA (*with a touch of impatience*): Which shall I do? Get the room ready, or pack your bag for you?

HJALMAR (*with an irritated look at* GREGERS): Pack the bag!—and get the room ready too!

GINA (*picks up the portmanteau*): Very well; I'll just put in the shirt and those other things we spoke of. (*She goes into the sitting room and closes the door after her.*)

GREGERS (*after a short pause*): It never occurred to me that things would come to this. Is it really necessary for you to leave your home?

HJALMAR (*wandering about restlessly*): What would you have me do? I wasn't made to bear unhappiness, Gregers. I need security; I must be surrounded by peace and comfort.

GREGERS: But you could find all that here, couldn't you? Why not try it? You have a splendid opportunity now to start afresh; why not begin again from here? And there's your invention to consider too; don't forget that.

HJALMAR: My invention! Don't even speak of that. That's a very doubtful proposition, I'm afraid.

GREGERS: Really? What do you mean?

HJALMAR: What on earth do you expect me to invent? Other people have invented practically everything already. It gets more difficult every day—

GREGERS: But I thought you'd worked so hard on it.

HJALMAR: It's all that damned Relling's fault!

GREGERS: Relling?

HJALMAR: Yes. He kept on telling me I had great inventive talent— that I would undoubtedly discover something to revolutionize photography.

GREGERS: I see! So it was Relling!

HJALMAR: But it's been a source of great happiness to me. Not so much the invention itself, but the fact that Hedvig had such faith in it. She believed in it as only a child can believe—unreservedly, whole heartedly—At least, I was fool enough to *think* she did.

GREGERS: Hedvig couldn't possibly deceive you—you *must* know that.

HJALMAR: I know nothing any more! She's the obstacle, you see. Hedvig's the one who's plunged my whole life into darkness.

GREGERS: Hedvig! Are you talking about *Hedvig*? How could she possibly plunge your life into darkness?

HJALMAR (*without answering*): I've loved that child more than anything on earth. Each time I came back to this humble room, she would run to meet me—and it was such a joy to see her blinking up at me with those sweet little eyes of hers so full of happiness. I loved her with all my heart—fool that I was! And I imagined that she loved me just as deeply in return.

GREGERS: You *imagined* it, you say?

HJALMAR: What else *can* I say now? I can get nothing out of Gina. Besides—she's totally unaware of the part the Ideal plays in this whole business. But I must open my heart to you, Gregers: I'm tormented by the thought that perhaps Hedvig never really cared for me at all.

GREGERS: And supposing she were to give you a great proof of her love? (*Listens.*) What's that? It sounded like the wild duck—

HJALMAR: Yes—it's the wild duck quacking; Father's in the attic.

GREGERS: Is he! (*His face lights up with joy.*) You'll see—you may soon have proof of how much your poor misunderstood Hedvig loves you.

HJALMAR: What proof could she possibly give me? I'd never dare believe any assurances of hers.

GREGERS: I'm positive Hedvig doesn't even know the meaning of deceit.

HJALMAR: I wouldn't count too much on that, Gregers. Heaven knows what Gina and Mrs. Sörby have sat here scheming and plotting. And Hedvig's no fool—she has sharp ears. That gift may not have been such a surprise to her after all. As a matter of fact, I thought I noticed something in her manner—

GREGERS: What's got into you, Hjalmar? What makes you say such things?

HJALMAR: I've had my eyes opened—that's all. You'll see—this deed of gift may be only the beginning; Mrs. Sörby has always had a great fondness for Hedvig, and now she's in a position to do anything she wants to for the child. They could snatch her away from me whenever they chose to do so.

GREGERS: Nonsense! Hedvig would never consent to leave you.

HJALMAR: Don't be so sure. Just think of all *they* have to offer her! And *I* who have loved her so deeply—! My greatest happiness would have been to take her hand and lead her through life, as one might lead a frightened child through a dark, empty room.

But—I'm convinced of it now!—the poor photographer up in his garret has never meant anything to her at all. She was just being shrewd; trying to keep on the good side of him until something better came along.

GREGERS: Come, Hjalmar—you know you don't believe that yourself.

HJALMAR: I don't know *what* to believe—that's the dreadful part of it—and I shall *never* know. You rely too much on the Ideal, my dear Gregers—otherwise you couldn't possibly doubt the truth of what I say. If those others were to come—laden with all their riches—and call out to the child: Leave him! You'll have a better life with us—

GREGERS: Yes? What then?

HJALMAR: And if I were to ask her: Hedvig, are you willing to give up that better life for me? (*With a scornful laugh*) You'd find out soon enough what her answer would be!

(*A pistol shot is heard in the attic.*)

GREGERS (*loudly and joyfully*): Hjalmar!

HJALMAR: There! He's at his shooting again!

GINA (*comes in*): Oh, Hjalmar—I wish Grandfather wouldn't bang away in there all by himself!

HJALMAR: I think I'll just look in—

GREGERS (*eagerly, with emotion*): Wait, Hjalmar. Do you know what that was?

HJALMAR: Of course I do.

GREGERS: No you don't; but *I* know. That was the proof!

HJALMAR: What proof?

GREGERS: That was the child's sacrifice to you. She's persuaded your father to shoot the wild duck.

HJALMAR: The wild duck!

GINA: Good gracious!

HJALMAR: What's the point of that?

GREGERS: She's sacrificed the thing she loved best in the world to *you*. She thought, if she did that, you'd come to love her again, you see.

HJALMAR (*tenderly, with emotion*): Poor child!

GINA: The things she thinks of!

GREGERS: All she wants is your love, Hjalmar. She can't live without it.

GINA (*fighting back her tears*): You see, Hjalmar!

HJALMAR: Where is she, Gina?

GINA (*sniffs*): She's in the kitchen, I suppose—poor little thing!

HJALMAR (*tears open the kitchen door and says*): Hedvig, come! Come to me, Hedvig! (*Looks round.*) No—she's not in here.

GINA: Then she must be in her room.

HJALMAR (*from outside*): She's not here either. (*Comes in again.*) She must have gone out.

GINA: Well—you wouldn't have her anywhere about the house.

HJALMAR: I hope she'll come home soon—so that I can tell her— Everything's going to be all right now, Gregers. I believe we'll be able to start a new life after all.

GREGERS (*quietly*): Thanks to the child; I knew it would be so.

(OLD EKDAL *appears at the door of his room; he is in full uniform and is busy buckling on his sword.*)

HJALMAR (*in astonishment*): Why, Father! Were you in there?

GINA: Don't tell me you've been shooting in your room?

EKDAL (*approaching, resentfully*): So you go hunting by yourself now, do you, Hjalmar?

HJALMAR (*anxious and bewildered*): I thought you were in the attic; wasn't it you who fired that shot in there?

EKDAL: Fired a shot? I? Hm.

GREGERS (*calls out to* HJALMAR): She's shot the wild duck herself!

HJALMAR: What can it mean! (*Rushes to the attic door, tears it open, looks in, and cries out.*) Hedvig!

GINA (*runs to the door*): God! What's happened?

HJALMAR (*goes into the attic*): She's lying on the floor!

GREGERS: What! Hedvig? (*Goes in to* HJALMAR.)

GINA (*simultaneously*): Hedvig! (*Inside the attic*) No, no, no!

EKDAL: Ho-ho! Is she going shooting too?

(HJALMAR, GINA *and* GREGERS *carry* HEDVIG *into the studio; her right hand hangs down with the pistol still clasped tightly in its fingers.*)

HJALMAR (*distracted*): The pistol must have gone off—she's wounded herself! Call for help! Help!

GINA (*rushes out into the hall and calls down the stairs*): Relling! Relling! Dr. Relling! Come quickly!

(HJALMAR *and* GREGERS *lay* HEDVIG *down on the sofa.*)

EKDAL (*quietly*): The forest takes revenge.

HJALMAR (*on his knees beside her*): She's beginning to come to. She's coming to—yes, yes.

GINA (*who has come in again*): Where is she wounded? I don't see
  anything—
  (RELLING *comes in hurriedly followed by* MOLVIK; *the latter without his waistcoat and necktie, and with his coat open.*)

RELLING: What's happening here?

GINA: They say Hedvig has shot herself.

HJALMAR: Quickly! Help us!

RELLING: Shot herself! (*He pushes the table aside and starts to
  examine her.*)

HJALMAR (*still kneeling, looks up at him anxiously*): It can't be
  serious, can it? Eh, Relling? She's hardly bleeding at all; it can't be
  serious?

RELLING: How did it happen?

HJALMAR: We don't know—!

GINA: She wanted to shoot the wild duck.

RELLING: The wild duck?

HJALMAR: The pistol must have gone off.

RELLING: Hm. I see.

EKDAL: The forest takes revenge. But I'm not afraid! Not I!
  (*Goes into the attic and slides the door shut after him.*)

HJALMAR: Relling—why don't you say something?

RELLING: The bullet entered the breast.

HJALMAR: Yes—but she's coming to—

RELLING: Can't you see that Hedvig's dead?

GINA (*bursts into tears*): My child! My little child!

GREGERS (*huskily*): In the boundless deep—

HJALMAR (*jumps up*): She must live, she *must*! For God's sake,
  Relling—if only for a moment. Just long enough for me to tell her
  how deeply I've loved her all the time!

RELLING: The bullet pierced her heart. Internal hemorrhage. Death
  must have been instantaneous.

HJALMAR: Oh, God! And I drove her from me like a dog! She died
  for love of me: she crept into the attic, filled with grief and terror,
  and died for love of me! (*Sobs.*) Never to be able to tell her!
  Never to be able to atone! (*Clenches his fists and looks upwards
  shouting.*) You, up there—! If you *are* there—! Why have you
  done this thing to me!

GINA: Hush, hush! You mustn't go on like that! We didn't deserve to
  keep her, I suppose.

MOLVIK: The child is not dead; it sleepeth.

RELLING: Rubbish.

HJALMAR (*becomes calm, goes over to the sofa, folds his arms, and looks down at* HEDVIG): She's so stiff—so still.

RELLING (*tries to loosen the hand holding the pistol*): She's holding it so tightly—so very tightly—

GINA: No, Relling—don't force her fingers. Let the gun be.

HJALMAR: She shall take it with her.

GINA: Yes; let her. But the child mustn't lie here—on show like this. She shall go to her own room. Help me, Hjalmar.

(HJALMAR *and* GINA *carry* HEDVIG *between them.*)

HJALMAR (*As they carry her*): Gina, Gina! How can you ever bear it!

GINA: We must try and help each other. At least *now* she belongs to both of us.

MOLVIK (*stretching out his arms and muttering*): Blessed be the Lord; to earth thou shalt return; to earth thou shalt return—

RELLING (*in a whisper*): Shut up, you fool—you're drunk.

(HJALMAR *and* GINA *carry the body out through the kitchen door.* RELLING *shuts it after them.* MOLVIK *slinks out into the hall.*)

RELLING (*goes over to* GREGERS *and says*): No one will ever make me believe this was an accident.

GREGERS (*who has been standing horrified, his face twitching*): How could this dreadful thing have happened. No one will ever know.

RELLING: The front of her dress was burned. She must have aimed the pistol at her heart and fired.

GREGERS: Hedvig has not died in vain. Didn't you see? His sorrow brought out all that is noblest in him.

RELLING: Most people are noble in the presence of death. One wonders how long this nobility of his will last.

GREGERS: Why shouldn't it last? Why shouldn't it increase and grow stronger with the years?

RELLING: The years! Before this year is out, little Hedvig will be no more to him than a theme on which to exercise his eloquence!

GREGERS: How dare you say that of Hjalmar Ekdal!

RELLING: We'll talk of this again when this year's grass has withered on her grave. You'll see: He'll be spouting about "the child snatched from her father's loving arms by an untimely death"; he'll be wallowing in a sea of self-pity and maudlin sentimentality. You wait. You'll see.

GREGERS: All I can say is—if *you* are right and *I* am wrong, then life is not worth living.

RELLING: Life would be quite pleasant all the same—if it were not for certain lunatics, certain fanatics, who hammer at our doors, insisting on some nonsense they call the Claim of the Ideal.

GREGERS (*gazing before him*): Then I'm glad my fate is what it is.

RELLING: And what *is* it, may I ask?

GREGERS (*starts to go*): To be thirteenth at table.

RELLING: The Hell it is. I wish I could believe it!

CURTAIN

Anton Chekhov

Anton Pavlovich Chekhov is one of the few great dramatists who was only sporadically a playwright. Most of Chekhov's creative energy was expended upon the short story and the short novel. His dramatic productions are comparatively few—six long plays, one of which, *Uncle Vanya*, was a revision of his earlier *The Wood Demon*, and several one-act plays. Nevertheless, four of these long plays, *The Sea Gull* (1896), *Uncle Vanya* (1897), *The Three Sisters* (1900), and *The Cherry Orchard* (1904) have long been ranked among the great classics of the drama.

Born on January 17, 1860 in Tanganrog, a provincial town in southern Russia on the Asov Sea, Chekhov was only a generation removed from serfdom. His grandfather, an ambitious and determined serf, had worked hard and saved enough money to buy freedom for himself and his family. He became the overseer of an estate and helped his sons to go into business. The writer's father, Pavel Chekhov, operated a small grocery store, but a love of music, which he expressed by organizing and leading a church choir, kept him away from his business too many hours to provide any kind of economic security for his wife and six children. Anton, the third-born son, and the other children were forced to spend many childhood hours behind the grocery counter while their father was training his choir. Despite their poverty and the frequent harsh treatment of their stern, religious father, the Chekhov children were fun-loving, vigorous, and ambitious. One of their favorite pastimes was presenting dramatic skits, frequently original satires of life in their provincial town. Anton was the most effective actor of this family troupe and evoked roars of laughter with his imitations.

The children were compelled to attend services in the Russian Orthodox Church and to sing in their father's choir. Years later the dramatist noted with bitterness, "I was brought up in religion and received a religious education; I sang in the choir, read from the Apostles and the Psalms in church, attended regularly at matins, and was compelled to assist at the altar and ring the bells. And what is the result? I remember my childhood as a pretty gloomy affair, and I'm not a bit religious now." Chekhov entered manhood an agnostic, but his early religious experience left its impact. He could not believe, but he longed for the spiritual security and peace that belief could provide.

Education, the Chekhov parents realized, was the sole means of advancement for their children, and they made certain that all of them attended school. In 1875, the two eldest boys, Alexander and Nikolai completed their studies in the local high school and left for Moscow to attend the University. The family could provide them no financial assistance, and they were expected to earn their own livelihood while studying. Not long after they established themselves in Moscow, they were joined by their family: Pavel Chekhov went bankrupt and unceremoniously left Tanganrog for a life of extreme poverty in Moscow.

Anton was left behind to complete his studies at the gymnasium, supporting himself by tutoring and doing odd jobs. During these three lonely years, he developed the independence, ambition, and overriding sense of responsibility that characterized him throughout his life. He not only supported himself but responded to the urgent pleas of his mother for monetary assistance by sending her part of his meager income. He applied himself diligently to his school work and when he was graduated he was awarded a small scholarship to continue his education at the University. He joined his family in their four-room basement apartment, bringing with him two paying boarders to supplement the family income, and he enrolled in the medical school. During his five years of medical study, Chekhov became the main support of his mother and younger brothers and sister by writing humorous sketches for the comic weeklies. The pay was meager, and he had to supply a massive quantity of material to earn a minimum income. Working under the most adverse conditions in the overcrowded apartment, Chekhov quickly became a prolific and professional humorist.

His course of study at the University demanded more time and energy each passing year, but before he received his degree, Chekhov wrote a play (which was not produced or published at that time), published over three hundred sketches and short stories in the comic weeklies, became the writer of a weekly column about Moscow life, and published a collection of his short stories. The divided career of this talented writer began as soon as he entered medical school. With the tremendous energy that was probably rooted in zest for life, ambition, and a strong sense of responsibility for his family, Chekhov attended classes, combed Moscow for material for his stories and his column, acceded to his passion for the drama by haunting the Moscow theaters, and still had time and energy for a widening circle of literary friends, for boisterous good times, and for serving as counselor to his bohemian older brothers who were debilitating their talents for writing and painting.

Six months after Dr. Chekhov began to practice medicine, he suffered his first hemorrhage from the tuberculosis which was to plague him for twenty years and end his life in 1904 at the age of forty-four. Chekhov managed for many years to deny to himself that the spells of violent coughing and the periodic hemorrhages were caused by the dreaded tuberculosis which had taken the lives of several members of his mother's family and which was to kill his brother Nikolai within a few years. When, in his late thirties, he could no longer ignore the severity of his illness, Chekhov never relinquished his self-imposed responsibility for the economic welfare of his family. He continued his double career and kept his house open to the increasing number of callers and the many friends with whom he surrounded himself. He remained always a humorous and witty companion, sharing with no one the spiritual anguish that created the atmosphere of his finest stories.

During his medical school years, Chekhov wrote for one reason only—money. He considered himself a journalist and entertained no illusions about the quality and value of the material he turned out rapidly under the pseudonym of Antosha Chekhonte. His work, however, did attract many readers, and in 1887, the editor of the St. Petersburg *New Times,* himself a writer, invited Chekhov to contribute stories to his influential newspaper. For the first time, Chekhov was free from the restrictions of the comic weeklies, and he began to publish short stories under his own name. A famous writer, Grigorovich, was so impressed by the quality of these stories that he wrote a letter to the unknown young writer praising his great talent but urging him not to waste it by dashing off his work so hurriedly and failing to take himself seriously. This letter and the increasing public response to his stories marked a turning point in Chekhov's literary career. He began to rewrite and polish his stories before he sent them off to be published; he became a dedicated and serious artist. Within a short time, Chekhov was an important figure in Russian literary circles. The increase in income that his reputation provided permitted him to take his family to the country for summers and to provide better living quarters in Moscow, but his continuing desire to elevate the family's standard of living kept him perpetually short of funds.

Many friends and admirers exhorted the short story writer to write a novel. Chekhov, however, found the novel form uncongenial. He had developed a concise technique of storytelling that was unsuited for the looser structure of the contemporary novel. That technique, however, he was able to utilize in drama, and he wrote a full length play, *Ivanov*. Its production in 1887 established him as an important dramatist. Chekhov, himself, was not at all sure of his dramatic talent. The staging of the play convinced him that he had not been understood, and before its St. Petersburg opening he revised it extensively. The favorable reviews did not convince him that he had achieved the communication he wanted by revising. The dismal failure of *The Wood Demon* (1889) enforced this conviction, and for seven years he abandoned the drama.

His literary reputation continued to grow. The publication of two volumes of short stories, *At Dusk* and *Tedious People,* brought him the coveted Pushkin Prize in 1888. The following year, to the dismay of his admirers and family, Chekhov suddenly decided to study at first hand the conditions of Sakhalin Island in Siberia where Russian criminals were exiled. He traveled overland to this remote prison island, and in 1894 published a two-volume report of the intolerable conditions he had seen. Of limited literary interest, the study probably prodded Russian officials to enact needed prison reforms. This work is unique in Chekhov's literary career. He generally viewed the artist as an objective observer of life rather than a propagandist, and though he devoted himself to caring for sick peasants and even to building schools with his own funds, he retained his artistic objectivity. The Sakhalin Island work may, in fact, have been undertaken to placate his social conscience.

A short time after he returned from his journey, Chekhov, the grandson of a serf, satisfied a long-standing ambition by purchasing an estate in Melikhovo not far from Moscow. During his five years in this country house, he wrote some of his greatest stories, and, disregarding his resolution to avoid the drama, *The Sea Gull*. Unfortunately, opening night in 1896 was disheartening. A leading actress who had been scheduled to appear in the play was replaced. Her vociferous claque had come to see her rather than Chekhov's play and they hissed and booed to show their disappointment. That night Chekhov renewed his vow never again to write for the stage. Succeeding performances of the drama, fortunately, were warmly received, and Chekhov was soon planning a new play.

At the age of thirty-seven, Chekhov suffered a very severe hemorrhage, and he was forced to leave Melikhovo for the more congenial climate of the Crimea. The writer traveled occasionally to the European Riviera, but most of the time he lived in Yalta, where he built a house. He missed the excitement of Moscow life and considered himself an exile, but his contact with the Moscow theater world actually increased at this time. In 1898 Nemirovich-Danchenko, co-founder and co-director with Stanislavsky, of a new theater called the Moscow Art Theater began to importune Chekhov to permit them to stage *The Sea Gull*. Still discouraged by the play's initial reception, Chekhov at first refused; finally he agreed, and a mutually beneficial relationship was begun. Stanislavsky's insistence upon realism and his demand that the actors thoroughly understand the characters they depicted provided Chekhov the kind of theater his new type of drama required. The new company made its impact on the history of theater with its staging of Chekhov's plays, and their need for new material eventually wrested from Chekhov *Uncle Vanya*, *The Three Sisters*, and, finally, *The Cherry Orchard*.

Chekhov's relationship with the Moscow Art Theater also affected his personal life. During rehearsals of *The Sea Gull* which he came to Moscow to attend he met and was attracted to an actress in the company, Olga Knipper. Because he knew that his illness was rapidly destroying him, Chekhov resisted marriage. In 1901, however, love and Olga overcame his reluctance. Olga's career in Moscow kept the couple apart for long periods, but the marriage brought much happiness to Chekhov during the final years of his life. He lacked the strength for intense concentrated work, and he put off beginning the new play he had promised his wife he would write for her company. Gradually, during the final year of his life, *The Cherry Orchard* took shape. Its premiere, on the writer's forty-fourth birthday, January 17,

1904, was a personal tribute to the dying writer. Within six months Russia's foremost dramatist died quietly in Badenweiser, a German health resort to which he had gone with his wife.

Anton Chekhov was a modest man who invariably expressed dissatisfaction with the quality of his literary work, and who never presumed to set down his artistic credo. He was, however, an indefatigable letter writer, and in some of the thousands of letters he wrote he consciously developed such a credo. One of the major tenets of his art was objectivity. The artist should observe and present life as it is, and he should not make his art a vehicle for the expression of his own opinions and beliefs. Chekhov's insistence on objectivity was undoubtedly conditioned by his scientific training. He drew his material from the squalid, frustrated, puzzled, struggling people with whom he came into contact as a medical doctor. Each of his stories attempts to present a fragment of life as it is—not as it should be, or as it might be, or as the artist imagines it. Almost instinctively, Chekhov allied himself with the realistic and naturalistic literary movements then developing in Europe. Unlike many of his European contemporaries, however, Chekhov never saw himself as a reformer. His aim was to recreate reality.

More important perhaps than his scientific training in the shaping of Chekhov's art, was the writer's introspective nature and his sensitivity to the individuality and integrity of his fellow man. The ethical code by which he lived was essentially Christian, with its emphasis upon sympathy for others and respect for their rights. Chekhov's letters and his literary work reveal that he did not simply pay lip service to such ethical strictures. He recognized that his own need for identity, his own inner fears and hopes mirrored those of every other person. Combined with this sensitivity for his fellow man was Chekhov's typically Russian proclivity for philosophical speculation. During the final quarter of the nineteenth century, Russia was beginning to respond to the new ideas that were sweeping Europe and to the undercurrent that would, within a few decades, produce a modern industrial nation. Old beliefs were being undermined and the educated sought new ideas and ideals. Many such ideals, for example Tolstoy's program for a return to the soil and the simple Christian life, were engendered by a need for absolute answers to life's problems. Russian intellectuals, made skeptical by increasing knowledge, longed for final answers, absolutes to replace the recently abandoned religious beliefs. Most Russians tended to ally themselves passionately with some social, political, or religious ideal. Chekhov, however, remained unallied and skeptical. A great admirer of Tolstoy and spiritually attracted by the great writer's ideas, he nevertheless could not accept Tolstoy's philosophy. To Chekhov, it, like all the other ideals currently available, was too dogmatic, too simple for the complexities of human life.

In his stories and dramas, Chekhov frequently satirized the tendency of contemporary intellectuals to ponder the meaning of life and to express soulfully their pessimism and self-pity; but he laughed, as he always did, with sympathy. In one of his stories, "Lights," for example, the main character denounces the pessimism of young people as a social fad, but he also declares that "thoughts of the transitoriness of life, its lack of meaning and aim, of the inevitability of death, of the shadows of the grave, are good and natural in old age, when they come as the products of years of inner travail."

To such thoughts, Chekhov apparently gave himself. His experiences as a doctor had convinced him that there must be some over-all design in nature, but whatever that unknown design might be, it did not provide a favored place for the human being. Passionately desiring the security of absolute belief but unable to ignore the evidence of reality and the intellect, Chekhov, an admirer of Darwin, eventually developed a vague belief in a developing world which would eventually bring man happiness—perhaps hundreds or thousands of years in the future. This belief he usually expressed through some character, such as Trofimoff, the student, in *The Cherry Orchard*, who declares, "Humanity is advancing towards the highest truth, the highest happiness which is possible on earth, and I am in the front ranks." The real world, however, provided no comfort to the anguished spirit of one who pondered life's aim and meaning. In a letter, Chekhov once wrote, "I have no political, religious and philosophical *Weltanschauung* yet. I change it every month, and so I have to restrict myself to describing how my heroes love, marry, have children, die, and how they talk." He was probably expressing his own spiritual state in "Terror," when he has a character declare: "I am afraid of everything. I am afraid because I do not understand what is the use of all this to anyone. I do not understand anyone or anything."

As a realist, Chekhov aimed to present not only the physical conditions of human life but also the equally real inner spiritual condition of mankind. To do so he required new techniques and a new form. He abandoned the traditional method of storytelling, with its emphasis upon action and plot, because it tended to dramatize and falsify life. Life was usually uneventful and tedious; the real drama of each life was revealed in subtle emotional experiences and spiritual states. Chekhov's stories are epiphanies—revelations through mood—of spiritual aspects of existence.

In the drama, Chekhov developed a similar technique. He rejected the prevailing theatricality of his time, and he rejected the Ibsen type of message drama. He expressed his dissatisfaction with the current drama in a letter following the production of his first play: "The playwrights of today begin their plays with angels, villains, and clowns. Now, look for these in the whole of Russia. Yes, you can find them, but such extreme characters are not required for a playwright. One is forced to wring them out of one's head, start perspiring and give it up as a bad job. I wanted to be original; I have not invented a single angel or villain, though I could not resist the clowns. I accused no one, justified nobody."

This dramatic credo emphasizes real people and life as it is lived; Chekhov developed it in the five plays that followed *Ivanov*. He eschewed the stock characters of drama; of more importance, he created a drama without villains or heroes, without central characters around whom the action develops. Some of Chekhov's characters have more important roles than others, but none is simply a butler or a governess, used to provide background for a central character or action. Each Chekhov character, no matter what his role, conveys to the audience his sense of his own human significance. In real life, every human being is the hero of his own life; the circle of his existence impinges upon the circles of others, but no matter what his social station, no matter how menial his life work, each person is central in his own consciousness and everyone else is peripheral. What Chekhov successfully and uniquely conveys in his dramas is the ultimate isolation of every man from all other human beings. No one's sense of self can ever be sufficiently extinguished to permit complete spiritual union with another human being. Not only the ensuing loneliness, but the knowledge that this sense of self will be extinguished by death creates the inner anguish of existence. The transitoriness of everything—of beauty, of present reality—mirrors one's own approaching extinction.

Chekhov evolved a dramatic technique for presenting this vision of reality, and in doing so cut across the traditional dramatic forms. It is not possible, for instance, to classify his plays as tragedies or comedies, or even to describe them as realistic, naturalistic, or impressionistic. While working on *The Cherry Orchard*, Chekhov declared again and again that he was writing a comedy, with elements of farce. Stanislavsky refused to present it as a comedy, and the dramatist was very discouraged by the director's handling of the drama during the rehearsals. Both men, of course, were right. Chekhov sees his characters from many angles. They all have fine qualities, and they all have weaknesses which are comical. For Chekhov, the line between the comic and the tragic is very thin. The conversation between Madame Ranevskaya and Lopahin in *The Cherry Orchard* is comical because she responds with irrelevancies to his pleas that she face the necessity of making practical use of her land. The comedy reveals Madame Ranevskaya's tragic inability to face reality. And the failure of communication between characters, typical of Chekhov's plays, though it makes us laugh also makes us aware of the fundamental isolation of each human being.

Without the traditional dependence upon story action, Chekhov's plays achieve their effect by creating a mood. Many of his dramatic techniques focus attention upon the transitoriness of life. Arrivals and leave-takings frame the drama and evoke the sadness of loss. The mood is reinforced by the nostalgic reminiscences of the characters and their expression of their fears of the uncertain future. Allusions to the beauty of nature, such as the cherry trees which are to be destroyed, also help to create the dominant mood of the plays. One of Chekhov's most effective techniques for evoking the mood that makes his audience feel the sadness and frustrations of existence is unrequited love. Seldom do two people in a Chekhov drama love each other. His characters are always "in love," each with someone who does not love him. If two characters do happen to respond to one another, their love is only temporary or they are frustrated by a failure of communication.

Chekhov's great achievement in the drama was to find the right form to present on stage the tedium of real life, the absorption of human beings in trivial details, and at the same time to reveal the subtle and complex emotions that people experience because they are isolated, lonely human beings alive in a world they do not understand, moving toward a destiny they fear and cannot control.

❦

BIBLIOGRAPHY

Bruford, Walter Horace. *Anton Chekhov*. New Haven, Conn.: Yale University Press, 1957.

Hingley, Ronald. *Chekhov: A Biographical and Critical Study*. London: Allen and Unwin, 1950.

Lucas, Frank Laurance. *The Drama of Chekhov, Synge, Yeats and Piran-dello.* London: Cassell, 1963.

Magarshack, David. *Chekhov the Dramatist.* New York: Auvergne Publishers, 1952.

Simmons, Ernest. *Chekhov: A Biography.* Boston: Little, Brown, 1962.

The Cherry Orchard

Translated by Stark Young

CHARACTERS

RANEVSKAYA, LYUBOFF ANDREEVNA	*a landowner*
ANYA	*her daughter, seventeen years old*
VARYA	*her adopted daughter, twenty-four years old*
GAYEFF, LEONID ANDREEVICH	*brother of Ranevskaya*
LOPAHIN, YERMOLAY ALEXEEVICH	*a merchant*
TROFIMOFF, PYOTR SERGEEVICH	*a student*
SEMYONOFF-PISHTCHIK, BORIS BORISOVICH	*a landowner*
CHARLOTTA IVANOVNA	*a governess*
EPIHODOFF, SEMYON PANTELEEVICH	*a clerk*
DUNYASHA	*a maid*
FIERS	*a valet, an old man of eighty-seven*
YASHA	*a young valet*
A PASSERBY *or* STRANGER	
THE STATIONMASTER	
A POST-OFFICE CLERK	
VISITORS, SERVANTS	

The action takes place on the estate of L. A. Ranevskaya.

(353)

ACT I

A room that is still called the nursery. One of the doors leads into Anya's room. Dawn, the sun will soon be rising. It is May, the cherry trees are in blossom but in the orchard it is cold, with a morning frost. The windows in the room are closed. Enter DUNYASHA *with a candle and* LOPAHIN *with a book in his hand.*

LOPAHIN: The train got in, thank God! What time is it?

DUNYASHA: It's nearly two. (*Blows out his candle.*) It's already daylight.

LOPAHIN: But how late was the train? Two hours at least. (*Yawning and stretching*) I'm a fine one, I am, look what a fool thing I did! I drove her on purpose just to meet them at the station, and then all of a sudden I'd overslept myself! Fell asleep in my chair. How provoking!—You could have waked me up.

DUNYASHA: I thought you had gone. (*Listening*) Listen, I think they are coming now.

LOPAHIN (*listening*): No—No, there's the luggage and one thing and another. (*A pause.*) Lyuboff Andreevna has been living abroad five years. I don't know what she is like now—She is a good woman. An easy-going, simple woman. I remember when I was a boy about fifteen, my father, who is at rest—in those days he ran a shop here in the village—hit me in the face with his fist, my nose was bleeding—We'd come to the yard together for something or other, and he was a little drunk. Lyuboff Andreevna, I can see her now, still so young, so slim, led me to the washbasin here in this very room, in the nursery. "Don't cry," she says, "little peasant, it will be well in time for your wedding"— (*A pause.*) Yes, little peasant—My father was a peasant truly, and here I am in a white waistcoat and yellow shoes. Like a pig rooting in a pastry shop— I've got this rich, lots of money, but if you really stop and think of it, I'm just a peasant—(*Turning the pages of a book*) Here I was reading a book and didn't get a thing out of it. Reading and went to sleep. (*A pause.*)

DUNYASHA: And all night long the dogs were not asleep, they know their masters are coming.

LOPAHIN: What is it, Dunyasha, you're so—

DUNYASHA: My hands are shaking. I'm going to faint.

LOPAHIN: You're just so delicate, Dunyasha. And all dressed up like a lady, and your hair all done up! Mustn't do that. Must know your place.

(*Enter* EPIHODOFF, *with a bouquet: he wears a jacket and highly polished boots with a loud squeak. As he enters he drops the bouquet.*)

EPIHODOFF (*picking up the bouquet*): Look, the gardener sent these, he says to put them in the dining room. (*Giving the bouquet to* DUNYASHA.)

LOPAHIN: And bring me some kvass.

DUNYASHA: Yes, sir.   (*Goes out.*)

EPIHODOFF: There is a morning frost now, three degrees of frost (*Sighing*) and the cherries all in bloom. I cannot approve of our climate—I cannot. Our climate can never quite rise to the occasion. Listen, Yermolay Alexeevich, allow me to subtend, I bought myself, day before yesterday, some boots and they, I venture to assure you, speak so that it is impossible. What could I grease them with?

LOPAHIN: Go on. You annoy me.

EPIHODOFF: Every day some misfortune happens to me. But I don't complain, I am used to it and I even smile.

(DUNYASHA *enters, serves* LOPAHIN *the kvass.*)

EPIHODOFF: I'm going. (*Stumbling over a chair and upsetting it*) There (*As if triumphant*) there, you see, pardon the expression, a circumstance like that, among others—It is simply quite remarkable.

(*Goes out.*)

DUNYASHA: And I must tell you, Yermolay Alexeevich, that Epihodoff has proposed to me.

LOPAHIN: Ah!

DUNYASHA: I don't know really what to—He is a quiet man but sometimes when he starts talking, you can't understand a thing he means. It's all very nice, and full of feeling, but just doesn't make any sense. I sort of like him. He loves me madly. He's a man that's unfortunate, every day there's something or other. They tease him around here, call him twenty-two misfortunes—

LOPAHIN (*cocking his ear*): Listen, I think they are coming—

DUNYASHA: They are coming! But what's the matter with me—I'm cold all over.

LOPAHIN: They're really coming. Let's go meet them. Will she recognize me? It's five years we haven't seen each other.

DUNYASHA: (*excitedly*): I'm going to faint this very minute. Ah, I'm going to faint!

(*Two carriages can be heard driving up to the house. LOPAHIN and DUNYASHA hurry out. The stage is empty. In the adjoining rooms a noise begins. FIERS hurries across the stage, leaning on a stick; he has been to meet LYUBOFF ANDREEVNA, and wears an old-fashioned livery and a high hat; he mutters something to himself, but you cannot understand a word of it. The noise offstage gets louder and louder. A voice "Look! Let's go through here—" LYUBOFF ANDREEVNA, ANYA and CHARLOTTA IVANOVNA, with a little dog on a chain, all of them dressed for traveling, VARYA, in a coat and kerchief, GAYEFF, SEMYONOFF-PISHTCHIK, LOPAHIN, DUNYASHA, with a bundle and an umbrella, servants with pieces of luggage—all pass through the room.*)

ANYA: Let's go through here. Mama, do you remember what room this is?

LYUBOFF ANDREEVNA (*happily, through her tears*): The nursery!

VARYA: How cold it is, my hands are stiff. (*To LYUBOFF ANDREEVNA*) Your rooms, the white one and the violet, are just the same as ever, Mama.

LYUBOFF ANDREEVNA: The nursery, my dear beautiful room—I slept here when I was little— (*Crying*) And now I am like a child— (*Kisses her brother and VARYA, then her brother again.*) And Varya is just the same as ever, looks like a nun. And I knew Dunyasha— (*Kisses DUNYASHA.*)

GAYEFF: The train was two hours late. How's that? How's that for good management?

CHARLOTTA (*to PISHTCHIK*): My dog he eats nuts too.

PISHTCHIK (*astonished*): Think of that!

(*Everybody goes out except ANYA and DUNYASHA.*)

DUNYASHA: We waited so long—(*Taking off ANYA's coat and hat.*)

ANYA: I didn't sleep all four nights on the way. And now I feel so chilly.

DUNYASHA: It was Lent when you left, there was some snow then, there was frost, and now? My darling (*Laughing and kissing her*), I waited so long for you, my joy, my life—I'm telling you now, I can't keep from it another minute.

ANYA (*wearily*): There we go again—

DUNYASHA: The clerk Epihodoff, proposed to me after Holy Week.

ANYA: You're always talking about the same thing—(*Arranging her hair*) I've lost all my hairpins— (*She is tired to the point of staggering.*)

DUNYASHA: I just don't know what to think. He loves me, loves me so!

ANYA (*looks in through her door, tenderly*): My room, my windows, it's just as if I had never been away. I'm home! Tomorrow morning I'll get up, I'll run into the orchard— Oh, if I only could go to sleep! I haven't slept all the way, I was tormented by anxiety.

DUNYASHA: Day before yesterday, Pyotr Sergeevich arrived.

ANYA (*joyfully*): Petya!

DUNYASHA: He's asleep in the bathhouse, he lives there. I am afraid, he says, of being in the way. (*Taking her watch from her pocket and looking at it*) Somebody ought to wake him up. It's only that Varvara Mikhailovna told us not to. Don't you wake him up, she said.

(*Enter* VARYA *with a bunch of keys at her belt.*)

VARYA: Dunyasha, coffee, quick—Mama is asking for coffee.

DUNYASHA: This minute.   (*Goes out.*)

VARYA: Well, thank goodness, you've come back. You are home again. (*Caressingly*) My darling is back! My precious is back!

ANYA: I've had such a time.

VARYA: I can imagine!

ANYA: I left during Holy Week, it was cold then. Charlotta talked all the way and did her tricks. Why did you fasten Charlotta on to me—?

VARYA: But you couldn't have traveled alone, darling; not at seventeen!

ANYA: We arrived in Paris, it was cold there and snowing. I speak terrible French. Mama lived on the fifth floor; I went to see her; there were some French people in her room, ladies, an old priest with his prayer book, and the place was full of tobacco smoke— very dreary. Suddenly I began to feel sorry for Mama, so sorry, I drew her to me, held her close and couldn't let her go. Then Mama kept hugging me, crying—yes—

VARYA (*tearfully*): Don't—oh, don't—

ANYA: Her villa near Mentone she had already sold, she had nothing left, nothing. And I didn't have a kopeck left. It was all we could do to get here. And Mama doesn't understand! We sit down to dinner at a station and she orders, insists on the most expensive things and gives the waiters rouble tips. Charlotta does the same.

Yasha too demands his share; it's simply dreadful. Mama has her butler, Yasha, we've brought him here—

VARYA: I saw the wretch.

ANYA: Well, how are things? Has the interest on the mortgage been paid?

VARYA: How could we?

ANYA: Oh, my God, my God—!

VARYA: In August the estate is to be sold—

ANYA: My God—!

LOPAHIN (*looking in through the door and mooing like a cow*): Moo-o-o— (*Goes away.*)

VARYA (*tearfully*): I'd land him one like that— (*Shaking her fist.*)

ANYA (*embracing* VARYA *gently*): Varya, has he proposed? (VARYA *shakes her head.*) But he loves you—Why don't you have it out with him, what are you waiting for?

VARYA: I don't think anything will come of it for us. He is very busy, he hasn't any time for me—And doesn't notice me. God knows, it's painful for me to see him—Everybody talks about our marriage, everybody congratulates us, and the truth is, there's nothing to it— it's all like a dream—(*In a different tone*) You have a brooch looks like a bee.

ANYA (*sadly*): Mama bought it. (*Going toward her room, speaking gaily, like a child*) And in Paris I went up in a balloon!

VARYA: My darling is back! My precious is back! (DUNYASHA *has returned with the coffee pot and is making coffee.* VARYA *is standing by the door.*) Darling, I'm busy all day long with the house and I go around thinking things. If only you could be married to a rich man, I'd be more at peace too, I would go all by myself to a hermitage—then to Kiev—to Moscow, and I'd keep going like that from one holy place to another —I would go on and on. Heavenly!

ANYA: The birds are singing in the orchard. What time is it now?

VARYA: It must be after two. It's time you were asleep, darling. (*Going into* ANYA's *room*) Heavenly!

(YASHA *enters with a lap robe and traveling bag. Crosses the stage airily.*)

YASHA: May I go through here?

DUNYASHA: We'd hardly recognize you, Yasha; you've changed so abroad!

YASHA: Hm— And who are you?

DUNYASHA: When you left here, I was like that— (*Her hand so high from the floor*) I'm Dunyasha, Fyodor Kozoyedoff's daughter. You don't remember!

YASHA: Hm— You little peach!

(*Looking around before he embraces her; she shrieks and drops a saucer;* YASHA *hurries out.*)

VARYA (*at the door, in a vexed tone*): And what's going on here?

DUNYASHA (*tearfully*): I broke a saucer—

VARYA: That's good luck.

ANYA: (*emerging from her room*): We ought to tell Mama beforehand: Petya is here—

VARYA: I told them not to wake him up.

ANYA (*pensively*): Six years ago our father died, a month later our brother Grisha was drowned in the river, such a pretty little boy, just seven. Mama couldn't bear it, she went away, went away without ever looking back— (*Shuddering*) How I understand her, if she only knew I did. (*A pause.*) And Petya Trofimoff was Grisha's tutor, he might remind—

(*Enter* FIERS; *he is in a jacket and white waistcoat. Goes to the coffee urn, busy with it.*)

FIERS: The mistress will have her breakfast here— (*Putting on white gloves*) Is the coffee ready? (*To* DUNYASHA, *sternly*) You! What about the cream?

DUNYASHA: Oh, my God— (*Hurrying out.*)

FIERS (*busy at the coffee urn*): Oh, you good-for-nothing—! (*Muttering to himself*) Come back from Paris— And the master used to go to Paris by coach— (*Laughing.*)

VARYA: Fiers, what are you—?

FIERS: At your service (*Joyfully*) My mistress is back! It's what I've been waiting for! Now I'm ready to die— (*Crying for joy.*)

(LYUBOFF ANDREEVNA, GAYEFF *and* SEMYONOFF-PISH-TCHIK *enter;* SEMYONOFF-PISHTCHIK *is in a podyovka of fine cloth and sharovary.* GAYEFF *enters; he makes gestures with his hands and body as if he were playing billiards.*)

LYUBOFF ANDREEVNA: How is it? Let me remember—Yellow into the corner! Duplicate in the middle!

GAYEFF: I cut into the corner. Sister, you and I slept here in this very room once, and now I am fifty-one years old, strange as that may seem—

LOPAHIN: Yes, time passes.

GAYEFF: What?

LOPAHIN: Time, I say, passes.

GAYEFF: And it smells like patchouli here.

ANYA: I'm going to bed. Good night, Mama. (*Kissing her mother.*)

LYUBOFF ANDREEVNA: My sweet little child (*Kissing her hands*) You're glad you are home? I still can't get myself together.

ANYA: Good-by, Uncle.

GAYEFF (*kissing her face and hands*): God be with you. How like your mother you are! (*To his sister*) Lyuba, at her age you were exactly like her.

(ANYA *shakes hands with* LOPAHIN *and* PISHTCHIK, *goes out and closes the door behind her.*)

LYUBOFF ANDREEVNA: She's very tired.

PISHTCHIK: It is a long trip, I imagine.

VARYA (*to* LOPAHIN *and* PISHTCHIK): Well, then, sirs? It's going on three o'clock, time for gentlemen to be going.

LYUBOFF ANDREEVNA (*laughing*): The same old Varya. (*Drawing her to her and kissing her*) There, I'll drink my coffee, then we'll all go. (FIERS *puts a small cushion under her feet.*) Thank you, my dear. I am used to coffee. Drink it day and night. Thank you, my dear old soul.

(*Kissing* FIERS.)

VARYA: I'll go see if all the things have come.   (*Goes out.*)

LYUBOFF ANDREEVNA: Is it really me sitting here? (*Laughing*) I'd like to jump around and wave my arms. (*Covering her face with her hands*) But I may be dreaming! God knows I love my country, love it deeply, I couldn't look out of the car window, I just kept crying. (*Tearfully*) However, I must drink my coffee. Thank you, Fiers, thank you, my dear old friend. I'm so glad you're still alive.

FIERS: Day before yesterday.

GAYEFF: He doesn't hear well.

LOPAHIN: And I must leave right now. It's nearly five o'clock in the morning, for Kharkov. What a nuisance! I wanted to look at you— talk— You are as beautiful as ever.

PISHTCHIK (*breathing heavily*): Even more beautiful— In your Paris clothes— It's a feast for the eyes—

LOPAHIN: Your brother, Leonid Andreevich here, says I'm a boor, a peasant money grubber, but that's all the same to me, absolutely. Let him say it. All I wish is you'd trust me as you used to, and your wonderful, touching eyes would look at me as they did. Merciful

God! My father was a serf; belonged to your grandfather and your father; but you, your own self, you did so much for me once that I've forgotten all that and love you like my own kin—more than my kin.

LYUBOFF ANDREEVNA: I can't sit still—I can't. (*Jumping up and walking about in great excitement*) I'll never live through this happiness— Laugh at me, I'm silly— My own little bookcase—! (*Kissing the bookcase*) My little table!

GAYEFF: And in your absence the nurse here died.

LYUBOFF ANDREEVNA (*sitting down and drinking coffee*): Yes, may she rest in Heaven! They wrote me.

GAYEFF: And Anastasy died. Cross-eyed Petrushka left me and lives in town now at the police officer's. (*Taking out of his pocket a box of hard candy and sucking a piece.*)

PISHTCHIK: My daughter, Dashenka—sends you her greetings—

LOPAHIN: I want to tell you something very pleasant, cheerful. (*Glancing at his watch*) I'm going right away. There's no time for talking. Well, I'll make it two or three words. As you know, your cherry orchard is to be sold for your debts; the auction is set for August 22nd, but don't you worry, my dear, you just sleep in peace, there's a way out of it. Here's my plan. Please listen to me. Your estate is only thirteen miles from town. They've run the railroad by it. Now if the cherry orchard and the land along the river were cut up into building lots and leased for summer cottages, you'd have at the very lowest twenty-five thousand roubles per year income.

GAYEFF: Excuse me, what rot!

LYUBOFF ANDREEVNA: I don't quite understand you, Yermolay Alexeevich.

LOPAHIN: At the very least you will get from the summer residents twenty-five roubles per year for a two-and-a-half acre lot and if you post a notice right off, I'll bet you anything that by autumn you won't have a single patch of land free, everything will be taken. In a word, my congratulations, you are saved. The location is wonderful, the river's so deep. Except, of course, it all needs to be tidied up, cleared— For instance, let's say, tear all the old buildings down and this house, which is no good any more, and cut down the old cherry orchard—

LYUBOFF ANDREEVNA: Cut down? My dear, forgive me, you don't understand at all. If there's one thing in the whole province that's interesting—not to say remarkable—it's our cherry orchard.

LOPAHIN: The only remarkable thing about this cherry orchard is that it's very big. There's a crop of cherries once every two years and even that's hard to get rid of. Nobody buys them.

GAYEFF: This orchard is even mentioned in the encyclopedia.

LOPAHIN (*glancing at his watch*): If we don't cook up something and don't get somewhere, the cherry orchard and the entire estate will be sold at auction on the twenty-second of August. Do get it settled then! I swear there is no other way out. Not a one!

FIERS: There was a time, forty-fifty years ago when the cherries were dried, soaked, pickled, cooked into jam and it used to be—

GAYEFF: Keep quiet, Fiers.

FIERS: And it used to be that the dried cherries were shipped by the wagon-load to Moscow and to Kharkov. And the money there was! And the dried cherries were soft then, juicy, sweet, fragrant— They had a way of treating them then—

LYUBOFF ANDREEVNA: And where is that way now?

FIERS: They have forgotten it. Nobody remembers it.

PISHTCHIK (*to* LYUBOFF ANDREEVNA): What's happening in Paris? How is everything? Did you eat frogs?

LYUBOFF ANDREEVNA: I ate crocodiles.

PISHTCHIK: Think of it—!

LOPAHIN: Up to now in the country there have been only the gentry and the peasants, but now in summer the villa people too are coming in. All the towns, even the least big ones, are surrounded with cottages. In about twenty years very likely the summer resident will multiply enormously. He merely drinks tea on the porch now, but it might well happen that on this two-and-a-half acre lot of his, he'll go in for farming, and then your cherry orchard would be happy, rich, splendid—

GAYEFF (*getting hot*): What rot!

(*Enter* VARYA *and* YASHA.)

VARYA: Here, Mama. Two telegrams for you. (*Choosing a key and opening the old bookcase noisily*) Here they are.

LYUBOFF ANDREEVNA: From Paris (*Tearing up the telegrams without reading them*) Paris, that's all over—

GAYEFF: Do you know how old this bookcase is, Lyuba? A week ago I pulled out the bottom drawer and looked, and there the figures were burned on it. The bookcase was made exactly a hundred years ago. How's that? Eh? You might celebrate its jubilee. It's an inanimate object, but all the same, be that as it may, it's a bookcase.

PISHTCHIK (*in astonishment*): A hundred years—! Think of it—!

GAYEFF: Yes—quite something—(*Shaking the bookcase*) Dear, honored bookcase! I saluted your existence, which for more than a hundred years has been directed toward the clear ideals of goodness and justice; your silent appeal to fruitful endeavor has not flagged in all the course of a hundred years, sustaining (*Tearfully*) through the generations of our family, our courage and our faith in a better future and nurturing in us ideals of goodness and of a social consciousness.

(*A pause.*)

LOPAHIN: Yes.

LYUBOFF ANDREEVNA: You're the same as ever, Lenya.

GAYEFF (*slightly embarrassed*): Carom to the right into the corner pocket. I cut into the side pocket!

LOPAHIN (*glancing at his watch*): Well, it's time for me to go.

YASHA (*handing medicine to* LYUBOFF ANDREEVNA): Perhaps you'll take the pills now—

PISHTCHIK: You should never take medicaments, dear madam— They do neither harm nor good— Hand them here, dearest lady. (*He takes the pillbox, shakes the pills out into his palm, blows on them, puts them in his mouth and washes them down with kvass.*) There! Now!

LYUBOFF ANDREEVNA (*startled*): Why, you've lost your mind!

PISHTCHIK: I took all the pills.

LOPAHIN: Such a glutton!

(*Everyone laughs.*)

FIERS: The gentleman stayed with us during Holy Week, he ate half a bucket of pickles— (*Muttering.*)

LYUBOFF ANDREEVNA: What is he muttering about?

VARYA: He's been muttering like that for three years. We're used to it.

YASHA: In his dotage.

(CHARLOTTA IVANOVNA *in a white dress—she is very thin, her corset laced very tight—with a lorgnette at her belt, crosses the stage.*)

LOPAHIN: Excuse me, Charlotta Ivanovna, I haven't had a chance yet to welcome you (*Trying to kiss her hand.*)

CHARLOTTA (*drawing her hand away*): If I let you kiss my hand, 'twould be my elbow next, then my shoulder—

LOPAHIN: No luck for me today. (*Everyone laughs.*) Charlotta Ivanovna, show us a trick!

CHARLOTTA: No. I want to go to bed.   (*Exit.*)

LOPAHIN: In three weeks we shall see each other. (*Kissing* LYUBOFF ANDREEVNA's *hand*) Till then, good-by. It's time. (*To* GAYEFF) See you soon. (*Kissing* PISHTCHIK) See you soon. (*Shaking* VARYA's *hand, then* FIERS' *and* YASHA's) I don't feel like going. (*To* LYUBOFF ANDREEVNA) If you think it over and make up your mind about the summer cottages, let me know and I'll arrange a loan of something like fifty thousand roubles. Think it over seriously.

VARYA (*angrily*): Do go on, anyhow, will you!

LOPAHIN: I'm going, I'm going—   (*Exit.*)

GAYEFF: Boor. However, pardon—Varya is going to marry him, it's Varya's little fiancé.

VARYA: Don't talk too much, Uncle.

LYUBOFF ANDREEVNA: Well, Varya, I should be very glad. He's a good man.

PISHTCHIK: A man, one must say truthfully—A most worthy—And my Dashenka—says also that—she says all sorts of things— (*Snoring but immediately waking up*) Nevertheless, dearest lady, oblige me—With a loan of two hundred and forty roubles— Tomorrow the interest on my mortgage has got to be paid—

VARYA (*startled*): There's not any money, none at all.

LYUBOFF ANDREEVNA: Really, I haven't got anything.

PISHTCHIK: I'll find it, somehow. (*Laughing*) I never give up hope. There, I think to myself, all is lost, I am ruined and lo and behold —a railroad is put through my land and—they paid me. And then, just watch, something else will turn up—if not today, then tomorrow—Dashenka will win two hundred thousand— She has a ticket.

LYUBOFF ANDREEVNA: We've finished the coffee, now we can go to bed.

FIERS (*brushing* GAYEFF's *clothes, reprovingly*): You put on the wrong trousers again. What am I going to do with you!

VARYA (*softly*): Anya is asleep. (*Opening the window softly*) Already the sun's rising—it's not cold. Look, Mama! What beautiful trees! My Lord, what air! The starlings are singing!

GAYEFF (*opening another window*): The orchard is all white. You haven't forgotten, Lyuba? That long lane there runs straight—as a strap stretched out. It glistens on moonlight nights. Do you remember? You haven't forgotten it?

LYUBOFF ANDREEVNA (*looking out of the window on to the orchard*): Oh, my childhood, my innocence! I slept in this nursery and looked out on the orchard from here, every morning happiness awoke with me, it was just as it is now, then, nothing has changed. (*Laughing with joy*) All, all white! Oh, my orchard! After a dark, rainy autumn and cold winter, you are young again and full of happiness. The heavenly angels have not deserted you— If I only could lift the weight from my breast, from my shoulders, if I could only forget my past!

GAYEFF: Yes, and the orchard will be sold for debt, strange as that may seem.

LYUBOFF ANDREEVNA: Look, our dear mother is walking through the orchard—In a white dress! (*Laughing happily*) It's she.

GAYEFF: Where?

VARYA: God be with you, Mama!

LYUBOFF ANDREEVNA: There's not anybody, it only seemed so. To the right, as you turn to the summerhouse, a little white tree is leaning there, looks like a woman— (*Enter* TROFIMOFF, *in a student's uniform, well worn, and glasses.*) What a wonderful orchard! The white masses of blossoms, the sky all blue.

TROFIMOFF: Lyuboff Andreevna! (*She looks around at him.*) I will just greet you and go immediately. (*Kissing her hand warmly*) I was told to wait until morning, but I hadn't the patience—

(LYUBOFF ANDREEVNA *looks at him puzzled.*)

VARYA (*tearfully*): This is Petya Trofimoff—

TROFIMOFF: Petya Trofimoff, the former tutor of your Grisha— Have I really changed so?

(LYUBOFF ANDREEVNA *embraces him; and crying quietly.*)

GAYEFF (*embarrassed*): There, there, Lyuba.

VARYA (*crying*): I told you, Petya, to wait til tomorrow.

LYUBOFF ANDREEVNA: My Grisha—My boy—Grisha—Son—

VARYA: What can we do, Mama? It's God's will.

TROFIMOFF (*in a low voice tearfully*): There, there—

LYUBOFF ANDREEVNA (*weeping softly*): My boy was lost, drowned— Why? Why, my friend? (*More quietly*) Anya is asleep there, and I am talking so loud—Making so much noise— But why, Petya? Why have you lost your looks? Why do you look so much older?

TROFIMOFF: A peasant woman on the train called me a mangy-looking gentleman.

LYUBOFF ANDREEVNA: You were a mere boy then, a charming young student, and now your hair's not very thick any more and you wear glasses. Are you really a student still? (*Going to the door.*)

TROFIMOFF: Very likely I'll be a perennial student.

LYUBOFF ANDREEVNA (*kissing her brother, then* VARYA): Well, go to bed— You've grown older too, Leonid.

PISHTCHIK (*following her*): So that's it, we are going to bed now. Oh, my gout! I'm staying here— I'd like, Lyuboff Andreevna, my soul, tomorrow morning— Two hundred and forty roubles—

GAYEFF: He's still at it.

PISHTCHIK: Two hundred and forty roubles— To pay interest on the mortgage.

LYUBOFF ANDREEVNA: I haven't any money, my dove.

PISHTCHIK: I'll pay it back, my dear— It's a trifling sum—

LYUBOFF ANDREEVNA: Oh, very well, Leonid will give— You give it to him, Leonid.

GAYEFF: Oh, certainly, I'll give it to him. Hold out your pockets.

LYUBOFF ANDREEVNA: What can we do, give it, he needs it— He'll pay it back.

(LYUBOFF ANDREEVNA, TROFIMOFF, PISHTCHIK *and* FIERS *go out.* GAYEFF, VARYA *and* YASHA *remain.*)

GAYEFF: My sister hasn't yet lost her habit of throwing money away. (*To* YASHA) Get away, my good fellow, you smell like hens.

YASHA (*with a grin*): And you are just the same as you used to be, Leonid Andreevich.

GAYEFF: What? (*To* VARYA) What did he say?

VARYA (*To* YASHA): Your mother has come from the village, she's been sitting in the servant's hall ever since yesterday, she wants to see you—

YASHA: The devil take her!

VARYA: Ach, shameless creature!

YASHA: A lot I need her! She might have come tomorrow.

(*Goes out.*)

VARYA: Mama is just the same as she was, she hasn't changed at all. If she could, she'd give away everything she has.

GAYEFF: Yes— If many remedies are prescribed for an illness, you may know the illness is incurable. I keep thinking, I wrack my brains, I have many remedies, a great many, and that means, really, I haven't any at all. It would be fine to inherit a fortune from somebody, it would be fine to marry off our Anya to a very rich man, it would be fine to go to Yaroslavl and try our luck with our old aunt, the Countess. Auntie is very, very rich.

VARYA (*crying*): If God would only help us!

GAYEFF: Don't bawl! Auntie is very rich but she doesn't like us. To begin with, Sister married a lawyer, not a nobleman— (ANYA *appears at the door.*) Married not a nobleman and behaved herself, you could say, not very virtuously. She is good, kind, nice, I love her very much, but no matter how much you allow for the extenuating circumstances, you must admit she's a depraved woman. You feel it in her slightest movement.

VARYA (*whispering*): Anya is standing in the door there.

GAYEFF: What? (*A pause.*) It's amazing, something got in my right eye. I am beginning to see poorly. And on Thursday, when I was in the District Court—

(ANYA *enters.*)

VARYA: But why aren't you asleep, Anya?

ANYA: I don't feel like sleeping. I can't.

GAYEFF: My little girl— (*Kissing* ANYA's *face and hands*) My child — (*Tearfully*) You are not my niece, you are my angel, you are everything to me. Believe me, believe—

ANYA: I believe you, Uncle. Everybody loves you, respects you— But dear Uncle, you must keep quiet, just keep quiet— What were you saying, just now, about my mother, about your own sister? What did you say that for?

GAYEFF: Yes, yes— (*Putting her hand up over his face*) Really, it's terrible! My God! Oh, God, save me! And today I made a speech to the bookcase— So silly! And it was only when I finished it that I could see it was silly.

VARYA: It's true, Uncle, you ought to keep quiet. Just keep quiet. That's all.

ANYA: If you kept quiet, you'd have more peace.

GAYEFF: I'll keep quiet. (*Kissing* ANYA's *and* VARYA's *hands*) I'll keep quiet. Only this, it's about business. On Thursday I was in the District Court; well, a few of us gathered around and a conversation began about this and that, about lots of things; apparently it will be possible to arrange a loan on a promissory note to pay the bank the interest due.

VARYA: If the Lord would only help us!

GAYEFF: Tuesday I shall go and talk it over again. (*To* VARYA) Don't bawl! (*To* ANYA) Your mother will talk to Lopahin; of course, he won't refuse her . . . And as soon as you rest up, you will go to Yaroslavl to your great-aunt, the Countess. There, that's how we will move from three directions, and the business is in the bag. We'll pay the interest. I am convinced of that— (*Putting a hard candy in his mouth*) On my honor I'll swear, by anything you like, that the estate shall not be sold! (*Excitedly*) By my happiness, I swear! Here's my hand, call me a worthless, dishonorable man, if I allow it to come up for auction! With all my soul I swear it!

ANYA (*a quieter mood returns to her; she is happy*): How good you are, Uncle, how clever! (*Embracing her uncle*) I feel easy now! I feel easy! I'm happy!

(FIERS *enters, reproachfully.*)

FIERS: Leonid Andreevich, have you no fear of God! When are you going to bed?

GAYEFF: Right away, right away. You may go, Fiers. For this once I'll undress myself. Well, children, beddy bye— More details tomorrow, and now, go to bed (*Kissing* ANYA *and* VARYA) I am a man of the eighties— It is a period that's not admired, but I can say, nevertheless, that I've suffered no little for my convictions in the course of my life. It is not for nothing that the peasant loves me. One must know the peasant! One must know from what—

ANYA: Again, Uncle!

VARYA: You, Uncle dear, keep quiet.

FIERS (*angrily*): Leonid Andreevich!

GAYEFF: I'm coming, I'm coming— Go to bed. A double bank into the side pocket! A clean shot— (*Goes out,* FIERS *hobbling after him.*)

ANYA: I feel easy now. I don't feel like going to Yaroslavl; I don't like Great-aunt, but still I feel easy. Thanks to Uncle. (*Sits down.*)

VARYA: I must get to sleep. I'm going. And there was unpleasantness here during your absence. In *t*he old servants' quarters, as you know, live only the old servants: Yephemushka, Polya, Yevstignay, well, and Karp. They began to let every sort of creature spend the night with them—I didn't say anything. But then I hear they've spread the rumor that I'd given orders to feed them nothing but beans. Out of stinginess, you see— And all that from Yevstignay— Very well, I think to myself. If that's the way it is, I think to myself, then you just wait. I call in Yevstignay— (*Yawning*) He comes— How is it, I say, that you, Yevstignay— You're such a fool— (*Glancing at* ANYA) Anitchka!—(*A pause.*) Asleep! (*Takes* ANYA *by her arm.*) Let's go to bed— Come on!— (*Leading her*) My little darling fell asleep! Come on— (*They go. Far away beyond the orchard a shepherd is playing on a pipe.* TROFIMOFF *walks across the stage and, seeing* VARYA *and* ANYA, *stops.*) Shh— She is asleep—asleep— Let's go, dear.

ANYA (*softly, half dreaming*): I'm so tired— All the bells!—Uncle— dear— And Mama and Uncle—Varya.

VARYA: Come on, my dear, come on. (*They go into Anya's room.*)

TROFIMOFF (*tenderly*): My little sun! My spring!

CURTAIN

ACT II

(*A field. An old chapel, long abandoned, with crooked walls, near it a well, big stones that apparently were once tombstones, and an old bench. A road to the estate of GAYEFF can be seen. On one side poplars rise, casting their shadows, the cherry orchard begins there. In the distance a row of telegraph poles; and far, far away, faintly traced on the horizon, is a large town, visible only in the clearest weather. The sun will soon be down. CHARLOTTA, YASHA and DUNYASHA are sitting on the bench; EPIHODOFF is standing near and playing the guitar; everyone sits lost in thought. CHARLOTTA wears an old peak cap (fourrage); she has taken a rifle from off her shoulders and is adjusting the buckle on the strap.*)

CHARLOTTA (*pensively*): I have no proper passport, I don't know how old I am—it always seems to me I'm very young. When I was a little girl, my father and mother traveled from fair to fair and gave performances, very good ones. And I did *salto mortale* and different tricks. And when Papa and Mama died, a German lady took me to live with her and began teaching me. Good. I grew up. And became a governess. But where I came from and who I am I don't know— Who my parents were, perhaps they weren't even married —I don't know. (*Taking a cucumber out of her pocket and beginning to eat it*) I don't know a thing. (*A pause.*) I'd like so much to talk but there's not anybody. I haven't anybody.

EPIHODOFF (*playing the guitar and singing*): "What care I for the noisy world, what care I for friends and foes."—How pleasant it is to play the mandolin!

DUNYASHA: That's a guitar, not a mandolin. (*Looking into a little mirror and powdering her face.*)

EPIHODOFF: For a madman who is in love this is a mandolin—

(*Singing*) "If only my heart were warm with the fire of requited love."

(YASHA *sings with him.*)

CHARLOTTA: How dreadfully these people sing— Phooey! Like jackals.

DUNYASHA (*to* YASHA): All the same what happiness to have been abroad.

YASHA: Yes, of course. I cannot disagree with you.

(*Yawning and then lighting a cigar.*)

EPIHODOFF: That's easily understood. Abroad everything long since attained its complete development.

YASHA: That's obvious.

EPIHODOFF: I am a cultured man. I read all kinds of remarkable books, but the trouble is I cannot discover my own inclinations, whether to live or to shoot myself, but nevertheless, I always carry a revolver on me. Here it is—(*Showing a revolver.*)

CHARLOTTA: That's done. Now I am going. (*Slinging the rifle over her shoulder*) You are a very clever man, Epihodoff, and a very terrible one; the women must love you madly. Brrrr-r-r-r! (*Going*) These clever people are all so silly, I haven't anybody to talk with. I'm always alone, alone, I have nobody and— Who I am, why I am, is unknown—   (*Goes out without hurrying.*)

EPIHODOFF: Strictly speaking, not touching on other subjects, I must state about myself, in passing, that fate treats me mercilessly, as a storm does a small ship. If, let us suppose, I am mistaken, then why, to mention one instance, do I wake up this morning, look and there on my chest is a spider of terrific size— There, like that. (*Showing the size with both hands*) And also I take some kvass to drink and in it I find something in the highest degree indecent, such as a cockroach. (*A pause.*) Have you read Buckle? (*A pause.*) I desire to trouble you, Avdotya Feodorovna, with a couple of words.

DUNYASHA: Speak.

EPIHODOFF: I have a desire to speak with you alone—(*Sighing.*)

DUNYASHA (*embarrassed*): Very well— But bring me my cape first— by the cupboard— It's rather damp here—

EPIHODOFF: Very well—I'll fetch it— Now I know what I should do with my revolver—

(*Takes the guitar and goes out playing.*)

YASHA: Twenty-two misfortunes! Between us he's a stupid man, it must be said. (*Yawning.*)

DUNYASHA: God forbid he should shoot himself. (*A pause.*) I've grown so uneasy, I'm always fretting. I was only a girl when I was taken into the master's house, and now I've lost the habit of simple living—and here are my hands white, white as a lady's. I've become so delicate, fragile, ladylike, afraid of everything—Frightfully so. And, Yasha, if you deceive me, I don't know what will happen to my nerves.

YASHA (*kissing her*): You little cucumber! Of course every girl must behave properly. What I dislike above everything is for a girl to conduct herself badly.

DUNYASHA: I have come to love you passionately, you are educated, you can discuss anything. (*A pause.*)

YASHA (*yawning*): Yes, sir—To my mind it is like this: If a girl loves someone, it means she is immoral. (*A pause.*) It is pleasant to smoke a cigar in the clear air—(*Listening*) They are coming here — It is the ladies and gentlemen—

(DUNYASHA *impulsively embraces him.*)

YASHA: Go to the house, as though you had been to bathe in the river, go by this path, otherwise, they might meet you and suspect me of making a rendezvous with you. That I cannot tolerate.

DUNYASHA (*with a little cough*): Your cigar has given me the headache.

(*Goes out.*)

(YASHA *remains, sitting near the chapel.* LYUBOFF ANDREEVNA, GAYEFF *and* LOPAHIN *enter.*)

LOPAHIN: We must decide definitely, time doesn't wait. Why, the matter's quite simple. Are you willing to lease your land for summer cottages or are you not? Answer in one word, yes or no? Just one word!

LYUBOFF ANDREEVNA: Who is it smokes those disgusting cigars out here—? (*Sitting down.*)

GAYEFF: The railroad running so near is a great convenience. (*Sitting down*) We made a trip to town and lunched there— Yellow in the side pocket! Perhaps I should go in the house first and play one game—

LYUBOFF ANDREEVNA: You'll have time.

LOPAHIN: Just one word! (*Imploringly*) Do give me your answer!

GAYEFF (*yawning*): What?

LYUBOFF ANDREEVNA (*looking in her purse*): Yesterday there was lots of money in it. Today there's very little. My poor Varya! For the sake of economy she feeds everybody milk soup, and in the

kitchen the old people get nothing but beans, and here I spend
money—senselessly— (*Dropping her purse and scattering gold
coins*) There they go scattering! (*She is vexed.*)

YASHA: Allow me, I'll pick them up in a second. (*Picking up the
coins.*)

LYUBOFF ANDREEVNA: If you will, Yasha. And why did I go in town
for lunch—? Your restaurant with its music is trashy, the table-
cloths smell of soap— Why drink so much, Lyonya? Why eat so
much? Why talk so much? Today in the restaurant you were
talking a lot again, and all of it beside the point. About the
seventies, about the decadents. And to whom? Talking to waiters
about the decadents!

LOPAHIN: Yes.

GAYEFF (*waving his hand*): I am incorrigible, that's evident— (*To
YASHA irritably*) What is it?—You are forever swirling around in
front of us?

YASHA (*laughing*): I cannot hear your voice without laughing.

GAYEFF (*to his sister*): Either I or he—

LYUBOFF ANDREEVNA: Go away, Yasha. Go on—

YASHA (*giving LYUBOFF ANDREEVNA her purse*): I am going right
away. (*Barely suppressing his laughter*) This minute.

(*Goes out.*)

LOPAHIN: The rich Deriganoff intends to buy your estate. They say
he is coming personally to the auction.

LYUBOFF ANDREEVNA: And where did you hear that?

LOPAHIN: In town they are saying it.

GAYEFF: Our Yaroslavl aunt promised to send us something, but
when and how much she will send, nobody knows—

LOPAHIN: How much will she send? A hundred thousand? Two
hundred?

LYUBOFF ANDREEVNA: Well—maybe ten, fifteen thousand—we'd be
thankful for that.

LOPAHIN: Excuse me, but such light-minded people as you are, such
odd, unbusinesslike people, I never saw. You are told in plain
Russian that your estate is being sold up and you just don't seem to
take it in.

LYUBOFF ANDREEVNA: But what are we to do? Tell us what?

LOPAHIN: I tell you every day. Every day I tell you the same thing.
Both the cherry orchard and the land have got to be leased for
summer cottages, it has to be done right now, quick— The auction

is right under your noses. Do understand! Once you finally decide that there are to be summer cottages, you will get all the money you want, and then you'll be saved.

LYUBOFF ANDREEVNA: Summer cottages and summer residents—it is so trivial, excuse me.

GAYEFF: I absolutely agree with you.

LOPAHIN: I'll either burst out crying, or scream, or faint. I can't bear it! You are torturing me! (*To* GAYEFF) You're a perfect old woman!

GAYEFF: What?

LOPAHIN: A perfect old woman! (*About to go.*)

LYUBOFF ANDREEVNA (*alarmed*): No, don't go, stay, my lamb, I beg you. Perhaps we will think of something!

LOPAHIN: What is there to think about?

LYUBOFF ANDREEVNA: Don't go, I beg you. With you here it is more cheerful anyhow— (*A pause.*) I keep waiting for something, as if the house were about to tumble down on our heads.

GAYEFF (*deep in thought*): Double into the corner pocket— Bank into the wide pocket—

LYUBOFF ANDREEVNA: We have sinned so much—

LOPAHIN: What sins have you—?

GAYEFF (*puts a hard candy into his mouth*): They say I've eaten my fortune up in hard candies— (*Laughing.*)

LYUBOFF ANDREEVNA: Oh, my sins—I've always thrown money around like mad, recklessly, and I married a man who accumulated nothing but debts. My husband died from champagne—he drank fearfully—and to my misfortune I fell in love with another man. I lived with him, and just at that time—it was my first punishment—a blow over the head: right here in the river my boy was drowned and I went abroad—went away for good, never to return, never to see this river again—I shut my eyes, ran away, beside myself, and he after me—mercilessly, brutally. I bought a villa near Mentone, because he fell ill there, and for three years I knew no rest day or night, the sick man exhausted me, my soul dried up. And last year when the villa was sold for debts, I went to Paris and there he robbed me of everything, threw me over, took up with another woman; I tried to poison myself—so stupid, so shameful— And suddenly I was seized with longing for Russia, for my own country, for my little girl— (*Wiping away her tears*) Lord, Lord, have mercy, forgive me my sins! Don't punish me any more! (*Getting a telegram out of her pocket*) I got this today from Paris, he asks forgiveness, begs me to return— (*Tears up the telegram.*) That sounds like music somewhere. (*Listening.*)

GAYEFF: It is our famous Jewish orchestra. You remember, four violins, a flute and double bass.

LYUBOFF ANDREEVNA: Does it still exist? We ought to get hold of it sometime and give a party.

LOPAHIN (*listening*): Can't hear it— (*Singing softly*) "And for money the Germans will frenchify a Russian." (*Laughing*) What a play I saw yesterday at the theatre, very funny!

LYUBOFF ANDREEVNA: And most likely there was nothing funny about it. You shouldn't look at plays, but look oftener at yourselves. How gray all your lives are, what a lot of idle things you say!

LOPAHIN: That's true. It must be said frankly this life of ours is idiotic — (*A pause*) My father was a peasant, an idiot, he understood nothing, he taught me nothing, he just beat me in his drunken fits and always with a stick. At bottom I am just as big a dolt and idiot as he was. I wasn't taught anything, my handwriting is vile, I write like a pig—I am ashamed for people to see it.

LYUBOFF ANDREEVNA: You ought to get married, my friend.

LOPAHIN: Yes—That's true.

LYUBOFF ANDREEVNA: To our Varya, perhaps. She is a good girl.

LOPAHIN: Yes.

LYUBOFF ANDREEVNA: She comes from simple people, and she works all day long, but the main thing is she loves you. And you, too, have liked her a long time.

LOPAHIN: Why not? I am not against it— She's a good girl. (*A pause.*)

GAYEFF: They are offering me a position in a bank. Six thousand a year— Have you heard that?

LYUBOFF ANDREEVNA: Not you! You stay where you are—

(FIERS *enters bringing an overcoat.*)

FIERS (*to* GAYEFF): Pray, Sir, put this on, it's damp.

GAYEFF (*putting on the overcoat*): You're a pest, old man.

FIERS: That's all right— This morning you went off without letting me know. (*Looking him over.*)

LYUBOFF ANDREEVNA: How old you've grown, Fiers!

FIERS: At your service.

LOPAHIN: She says you've grown very old!

FIERS: I've lived a long time. They were planning to marry me off before your papa was born. (*Laughing*) And at the time the serfs were freed I was already the head footman. I didn't want to be freed then, I stayed with the masters—(*A pause.*) And I remember, everybody was happy, but what they were happy about they didn't know themselves.

LOPAHIN: In the old days it was fine. At least they flogged.

FIERS (*not hearing*): But, of course. The peasants stuck to the masters, the masters stuck to the peasants, and now everything is all smashed up, you can't tell about anything.

GAYEFF: Keep still, Fiers. Tomorrow I must go to town. They have promised to introduce me to a certain general who might make us a loan.

LOPAHIN: Nothing will come of it. And you can rest assured you won't pay the interest.

LYUBOFF ANDREEVNA: He's just raving on. There aren't any such generals.

(TROFIMOFF, ANYA *and* VARYA *enter.*)

GAYEFF: Here they come.

ANYA: There is Mama sitting there.

LYUBOFF ANDREEVNA (*tenderly*): Come, come—My darlings—(*Embracing* ANYA *and* VARYA) If you only knew how I love you both! Come sit by me—there—like that.

(*Everybody sits down.*)

LOPAHIN: Our perennial student is always strolling with the young ladies.

TROFIMOFF: It's none of your business.

LOPAHIN: He will soon be fifty and he's still a student.

TROFIMOFF: Stop your stupid jokes.

LOPAHIN: But why are you so peevish, you queer duck?

TROFIMOFF: Don't you pester me.

LOPAHIN (*laughing*): Permit me to ask you, what do you make of me?

TROFIMOFF: Yermolay Alexeevich, I make this of you: you are a rich man, you'll soon be a millionaire. Just as it is in the metabolism of nature, a wild beast is needed to eat up everything that comes his way; so you, too, are needed.

(*Everyone laughs.*)

VARYA: Petya, you'd better tell us about the planets.

LYUBOFF ANDREEVNA: No, let's go on with yesterday's conversation.

TROFIMOFF: What was it about?

GAYEFF: About the proud man.

TROFIMOFF: We talked a long time yesterday, but didn't get anywhere. In a proud man, in your sense of the word, there is something mystical. Maybe you are right, from your standpoint, but if we are to discuss it in simple terms, without whimsy, then what pride can there be, is there any sense in it, if man physiologically is poorly constructed, if in the great majority he is crude, unintelligent, profoundly miserable. One must stop admiring oneself. One must only work.

GAYEFF: All the same, you will die.

TROFIMOFF: Who knows? And what does it mean—you will die? Man may have a hundred senses, and when he dies only the five that are known to us may perish, and the remaining ninety-five go on living.

LYUBOFF ANDREEVNA: How clever you are, Petya!

LOPAHIN (*ironically*): Terribly!

TROFIMOFF: Humanity goes forward, perfecting its powers. Everything that's unattainable now will some day become familiar, understandable; it is only that one must work and must help with all one's might those who seek the truth. With us in Russia so far only a very few work. The great majority of the intelligentsia that I know are looking for nothing, doing nothing, and as yet have no capacity for work. They call themselves intelligentsia, are free and easy with the servants, treat the peasants like animals, educate themselves poorly, read nothing seriously, do absolutely nothing; about science they just talk and about art they understand very little. Every one of them is serious, all have stern faces; they all talk of nothing but important things, philosophize, and all the time everybody can see that the workmen eat abominably, sleep without any pillows, thirty or forty to a room, and everywhere there are bedbugs, stench, dampness, moral uncleanness— And apparently with us, all the fine talk is only to divert the attention of ourselves and of others. Show me where we have the day nurseries they are always talking so much about, where are the reading rooms? They only write of these in novels, for the truth is there are not any at all. There is only filth, vulgarity, orientalism— I am afraid of very serious faces and dislike them. I'm afraid of serious conversations. Rather than that let's just keep still.

LOPAHIN· You know I get up before five o'clock in the morning and work from morning till night. Well, I always have money, my own and other people's, on hand, and I see what the people around me are. One has only to start doing something to find out how few honest and decent people there are. At times when I can't go to sleep, I think: Lord, thou gavest us immense forests, unbounded fields and the widest horizons, and living in the midst of them we should indeed be giants—

LYUBOFF ANDREEVNA: You feel the need for giants— They are good only in fairy tales, anywhere else they only frighten us.

(*At the back of the stage* EPIHODOFF *passes by, playing the guitar.*)

LYUBOFF ANDREEVNA (*lost in thought*): Epihodoff is coming—

ANYA (*lost in thought*): Epihodoff is coming.

GAYEFF: The sun has set, ladies and gentlemen.

TROFIMOFF: Yes.

GAYEFF (*not loud and as if he were declaiming*): Oh, Nature, wonderful, you gleam with eternal radiance, beautiful and indifferent, you, whom we call Mother, combine in yourself both life and death, you give life and you take it away.

VARYA (*beseechingly*): Uncle!

ANYA: Uncle, you're doing it again!

TROFIMOFF: You'd better bank the yellow into the side pocket.

GAYEFF: I'll be quiet, quiet.

(*All sit absorbed in their thoughts. There is only the silence.* FIERS *is heard muttering to himself softly. Suddenly a distant sound is heard, as if from the sky, like the sound of a snapped string, dying away, mournful.*)

LYUBOFF ANDREEVNA: What's that?

LOPAHIN: I don't know. Somewhere far off in a mine shaft a bucket fell. But somewhere very far off.

GAYEFF: And it may be some bird—like a heron.

TROFIMOFF: Or an owl—

LYUBOFF ANDREEVNA (*shivering*): It's unpleasant, somehow. (*A pause.*)

FIERS: Before the disaster it was like that. The owl hooted and the samovar hummed without stopping, both.

GAYEFF: Before what disaster?

FIERS: Before the emancipation.

(*A pause.*)

LYUBOFF ANDREEVNA: You know, my friends, let's go. Twilight is falling. (*To* ANYA) You have tears in your eyes— What is it, my dear little girl? (*Embracing her.*)

ANYA: It's just that, Mama. It's nothing.

TROFIMOFF: Somebody is coming.

> (*A* STRANGER *appears in a shabby white cap, and an overcoat; he is a little drunk.*)

THE STRANGER: Allow me to ask you, can I go straight through here to the station?

GAYEFF: You can. Go by that road.

THE STRANGER: I am heartily grateful to you. (*Coughing*) The weather is splendid— (*Declaiming*) Brother of mine, suffering brother— Go out to the Volga, whose moans— (*To* VARYA) Mademoiselle, grant a hungry Russian man some thirty kopecks—

(VARYA *is frightened and gives a shriek.*)

LOPAHIN (*angrily*): There's a limit to everything.

LYUBOFF ANDREEVNA (*flustered*): Take this— Here's this for you— (*Searching in her purse*) No silver— It's all the same, here's a gold piece for you—

THE STRANGER: I am heartily grateful to you.

> (*Goes out. Laughter.*)

VARYA (*frightened*): I'm going—I'm going— Oh; Mama, you poor little Mama! There's nothing in the house for people to eat, and you gave him a gold piece.

LYUBOFF ANDREEVNA: What is to be done with me, so silly? I shall give you all I have in the house. Yermolay Alexeevich, you will lend me some this once more!—

LOPAHIN: Agreed.

LYUBOFF ANDREEVNA: Let's go, ladies and gentlemen, it's time. And here, Varya, we have definitely made a match for you, I congratulate you.

VARYA (*through her tears*): Mama, that's not something to joke about.

LOPAHIN: Achmelia, get thee to a nunnery.

GAYEFF: And my hands are trembling; it is a long time since I have played billiards.

LOPAHIN: Achmelia, Oh nymph, in thine orisons be all my sins remember'd—

LYUBOFF ANDREEVNA: Let's go, my dear friends, it will soon be suppertime.

VARYA: He frightened me. My heart is thumping so!

LOPAHIN: I remind you, ladies and gentlemen: August 22nd the cherry orchard will be auctioned off. Think about that!—Think!—

> (*All go out except* TROFIMOFF *and* ANYA.)

ANYA (*laughing*): My thanks to the stranger, he frightened Varya, now we are alone.

TROFIMOFF: Varya is afraid we might begin to love each other and all day long she won't leave us to ourselves. With her narrow mind she cannot understand that we are above love. To sidestep the petty and illusory, which prevent our being free and happy, that is the aim and meaning of our life. Forward! We march on irresistibly toward the bright star that burns there in the distance. Forward! Do not fall behind, friends!

ANYA (*extending her arms upward*): How well you talk! (*A pause.*) It's wonderful here today!

TROFIMOFF: Yes, the weather is marvelous.

ANYA: What have you done to me, Petya, why don't I love the cherry orchard any longer the way I used to? I loved it so tenderly, it seemed to me there was not a better place on earth than our orchard.

TROFIMOFF: All Russia is our orchard. The earth is immense and beautiful, and on it are many wonderful places. (*A pause.*) Just think, Anya: your grandfather, great-grandfather and all your ancestors were slave owners, in possession of living souls, and can you doubt that from every cherry in the orchard, from every leaf, from every trunk, human beings are looking at you, can it be that you don't hear their voices? To possess living souls, well, that depraved all of you who lived before and who are living now, so that your mother and you, and your uncle no longer notice that you live by debt, at somebody else's expense, at the expense of those very people whom you wouldn't let past your front door— We are at least two hundred years behind the times, we have as yet absolutely nothing, we have no definite attitude toward the past, we only philosophize, complain of our sadness or drink vodka. Why, it is quite clear that to begin to live in the present we must first atone for our past, must be done with it; and we can atone for it only through suffering, only through uncommon, incessant labor. Understand that, Anya.

ANYA: The house we live in ceased to be ours long ago, and I'll go away, I give you my word.

TROFIMOFF: If you have the household keys, throw them in the well and go away. Be free as the wind.

ANYA (*transported*): How well you said that!

TROFIMOFF: Believe me, Anya, believe me! I am not thirty yet, I am young, I am still a student, but I have already borne so much!

Every winter I am hungry, sick, anxious, poor as a beggar, and—where has destiny not chased me, where haven't I been! And yet, my soul has always, every minute, day and night, been full of inexplicable premonitions. I have a premonition of happiness, Anya, I see it already—

ANYA (*pensively*): The moon is rising.

(EPIHODOFF *is heard playing on the guitar, always the same sad song. The moon rises. Somewhere near the poplars* VARYA *is looking for* ANYA *and calling "Anya where are you?"*)

TROFIMOFF: Yes, the moon is rising. (*A pause.*) Here is happiness, here it comes, comes always nearer and nearer, I hear its footsteps now. And if we shall not see it, shall not come to know it, what does that matter? Others will see it!

VARYA (*off*): Anya! Where are you?

TROFIMOFF: Again, that Varya! (*Angrily*) It's scandalous!

ANYA: Well, let's go to the river. It's lovely there.

TROFIMOFF: Let's go.   (*They go out.*)

VARYA (*off*): Anya! Anya!

CURTAIN

ACT III

(*The drawing room, separated by an arch from the ballroom. A chandelier is lighted. A Jewish orchestra is playing—the same that was mentioned in Act Two. Evening. In the ballroom they are dancing* grand rond. *The voice of* SEMYONOFF-PISHTCHIK "Promenade à une paire!" *They enter the drawing room; in the first couple are* PISHTCHIK *and* CHARLOTTA IVANOVNA; *in the second,* TROFIMOFF *and* LYUBOFF ANDREEVNA; *in the third,* ANYA *with the* POST-OFFICE CLERK; *in the fourth,* VARYA *with the* STATIONMASTER, *et cetera—*VARYA *is crying softly and wipes away her tears while she is dancing.* DUNYASHA *is in the last couple through the drawing room,* PISHTCHIK *shouts* "Grand rond, balancez!" *and* "Les Cavaliers à genoux et remerciez vos dames!"*

FIERS *in a frock coat goes by with seltzer water on a tray.* PISHTCHIK *and* TROFIMOFF *come into the drawing room.*)

PISHTCHIK: I am full-blooded, I have had two strokes already, and dancing is hard for me, but as they say, if you are in a pack of dogs, you may bark and bark, but you must still wag your tail. At that, I have the health of a horse. My dear father—he was a great joker—may he dwell in Heaven—used to talk as if our ancient line, the Semyonoff-Pishtchiks, were descended from the very horse that Caligula made a Senator—(*Sitting down*) But here's my trouble: I haven't any money. A hungry dog believes in nothing but meat—(*Snoring but waking at once*) And the same way with me—I can't talk about anything but money.

TROFIMOFF: Well, to tell you the truth, there is something of a horse about your figure.

PISHTCHIK: Well—a horse is a fine animal— You can sell a horse— (*The sound of playing billiards comes from the next room.* VARYA *appears under the arch to the ballroom.*)

TROFIMOFF (*teasing*): Madam Lopahin! Madam Lopahin!

VARYA (*angrily*): A mangy-looking gentleman!

TROFIMOFF: Yes, I am a mangy-looking gentleman, and proud of it!

VARYA (*in bitter thought*): Here we have gone and hired musicians and what are we going to pay them with?   (*Goes out.*)

TROFIMOFF (*to* PISHTCHIK): If the energy you have wasted in the course of your life trying to find money to pay the interest had gone into something else, you could very likely have turned the world upside down before you were done with it.

PISHTCHIK: Nietzsche—the philosopher—the greatest—the most celebrated—a man of tremendous mind—says in his works that one may make counterfeit money.

TROFIMOFF: And have you read Nietzsche?

PISHTCHIK: Well—Dashenka told me. And I'm in such a state now that I could make counterfeit money myself— Day after tomorrow three hundred and ten roubles must be paid—one hundred and thirty I've on hand— (*Feeling in his pockets, alarmed*) The money is gone! I have lost the money! (*Tearfully*) Where is the money? (*Joyfully*) Here it is, inside the lining—I was in quite a sweat—

(LYUBOFF ANDREEVNA *and* CHARLOTTA IVANOVNA *come in.*)

LYUBOFF ANDREEVNA (*humming lazginka, a Georgian dance*): Why does Leonid take so long? What's he doing in town? (*To* DUNYASHA) Dunyasha, offer the musicians some tea—

TROFIMOFF: In all probability the auction did not take place.

LYUBOFF ANDREEVNA: And the musicians came at an unfortunate moment and we planned the ball at an unfortunate moment— Well, it doesn't matter. (*Sitting down and singing softly.*)

CHARLOTTA (*gives* PISHTCHIK *a deck of cards*): Here is a deck of cards for you, think of some one card.

PISHTCHIK: I have thought of one.

CHARLOTTA: Now, shuffle the deck. Very good. Hand it here; oh, my dear Monsieur Pishtchik. *Ein, zwei, drei!* Now look for it, it's in your coat pocket—

PISHTCHIK (*getting a card out of his coat pocket*): The eight of spades, that's absolutely right! (*Amazed*) Fancy that!

CHARLOTTA (*holding a deck of cards in her palm; to* TROFIMOFF): Tell me quick now, which card is on top?

TROFIMOFF: What is it? Well—the Queen of Spades.

CHARLOTTA: Right! (*To* PISHTCHIK) Well? Which card's on top?

PISHTCHIK: The Ace of Hearts.

CHARLOTTA: Right! (*Strikes the deck against her palm; the deck of cards disappears.*) And what beautiful weather we are having today!

(*A mysterious feminine voice answers her, as if from under the floor, "Oh, yes. The weather is splendid, madame." "You are so nice, you're my ideal—" The voice "Madame, you too please me greatly."*)

THE STATIONMASTER (*applauding*): Madam Ventriloquist, bravo!

PISHTCHIK (*amazed*): Fancy that! Most charming Charlotta Ivanovna—I am simply in love with you.

CHARLOTTA: In love? (*Shrugging her shoulders*) Is it possible that you can love? *Guter menschaber schlachter musikant.*

TROFIMOFF (*slapping* PISHTCHIK *on the shoulder*): You horse, you—

CHARLOTTA: I beg your attention, one more trick. (*Taking a lap robe from the chair*) Here is a very fine lap robe—I want to sell it— (*Shaking it out*) Wouldn't somebody like to buy it?

PISHTCHIK (*amazed*): Fancy that!

CHARLOTTA: *Ein, zwei, drei!*

(*She quickly raises the lowered robe, behind it stands* ANYA, *who curtesys, runs to her mother, embraces her and runs back into the ballroom amid the general delight.*)

LYUBOFF ANDREEVNA (*applauding*): Bravo, bravo—!

CHARLOTTA: Now again! *Ein, zwei, drei!*

(*Lifting the robe: behind it stands* VARYA, *she bows.*)

PISHTCHIK (*amazed*): Fancy that!

CHARLOTTA: That's all. (*Throwing the robe at* PISHTCHIK, *curtseying and running into the ballroom.*)

PISHTCHIK (*hurrying after her*): You little rascal— What a girl! What a girl! (*Goes out.*)

LYUBOFF ANDREEVNA: And Leonid is not here yet. What he's doing in town so long, I don't understand! Everything is finished there, either the estate is sold by now, or the auction didn't take place. Why keep it from us so long?

VARYA (*trying to comfort her*): Uncle has bought it, I am sure of that.

TROFIMOFF (*mockingly*): Yes.

VARYA: Great-aunt sent him power of attorney to buy it in her name and transfer the debt. She did this for Anya. And I feel certain, God willing, that Uncle will buy it.

LYUBOFF ANDREEVNA: Our Yaroslavl great-aunt has sent fifteen thousand to buy the estate in her name— She doesn't trust us, but that wouldn't be enough to pay the interest even— (*Covering her face with her hands*) Today my fate will be decided, my fate—

TROFIMOFF (*teasing* VARYA): Madam Lopahin!

VARYA (*angrily*): Perennial student! You have already been expelled from the University twice.

LYUBOFF ANDREEVNA: But why are you angry, Varya? He teases you about Lopahin, what of it? Marry Lopahin if you want to, he is a good man, interesting. If you don't want to, don't marry him; darling, nobody is making you do it.

VARYA: I look at this matter seriously, Mama, one must speak straight out. He's a good man, I like him.

LYUBOFF ANDREEVNA: Then marry him. What there is to wait for I don't understand!

VARYA: But I can't propose to him myself, Mama. It's two years now; everyone has been talking to me about him, everyone talks, and he either remains silent or jokes. I understand. He's getting rich, he's busy with his own affairs, and has no time for me. If there were money, ever so little, even a hundred roubles, I would drop everything, and go far away. I'd go to a nunnery.

TROFIMOFF: How saintly!

VARYA (*to* TROFIMOFF): A student should be intelligent! (*In a low voice, tearfully*) How homely you have grown, Petya, how old you've got. (*To* LYUBOFF ANDREEVNA, *no longer crying*) It is just that I can't live without working, Mama. I must be doing something every minute.

(YASHA *enters*)

YASHA (*barely restraining his laughter*): Epihodoff has broken a billiard cue!—   (*Goes out.*)

VARYA: But why is Epihodoff here? Who allowed him to play billiards? I don't understand these people—   (*Goes out.*)

LYUBOFF ANDREEVNA: Don't tease her, Petya; you can see she has troubles enough without that.

TROFIMOFF: She is just too zealous. Sticking her nose into things that are none of her business. All summer she gave us no peace, neither me nor Anya; she was afraid a romance would spring up between us. What business is that of hers? And besides I haven't shown any signs of it. I am so remote from triviality. We are above love!

LYUBOFF ANDREEVNA: Well, then, I must be beneath love. (*Very anxiously*) Why isn't Leonid here? Just to tell us whether the estate is sold or not? Calamity seems to me so incredible that I don't know what to think, I'm lost—I could scream this minute—I could do something insane. Save me, Petya. Say something, do say. . . .

TROFIMOFF: Whether the estate is sold today or is not sold—is it not the same? There is no turning back, the path is all grown over. Calm yourself, my dear, all that was over long ago. One mustn't deceive oneself, one must for once at least in one's life look truth straight in the eye.

LYUBOFF ANDREEVNA: What truth? You see where the truth is and where the untruth is, but as for me, it's as if I had lost my sight, I see nothing. You boldly decide all important questions, but tell me, my dear boy, isn't that because you are young and haven't had time yet to suffer through any one of your problems? You look boldly ahead, and isn't that because you don't see and don't expect anything terrible, since life is still hidden from your young eyes? You are braver, more honest, more profound than we are, but stop and think, be magnanimous, have a little mercy on me, just a little. Why, I was born here. My father and mother lived here and my grandfather. I love this house, I can't imagine my life without the cherry orchard and if it is very necessary to sell it, then sell me along with the orchard— (*Embracing* TROFIMOFF *and kissing him on the forehead*) Why, my son was drowned here—(*Crying*) Have mercy on me, good, kind man.

TROFIMOFF: You know I sympathize with you from the bottom of my heart.

LYUBOFF ANDREEVNA: But that should be said differently, differently —(*Taking out her handkerchief; a telegram falls on the floor.*) My heart is heavy today, you can't imagine how heavy. It is too noisy for me here, my soul trembles at every sound, I tremble all over and yet I can't go off to myself, when I am alone the silence frightens me. Don't blame me, Petya—I love you as one of my own. I should gladly have given you Anya's hand, I assure you, only, my dear, you must study and finish your course. You do nothing. Fate simply flings you about from place to place, and that's so strange— Isn't that so? Yes? And you must do something about your beard, to make it grow somehow— (*Laughing*) You look funny!

TROFIMOFF (*picking up the telegram*): I do not desire to be beautiful.

LYUBOFF ANDREEVNA: This telegram is from Paris. I get one every day. Yesterday and today too. That wild man has fallen ill again, something is wrong again with him— He asks forgiveness, begs me to come, and really I ought to make a trip to Paris and stay awhile near him. Your face looks stern, Petya, but what is there to do, my dear, what am I to do, he is ill, he is alone, unhappy and who will look after him there, who will keep him from doing the wrong thing, who will give him his medicine on time? And what is there to hide or keep still about? I love him, that's plain. I love him, love him— It's a stone about my neck, I'm sinking to the bottom with it, but I love that stone and live without it I cannot. (*Pressing* TROFIMOFF's *hand*) Don't think harshly of me, Petya, don't say anything to me, don't—

TROFIMOFF (*tearfully*): Forgive my frankness, for God's sake! Why, he picked your bones.

LYUBOFF ANDREEVNA: No, no, no, you must not talk like that. (*Stopping her ears.*)

TROFIMOFF: But he is a scoundrel, only you, you are the only one that doesn't know it. He is a petty scoundrel, a nonentity—

LYUBOFF ANDREEVNA (*angry but controlling herself*): You are twenty-six years old or twenty-seven, but you are still a schoolboy in the second grade!

TROFIMOFF: Very well!

LYUBOFF ANDREEVNA: You should be a man—at your age you should understand people who love. And you yourself should love someone—you should fall in love! (*Angrily*) Yes, yes! And there is no purity in you; you are simply smug, a ridiculous crank, a freak—

TROFIMOFF (*horrified*): What is she saying!

LYUBOFF ANDREEVNA: "I am above love!" You are not above love, Petya, you are, as our Fiers would say, just a good-for-nothing. Imagine, at your age, not having a mistress—!

TROFIMOFF (*horrified*): This is terrible! What is she saying! (*Goes quickly into the ballroom, clutching his head.*) This is horrible—I can't bear it, I am going—(*Goes out but immediately returns.*) All is over between us. (*Goes out into the hall.*)

LYUBOFF ANDREEVNA (*shouting after him*): Petya, wait! You funny creature, I was joking! Petya! (*In the hall you hear someone running up the stairs and suddenly falling back down with a crash. You hear* ANYA *and* VARYA *scream but immediately you hear laughter.*) What's that?

(ANYA *runs in laughing.*)

ANYA: Petya fell down the stairs!   (*Runs out.*)

LYUBOFF ANDREEVNA: What a funny boy that Petya is—! (*The* STATIONMASTER *stops in the center of the ballroom and begins to recite "The Sinner" by A. Tolstoi. They listen to him but he has recited only a few lines when the strains of a waltz are heard from the hall and the recitation is broken off. They all dance.* TROFIMOFF, ANYA, VARYA *and* LYUBOFF ANDREEVNA *come in from the hall*) But, Petya—but, dear soul—I beg your forgiveness— Let's go dance.

(*She dances with* TROFIMOFF. ANYA *and* VARYA *dance.* FIERS *enters, leaving his stick by the side door.* YASHA *also comes into the drawing room and watches the dancers.*)

YASHA: What is it, Grandpa?

FIERS: I don't feel very well. In the old days there were generals, barons, admirals dancing at our parties, and now we send for the post-office clerk and the stationmaster, and even they are none too anxious to come. Somehow I've grown feeble. The old master, the grandfather, treated everybody with sealing-wax for all sicknesses. I take sealing-wax every day, have done so for twenty-odd years or more; it may be due to that that I'm alive.

YASHA: You are tiresome, Grandpa. (*Yawning*) Why don't you go off and die?

FIERS: Aw, you—good-for-nothing!— (*Muttering.*)

(TROFIMOFF *and* LYUBOFF ANDREEVNA *dance in the ballroom and then in the drawing room.*)

LYUBOFF ANDREEVNA: *Merci.* I'll sit down awhile—(*Sitting down*) I'm tired.

(ANYA *enters, agitated.*)

ANYA: And just now in the kitchen some man was saying that the cherry orchard had been sold today.

LYUBOFF ANDREEVNA: Sold to whom?

ANYA: He didn't say who to. He's gone.

(*Dancing with* TROFIMOFF, *they pass into the ballroom.*)

YASHA: It was some old man babbling there. A stranger.

FIERS: And Leonid Andreevich is still not here, he has not arrived. The overcoat he has on is light, mid-season—let's hope he won't catch cold. Ach, these young things!

LYUBOFF ANDREEVNA: I shall die this minute. Go, Yasha, find out who it was sold to.

YASHA: But he's been gone a long time, the old fellow. (*Laughing.*)

LYUBOFF ANDREEVNA (*with some annoyance*): Well, what are you laughing at? What are you so amused at?

YASHA: Epihodoff is just too funny. An empty-headed man. Twenty-two misfortunes!

LYUBOFF ANDREEVNA: Fiers, if the estate is sold, where will you go?

FIERS: Wherever you say, there I'll go.

LYUBOFF ANDREEVNA: Why do you look like that? Aren't you well? You know you ought to go to bed—

FIERS: Yes—(*With a sneer*) I go to bed and without me who's going to serve, who'll take care of things? I'm the only one in the whole house.

YASHA (*to* LYUBOFF ANDREEVNA): Lyuboff Andreevna, let me ask a favor of you, do be so kind! If you ever go back to Paris, take me with you, please do! It's impossible for me to stay here. (*Looking around him, and speaking in a low voice*) Why talk about it? You can see for yourself it's an uncivilized country, an immoral people and not only that, there's the boredom of it. The food they give us in that kitchen is abominable and there's that Fiers, too, walking about and muttering all kinds of words that are out of place. Take me with you, be so kind!

(PISHTCHIK *enters.*)

PISHTCHIK: Allow me to ask you— for a little waltz, most beautiful lady— (LYUBOFF ANDREEVNA *goes with him.*) Charming lady, I must borrow a hundred and eighty roubles from you— will borrow— (*Dancing*) a hundred and eighty roubles— (*They pass into the ballroom.*)

YASHA (*singing low*): "Wilt thou know the unrest in my soul!"

(*In the ballroom a figure in a gray top hat and checked trousers waves both hands and jumps about; there are shouts of "Bravo, Charlotta Ivanovna!"*)

DUNYASHA (*stopping to powder her face*): The young lady orders me to dance—there are a lot of gentlemen and very few ladies—but dancing makes my head swim and my heart thump. Fiers Nikolaevich, the post-office clerk said something to me just now that took my breath away.

(*The music plays more softly.*)

FIERS: What did he say to you?

DUNYASHA: You are like a flower, he says.

YASHA (*yawning*): What ignorance—!   (*Goes out.*)

DUNYASHA: Like a flower—I am such a sensitive girl, I love tender words awfully.

FIERS: You'll be getting your head turned.

(EPIHODOFF *enters.*)

EPIHODOFF: Avdotya Feodorovna, you don't want to see me— It's as if I were some sort of insect. (*Sighing*) Ach, life!

DUNYASHA: What do you want?

EPIHODOFF: Undoubtedly you may be right. (*Sighing*) But of course, if one considers it from a given point of view, then you, I will allow myself so to express it, forgive my frankness, absolutely led me into a state of mind. I know my fate, every day some misfortune happens to me, but I have long since become accustomed to that, and so I look on my misfortunes with a smile. You gave me your word and, although I—

DUNYASHA: I beg you, we'll talk later on, but leave me now in peace. I'm in a dream now. (*Playing with her fan.*)

EPIHODOFF: I have a something wrong happens every day—I will allow myself so to express it—I just smile, I even laugh.

(VARYA *enters from the ballroom.*)

VARYA: You are not gone yet, Semyon? What a really disrespectful man you are! (*To* DUNYASHA) Get out of here, Dunyasha. (*To* EPIHODOFF) You either play billiards and break a cue or you walk about the drawing room like a guest.

EPIHODOFF: Allow me to tell you, you cannot make any demands on me.

VARYA: I'm not making any demands on you, I'm talking to you. All you know is to walk from place to place but not do any work. We keep a clerk, but what for, nobody knows.

EPIHODOFF (*offended*): Whether I work, whether I walk, whether I eat, or whether I play billiards are matters to be discussed only by people of understanding and my seniors.

VARYA: You dare to say that to me! (*Flying into a temper*) You dare? So I don't understand anything? Get out of here! This minute!

EPIHODOFF (*alarmed*): I beg you to express yourself in a delicate manner.

VARYA (*beside herself*): This very minute, get out of here! Get out! (*He goes to the door; she follows him.*) Twenty-two misfortunes! Don't you dare breathe in here! Don't let me set eyes on you! (EPIHODOFF *has gone out, but his voice comes from outside the door "I shall complain about you."*) Ah, you are coming back? (*Grabbing the stick that* FIERS *put by the door*) Come on, come— come on, I'll show you— Ah, you are coming? You are coming? Take that then—!

(*She swings the stick, at the very moment when* LOPAHIN *is coming in.*)

LOPAHIN: Most humbly, I thank you.

VARYA (*angrily and ironically*): I beg your pardon!

LOPAHIN: It's nothing at all. I humbly thank you for the pleasant treat.

VARYA: It isn't worth your thanks. (*Moving away, then looking back and asking gently*) I haven't hurt you?

LOPAHIN: No, it's nothing. There's a great bump coming though. (*Voices in the ballroom "Lopahin has come back." "Yermolay Alexeevich!"*)

(PISHTCHIK *enters.*)

PISHTCHIK: See what we see, hear what we hear—! (*He and* LOPAHIN *kiss one another.*) You smell slightly of cognac, my dear, my good old chap. And we are amusing ourselves here too.

(LYUBOFF ANDREEVNA *enters.*)

LYUBOFF ANDREEVNA: Is that you, Yermolay Alexeevich? Why were you so long? Where is Leonid?

LOPAHIN: Leonid Andreevich got back when I did, he's coming.

LYUBOFF ANDREEVNA (*agitated*): Well, what? Was there an auction? Do speak!

LOPAHIN (*embarrassed, afraid of showing the joy he feels*): The auction was over by four o'clock— We were late for the train, had to wait till half-past nine. (*Sighing heavily*) Ugh, my head's swimming a bit!

(GAYEFF *enters; with his right hand he carries his pur-chases, with his left he wipes away his tears.*)

LYUBOFF ANDREEVNA: Lyona, what? Lyona, eh? (*Impatiently, with tears in her eyes*) Quick, for God's sake—

GAYEFF (*not answering her, merely waving his hand; to* FIERS, *crying*): Here, take it— There are anchovies, some Kertch herrings — I haven't eaten anything all day— What I have suffered! (*The door into the billiard room is open; you hear the balls clicking and* YASHA's *voice "Seven and eighteen!"* GAYEFF's *expression changes, he is no longer crying.*) I'm terribly tired. You help me change, Fiers. (*Goes to his room through the ballroom,* FIERS *behind him.*)

PISHTCHIK: What happened at the auction? Go on, tell us!

LYUBOFF ANDREEVNA: Is the cherry orchard sold?

LOPAHIN: It's sold.

LYUBOFF ANDREEVNA: Who bought it?

LOPAHIN: I bought it. (*A pause.* LYUBOFF ANDREEVNA *is overcome. She would have fallen had she not been standing near the chair and table.* VARYA *takes the keys from her belt, throws them on the floor in the middle of the drawing room and goes out.*) I bought it. Kindly wait a moment, ladies and gentlemen, everything is muddled up in my head, I can't speak— (*Laughing*) We arrived at the auction, Deriganoff was already there. Leonid Andreevich had only fifteen thousand and Deriganoff right off bids thirty over and above indebtedness. I see how things are, I match him with forty thousand. He forty-five. I fifty-five. That is to say he raises it by fives, I by tens.—So it ended. Over and above the indebtedness, I bid up to ninety thousand, it was knocked down to me. The cherry orchard is mine now. Mine! (*Guffawing*) My God, Lord, the cherry orchard is mine! Tell me I'm drunk, out of my head, that I'm imagining all this— (*Stamps his feet*) Don't laugh at me! If only my father and grandfather could rise from their graves and see this whole business, see how their Yermolay, beaten, half-illiterate Yermolay, who used to run around barefoot in winter, how that very Yermolay has bought an estate that nothing in the world can beat. I bought the estate where grandfather and father were slaves, where you wouldn't even let me in the kitchen. I am asleep, it's only some dream of mine, it only seems so to me— That's nothing but the fruit of your imagination, covered with the darkness of the unknown— (*Picking up the keys, with a gentle smile*) She threw down the keys, wants to show she is not mistress any more— (*Jingling the keys*) Well, it's all the same. (*The orchestra is heard tuning up*) Hey, musicians, play, I want to hear you! Come on, everybody, and see how Yermolay Lopahin will swing the ax in the cherry orchard, how the trees will fall to the ground! We are going to build villas and our grandsons and great-grandsons will see a new life here— Music, play! (*The music is playing.* LYUBOFF ANDREEVNA *has sunk into a chair, crying bitterly.* LOPAHIN *reproachfully*) Why, then, didn't you listen to me? My poor dear, it can't be undone now. (*With tears*) Oh, if this could all be over soon, if somehow our awkward, unhappy life would be changed!

PISHTCHIK (*taking him by the arm, in a low voice*): She is crying. Come on in the ballroom, let her be by herself— Come on— (*Taking him by the arm and leading him into the ballroom.*)

LOPAHIN: What's the matter? Music, there, play up! (*Sarcastically*) Everything is to be as I want it! Here comes the new squire, the owner of the cherry orchard. (*Quite accidentally, he bumps into the little table, and very nearly upsets the candelabra.*) I can pay for everything!

(*Goes out with* PISHTCHIK. *There is nobody left either in the ballroom or the drawing room but* LYUBOFF ANDREEVNA, *who sits all huddled up and crying bitterly. The music plays softly.* ANYA *and* TROFIMOFF *enter hurriedly.* ANYA *comes up to her mother and kneels in front of her.* TROFIMOFF *remains at the ballroom door.*)

ANYA: Mama—! Mama, you are crying? My dear, kind, good Mama, my beautiful, I love you—I bless you. The cherry orchard is sold, it's not ours any more, that's true, true; but don't cry, Mama, you've your life still left you, you've your good, pure heart ahead of you— Come with me, come on, darling, away from here, come on— We will plant a new orchard, finer than this one, you'll see it, you'll understand; and joy, quiet, deep joy will sink into your heart, like the sun at evening, and you'll smile, Mama! Come, darling, come on!

CURTAIN

ACT IV

(*The same setting as in Act One. There are neither curtains on the windows nor are there any pictures on the walls. Only a little furniture remains piled up in one corner as if for sale. A sense of emptiness is felt. Near the outer door, at the rear of the stage, is a pile of suitcases, traveling bags, and so on. The door on the left is open, and through it* VARYA's *and* ANYA's *voices are heard.* LOPAHIN *is standing waiting.* YASHA *is holding a tray with glasses of champagne. In the hall* EPIHODOFF *is tying up a box, offstage at the rear there is a hum. It is the peasants who have come to say good-by.* GAYEFF's *voice "Thanks, brothers, thank you."*)

YASHA: The simple folk have come to say good-by. I am of the opinion, Yermolay Alexeevich, that the people are kind enough but don't understand anything.

(*The hum subsides.* LYUBOFF ANDREEVNA *enters through the hall with* GAYEFF; *she is not crying, but is pale, her face quivers, she is not able to speak.*)

GAYEFF: You gave them your purse, Lyuba. Mustn't do that! Mustn't do that!

LYUBOFF ANDREEVNA: I couldn't help it! I couldn't help it!

(*Both go out.*)

LOPAHIN (*calling through the door after them*): Please, I humbly beg you! A little glass at parting. I didn't think to bring some from town, and at the station I found just one bottle. Please! (*A pause.*) Well, then, ladies and gentlemen! You don't want it? (*Moving away from the door*) If I'd known that, I wouldn't have bought it. Well, then I won't drink any either. (YASHA *carefully sets the tray down on a chair.*) At least, you have some, Yasha.

YASHA: To those who are departing! Pleasant days to those who stay behind! (*Drinking*) This champagne is not the real stuff, I can assure you.

LOPAHIN: Eight roubles a bottle. (*A pause.*) It's devilish cold in here.

YASHA: They didn't heat up today, we are leaving anyway. (*Laughing.*)

LOPAHIN: What are you laughing about?

YASHA: For joy.

LOPAHIN: Outside it's October, but it's sunny and still, like summer. Good for building. (*Looking at his watch, then through the door*) Ladies and gentlemen, bear in mind we have forty-six minutes in all till train time! Which means you have to go to the station in twenty minutes. Hurry up a little.

(*TROFIMOFF enters from outside in an overcoat.*)

TROFIMOFF: Seems to me it is time to go. The carriages are ready. The devil knows where my rubbers are. They've disappeared. (*In the door*) Anya, my rubbers are not here! I can't find them.

LOPAHIN: And I have to go to Harkoff. I'm going on the same train with you. I'm going to live in Harkoff all winter. I've been dilly-dallying along with you, I'm tired of doing nothing. I can't be without work, look, I don't know what to do with my hands here, see, they are dangling somehow, as if they didn't belong to me.

TROFIMOFF: We are leaving right away, and you'll set about your useful labors again.

LOPAHIN: Here, drink a glass.

TROFIMOFF: I shan't.

LOPAHIN: It's to Moscow now?

TROFIMOFF: Yes. I'll see them off to town, and tomorrow to Moscow.

LOPAHIN: Yes— Maybe the professors are not giving their lectures. I imagine they are waiting till you arrive.

TROFIMOFF: That's none of your business.

LOPAHIN: How many years is it you've been studying at the University?

TROFIMOFF: Think of something newer. This is old and flat. (*Looking for his rubbers*) You know, perhaps, we shall not see each other again; therefore, permit me to give you one piece of advice at parting! Don't wave your arms! Cure yourself of that habit—of arm waving. And also of building summer cottages, figuring that the summer residents will in time become individual landowners; figuring like that is arm waving too— Just the same, however, I like you. You have delicate soft fingers like an artist, you have a delicate soft heart—

LOPAHIN (*embracing him*): Good-by, my dear boy. Thanks for everything. If you need it, take some money from me for the trip.

TROFIMOFF: Why should I? There's no need for it.

LOPAHIN: But you haven't any!

TROFIMOFF: I have. Thank you. I got some for a translation. Here it is in my pocket. (*Anxiously*) But my rubbers are gone.

VARYA (*from another room*): Take your nasty things! (*Throws a pair of rubbers on to the stage.*)

TROFIMOFF: But what are you angry about, Varya? Hm— Why, these are not my rubbers.

LOPAHIN: In the spring I planted twenty-seven hundred acres of poppies and now I've made forty thousand clear. And when my poppies were in bloom, what a picture it was! So look, as I say, I've made forty thousand, which means I'm offering you a loan because I can afford to. Why turn up your nose? I'm a peasant—I speak straight out.

TROFIMOFF: Your father was a peasant, mine—an apothecary—and from that absolutely nothing follows. (LOPAHIN *takes out his wallet.*) Leave it alone, leave it alone— If you gave me two hundred thousand even, I wouldn't take it. I am a free man. And everything that you all value so highly and dearly, both rich man and beggars, has not the slightest power over me, it's like a mere feather floating in the air. I can get along without you, I can pass you by, I am strong and proud. Humanity is moving toward the loftiest truth, toward the loftiest happiness that is possible on earth and I am in the front ranks.

LOPAHIN: Will you get there?

TROFIMOFF: I'll get there. (*A pause.*) I'll get there, or I'll show the others the way to get there.

(*In the distance is heard the sound of an ax on a tree.*)

LOPAHIN: Well, good-by, my dear boy. It's time to go. We turn up our noses at one another, but life keeps on passing. When I work a long time without stopping, my thoughts are clearer, and it seems as if I, too, know what I exist for, and, brother, how many people are there in Russia who exist, nobody knows for what! Well, all the same, it's not that that keeps things circulating. Leonid Andreevich, they say, has accepted a position—he'll be in a bank, six thousand a year—the only thing is he won't stay there, he's very lazy—

ANYA (*in the doorway*): Mama begs of you until she's gone, not to cut down the orchard.

TROFIMOFF: Honestly, haven't you enough tact to—(*Goes out through the hall.*)

LOPAHIN: Right away, right away— What people, really!

(*Goes out after him.*)

ANYA: Has Fiers been sent to the hospital?

YASHA: I told them to this morning. They must have sent him.

ANYA (*to* EPIHODOFF, *who is passing through the room*): Semyon Panteleevich, please inquire whether or not they have taken Fiers to the hospital.

YASHA (*huffily*): This morning, I told Igor. Why ask ten times over!

EPIHODOFF: The venerable Fiers, according to my conclusive opinion, is not worth mending, he ought to join his forefathers. And I can only envy him. (*Putting a suitcase on a hatbox and crushing it*) Well, there you are, of course. I knew it. (*Goes out.*)

YASHA (*mockingly*): Twenty-two misfortunes—

VARYA (*on the other side of the door*): Have they taken Fiers to the hospital?

ANYA: They have.

VARYA: Then why didn't they take the letter to the doctor?

ANYA: We must send it on after them— (*Goes out.*)

VARYA (*from the next room*): Where is Yasha? Tell him his mother has come, she wants to say good-by to him.

YASHA (*waving his hand*): They merely try my patience.

(DUNYASHA *has been busying herself with the luggage; now when* YASHA *is left alone, she goes up to him.*)

DUNYASHA: If you'd only look at me once, Yasha. You are going away—leaving me— (*Crying and throwing herself on his neck.*)

YASHA: Why are you crying? (*Drinking champagne*) In six days I'll be in Paris again. Tomorrow we will board the express train and dash off out of sight; somehow, I can't believe it. *Vive la France!* It doesn't suit me here—I can't live here— Can't help that. I've seen enough ignorance—enough for me. (*Drinking champagne*) Why do you cry? Behave yourself properly, then you won't be crying.

DUNYASHA (*powdering her face, looking into a small mirror*): Send me a letter from Paris. I loved you, Yasha, you know, loved you so! I am a tender creature, Yasha!

YASHA: They are coming here. (*Bustling about near the suitcases, humming low.*)

(LYUBOFF ANDREEVNA, GAYEFF, ANYA *and* CHARLOTTA IVANOVNA *enter.*)

GAYEFF: We should be going. There is very little time left. (*Looking at* YASHA) Who is it smells like herring!

LYUBOFF ANDREEVNA: In about ten minutes let's be in the carriage— (*Glancing around the room*) Good-by, dear house, old Grandfather. Winter will pass, spring will be here; but you won't be here any longer, they'll tear you down. How much these walls have seen! (*Kissing her daughter warmly*) My treasure, you are beaming, your eyes are dancing like two diamonds. Are you happy? Very?

ANYA: Very! It's the beginning of a new life, Mama!

GAYEFF (*gaily*): Yes, indeed, everything is fine now. Before the sale of the cherry orchard, we all were troubled, distressed, and then when the question was settled definitely, irrevocably, we all calmed down and were even cheerful— I'm a bank official. I am a financier now— Yellow ball into the side pocket, anyway, Lyuba, you look better, no doubt about that.

LYUBOFF ANDREEVNA: Yes. My nerves are better, that's true. (*They hand her her hat and coat.*) I sleep well. Carry out my things, Yasha. It's time. (*To* ANYA) My little girl, we shall see each other again soon— I am going to Paris, I shall live there on the money your Yaroslavl great-aunt sent for the purchase of the estate—long live Great-aunt! But that money won't last long.

ANYA: Mama, you'll come back soon, soon— Isn't that so? I'll prepare myself, pass the examination at high school, and then I'll work, I will help you. We'll read all sorts of books together. Mama, isn't that so? (*Kissing her mother's hands*) We'll read in the autumn evenings, read lots of books, and a new, wonderful world will open up before us— (*Daydreaming*) Mama, do come—

LYUBOFF ANDREEVNA: I'll come, my precious. (*Embracing her daughter.*)

(LOPAHIN *enters with* CHARLOTTA *who is softly humming a song.*)

GAYEFF: Lucky Charlotta: she's singing!

CHARLOTTA (*taking a bundle that looks like a baby wrapped up*): My baby, bye, bye— (*A baby's cry is heard: "Ooah, ooah—!"*) Hush, my darling, my dear little boy. (*"Ooah, ooah—!"*) I am so sorry for you! (*Throwing the bundle back*) Will you please find me a position? I cannot go on like this.

LOPAHIN: We will find something, Charlotta Ivanovna, don't worry.

GAYEFF: Everybody is dropping us, Varya is going away.—All of a sudden we are not needed.

CHARLOTTA: I have no place in town to live. I must go away. (*Humming*) It's all the same—

(PISHTCHIK *enters.*)

LOPAHIN: The freak of nature—!

PISHTCHIK (*out of breath*): Ugh, let me catch my breath—I'm exhausted— My honored friends— Give me some water—

GAYEFF: After money, I suppose? This humble servant will flee from sin! (*Goes out.*)

PISHTCHIK: It's a long time since I was here— Most beautiful lady— (*To* LOPAHIN) You here—? Glad to see you—a man of the greatest intellect— Here— Take it— (*Giving* LOPAHIN *some money*) Four hundred roubles— That leaves eight hundred and forty I still owe you—

LOPAHIN (*with astonishment, shrugging his shoulders*): I must be dreaming. But where did you get it?

PISHTCHIK: Wait—I'm hot— Most extraordinary event. Some Englishmen came and found on my land some kind of white clay— (*To* LYUBOFF ANDREEVNA) And four hundred for you—Beautiful lady—Wonderful lady— (*Handing over the money*) The rest later. (*Taking a drink of water*) Just now a young man was saying on the train that some great philosopher recommends jumping off roofs—"Jump!" he says, and "therein lies the whole problem." (*With astonishment*) You don't say! Water!

LOPAHIN: And what Englishmen were they?

PISHTCHIK: I leased them the parcel of land with the clay for twenty-four years— And now, excuse me, I haven't time—I must run along—I'm going to Znoykoff's—To Kardamonoff's— I owe everybody— (*Drinking*) I wish you well—I'll drop in on Thursday—

LYUBOFF ANDREEVNA: We are moving to town right away, and tomorrow I'm going abroad—

PISHTCHIK: What? (*Alarmed*) Why to town? That's why I see furniture—Suitcases— Well, no matter— (*Tearfully*) No matter— Men of the greatest minds—those Englishmen— No matter— Good luck! God will help you— No matter— Everything in this world comes to an end—(*Kissing* LYUBOFF ANDREEVNA'S *hand*) And should the report reach you that my end has come, think of that well-known horse and say: "There was once on earth a so and so—Semyonoff Pishtchik— The kingdom of Heaven be his." Most remarkable weather—yes— (*Going out greatly disconcerted, but*

immediately returning and speaking from the door) Dashenka
sends her greetings!

(Goes out.)

LYUBOFF ANDREEVNA: And now we can go. I am leaving with two
worries. First, that Fiers is sick. *(Glancing at her watch)* We still
have five minutes—

ANYA: Mama, Fiers has already been sent to the hospital. Yasha sent
him off this morning.

LYUBOFF ANDREEVNA: My second worry—is Varya. She is used to
getting up early and working, 'and now without any work she is
like a fish out of water. She has grown thin, pale and cries all the
time, poor thing— *(A pause.)* You know this, Yermolay Alexeevich: I dreamed—of marrying her to you. And there was every
sign of your getting married. *(Whispering to ANYA, who beckons
to CHARLOTTA; both go out.)* She loves you, you are fond of her,
and I don't know, don't know why it is you seem to avoid each
other—I don't understand it!

LOPAHIN: I don't understand it either, I must confess. It's all strange
somehow— If there's still time, I am ready right now even— Let's
finish it up— and *basta,* but without you I feel I won't propose.

LYUBOFF ANDREEVNA: But that's excellent. Surely it takes only a
minute. I'll call her at once.

LOPAHIN: And to fit the occasion there's the champagne. *(Looking at
the glasses)* Empty, somebody has already drunk them. (YASHA
coughs.) That's what's called lapping it up—

LYUBOFF ANDREEVNA *(vivaciously)*: Splendid! We'll go out— Yasha,
allez! I'll call her— *(Through the door)* Varya, drop everything
and come here. Come on!

(Goes out with YASHA.)

LOPAHIN *(Looking at his watch)*: Yes—
*(A pause. Behind the door you hear smothered laughter, whispering,
finally VARYA enters.)*

VARYA *(looking at the luggage a long time)*: That's strange, I just
can't find it—

LOPAHIN: What are you looking for?

VARYA: I packed it myself and don't remember where. *(A pause.)*

LOPAHIN: Where do you expect to go now, Varvara Mikhailovna?

VARYA: I? To Regulin's. I agreed to go there to look after the house—
As a sort of housekeeper.

LOPAHIN: That's in Yashnevo? It's nigh on to seventy miles. *(A
pause.)* And here ends life in this house—

VARYA (*examining the luggage*): But where is it? Either I put it in the trunk, perhaps— Yes, life in this house is ended—it won't be any more—

LOPAHIN: And I am going to Harkoff now—By the next train. I've a lot to do. And I am leaving Epihodoff—on the ground here—I've hired him.

VARYA: Well!

LOPAHIN: Last year at this time it had already been snowing, if you remember, and now it's quiet, it's sunny. It's only that it's cold, about three degrees of frost.

VARYA: I haven't noticed. (*A pause.*) And besides our thermometer is broken— (*A pause. A voice from the yard through the door*) Yermolay Alexeevich—

LOPAHIN (*as if he had been expecting this call for a long time*): This minute! (*Goes out quickly.*)

(VARYA, *sitting on the floor, putting her head on a bundle of clothes, sobs quietly. The door opens,* LYUBOFF ANDREEVNA *enters cautiously.*)

VARYA (*she is not crying any longer, and has wiped her eyes*): Yes, it's time, Mama. I can get to Regulin's today, if we are just not too late for the train— (*Through the door*) Anya, put your things on! (ANYA, *then* GAYEFF *and* CHARLOTTA IVANOVNA *enter.* GAYEFF *has on a warm overcoat, with a hood. The servants gather, also the drivers.* EPIHODOFF *busies himself with the luggage.*) Now we can be on our way.

ANYA (*joyfully*): On óur way!

GAYEFF: My friends, my dear, kind friends! Leaving this house forever, can I remain silent, can I restrain myself from expressing, as we say, farewell, those feelings that fill now my whole being—

ANYA (*beseechingly*): Uncle!

VARYA: Dear Uncle, don't!

GAYEFF (*dejectedly*): Bank the yellow into the side pocket— I am silent—

(TROFIMOFF *and then* LOPAHIN *enter.*)

TROFIMOFF: Well, ladies and gentlemen, it's time to go!

LOPAHIN: Epihodoff, my coat!

LYUBOFF ANDREEVNA: I'll sit here just a minute more. It's as if I had never seen before what the walls in this house are like, what kind of ceilings, and now I look at them greedily, with such tender love—

GAYEFF: I remember when I was six years old, on Trinity Day, I sat in this window and watched my father going to Church—

LYUBOFF ANDREEVNA: Are all the things taken out?

LOPAHIN: Everything, I think. (*Putting on his overcoat. To* EPIHODOFF) Epihodoff, you see that everything is in order.

EPIHODOFF (*talking in a hoarse voice*): Don't worry, Yermolay Alexeevich!

LOPAHIN: Why is your voice like that?

EPIHODOFF: Just drank some water, swallowed something.

YASHA (*with contempt*): The ignorance—

LYUBOFF ANDREEVNA: We are going and there won't be a soul left here—

LOPAHIN: Till spring.

VARYA (*she pulls an umbrella out from a bundle, it looks as if she were going to hit someone;* LOPAHIN *pretends to be frightened*): What do you, what do you— I never thought of it.

TROFIMOFF: Ladies and gentlemen, let's get in the carriages— It's time! The train is coming any minute.

VARYA: Petya, here they are, your rubbers, by the suitcase. (*Tearfully*) And how dirty yours are, how old—!

TROFIMOFF (*putting on the rubbers*): Let's go, ladies and gentlemen!

GAYEFF (*greatly embarrassed, afraid he will cry*): The train— The station— Cross into the side, combination off the white into the corner—

LYUBOFF ANDREEVNA: Let's go!

LOPAHIN: Everybody here? Nobody there? (*Locking the side door on the left*) Things are stored here, it must be locked up, let's go!

ANYA: Good-by, house! Good-by, the old life!

TROFIMOFF: Long live the new life!

(*Goes out with* ANYA. VARYA *casts a glance around the room and, without hurrying, goes out.* YASHA *and* CHARLOTTA, *with her dog, go out.*)

LOPAHIN: And so, till spring. Out, ladies and gentlemen— Till we meet.   (*Goes out.*)

(LYUBOFF ANDREEVNA *and* GAYEFF *are left alone. As if they had been waiting for this, they throw themselves on one another's necks sobbing, but smothering their sobs as if afraid of being heard.*)

GAYEFF (*in despair*): Oh, Sister, Sister—

LYUBOFF ANDREEVNA: Oh, my dear, my lovely, beautiful orchard! My life, my youth, my happiness, good-by!

ANYA (ANYA'S *voice, gaily, appealingly*): Mama—!

TROFIMOFF (TROFIMOFF'S *voice, gaily, excitedly*): Aaooch!

LYUBOFF ANDREEVNA: For the last time, just to look at the walls, at the window— My dear mother used to love to walk around in this room—

GAYEFF: Oh, Sister, Sister—!

ANYA (ANYA'S *voice*): Mama—!

TROFIMOFF (TROFIMOFF'S *voice*): Aaooch—!

LYUBOFF ANDREEVNA: We are coming!   (*They go out.*)

(*The stage is empty. You hear the keys locking all the doors, then the carriages drive off. It grows quiet. In the silence you hear the dull thud of an ax on a tree, a lonely, mournful sound. Footsteps are heard. From the door on the right* FIERS *appears. He is dressed as usual, in a jacket and a white waistcoat, slippers on his feet. He is sick.*)

FIERS (*going to the door and trying the knob*): Locked. They've gone. (*Sitting down on the sofa*) They forgot about me— No matter— I'll sit here awhile— And Leonid Andreevich, for sure, didn't put on his fur coat, he went off with his topcoat— (*Sighing anxiously*) And I didn't see to it— The young saplings! (*He mutters something that cannot be understood*) Life has gone by, as if I hadn't lived at all— (*Lying down*) I'll lie down awhile— You haven't got any strength, nothing is left, nothing— Ach, you— good-for-nothing— (*He lies still.*)

(*There is a far-off sound as if out of the sky, the sound of a snapped string, dying away, sad. A stillness falls, and there is only the thud of an ax on a tree, far away in the orchard.*)

CURTAIN

Eugene O'Neill

*E*ugene Gladstone O'Neill, America's greatest dramatist, was born in a Broadway hotel in the heart of the New York theater district on October 6, 1888. The son of a nationally known actor, he spent the early years of his life in hotel rooms and theaters. Long before most children have seen their first play, O'Neill knew the theater thoroughly. And when he began to write his early one-act plays, he rejected the romantic melodrama of the contemporary American stage and became the champion of realistic drama.

The dramatist's father, James O'Neill, became famous and prosperous playing Edmond Dantes in *The Count of Monte Cristo*. The son of impoverished Irish immigrants, he had to leave school at the age of ten. He was a hard-working, forceful young man with a real acting talent and, until he took over the role of Dantes, was becoming known as a fine Shakespearean actor. He never forgot his early years of poverty and tended to be parsimonious, but he was determined to ensure that his two sons received the education he had missed. At seven, Eugene was enrolled in a Roman Catholic boarding school, Mount Saint Vincent, not far from New York City. The school was run by nuns, and the boy received an intensive religious indoctrination. Though he was soon to reject Catholicism, this early training made O'Neill an absolutist. He completed his high school work at another boarding school, Betts Academy, in Connecticut. He was an indifferent student, but he early became an avid reader, discovering, during his senior year at the academy, the plays of Ibsen and Bernard

Shaw. These writers expressed for him what he already felt was wrong with the dramas he was attending in New York, and they demonstrated what realistic drama could achieve. At this stage of his life, however, O'Neill entertained no thoughts of a theatrical career for himself. Graduates of Betts Academy generally entered Yale, but O'Neill, already steering his own course, refused to follow the path of his classmates, and in 1906 he entered Princeton.

He was a comparatively worldly wise college freshman, having been introduced by his brother, Jamie, ten years his senior, to the glitter of the Broadway theater world. He attended the theater regularly and accompanied his hard-drinking brother on his rounds of the New York saloons. The prescribed courses at Princeton made little impression upon him, but he did respond enthusiastically to a book he discovered on his own, Nietzsche's *Thus Spake Zarathustra*. Nietzsche provided a substitute for the Catholicism O'Neill had renounced and a voice for the social and intellectual rebellion that had been brewing within him. O'Neill did not complete his freshman year. He was suspended for some schoolboy prank, and he withdrew from college to join his brother in New York. His disappointed father tried to help him by arranging for a job, but the eighteen-year-old O'Neill joined his brother in a pattern of wild, self-destructive drinking and living. It took O'Neill less than three years to journey from a secluded dormitory room at Princeton to a vermin-infested cell at Jimmy the Priest's, a Fulton Street rooming-house and saloon that harbored human derelicts. "One couldn't go any lower," O'Neill later said of the place, which he used as the setting for *The Iceman Cometh*. "Gorky's Night's Lodging was an ice cream parlor in comparison."

On the steep, anguished road down to this spiritual and physical "hell-hole," O'Neill married a girl of whom his father disapproved. He spent one week with his young bride before leaving for a South American mining expedition. During the journey to Honduras he contracted malaria, and he was soon back in New York. He avoided his wife, appealing to his father for help. Eventually, a divorce was arranged; O'Neill was not to meet the offspring of his brief marriage until the boy, Eugene O'Neill, Jr., was ten years old. Driven by psychological needs and emotional problems that he could neither understand nor control, O'Neill suddenly, in 1910, became a seaman aboard a Norwegian sailing vessel. In the vast loneliness of the ocean setting, he discovered a release from tension, a sense of spiritual belonging that he did not even realize he had been seeking. In the autobiographical drama of his final years, *A Long Day's Journey into Night*, he describes this important experience:

> . . . for a moment I lost myself—actually lost my life. I was set free! I dissolved in the sea, became white sails and flying spray, became beauty and rhythm, became moonlight and the ship and the high dim-starred sky! I belonged without past or future, within peace and unity and a wild joy, within something greater than my own life, or the life of Man, to Life itself.

This mystical experience probably reflected O'Neill's unrecognized spiritual quest for a substitute for his lost faith, and it paved the way for his later acceptance, at least temporarily, of the Jungian concept of a racial unconscious and of the Nietzschean idea of a Life Force greater than the individual man. Though the experience left an indelible mark upon O'Neill, it did not slow his journey downward. He jumped ship in Buenos Aires and quickly drank up his accumulated pay. After trying a few jobs, he took to begging for money to keep himself drunk. Eventually, he sobered sufficiently to sign on as a seaman aboard a vessel headed for New York. There, he again drank up his pay, sharing a room at Jimmy the Priest's with a sailor friend. After another trip to sea, he settled down to staying drunk, and in 1912 reached the low point of his descent with a suicide attempt.

His spiritual ascent from these lower depths began with an agreement with his father to spend the summer with his family in their New London, Connecticut summer home and work on a local newspaper as a reporter. A short time later a touch of tuberculosis sent O'Neill to a sanitarium for about six months. During this period of enforced confinement and routine living, he began to write. He returned to New London to complete his recuperation and, by 1914, he had written enough one-act plays to publish, with the financial assistance of his father, a collection entitled *Thirst, and Other One-Act Plays*. O'Neill was now determined to become a playwright and he decided to seek help. He enrolled in George Pierce Baker's playwrighting course at Yale, spending a year in New Haven. Though he was accepted for a second year of study and apparently planned to return, at the last minute he withdrew and went to New York. He continued drinking heavily, but he did not stop writing. In the summer of 1916, a chance meeting with a group of theatrical enthusiasts who were establishing a summer theater in Provincetown gave O'Neill his first public hearing. In the converted wharf the group was using for a theater, O'Neill's one-act *Bound East for Cardiff* was an immediate success. When the group opened an off-Broadway theater in New York's Greenwich Village, O'Neill had an enthusiastic group of actors and directors eager to stage his early dramas.

He saved his first long work, *Beyond the Horizon,* for a Broadway production. When it was finally staged in 1920, after many delays, it won him a Pulitzer Prize and firmly established him as the leading playwright of a new era in American drama. That same year, the Provincetown Players produced *The Emperor Jones,* which revealed O'Neill as a dramatist eager to experiment with new techniques and responsive to contemporary ideas that sought to explain, in psychological terms, human conduct and human life. The influence of Jung is dominant in this play which uses the techniques of expressionistic theater. In other plays, such as *Strange Interlude* (1928), the Freudian influence is pervasive. If O'Neill's aim, as he once noted, was to dramatize the "ancient problem of the relation between man and God," he did not hesitate to use the concepts of the modern world and to introduce uncommon theatrical techniques into his plays. In *Strange Interlude,* for instance, he made extensive use of the soliloquy to depict the inner responses and thoughts of his characters; and in *The Great God Brown* the actors don masks when they express the inner, repressed personality of the characters.

O'Neill's second major Broadway play, *Anna Christie,* produced in 1921, was also awarded a Pulitzer Prize; he was to win still a third for *Strange Interlude.* Not all his dramas were so well received, but by the time *Desire under the Elms* was staged in 1924 O'Neill's reputation was secure and was bringing him to the attention of foreign critics and audiences. In 1936, he received the Nobel Prize for Literature. Few dramatists have been accorded this honor, and O'Neill was the first and only American playwright who has won the award.

During the years of his most intense creativity, the dramatist's private life was far from placid. Passionate love affairs absorbed much of his attention, but in 1918 he married for a second time. His wife, Agnes Boulton, who was also a writer, bore him two children. The marriage lasted for about ten years, though some time before it ended in divorce, O'Neill had fallen in love with an actress, Carlotta Monterey. In 1929, they were married, and this time the marriage endured. With Carlotta, O'Neill began to live a secluded routine life. He gave up liquor completely, and, for the most part, lived away from New York. Broadway theater audiences, however, saw few seasons go by without an O'Neill production, either a new play or a revival. *Mourn-*

ing Becomes Electra, a trilogy based upon the Greek story of Aga-
memnon and his family, was staged in 1931. Two years later,
O'Neill's only comedy, *Ah Wilderness,* opened to rave reviews and
ran for 289 performances. Then, for more than a decade, O'Neill
offered no new play; he worked during this period on a cycle of
historical dramas, many of which he later destroyed. *The Iceman
Cometh* in 1946 was the last New York opening of a new O'Neill
play during the author's lifetime. *A Long Day's Journey into Night*
and *A Touch of the Poet* were produced posthumously.

Nearing his sixtieth year, O'Neill became the victim of a rare and
terrible disease of the nervous system, paralysis agitans. During the
final five years of his life, he was able to do little writing and he
seldom appeared in public. On November 27, 1953 he died. At his
request, he was buried without religious ceremony with only his wife,
nurse, and doctor present. The simple stone marking his grave in
Forest Hills cemetery, on the outskirts of Boston, bears a single word:
"O'Neill."

Desire under the Elms and most of the forty odd plays that
O'Neill wrote are tragedies. The deeply troubled young man who
tried to commit suicide at Jimmy the Priest's retained his vision of
human existence as a tragic losing battle against conditions inimical to
the human being. Probably because of his early religious training,
O'Neill had the kind of temperament that rejected compromise and
middle-of-the-road positions. He rejected God, but he could not do
without a substitute for the God he no longer believed in. "The
playwright today," he once wrote, "must dig at the roots of the
sickness of today as he feels it—the death of the old God and the
failure of science and materialism to give any satisfying new One for
the surviving primitive religious instinct to find a meaning for life in,
and to comfort its fears of death with." Absolutist that he was, O'Neill
sought the single answer, the single concept that could reconcile the
contradictions that seemed to him to make up existence. As he noted,
"the curse of being an extremist is that every ideal remains single and
alone, demanding all-or-nothing or destruction . . . what haunted,
haunting ghosts we are."

The human tragedy, as O'Neill at first sensed it and then later
understood it, is that man is trapped on all levels of experience by
irreconcilable opposites—life and death, goodness and evil, ugliness
and beauty, love and hatred. Man may achieve grandeur in his
struggle against the reality of existence, but never happiness or success. A man, for instance, who is driven by a need for self-assertion,

achieves strength and power in his egoism, but he throttles his equally strong drive for selfless love. Both the need for self-assertion and the need for unselfish love are part of the human personality, and the fulfillment of one need denies the other. The irreconcilable forces of idealism and realism, love and hate, sensitivity and coarseness, creativity and destructiveness tear at man's spirit. No reconciliation is possible and man can only devote his life to a search for identity.

To understand this tragic vision as it affects O'Neill's dramas, it is helpful to recognize its source in the playwright's own early emotional development. The tensions from which the young O'Neill suffered, he dramatized covertly in most of his tragedies and overtly in the autobiographical *A Long Day's Journey into Night,* which he considered so revealing that he would not permit its production or publication during his lifetime. In the play, O'Neill described the central trauma of his young manhood, the discovery that his mother, whom he loved and idealized, was a narcotics addict. With this play and the biographies now available, we can recognize that O'Neill's emotional response to his mother and father shaped his vision of tragic irreconcilables.

Ella and James O'Neill married for love and remained in love, but their personalities responded to psychological needs that their marriage could not satisfy. James O'Neill was an expansive personality. He enjoyed the convivial atmosphere of the barroom, the applause and praise of audiences, the unsettled life of the touring actor. His wife, who had been educated in a convent school, needed the security of a settled home, of a close family life. She was a soft, idealistic, affectionate woman who lavished upon her two surviving sons much love and attention. A tragic accident, the suffocation of her second son in his cradle, gave a focus to all the suppressed facets of her personality. She was away on tour with her husband when the child died, and she blamed herself and the kind of life she had to lead for the loss. She was deeply upset by the tragedy, and when her third son, Eugene, was born she required sedatives. She continued to use them, gradually becoming addicted. Her eldest son was deeply hurt by the discovery of his mother's condition, and he and Mr. O'Neill sheltered Eugene from the truth as long as they could.

O'Neill's reaction to the discovery of his mother's addiction was extreme. His idealized image of his mother was tarnished, yet he could not eradicate his deep love for her. He could not be reconciled to the reality, but he had to live with it. Both sons, as the autobiographical drama indicates, tended to protect their mother by placing the responsibility for her illness upon the father and the kind of life he forced her to lead. The ordinary Oedipal relationship between male children and the parents was intensified in the O'Neill family. In his dramas, O'Neill allies with the paternal archetype sternness, hardness, egoism, materialism; and with the maternal, soft gentleness, self-sacrifice, sensitivity, idealism, and a hunger for love. In the earlier plays these opposites are dramatized in separate characters. In the later and major works, they merge as antithetical forces at work within all personalities. The father and son of *Desire under the Elms* illustrate this fusion of opposites within the same personality. Ephraim Cabot is the harsh, tyrannical father, self-absorbed and driven by an almost maniacal need for self-identity. At the same time, Ephraim expresses the opposing needs within him by seeking the companionship of the placid cows. The maternal spirit, which hovers over the house like the two elms above it, is dominant in Eben, who seeks revenge because his father has destroyed that spirit. Yet, as his brothers point out, Eben is like his father. The tragedy for Ephraim and Eben and for most of O'Neill's characters evolves from their inability to resolve the opposing forces that tear at them.

O'Neill recognized how much a product of psychological drives the human being was, and he determined to write tragedy in terms of those drives. His insistence upon presenting his characters realistically and in realistic settings made him, from the outset, an enemy of the prevailing melodrama that dominated the American theater. Many of the characters and situations he depicted were brutal and sordid, and he was often characterized as a naturalist, a writer intent upon presenting the sordid aspects of life to reveal a sociological or biological cause of the human condition. He was also, not infrequently, linked by critics with various other literary and dramatic movements, but he objected strenuously and with much justification to such labels. "To be called a 'sordid realist' one day, a 'grim pessimistic Naturalist' the next, a 'lying Moral Romanticist' the next, etc. is quite perplexing—not to add the *Times* editorial that settled *Desire* once and for all by calling it a 'Neo-Primitive, a Matisse of the drama, as it were.'" In that same letter O'Neill went on to declare that he saw himself as a melting pot for every available dramatic approach and technique which he boiled down to create his own individual method. His aim as a dramatist, he declared, was "to see the transfiguring nobility of tragedy, in as near the Greek sense as one can grasp it, in seemingly the most ignoble, debased lives."

Desire under the Elms is probably the first of O'Neill's tragedies in which this aim is clearly discernible. His study of the Greek tragedians is apparent in the small cast of major characters, the family situation, the Medean murder of a child by its mother, the ennobling struggle of the old farmer against fate. In the same letter in which he set forth this aim, O'Neill also stated that in all his work, he was trying to

> interpret Life in terms of lives, never just lives in terms of character. I'm always acutely conscious of the Force behind—Fate, God, our biological past creating our present, whatever one calls it—Mystery certainly—and of the one eternal tragedy of Man in his glorious, self-destructive struggle to make the Force express him instead of being, as an animal is, an infinitesimal incident in its expression.

There is perhaps no better description of O'Neill's tragic story of a New England farmer's struggle to assert himself against the harsh forces of his world.

Desire under the Elms had its premiere on November 11, 1924 in an off-Broadway theater. The newspaper reviewers displayed no enthusiasm for it, but audiences continued to fill the small theater for each performance. As a result it was moved to a larger theater on Broadway. At once a controversy erupted. A vociferous minority declared this essentially Greek drama immoral and perverse. The denouncers of the play found a voice when the legal authorities in Los Angeles arrested the manager and actors of a touring troupe staging the play. They were accused of presenting a lewd, obscene, and immoral play and were brought to trial. The jury of twelve listened to the denunciations of the prosecutor and then to the arguments of defense counsel. Only four of the twelve were not persuaded that the play was immoral, and the trial ended in a hung jury. At the time the notoriety of these proceedings filled the theater; eventually, the essential greatness of *Desire Under the Elms* won for it an audience that has continued to grow and applaud it. The drama has been declared by many critics O'Neill's greatest tragedy, and its position among the great dramas of the world now seems secure.

≈≈

BIBLIOGRAPHY

Alexander, Doris. *The Tempering of Eugene O'Neill*. New York: Harcourt, Brace & World, 1962.

Cargill, Oscar, (ed.). *O'Neill and His Plays: Four Decades of Criticism.*
   New York: New York University Press, 1963.
Carpenter, Frederick. *Eugene O'Neill.* New York: Twayne Publishers,
   1964.
Falk, Doris. *Eugene O'Neill and the Tragic Tension.* New Brunswick,
   N.J.: Rutgers University Press, 1958.
Gassner, John. *O'Neill: A Collection of Critical Essays.* Englewood Cliffs,
   N.J.: Prentice-Hall, 1964.
Gelb, Arthur and Barbara. *O'Neill.* New York: Harper & Row, 1962.

Desire under the Elms

CHARACTERS

EPHRAIM CABOT

SIMEON

PETER $\Big\}$ *his sons*

EBEN

ABBIE PUTNAM

Young GIRL, *two* FARMERS, *the* FIDDLER, *a* SHERIFF, *and other folk from the neighboring farms.*

The action of the entire play takes place in, and immediately outside of, the Cabot farmhouse in New England, in the year 1850. The south end of the house faces front to a stone wall with a wooden gate at center opening on a country road. The house is in good condition but in need of paint. Its walls are a sickly grayish, the green of the shutters faded. Two enormous elms are on each side of the house. They bend their trailing branches down over the roof. They appear to protect and at the same time subdue. There is a sinister maternity in their aspect, a crushing, jealous absorption. They have developed from their intimate contact with the life of man in the house an appalling humaneness. They brood oppressively over the house. They are like exhausted women resting their sagging breasts and hands and hair on its roof, and when it rains their tears trickle down monotonously and rot on the shingles.

There is a path running from the gate around the right corner of the house to the front door. A narrow porch is on this side. The end wall facing us has two windows in its upper story, two larger ones on the floor below. The two upper are those of the father's bedroom and that of the brothers. On the left, ground floor, is the kitchen—on the right, the parlor, the shades of which are always drawn down.

❧❧

PART I
SCENE I

(Exterior of the farmhouse. It is sunset of a day at the beginning of summer in the year 1850. There is no wind and everything is still. The sky above the roof is suffused with deep colors, the green of the elms glows, but the house is in shadow, seeming pale and washed out by contrast.

A door opens and EBEN CABOT *comes to the end of the porch and stands looking down the road to the right. He has a large bell in his hand and this he swings mechanically, awakening a deafening clangor. Then he puts his hands on his hips and stares up at the sky. He sighs with a puzzled awe and blurts out with halting appreciation.)*

EBEN: God! Purty! *(His eyes fall and he stares about him frowningly. He is twenty-five, tall and sinewy. His face is well-formed, good-looking, but its expression is resentful and defensive. His defiant, dark eyes remind one of a wild animal's in captivity. Each day is a cage in which he finds himself trapped but inwardly unsubdued. There is a fierce repressed vitality about him. He has black hair, mustache, a thin curly trace of beard. He is dressed in rough farm clothes.*

He spits on the ground with intense disgust, turns and goes back into the house.

SIMEON *and* PETER *come in from their work in the fields. They are tall men, much older than their half-brother [*SIMEON *is thirty-nine and* PETER *thirty-seven], built on a squarer, simpler model, fleshier in body, more bovine and homelier in face, shrewder and more practical. Their shoulders stoop a bit from years of farm work. They clump heavily along in their clumsy thick-soled boots caked with earth. Their clothes, their faces, hands, bare arms and* *throats are earth-stained. They smell of earth. They stand together for a moment in front of the house and, as if with the one impulse, stare dumbly up at the sky, leaning on their hoes. Their faces have a compressed, unresigned expression. As they look upward, this softens.)*

SIMEON (*grudgingly*): Purty.

PETER: Ay-eh.

SIMEON (*suddenly*): Eighteen year ago.

PETER: What?

SIMEON: Jenn. My woman. She died.

PETER: I'd fergot.

SIMEON: I rec'lect—now an' agin. Makes it lonesome. She'd hair long's a hoss' tail—an' yaller like gold!

PETER: Waal—she's gone. (*This with indifferent finality—then after a pause*) They's gold in the West, Sim.

SIMEON (*still under the influence of sunset—vaguely*): In the sky?

PETER: Waal—in a manner o' speakin'—thar's the promise. (*Growing excited*) Gold in the sky—in the West—Golden Gate—Californi-a!—Goldest West!—fields o' gold!

SIMEON (*excited in his turn*): Fortunes layin' just atop o' the ground waitin' t' be picked! Solomon's mines, they says! (*For a moment they continue looking up at the sky—then their eyes drop.*)

PETER (*with sardonic bitterness*): Here—it's stones atop o' the ground—stones atop o' stones—makin' stone walls—year atop o' year—him 'n' yew 'n' me 'n' then Eben—makin' stone walls fur him to fence us in!

SIMEON: We've wuked. Give our strength. Give our years. Plowed 'em under in the ground—(*he stamps rebelliously*)—rottin'—makin' soil for his crops! (*A pause.*) Waal—the farm pays good for hereabouts.

PETER: If we plowed in Californi-a, they'd be lumps o' gold in the furrow!

SIMEON: Californi-a's t'other side o' earth, a'most. We got t' calc'late—

PETER (*after a pause*): 'Twould be hard fur me, too, to give up what we've 'arned here by our sweat. (*A pause*, EBEN *sticks his head out of the dining-room window, listening.*)

SIMEON: Ay-eh. (*A pause.*) Mebbe—he'll die soon.

PETER (*doubtfully*): Mebbe.

SIMEON: Mebbe—fur all we knows—he's dead now.

PETER: Ye'd need proof.

SIMEON: He's been gone two months—with no word.

PETER: Left us in the fields an evenin' like this. Hitched up an' druv off into the West. That's plum onnateral. He hain't never been off this farm 'ceptin' t' the village in thirty year or more, not since he married Eben's maw. (*A pause. Shrewdly*) I calc'late we might git him declared crazy by the court.

SIMEON: He skinned 'em too slick. He got the best o' all on 'em. They'd never b'lieve him crazy. (*A pause.*) We got t' wait—till he's under ground.

EBEN (*with a sardonic chuckle*): Honor thy father! (*They turn, startled, and stare at him. He grins, then scowls.*) I pray he's died. (*They stare at him. He continues matter-of-factly*) Supper's ready.

SIMEON and PETER (*together*): Ay-eh.

EBEN (*gazing up at the sky*): Sun's downin' purty.

SIMEON and PETER (*together*): Ay-eh. They's gold in the West.

EBEN: Ay-eh. (*Pointing*) Yonder atop o' the hill pasture, ye mean?

SIMEON and PETER (*together*): In Californi-a!

EBEN: Hunh? (*Stares at them indifferently for a second, then drawls*) Waal—supper's gittin' cold. (*He turns back into kitchen.*)

SIMEON (*startled—smacks his lips*): I air hungry!

PETER (*sniffing*): I smells bacon!

SIMEON (*with hungry appreciation*): Bacon's good!

PETER (*in same tone*): Bacon's bacon! (*They turn, shouldering each other, their bodies bumping and rubbing together as they hurry clumsily to their food, like two friendly oxen toward their evening meal. They disappear around the right corner of house and can be heard entering the door.*)

(CURTAIN.)

SCENE II

(*The color fades from the sky. Twilight begins. The interior of the kitchen is now visible. A pine table is at center, a cookstove in the right rear corner, four rough wooden chairs, a tallow candle on the table. In the middle of the rear wall is fastened a big advertising poster with a ship in full sail and the word "California" in big letters. Kitchen utensils hang from nails. Everything is neat and in order but the atmosphere is of a men's camp kitchen rather than that of a home.*

Places for three are laid. EBEN takes boiled potatoes and bacon from the stove and puts them on the table, also a loaf of bread and a crock of water. SIMEON *and* PETER *shoulder in, slump down in their chairs without a word.* EBEN *joins them. The three eat in silence for a moment, the two elder as naturally unrestrained as beasts of the field,* EBEN *picking at his food without appetite, glancing at them with a tolerant dislike.*)

SIMEON (*suddenly turns to* EBEN): Looky here! Ye'd oughtn't t' said that, Eben.

PETER: 'Twa'n't righteous.

EBEN: What?

SIMEON: Ye prayed he'd died.

EBEN: Waal—don't yew pray it? (*A pause.*)

PETER: He's our Paw.

EBEN (*violently*): Not mine!

SIMEON (*dryly*): Ye'd not let no one else say that about yer Maw! Ha! (*He gives one abrupt sardonic guffaw.* PETER *grins.*)

EBEN (*very pale*): I meant—I hain't his'n—I hain't like him—he hain't me!

PETER (*dryly*): Wait till ye've growed his age!

EBEN (*intensely*): I'm Maw—every drop o' blood! (*A pause. They stare at him with indifferent curiosity.*)

PETER (*reminiscently*): She was good t' Sim 'n' me. A good Step-maw's scurse.

SIMEON: She was good t' everyone.

EBEN (*greatly moved, gets to his feet and makes an awkward bow to each of them—stammering*): I be thankful t' ye. I'm her—her heir. (*He sits down in confusion.*)

PETER (*after a pause—judicially*): She was good even t' him.

EBEN (*fiercely*): An' fur thanks he killed her!

SIMEON (*after a pause*): No one never kills nobody. It's allus somethin'. That's the murderer.

EBEN: Didn't he slave Maw t' death?

PETER: He's slaved himself t' death. He's slaved Sim 'n' me 'n' yew t' death—on'y none o' us hain't died—yit.

SIMEON: It's somethin'—drivin' him—t' drive us!

EBEN (*vengefully*): Waal—I hold him t' jedgment! (*Then scornfully*) Somethin'! What's somethin'?

SIMEON: Dunno.

EBEN (*sardonically*): What's drivin' yew to Californi-a, mebbe? (*They look at him in surprise.*) Oh, I've heerd ye! (*Then, after a pause*) But ye'll never go t' the gold fields!

PETER (*assertively*): Mebbe!

EBEN: Whar'll ye git the money?

PETER: We kin walk. It's an a'mighty ways—Californi-a—but if yew was t' put all the steps we've walked on this farm end t' end we'd be in the moon!

EBEN: The Injuns'll skulp ye on the plains.

SIMEON (*with grim humor*): We'll mebbe make 'em pay a hair fur a hair!

EBEN (*decisively*): But t'ain't that. Ye won't never go because ye'll wait here fur yer share o' the farm, thinkin' allus he'll die soon.

SIMEON (*after a pause*): We've a right.

PETER: Two-thirds belongs t'us.

EBEN (*jumping to his feet*): Ye've no right! She wa'n't yewr Maw! It was her farm! Didn't he steal it from her? She's dead. It's my farm.

SIMEON (*sardonically*): Tell that t' Paw—when he comes! I'll bet ye a dollar he'll laugh—fur once in his life. Ha! (*He laughs himself in one single mirthless bark.*)

PETER (*amused in turn, echoes his brother*): Ha!

SIMEON (*after a pause*): What've ye got held agin us, Eben? Year arter year it's skulked in yer eye—somethin'.

PETER: Ay-eh.

EBEN: Ay-eh. They's somethin'. (*Suddenly exploding*) Why didn't ye never stand between him 'n' my Maw when he was slavin' her to her grave—t' pay her back fur the kindness she done t' yew? (*There is a long pause. They stare at him in surprise.*)

SIMEON: Waal—the stock'd got t' be watered.

PETER: 'R they was woodin' t' do.

SIMEON: 'R plowin'.

PETER: 'R hayin'.

SIMEON: 'R spreadin' manure.

PETER: 'R weedin'.

SIMEON: 'R prunin'.

PETER: 'R milkin'.

EBEN (*breaking in harshly*): An' makin' walls—stone atop o' stone—makin' walls till yer heart's a stone ye heft up out o' the way o' growth onto a stone wall t' wall in yer heart!

SIMEON (*matter-of-factly*): We never had no time t' meddle.

PETER (*to* EBEN): Yew was fifteen afore yer Maw died—an' big fur yer age. Why didn't ye never do nothin'?

EBEN (*harshly*): They was chores t' do, wa'n't they? (*A pause—then slowly*) It was on'y arter she died I come to think o' it. Me cookin'

—doin' her work—that made me know her, suffer her sufferin'—
she'd come back t' help—come back t' bile potatoes—come back t'
fry bacon—come back t' bake biscuits—come back all cramped up
t' shake the fire, an' carry ashes, her eyes weepin' an' bloody with
smoke an' cinders same's they used t' be. She still comes back—
stands by the stove thar in the evenin'—she can't find it naterel
sleepin' an' restin' in peace. She can't git used t' bein' free—even
in her grave.

SIMEON: She never complained none.

EBEN: She'd got too tired. She'd got too used t' bein' too tired. That
was what he done. (*With vengeful passion*) An' sooner'r later, I'll
meddle. I'll say the thin's I didn't say then t' him! I'll yell 'em at
the top o' my lungs. I'll see t' it my Maw gits some rest an' sleep in
her grave! (*He sits down again, relapsing into a brooding silence.
They look at him with a queer indifferent curiosity.*)

PETER (*after a pause*): Whar in tarnation d'ye s'pose he went, Sim?

SIMEON: Dunno. He druv off in the buggy, all spick an' span, with
the mare all breshed an' shiny, druv off clackin' his tongue an'
wavin' his whip. I remember it right well. I was finishin' plowin',
it was spring an' May an' sunset, an' gold in the West, an' he druv
off into it. I yells "Whar ye goin', Paw?" an' he hauls up by the
stone wall a jiffy. His old snake's eyes was glitterin' in the sun like
he'd been drinkin' a jugful an' he says with a mule's grin: "Don't
ye run away till I come back!"

PETER: Wonder if he knowed we was wantin' fur Californi-a?

SIMEON: Mebbe. I didn't say nothin' and he says, lookin' kinder
queer an' sick: "I been hearin' the hens cluckin' an' the roosters
crowin' all the durn day. I been listenin' t' the cows lowin' an'
everythin' else kickin' up till I can't stand it no more. It's spring
an' I'm feelin' damned," he says. "Damned like an old bare hickory
tree fit on'y fur burnin'," he says. An' then I calc'late I must've
looked a mite hopeful, fur he adds real spry and vicious: "But
don't git no fool idee I'm dead. I've sworn t' live a hundred an' I'll
do it, if on'y t' spite yer sinful greed! An' now I'm ridin' out t' learn
God's message t' me in the spring, like the prophets done. An' yew
git back t' yer plowin'," he says. An' he druv off singin' a hymn. I
thought he was drunk—'r I'd stopped him goin'.

EBEN (*scornfully*): No, ye wouldn't! Ye're scared o' him. He's
stronger—inside—than both o' ye put together!

PETER (*sardonically*): An' yew—be yew Samson?

EBEN: I'm gittin' stronger. I kin feel it growin' in me—growin' an' growin'—till it'll bust out—! (*He gets up and puts on his coat and a hat. They watch him, gradually breaking into grins.* EBEN *avoids their eyes sheepishly.*) I'm goin' out fur a spell—up the road.

PETER: T' the village?

SIMEON: T' see Minnie?

EBEN (*defiantly*): Ay-eh!

PETER (*jeeringly*): The Scarlet Woman!

SIMEON: Lust—that's what's growin' in ye!

EBEN: Waal—she's purty!

PETER: She's been purty fur twenty year!

SIMEON: A new coat o' paint'll make a heifer out of forty.

EBEN: She hain't forty!

PETER: If she hain't, she's teeterin' on the edge.

EBEN (*desperately*): What d'yew know—

PETER: All they is . . . Sim knew her—an' then me arter—

SIMEON: An' Paw kin tell yew somethin' too! He was fust!

EBEN: D'ye mean t' say he . . . ?

SIMEON (*with a grin*): Ay-eh! We air his heirs in everythin'!

EBEN (*intensely*): That's more to it! That grows on it! It'll bust soon! (*Then violently*) I'll go smash my fist in her face! (*He pulls open the door in rear violently.*)

SIMEON (*with a wink at* PETER—*drawlingly*): Mebbe—but the night's wa'm—purty—by the time ye git thar mebbe ye'll kiss her instead!

PETER: Sart'n he will! (*They both roar with coarse laughter.* EBEN *rushes out and slams the door—then the outside front door—comes around the corner of the house and stands still by the gate, staring up at the sky.*)

SIMEON (*looking after him*): Like his Paw.

PETER: Dead spit an' image!

SIMEON: Dog'll eat dog!

PETER: Ay-eh. (*Pause. With yearning*) Mebbe a year from now we'll be in Californi-a.

SIMEON: Ay-eh. (*A pause. Both yawn.*) Let's git t'bed. (*He blows out the candle. They go out door in rear.* EBEN *stretches his arms up to the sky—rebelliously.*)

EBEN: Waal—thar's a star, an' somewhar's they's him, an' here's me, an' thar's Min up the road—in the same night. What if I does kiss her? She's like t'night, she's soft 'n' wa'm, her eyes kin wink like a star, her mouth's wa'm, her arms're wa'm, she smells like a wa'm plowed field, she's purty . . . Ay-eh! By God A'mighty she's purty, an' I don't give a damn how many sins she's sinned afore mine or who she's sinned 'em with, my sin's as purty as any one on 'em! (*He strides off down the road to the left.*)

SCENE III

(*It is the pitch darkness just before dawn.* EBEN *comes in from the left and goes around to the porch, feeling his way, chuckling bitterly and cursing half-aloud to himself.*)

EBEN: The cussed old miser! (*He can be heard going in the front door. There is a pause as he goes upstairs, then a loud knock on the bedroom door of the brothers.*) Wake up!

SIMEON (*startedly*): Who's thar?

EBEN (*pushing open the door and coming in, a lighted candle in his hand. The bedroom of the brothers is revealed. Its ceiling is the sloping roof. They can stand upright only close to the center dividing wall of the upstairs.* SIMEON *and* PETER *are in a double bed, front.* EBEN'*s cot is to the rear.* EBEN *has a mixture of silly grin and vicious scowl on his face*): I be!

PETER (*angrily*): What in hell's-fire . . . ?

EBEN: I got news fur ye! Ha! (*He gives one abrupt sardonic guffaw.*)

SIMEON (*angrily*): Couldn't ye hold it 'til we'd got our sleep?

EBEN: It's nigh sunup. (*Then explosively*) He's gone an' married agen!

SIMEON *and* PETER (*explosively*): Paw?

EBEN: Got himself hitched to a female 'bout thirty-five—an' purty, they says . . .

SIMEON (*aghast*): It's a durn lie!

PETER: Who says?

SIMEON: They been stringin' ye!

EBEN: Think I'm a dunce, do ye? The hull village says. The preacher from New Dover, he brung the news—told it t'our preacher— New Dover, that's whar the old loon got himself hitched—that's whar the woman lived—

PETER (*no longer doubting—stunned*): Waal . . . !

SIMEON (*the same*): Waal . . . !

EBEN (*sitting down on a bed—with vicious hatred*): Ain't he a devil out o' hell? It's jest t' spite us—the damned old mule!

PETER (*after a pause*): Everythin'll go t' her now.

SIMEON: Ay-eh. (*A pause—dully*) Waal—if it's done—

PETER: It's done us. (*Pause—then persuasively*) They's gold in the fields o' Californi-a, Sim. No good a-stayin' here now.

SIMEON: Jest what I was a-thinkin'. (*Then with decision*) S'well fust's last! Let's light out and git this mornin'.

PETER: Suits me.

EBEN: Ye must like walkin'.

SIMEON (*sardonically*): If ye'd grow wings on us we'd fly thar!

EBEN: Ye'd like ridin' better—on a boat, wouldn't ye? (*Fumbles in his pocket and takes out a crumpled sheet of foolscap.*) Waal, if ye sign this ye kin ride on a boat. I've had it writ out an' ready in case ye'd ever go. It says fur three hundred dollars t' each ye agree yewr shares o' the farm is sold t' me. (*They look suspiciously at the paper. A pause.*)

SIMEON (*wonderingly*): But if he's hitched agen—

PETER: An' whar'd yew git that sum o' money, anyways?

EBEN (*cunningly*): I know whar it's hid. I been waitin'—Maw told me. She knew whar it lay fur years, but she was waitin' . . . It's her'n—the money he hoarded from her farm an' hid from Maw. It's my money by rights now.

PETER: Whar's it hid?

EBEN (*cunningly*): Whar yew won't never find it without me. Maw spied on him—'r she'd never knowed. (*A pause. They look at him suspiciously, and he at them.*) Waal, is it fa'r trade?

SIMEON: Dunno.

PETER: Dunno.

SIMEON (*looking at window*): Sky's grayin'.

PETER: Ye better start the fire, Eben.

SIMEON: An' fix some vittles.

EBEN: Ay-eh. (*Then with a forced jocular heartiness*) I'll git ye a good one. If ye're startin' t' hoof it t' Californi-a ye'll need somethin' that'll stick t' yer ribs. (*He turns to the door, adding meaningly*) But ye kin ride on a boat if ye'll swap. (*He stops at the door and pauses. They stare at him.*)

SIMEON (*suspiciously*): Whar was ye all night?

EBEN (*defiantly*): Up t' Min's. (*Then slowly*) Walkin' thar, fust I felt 's if I'd kiss her; then I got a-thinkin' o' what ye'd said o' him an' her an' I says, I'll bust her nose fur that! Then I got t' the village an' heerd the news an' I got madder'n hell an' run all the way t' Min's not knowin' what I'd do— (*He pauses—then sheepishly but more defiantly*) Waal—when I seen her, I didn't hit her—nor I didn't kiss her nuther—I begun t' beller like a calf an' cuss at the same time, I was so durn mad—an' she got scared—an' I jest grabbed holt an' tuk her! (*Proudly*) Yes, sirree! I tuk her. She may've been his'n—an' your'n, too—but she's mine now!

SIMEON (*dryly*): In love, air yew?

EBEN (*with lofty scorn*): Love! I don't take no stock in sech slop!

PETER (*winking at* SIMEON): Mebbe Eben's aimin' t' marry, too.

SIMEON: Min'd make a true faithful he'pmeet! (*They snicker.*)

EBEN: What do I care fur her—'ceptin' she's round an' wa'm? The p'int is she was his'n—an' now she belongs t' me! (*He goes to the door—then turns—rebelliously*) An' Min hain't sech a bad un. They's worse'n Min in the world, I'll bet ye! Wait'll we see this cow the Old Man's hitched t'! She'll beat Min, I got a notion! (*He starts to go out.*)

SIMEON (*suddenly*): Mebbe ye'll try t' make her your'n, too?

PETER: Ha! (*He gives a sardonic laugh of relish at this idea.*)

EBEN (*spitting with disgust*): Her—here—sleepin' with him—stealin' my Maw's farm! I'd as soon pet a skunk 'r kiss a snake! (*He goes out. The two stare after him suspiciously. A pause. They listen to his steps receding.*)

PETER: He's startin' the fire.

SIMEON: I'd like t' ride t' Californi-a—but—

PETER: Min might o' put some scheme in his head.

SIMEON: Mebbe it's all a lie 'bout Paw marryin'. We'd best wait an' see the bride.

PETER: An' don't sign nothin' till we does!

SIMEON: Nor till we've tested it's good money! (*Then with a grin*) But if Paw's hitched we'd be sellin' Eben somethin' we'd never git nohow!

PETER: We'll wait an' see. (*Then with sudden vindictive anger*) An' till he comes, let's yew 'n' me not wuk a lick, let Eben tend to thin's if he's a mind t', let's us jest sleep an' eat an' drink likker, an' let the hull damned farm go t' blazes!

SIMEON (*excitedly*): By God, we've 'arned a rest! We'll play rich fur a change. I hain't a-going to stir outa bed till breakfast's ready.

PETER: An' on the table!

SIMEON (*after a pause—thoughtfully*): What d'ye calc'late she'll be like—our new Maw? Like Eben thinks?

PETER: More'n likely.

SIMEON (*vindictively*): Waal—I hope she's a she-devil that'll make him wish he was dead an' livin' in the pit o' hell fur comfort!

PETER (*fervently*): Amen!

SIMEON (*imitating his father's voice*): "I'm ridin' out t' learn God's message t' me in the spring like the prophets done," he says. I'll bet right then an' thar he knew plumb well he was goin' whorin', the stinkin' old hypocrite!

SCENE IV

(*Same as Scene II—shows the interior of the kitchen with a lighted candle on table. It is gray dawn outside.* SIMEON *and* PETER *are just finishing their breakfast.* EBEN *sits before his plate of untouched food, brooding frowningly.*)

PETER (*glancing at him rather irritably*): Lookin' glum don't help none.

SIMEON (*sarcastically*): Sorrowin' over his lust o' the flesh!

PETER (*with a grin*): Was she yer fust?

EBEN (*angrily*): None o' yer business. (*A pause.*) I was thinkin' o' him. I got a notion he's gittin' near—I kin feel him comin' on like yew kin feel malaria chill afore it takes ye.

PETER: It's too early yet.

SIMEON: Dunno. He'd like t' catch us nappin'—jest t' have somethin' t' hoss us 'round over.

PETER (*mechanically gets to his feet.* SIMEON *does the same*): Waal —let's git t' wuk. (*They both plod mechanically toward the door before they realize. Then they stop short.*)

SIMEON (*grinning*): Ye're a cussed fool, Pete—and I be wuss! Let him see we hain't wukin'! We don't give a durn!

PETER (*as they go back to the table*): Not a damned durn! It'll serve t' show him we're done with him. (*They sit down again.* EBEN *stares from one to the other with surprise.*)

SIMEON (*grins at him*): We're aimin' t' start bein' lilies o' the field.

PETER: Nary a toil 'r spin 'r lick o' wuk do we put in!

SIMEON: Ye're sole owner—till he comes—that's what ye wanted. Waal, ye got t' be sole hand, too.

PETER: The cows air bellerin'. Ye better hustle at the milkin'.

EBEN (*with excited joy*): Ye mean ye'll sign the paper?

SIMEON (*dryly*): Mebbe.

PETER: Mebbe.

SIMEON: We're considerin'. (*Peremptorily*) Ye better git t' wuk.

EBEN (*with queer excitement*): It's Maw's farm agen! It's my farm!

Them's my cows! I'll milk my durn fingers off fur cows o' mine! (*He goes out door in rear, they stare after him indifferently.*)

SIMEON: Like his Paw.

PETER: Dead spit 'n' image!

SIMEON: Waal—let dog eat dog! (EBEN *comes out of front door and around the corner of the house. The sky is beginning to grow flushed with sunrise.* EBEN *stops by the gate and stares around him with glowing, possessive eyes. He takes in the whole farm with his embracing glance of desire.*)

EBEN: It's purty! It's damned purty! It's mine! (*He suddenly throws his head back boldly and glares with hard, defiant eyes at the sky.*) Mine, d'ye hear? Mine! (*He turns and walks quickly off left, rear, toward the barn. The two brothers light their pipes.*)

SIMEON (*putting his muddy boots up on the table, tilting back his chair, and puffing defiantly*): Waal—this air solid comfort—fur once.

PETER: Ay-eh. (*He follows suit. A pause. Unconsciously they both sigh.*)

SIMEON (*suddenly*): He never was much o' a hand at milkin', Eben wa'n't.

PETER (*with a snort*): His hands air like hoofs! (*A pause.*)

SIMEON: Reach down the jug thar! Let's take a swaller. I'm feelin' kind o' low.

PETER: Good idee! (*He does so—gets two glasses—they pour out drinks of whisky.*) Here's t' the gold in Californi-a!

SIMEON: An' luck t' find it! (*They drink—puff resolutely—sigh—take their feet down from the table.*)

PETER: Likker don't pear t' sot right.

SIMEON: We hain't used t' it this early. (*A pause. They become very restless.*)

PETER: Gittin' close in this kitchen.

SIMEON (*with immense relief*): Let's git a breath o' air. (*They arise briskly and go out rear—appear around house and stop by the gate. They stare up at the sky with a numbed appreciation.*)

PETER: Purty!

SIMEON: Ay-eh. Gold's t' the East now.

PETER: Sun's startin' with us fur the Golden West.

SIMEON (*staring around the farm, his compressed face tightened, unable to conceal his emotion*): Waal—it's our last mornin' mebbe.

PETER (*the same*): Ay-eh.

SIMEON (*stamps his foot on the earth and addresses it desperately*): Waal—ye've thirty year o' me buried in ye—spread out over ye—blood an' bone an' sweat—rotted away—fertilizin' ye—richin' yer soul—prime manure, by God, that's what I been t' ye!

PETER: Ay-eh! An' me!

SIMEON: An' yew, Peter. (*He sighs—then spits.*) Waal—no use'n cryin' over spilt milk.

PETER: They's gold in the West—an' freedom, mebbe. We been slaves t' stone walls here.

SIMEON (*defiantly*): We hain't nobody's slaves from this out—nor no thin's slaves nuther. (*A pause—restlessly*) Speakin' o' milk, wonder how Eben's managin'?

PETER: I s'pose he's managin'.

SIMEON: Mebbe we'd ought t' help—this once.

PETER: Mebbe. The cows knows us.

SIMEON: An' likes us. They don't know him much.

PETER: An' the hosses, an' pigs, an' chickens. They don't know him much.

SIMEON: They knows us like brothers—an' likes us! (*Proudly*) Hain't we raised 'em t' be fust-rate, number one prize stock?

PETER: We hain't—not no more.

SIMEON (*dully*): I was fergittin'. (*Then resignedly*) Waal, let's go help Eben a spell an' git waked up.

PETER: Suits me. (*They are starting off down left, rear, for the barn when* EBEN *appears from there hurrying toward them, his face excited.*)

EBEN (*breathlessly*): Waal—har they be! The old mule an' the bride! I seen 'em from the barn down below at the turnin'.

PETER: How could ye tell that far?

EBEN: Hain't I as far-sight as he's near-sight? Don't I know the mare 'n' buggy, an' two people settin' in it? Who else . . . ? An' I tell ye I kin feel 'em a-comin', too! (*He squirms as if he had the itch.*)

PETER (*beginning to be angry*): Waal—let him do his own unhitchin'!

SIMEON (*angry in his turn*): Let's hustle in an' git our bundles an' be a-goin' as he's a-comin'. I don't want never t' step inside the door agen arter he's back. (*They both start back around the corner of the house.* EBEN *follows them.*)

EBEN (*anxiously*): Will ye sign it afore ye go?

PETER: Let's see the color o' the old skinflint's money an' we'll sign. (*They disappear left. The two brothers clump upstairs to get their bundles.* EBEN *appears in the kitchen, runs to the window, peers out, comes back and pulls up a strip of flooring in under stove, takes out a canvas bag and puts it on table, then sets the floorboard back in place. The two brothers appear a moment after. They carry old carpet bags.)*

EBEN (*puts his hand on bag guardingly*): Have ye signed?

SIMEON (*shows paper in his hand*): Ay-eh. (*Greedily*) Be that the money?

EBEN (*opens bag and pours out pile of twenty-dollar gold pieces*): Twenty-dollar pieces—thirty on 'em. Count 'em. (PETER *does so, arranging them in stacks of five, biting one or two to test them.*)

PETER: Six hundred. (*He puts them in bag and puts it inside his shirt carefully.*)

SIMEON (*handing paper to* EBEN): Har ye be.

EBEN (*after a glance, folds it carefully and hides it under his shirt—gratefully*): Thank yew.

PETER: Thank yew fur the ride.

SIMEON: We'll send ye a lump o' gold fur Christmas. (*A pause.* EBEN *stares at them and they at him.*)

PETER (*awkwardly*): Waal—we're a-goin'.

SIMEON: Comin' out t' the yard?

EBEN: No. I'm waitin' in here a spell. (*Another silence. The brothers edge awkwardly to door in rear—then turn and stand.*)

SIMEON: Waal—good-by.

PETER: Good-by.

EBEN: Good-by. (*They go out. He sits down at the table, faces the stove and pulls out the paper. He looks from it to the stove. His face, lighted up by the shaft of sunlight from the window, has an expression of trance. His lips move. The two brothers come out to the gate.*)

PETER (*looking off toward barn*): Thar he be—unhitchin'.

SIMEON (*with a chuckle*): I'll bet ye he's riled!

PETER: An' thar she be.

SIMEON: Let's wait 'n' see what our new Maw looks like.

PETER (*with a grin*): An' give him our partin' cuss!

SIMEON (*grinning*): I feel like raisin' fun. I feel light in my head an' feet.

PETER: Me, too I feel like laffin' till I'd split up the middle.

SIMEON: Reckon it's the likker?

PETER: No. My feet feel itchin' t' walk an' walk—an' jump high over thin's—an' . . . .

SIMEON: Dance? (*A pause.*)

PETER (*puzzled*): It's plumb onnateral.

SIMEON (*a light coming over his face*): I calc'late it's 'cause school's out. It's holiday. Fur once we're free!

PETER (*dazedly*): Free?

SIMEON: The halter's broke—the harness is busted—the fence bars is down—the stone walls air crumblin' an' tumblin'! We'll be kickin' up an' tearin' away down the road!

PETER (*drawing a deep breath—oratorically*): Anybody that wants this stinkin' old rock-pile of a farm kin hev it. 'Tain't our'n, no sirree!

SIMEON (*takes the gate off its hinges and puts it under his arm*): We harby 'bolishes shet gates an' open gates, an' all gates, by thunder!

PETER: We'll take it with us fur luck an' let 'er sail free down some river.

SIMEON (*as a sound of voices comes from left, rear*): Har they comes! (*The two brothers congeal into two stiff, grim-visaged statues. EPHRAIM CABOT and ABBIE PUTNAM come in. CABOT is seventy-five, tall and gaunt, with great, wiry, concentrated power, but stoop-shouldered from toil. His face is as hard as if it were hewn out of a boulder, yet there is a weakness in it, a petty pride in its own narrow strength. His eyes are small, close together, and extremely near-sighted, blinking continually in the effort to focus on objects, their stare having a straining, ingrowing quality. He is dressed in his dismal black Sunday suit. ABBIE is thirty-five, buxom, full of vitality. Her round face is pretty but marred by its rather gross sensuality. There is strength and obstinacy in her jaw, a hard determination in her eyes, and about her whole personality the same unsettled, untamed, desperate quality which is so apparent in EBEN.*)

CABOT (*as they enter—a queer strangled emotion in his dry cracking voice*): Har we be t' hum, Abbie.

ABBIE (*with lust for the word*): Hum! (*Her eyes gloating on the house without seeming to see the two stiff figures at the gate.*) It's purty—purty! I can't b'lieve it's r'ally mine.

CABOT (*sharply*): Yewr'n? Mine! (*He stares at her penetratingly. She stares back. He adds relentingly*) Our'n—mebbe! It was lonesome too long. I was growin' old in the spring. A hum's got t' hev a woman.

ABBIE (*her voice taking possession*): A woman's got t' hev a hum!

CABOT (*nodding uncertainly*): Ay-eh. (*Then irritably*) Whar be they? Ain't thar nobody about—'r wukin'—r' nothin'?

ABBIE (*sees the brothers. She returns their stare of cold appraising contempt with interest—slowly*): Thar's two men loafin' at the gate an' starin' at me like a couple o' strayed hogs.

CABOT (*straining his eyes*): I kin see 'em—but I can't make out. . . .

SIMEON: It's Simeon.

PETER: It's Peter.

CABOT (*exploding*): Why hain't ye wukin'?

SIMEON (*dryly*): We're waitin' t' welcome ye hum—yew an' the bride!

CABOT (*confusedly*): Huh? Waal—this be yer new Maw, boys. (*She stares at them and they at her.*)

SIMEON (*turns away and spits contemptuously*): I see her!

PETER (*spits also*): An' I see her!

ABBIE (*with the conqueror's conscious superiority*): I'll go in an' look at *my* house. (*She goes slowly around to porch.*)

SIMEON (*with a snort*): *Her* house!

PETER (*calls after her*): Ye'll find Eben inside. Ye better not tell him it's *yewr* house.

ABBIE (*mouthing the name*): Eben. (*Then quietly*) I'll tell Eben.

CABOT (*with a contemptuous sneer*): Ye needn't heed Eben. Eben's a dumb fool—like his Maw—soft an' simple!

SIMEON (*with his sardonic burst of laughter*): Ha! Eben's a chip o' yew—spit 'n' image—hard 'n' bitter's a hickory tree! Dog'll eat dog. He'll eat ye yet, old man!

CABOT (*commandingly*): Ye git t' wuk!

SIMEON (*as ABBIE disappears in house—winks at PETER and says tauntingly*): So that thar's our new Maw, be it? Whar in hell did ye dig her up? (*He and PETER laugh.*)

PETER: Ha! Ye'd better turn her in the pen with the other sows. (*They laugh uproariously, slapping their thighs.*)

CABOT (*so amazed at their effrontery that he stutters in confusion*): Simeon! Peter! What's come over ye? Air ye drunk?

SIMEON: We're free, old man—free o' yew an' the hull damned farm! (*They grow more and more hilarious and excited.*)

PETER: An' we're startin' out fur the gold fields o' Californi-a!

SIMEON: Ye kin take this place an' burn it!

PETER: An' bury it—fur all we cares!

SIMEON: We're free, old man! (*He cuts a caper.*)

PETER: Free! (*He gives a kick in the air.*)

SIMEON (*in a frenzy*): Whoop!

PETER: Whoop! (*They do an absurd Indian war dance about the old*

*man who is petrified between rage and the fear that they are
insane.*)

SIMEON: We're free as Injuns! Lucky we don't sculp ye!

PETER: An' burn yer barn an' kill the stock!

SIMEON: An' rape yer new woman! Whoop! (*He and* PETER *stop
their dance, holding their sides, rocking with wild laughter.*)

CABOT (*edging away*): Lust fur gold—fur the sinful, easy gold o'
Californi-a! It's made ye mad!

SIMEON (*tauntingly*): Wouldn't ye like us to send ye back some
sinful gold, ye old sinner?

PETER: They's gold besides what's in Californi-a! (*He retreats back
beyond the vision of the old man and takes the bag of money and
flaunts it in the air above his head, laughing.*)

SIMEON: And sinfuller, too!

PETER: We'll be voyagin' on the sea! Whoop! (*He leaps up and
down.*)

SIMEON: Livin' free! Whoop! (*He leaps in turn.*)

CABOT (*suddenly roaring with rage*): My cuss on ye!

SIMEON: Take our'n in trade fur it! Whoop!

CABOT: I'll hev ye both chained up in the asylum!

PETER: Ye old skinflint! Good-by!

SIMEON: Ye old blood sucker! Good-by!

CABOT: Go afore I . . . !

PETER: Whoop! (*He picks a stone from the road.* SIMEON *does the
same.*)

SIMEON: Maw'll be in the parlor.

PETER: Ay-eh! One! Two!

CABOT (*frightened*): What air ye . . . ?

PETER: Three! (*They both throw, the stones hitting the parlor window with a crash of glass, tearing the shade.*)

SIMEON: Whoop!

PETER: Whoop!

CABOT (*in a fury now, rushing toward them*): If I kin lay hands on
ye—I'll break yer bones fur ye! (*But they beat a capering retreat
before him,* SIMEON *with the gate still under his arm.* CABOT *comes
back, panting with impotent rage. Their voices as they go off take
up the song of the gold-seekers to the old tune of "Oh, Susannah!"*)

> "I jumped aboard the Liza ship,
> And traveled on the sea,
> And every time I thought of home
> I wished it wasn't me!

Oh! Californi'a,
That's the land fur me!
I'm off to Californi-a!
With my wash bowl on my knee."

(*In the meantime, the window of the upper bedroom on right is raised and* ABBIE *sticks her head out. She looks down at* CABOT—*with a sigh of relief.*)

ABBIE: Waal—that's the last o' them two, hain't it? (*He doesn't answer. Then in possessive tones*) This here's a nice bedroom, Ephraim. It's a r'al nice bed. Is it my room, Ephraim?

CABOT (*grimly—without looking up*): Our'n! (*She cannot control a grimace of aversion and pulls back her head slowly and shuts the window. A sudden horrible thought seems to enter* CABOT's *head.*) They been up to somethin'! Mebbe—mebbe, they've pizened the stock—'r somethin'! (*He almost runs off down toward the barn. A moment later the kitchen door is slowly pushed open and* ABBIE *enters. For a moment she stands looking at* EBEN. *He does not notice her at first. Her eyes take him in penetratingly with a calculating appraisal of his strength as against hers. But under this her desire is dimly awakened by his youth and good looks. Suddenly he becomes conscious of her presence and looks up. Their eyes meet. He leaps to his feet, glowering at her speechlessly.*)

ABBIE (*in her most seductive tones which she uses all through this scene*): Be you—Eben? I'm Abbie— (*She laughs.*) I mean, I'm yer new Maw.

EBEN (*viciously*): No, damn ye!

ABBIE (*as if she hadn't heard—with a queer smile*): Yer Paw's spoke a lot o' yew. . . .

EBEN: Ha!

ABBIE: Ye mustn't mind him. He's an old man. (*A long pause. They stare at each other.*) I don't want t' pretend playin' Maw t' ye, Eben. (*Admiringly*) Ye're too big an' too strong fur that. I want t' be frens with ye. Mebbe with me fur a fren ye'd find ye'd like livin' here better. I kin make it easy fur ye with him, mebbe. (*With a scornful sense of power*) I calc'late I kin git him t' do most anythin' fur me.

EBBEN (*with bitter scorn*): Ha! (*They stare again,* EBEN *obscurely moved, physically attracted to her—in forced stilted tones*) Yew kin go t' the devil!

ABBIE (*calmly*): If cussin' me does ye good, cuss all ye've a mind t'. I'm all prepared t' have ye agin me—at fust. I don't blame ye nuther. I'd feel the same at any stranger comin' t' take my Maw's place. (*He shudders. She is watching him carefully.*) Yew must've cared a lot fur yewr Maw, didn't ye? My Maw died afore I'd growed. I don't remember her none. (*A pause.*) But yew won't hate me long, Eben. I'm not the wust in the world—an' yew an' me've got a lot in common. I kin tell that by lookin' at ye. Waal—I've had a hard life, too—oceans o' trouble an' nuthin' but wuk fur reward. I was a orphan early an' had t' wuk fur others in other folks' hums. Then I married an' he turned out a drunken spreer an' so he had to wuk fur others an' me too agen in other folks' hums, an' the baby died, an' my husband got sick an' died too, an' I was glad sayin' now I'm free fur once, on'y I diskivered right away all I was free fur was t' wuk agen in other folks' hums, doin' other folks' wuk till I'd most give up hope o' ever doin' my own wuk in my own hum, an' then your Paw come. . . . (CABOT *appears returning from the barn. He comes to the gate and looks down the road the brothers have gone. A faint strain of their retreating voices is heard: "Oh, Californi-a! That's the place for me." He stands glowering, his fist clenched, his face grim with rage.*)

EBEN (*fighting against his growing attraction and sympathy—harshly*): An' bought yew—like a harlot! (*She is stung and flushes angrily. She has been sincerely moved by the recital of her troubles. He adds furiously*) An' the price he's payin' ye—this farm—was my Maw's, damn ye!—an' mine now!

ABBIE (*with a cool laugh of confidence*): Yewr'n? We'll see 'bout that! (*Then strongly*) Waal—what if I did need a hum? What else'd I marry an old man like him fur?

EBEN (*maliciously*): I'll tell him ye said that!

ABBIE (*smiling*): I'll say ye're lyin' a-purpose—an' he'll drive ye off the place!

EBEN: Ye devil!

ABBIE (*defying him*): This be my farm—this be my hum—this be my kitchen—!

EBEN (*furiously, as if he were going to attack her*): Shut up, damn ye!

ABBIE (*walks up to him—a queer coarse expression of desire in her face and body—slowly*): An' upstairs—that be my bedroom—an' my bed! (*He stares into her eyes, terribly confused and torn. She adds softly*) I hain't bad nor mean—'ceptin' fur an enemy—but I got t' fight fur what's due me out o' life, if I ever 'spect t' git it.

(*Then putting her hand on his arm—seductively*) Let's yew 'n' me be frens, Eben.

EBEN (*stupidly—as if hypnotized*): Ay-eh. (*Then furiously flinging off her arm*) No, ye durned old witch! I hate ye! (*He rushes out the door.*)

ABBIE (*looks after him smiling satisfiedly—then half to herself, mouthing the word*): Eben's nice. (*She looks at the table, proudly.*) I'll wash up *my* dishes now. (EBEN *appears outside, slamming the door behind him. He comes around corner, stops on seeing his father, and stands staring at him with hate.*)

CABOT (*raising his arms to heaven in the fury he can no longer control*): Lord God o' Hosts, smite the undutiful sons with Thy wust cuss!

EBEN (*breaking in violently*): Yew 'n' yewr God! Allus cussin' folks —allus naggin' 'em!

CABOT (*oblivious to him—summoningly*): God o' the old! God o' the lonesome!

EBEN (*mockingly*): Naggin' His sheep t' sin! T' hell with yewr God! (CABOT *turns. He and* EBEN *glower at each other.*)

CABOT (*harshly*): So it's yew. I might've knowed it. (*Shaking his finger threateningly at him*) Blasphemin' fool! (*Then quickly*) Why hain't ye t' wuk?

EBEN: Why hain't yew? They've went. I can't wuk it all alone.

CABOT (*contemptuously*): Nor noways! I'm wuth ten o' ye yit, old's I be! Ye'll never be more'n half a man! (*Then, matter-of-factly*) Waal—let's git t' the barn. (*They go. A last faint note of the "Californi-a" song is heard from the distance.* ABBIE *is washing her dishes.*)

CURTAIN

❧❧

PART II

SCENE I

(*The exterior of the farmhouse, as in Part I—a hot Sunday afternoon two months later.* ABBIE, *dressed in her best, is discovered sitting in a rocker at the end of the porch. She rocks listlessly, enervated by the heat, staring in front of her with bored, half-closed eyes.*

EBEN *sticks his head out of his bedroom window. He looks around furtively and tries to see—or hear—if anyone is on the porch, but although he has been careful to make no noise,* ABBIE *has sensed his movement. She stops rocking, her face grows animated and eager, she waits attentively.* EBEN *seems to feel her presence, he scowls back his thoughts of her and spits with exaggerated disdain—then withdraws back into the room.* ABBIE *waits, holding her breath as she listens with passionate eagerness for every sound within the house.*

EBEN *comes out. Their eyes meet. His falter, he is confused, he turns away and slams the door resentfully. At this gesture,* ABBIE *laughs tantalizingly, amused but at the same time piqued and irritated. He scowls, strides off the porch to the path and starts to walk past her to the road with a grand swagger of ignoring her existence. He is dressed in his store suit, spruced up, his face shines from soap and water.* ABBIE *leans forward on her chair, her eyes hard and angry now, and, as he passes her, gives a sneering, taunting chuckle.*)

EBEN (*stung—turns on her furiously*): What air yew cacklin' 'bout?
ABBIE (*triumphant*): Yew!
EBEN: What about me?
ABBIE: Ye look all slicked up like a prize bull.
EBEN (*with a sneer*): Waal—ye hain't so durned purty yerself, be ye? (*They stare into each other's eyes, his held by hers in spite of himself, hers glowingly possessive. Their physical attraction becomes a palpable force quivering in the hot air.*)
ABBIE (*softly*): Ye don't mean that, Eben. Ye may think ye mean it, mebbe, but ye don't. Ye can't. It's agin nature, Eben. Ye been fightin' yer nature ever since the day I come—tryin' t' tell yerself I hain't purty t'ye. (*She laughs a low humid laugh without taking her eyes from his. A pause—her body squirms desirously—she murmurs languorously*) Hain't the sun strong an' hot? Ye kin feel it burnin' into the earth—Nature—makin' thin's grow—bigger 'n' bigger—burnin' inside ye—makin' thin's grow—bigger 'n' bigger —burnin' inside ye—makin' ye want t' grow—into somethin' else —till ye're jined with it—an' it's your'n—but it owns ye, too—an' makes ye grow bigger—like a tree—like them elums— (*She laughs again softly, holding his eyes. He takes a step toward her, compelled against his will.*) Nature'll beat ye, Eben. Ye might's well own up t' it fust 's last.
EBEN (*trying to break from her spell—confusedly*): If Paw'd hear ye

goin' on. . . . (*Resentfully*) But ye've made such a damned idjit
out o' the old devil . . . ! (ABBIE *laughs.*)

ABBIE: Waal—hain't it easier fur yew with him changed softer?

EBEN (*defiantly*): No. I'm fightin' him—fightin' yew—fightin' fur
Maw's rights t' her hum! (*This breaks her spell for him. He
glowers at her.*) An' I'm onto ye. Ye hain't foolin' me a mite. Ye're
aimin' t' swaller up everythin' an' make it your'n. Waal, you'll
find I'm a heap sight bigger hunk nor yew kin chew! (*He turns
from her with a sneer.*)

ABBIE (*trying to regain her ascendancy—seductively*): Eben!

EBEN: Leave me be! (*He starts to walk away.*)

ABBIE (*more commandingly*): Eben!

EBEN (*stops—resentfully*): What d'ye want?

ABBIE (*trying to conceal a growing excitement*): Whar air ye goin'?

EBEN (*with malicious nonchalance*): Oh—up the road a spell.

ABBIE: T' the village?

EBEN (*airly*): Mebbe.

ABBIE (*excitedly*): T' see that Min, I s'pose?

EBEN: Mebbe.

ABBIE (*weakly*): What d'ye want t' waste time on her fur?

EBEN (*revenging himself now—grinning at her*): Ye can't beat Nature, didn't ye say? (*He laughs and again starts to walk away.*)

ABBIE (*bursting out*): An ugly old hake!

EBEN (*with a tantalizing sneer*): She's purtier'n yew be!

ABBIE: That every wuthless drunk in the country has. . . .

EBEN (*tauntingly*): Mebbe—but she's better'n yew. She owns up fa'r
'n' squar' t' her doin's.

ABBIE (*furiously*): Don't ye dare compare. . . .

EBEN: She don't go sneakin' an' stealin'—what's mine.

ABBIE (*savagely seizing on his weak point*): Your'n? Yew mean—my
farm?

EBEN: I mean the farm yew sold yerself fur like any other old whore
—my farm!

ABBIE (*stung—fiercely*): Ye'll never live t' see the day when even a
stinkin' weed on it 'll belong t' ye! (*Then in a scream*) Git out o'
my sight! Go on t' yer slut—disgracin' yer Paw 'n' me! I'll git yer
Paw t' horsewhip ye off the place if I want t'! Ye're only livin'
here 'cause I tolerate ye! Git along! I hate the sight o' ye! (*She
stops, panting and glaring at him.*)

EBEN (*returning her glance in kind*): An' I hate the sight o' yew!

(*He turns and strides off up the road. She follows his retreating figure with concentrated hate. Old* CABOT *appears coming up from the barn. The hard, grim expression of his face has changed. He seems in some queer way softened, mellowed. His eyes have taken on a strange, incongruous dreamy quality. Yet there is no hint of physical weakness about him—rather he looks more robust and younger.* ABBIE *sees him and turns away quickly with unconcealed aversion. He comes slowly up to her.*)

CABOT (*mildly*): War yew an' Eben quarrelin' agen?

ABBIE (*shortly*): No.

CABOT: Ye was talkin' a'mighty loud. (*He sits down on the edge of porch.*)

ABBIE (*snappishly*): If ye heerd us they hain't no need askin' questions.

CABOT: I didn't hear what ye said.

ABBIE (*relieved*): Waal—it wa'n't nothin' t' speak on.

CABOT (*after a pause*): Eben's queer.

ABBIE (*bitterly*): He's the dead spit 'n' image o' yew!

CABOT (*queerly interested*): D'ye think so, Abbie? (*After a pause, ruminatingly*) Me 'n' Eben's allus fit 'n' fit. I never could b'ar him noways. He's so thunderin' soft—like his Maw.

ABBIE (*scornfully*): Ay-eh! 'Bout as soft as yew be!

CABOT (*as if he hadn't heard*): Mebbe I been too hard on him.

ABBIE (*jeeringly*): Waal—ye're gittin' soft now—soft as slop! That's what Eben was sayin'.

CABOT (*his face instantly grim and ominous*): Eben was sayin'? Waal, he'd best not do nothin' t' try me 'r he'll soon diskiver. . . . (*A pause. She keeps her face turned away. His gradually softens. He stares up at the sky.*) Purty, hain't it?

ABBIE (*crossly*): I don't see nothin' purty.

CABOT: The sky. Feels like a wa'm field up thar.

ABBIE (*sarcastically*): Air yew aimin' t' buy up over the farm too? (*She snickers contemptuously.*)

CABOT (*strangely*): I'd like t' own my place up thar. (*A pause.*) I'm gittin' old, Abbie. I'm gittin' ripe on the bough. (*A pause. She stares at him mystified. He goes on.*) It's allus lonesome cold in the house—even when it's bilin' hot outside. Hain't yew noticed?

ABBIE: No.

CABOT: It's wa'm down t' the barn—nice smellin' an' warm—with the cows. (*A pause.*) Cows is queer.

ABBIE: Like yew?

CABOT: Like Eben. (*A pause.*) I'm gittin' t' feel resigned t' Eben—jest as I got t' feel 'bout his Maw. I'm gittin' t' learn to b'ar his softness —jest like her'n. I calc'late I c'd a'most take t' him—if he wa'n't sech a dumb fool! (*A pause.*) I s'pose it's old age a-creepin' in my bones.

ABBIE (*indifferently*): Waal—ye hain't dead yet.

CABOT (*roused*): No, I hain't, yew bet—not by a hell of a sight—I'm sound 'n' tough as hickory! (*Then moodily*) But arter three score and ten the Lord warns ye t' prepare. (*A pause.*) That's why Eben's come in my head. Now that his cussed sinful brothers is gone their path t' hell, they's no one left but Eben.

ABBIE (*resentfully*): They's me, hain't they? (*Agitatedly*) What's all this sudden likin' ye tuk to Eben? Why don't ye say nothin' 'bout me? Hain't I yer lawful wife?

CABOT (*simply*): Ay-eh. Ye be. (*A pause—he stares at her desirously —his eyes grow avid—then with a sudden movement he seizes her hands and squeezes them, declaiming in a queer camp meeting preacher's tempo*) Yew air my Rose o' Sharon! Behold, yew air fair; yer eyes air doves; yer lips air like scarlet; yer two breasts air like two fawns; yer navel be like a round goblet; yer belly be like a heap o' wheat. . . . (*He covers her hand with kisses. She does not seem to notice. She stares before her with hard angry eyes.*)

ABBIE (*jerking her hands away—harshly*): So ye're plannin' t' leave the farm t' Eben, air ye?

CABOT (*dazedly*): Leave. . . ? (*Then with resentful obstinacy*) I hain't a-givin' it t' no one!

ABBIE (*remorselessly*): Ye can't take it with ye.

CABOT (*thinks a moment—then reluctantly*): No, I calc'late not. (*After a pause—with a strange passion*) But if I could, I would, by the Etarnal! 'R if I could, in my dyin' hour, I'd set it afire an' watch it burn—this house an' every ear o' corn an' every tree down t' the last blade o' hay! I'd sit an' know it was all a-dying with me an' no one else'd ever own what was mine, what I'd made out o' nothin' with my own sweat 'n' blood! (*A pause—then he adds with a queer affection*) 'Ceptin' the cows. Them I'd turn free.

ABBIE (*harshly*): An' me?

CABOT (*with a queer smile*): Ye'd be turned free, too.

ABBIE (*furiously*): So that's the thanks I git fur marrin' ye—t' have ye change kind to Eben who hates ye, an' talk o' turnin' me out in the road.

CABOT (*hastily*): Abbie! Ye know I wa'n't. . . .

ABBIE (*vengefully*): Just let me tell ye a thing or two 'bout Eben! Whar's he gone? T' see that harlot, Min! I tried fur t' stop him. Disgracin' yew an' me—on the Sabbath, too!

CABOT (*rather guiltily*): He's a sinner—nateral-born. It's lust eatin' his heart.

ABBIE (*enraged beyond endurance—wildly vindictive*): An' his lust fur me! Kin ye find excuses fur that?

CABOT (*stares at her—after a dead pause*): Lust—fur yew?

ABBIE (*defiantly*): He was tryin' t' make love t' me—when ye heerd us quarrelin'.

CABOT (*stares at her—then a terrible expression of rage comes over his face—he springs to his feet shaking all over*): By the A'mighty God—I'll end him!

ABBIE (*frightened now for* EBEN): No! Don't ye!

CABOT (*violently*): I'll git the shotgun an' blow his soft brains t' the top o' them elums!

ABBIE (*throwing her arms around him*): No, Ephraim!

CABOT (*pushing her away violently*): I will, by God!

ABBIE (*in a quieting tone*): Listen, Ephraim. 'Twa'n't nothin' bad—on'y a boy's foolin'—'twa'n't meant serious—jest jokin' an' teasin'. . . .

CABOT: Then why did ye say—lust?

ABBIE: It must hev sounded wusser'n I meant. An' I was mad at thinkin'—ye'd leave him the farm.

CABOT (*quieter but still grim and cruel*): Waal then, I'll horsewhip him off the place if that much'll content ye.

ABBIE (*reaching out and taking his hand*): No. Don't think o' me! Ye mustn't drive him off. 'Tain't sensible. Who'll ye get to help ye on the farm? They's no one hereabouts.

CABOT (*considers this—then nodding his appreciation*): Ye got a head on ye. (*Then irritably*) Waal, let him stay. (*He sits down on the edge of the porch. She sits beside him. He murmurs contemptuously*) I oughtn't t' git riled so—at that 'ere fool calf. (*A pause.*) But har's the p'int. What son o' mine'll keep on here t' the farm—when the Lord does call me? Simeon an' Peter air gone t' hell—an' Eben's follerin' 'em.

ABBIE: They's me.

CABOT: Ye're on'y a woman.

ABBIE: I'm yewr wife.

CABOT: That hain't me. A son is me—my blood—mine. Mine ought t' git mine. An' then it's still mine—even though I be six foot under. D'ye see?

ABBIE (*giving him a look of hatred*): Ay-eh. I see. (*She becomes very thoughtful, her face growing shrewd, her eyes studying* CABOT *craftily.*)

CABOT: I'm gittin' old—ripe on the bough. (*Then with a sudden forced reassurance*) Not but what I hain't a hard nut t' crack even yet—an' fur many a year t' come! By the Eternal, I kin break most o' the young fellers' backs at any kind o' work any day o' the year!

ABBIE (*suddenly*): Mebbe the Lord'll give *us* a son.

CABOT (*turns and stares at her eagerly*): Ye mean—a son—t' me 'n' yew?

ABBIE (*with a cajoling smile*): Ye're a strong man yet, hain't ye? 'Tain't noways impossible, be it? We know that. Why d'ye stare so? Hain't ye never thought o' that afore? I been thinkin' o' it all along. Ay-eh—an' I been prayin' it'd happen, too.

CABOT (*his face growing full of joyous pride and a sort of religious ecstasy*): Ye been prayin', Abbie?—fur a son?—t' us?

ABBIE: Ay-eh. (*With a grim resolution*) I want a son now.

CABOT (*excitedly clutching both of her hands in his*): It'd be the blessin' o' God, Abbie—the blessin' o' God A'mighty on me—in my old age—in my lonesomeness! They hain't nothin' I wouldn't do fur ye then, Abbie. Ye'd hev on'y t' ask it—anythin' ye'd a mind t'!

ABBIE (*interrupting*): Would ye will the farm t' me then—t' me an' it . . .

CABOT (*vehemently*): I'd do anythin' ye axed, I tell ye! I swar it! May I be everlastin' damned t' hell if I wouldn't! (*He sinks to his knees pulling her down with him. He trembles all over with the fervor of his hopes.*) Pray t' the Lord agen, Abbie. It's the Sabbath! I'll jine ye! Two prayers air better nor one. "An' God hearkened unto Rachel"! An' God hearkened unto Abbie! Pray Abbie! Pray fur him to hearken! (*He bows his head, mumbling. She pretends to do likewise but gives him a side glance of scorn and triumph.*)

SCENE II

(*About eight in the evening. The interior of the two bedrooms on the top floor is shown—*EBEN *is sitting on the side of his bed in the room on the left. On account of the heat he has taken off everything but his undershirt and pants. His feet are bare. He faces front, brooding moodily, his chin propped on his hands, a desperate expression on his face.*

In the other room CABOT *and* ABBIE *are sitting side by side on the edge of their bed, an old four-poster with feather mattress. He is in his night shirt, she in her nightdress. He is still in the queer, excited mood into which the notion of a son has thrown him. Both rooms are lighted dimly and flickeringly by tallow candles.)*

CABOT: The farm needs a son.

ABBIE: I need a son.

CABOT: Ay-eh. Sometimes ye air the farm an' sometimes the farm be yew. That's why I clove t' ye in my lonesomeness. (*A pause. He pounds his knee with his fist.*) Me an' the farm has got t' beget a son!

ABBIE: Ye'd best go t' sleep. Ye're gittin' thin's all mixed.

CABOT (*with an impatient gesture*): No, I hain't. My mind's clear's a well. Ye don't know me, that's it. (*He stares hopelessly at the floor.*)

ABBIE (*indifferently*): Mebbe. (*In the next room* EBEN *gets up and paces up and down distractedly.* ABBIE *hears him. Her eyes fasten on the intervening wall with concentrated attention.* EBEN *stops and stares. Their hot glances seem to meet through the wall. Unconsciously he stretches out his arms for her and she half rises. Then aware, he mutters a curse at himself and flings himself face downward on the bed, his clenched fists above his head, his face buried in the pillow.* ABBIE *relaxes with a faint sigh but her eyes remain fixed on the wall; she listens with all her attention for some movement from* EBEN.)

CABOT (*suddenly raises his head and looks at her—scornfully*): Will ye ever know me—'r will any man 'r woman? (*Shaking his head*) No. I calc'late 't wa'n't t' be. (*He turns away.* ABBIE *looks at the wall. Then, evidently unable to keep silent about his thoughts, without looking at his wife, he puts out his hand and clutches her knee. She starts violently, looks at him, sees he is not watching her, concentrates again on the wall and pays no attention to what he says.*) Listen, Abbie. When I come here fifty odd year ago—I was jest twenty an' the strongest an' hardest ye ever seen—ten times as strong an' fifty times as hard as Eben. Waal—this place was nothin' but fields o' stones. Folks laughed when I tuk it. They couldn't know what I knowed. When ye kin make corn sprout out o' stones, God's livin' in yew! They wa'n't strong enuf fur that! They reckoned God was easy. They laughed. They don't laugh no more. Some died hereabouts. Some went West an' died. They're all under ground—fur follerin' arter an easy God. God hain't easy.

(*He shakes his head slowly.*) An' I growed hard. Folks kept allus sayin' he's a hard man like 'twas sinful t' be hard, so's at last I said back at 'em: Waal then, by thunder, ye'll git me hard an' see how ye like it! (*Then suddenly*) But I give in t' weakness once. 'Twas arter I'd been here two year. I got weak—despairful—they was so many stones. They was a party leavin', givin' up, goin' West. I jined 'em. We tracked on 'n' on. We come t' broad medders, plains, whar the soil was black an' rich as gold. Nary a stone. Easy. Ye'd on'y to plow an' sow an' then set an' smoke yer pipe an' watch thin's grow. I could o' been a rich man—but somethin' in me fit me an' fit me—the voice o' God sayin': "This hain't wuth nothin' t' Me. Get ye back t' hum!" I got afeerd o' that voice an' I lit out back t' hum here, leavin' my claim an' crops t' whoever'd a mind t' take 'em. Ay-eh. I actoolly give up what was rightful mine! God's hard, not easy! God's in the stones! Build my church on a rock— out o' stones an' I'll be in them! That's what He meant t' Peter! (*He sighs heavily—a pause.*) Stones. I picked 'em up an' piled 'em into walls. Ye kin read the years o' my life in them walls, every day a hefted stone, climbin' over the hills up and down, fencin' in the fields that was mine, whar I'd made thin's grow out o' nothin'— like the will o' God, like the servant o' His hand. It wa'n't easy. It was hard an' He made me hard fur it. (*He pauses.*) All the time I kept gittin' lonesomer. I tuk a wife. She bore Simeon an' Peter. She was a good woman. She wuked hard. We was married twenty year. She never knowed me. She helped but she never knowed what she was helpin'. I was allus lonesome. She died. After that it wa'n't so lonesome fur a spell. (*A pause.*) I lost count o' the years. I had no time t' fool away countin' 'em. Sim an' Peter helped. The farm growed. It was all mine! When I thought o' that I didn't feel lonesome. (*A pause.*) But ye can't hitch yer mind t' one thin' day an' night. I tuk another wife—Eben's Maw. Her folks was contestin' me at law over my deeds t' the farm—my farm! That's why Eben keeps a-talkin' his fool talk o' this bein' his Maw's farm. She bore Eben. She was purty—but soft. She tried t' be hard. She couldn't. She never knowed me nor nothin'. It was lonesomer 'n hell with her. After a matter o' sixteen odd years, she died. (*A pause.*) I lived with the boys. They hated me 'cause I was hard. I hated them 'cause they was soft. They coveted the farm without knowin' what it meant. It made me bitter 'n wormwood. It aged me—them coveting what I'd made fur mine. Then this spring the call come—the voice o' God cryin' in my wilderness, in my lonesomeness—t' go out an' seek an' find! (*Turning to her with strange passion*) I sought ye an' I found ye! Yew air my Rose o' Sharon! Yer eyes air like. . . . (*She has turned a blank face, resentful eyes to his. He stares at her for a moment—then harshly*) Air ye any the wiser fur all I've told ye?

ABBIE (*confusedly*): Mebbe.

CABOT (*pushing her away from him—angrily*): Ye don't know nothin'—nor never will. If ye don't hev a son t' redeem ye . . . (*This in a tone of cold threat.*)

ABBIE (*resentfully*): I've prayed, hain't I?

CABOT (*bitterly*): Pray agen—fur understandin'!

ABBIE (*a veiled threat in her tone*): Ye'll have a son out o' me, I promise ye.

CABOT: How kin ye promise?

ABBIE: I got second-sight mebbe. I kin foretell. (*She gives a queer smile.*)

CABOT: I believe ye have. Ye give me the chills sometimes. (*He shivers.*) It's cold in this house. It's oneasy. They's thin's pokin' about in the dark—in the corners. (*He pulls on his trousers, tucking in his night shirt, and pulls on his boots.*)

ABBIE (*surprised*): Whar air ye goin'?

CABOT (*queerly*): Down whar it's restful—whar it's warm—down t' the barn. (*Bitterly*) I kin talk t' the cows. They know. They know the farm an' me. They'll give me peace. (*He turns to go out the door.*)

ABBIE (*a bit frightenedly*): Air ye ailin' tonight, Ephraim?

CABOT: Growin'. Growin' ripe on the bough. (*He turns and goes, his boots clumping down the stairs.* EBEN *sits up with a start, listening.* ABBIE *is conscious of his movement and stares at the wall.* CABOT *comes out of the house around the corner and stands by the gate, blinking at the sky. He stretches up his hands in a tortured gesture*) God A'mighty, call from the dark! (*He listens as if expecting an answer. Then his arms drop, he shakes his head and plods off toward the barn.* EBEN *and* ABBIE *stare at each other through the wall.* EBEN *sighs heavily and* ABBIE *echoes it. Both become terribly nervous, uneasy. Finally* ABBIE *gets up and listens, her ear to the wall. He acts as if he saw every move she was making, he becomes resolutely still. She seems driven into a decision—goes out the door in rear determinedly. His eyes follow her. Then as the door of his room is opened softly, he turns away, waits in an attitude of strained fixity.* ABBIE *stands for a second staring at*

*him, her eyes burning with desire. Then with a little cry she runs
over and throws her arms about his neck, she pulls his head back
and covers his mouth with kisses. At first, he submits dumbly; then
he puts his arms about her neck and returns her kisses, but finally,
suddenly aware of his hatred, he hurls her away from him, springing to his feet. They stand speechless and breathless, panting like
two animals.)*

ABBIE (*at last—painfully*): Ye shouldn't, Eben—ye shouldn't—I'd
make ye happy!

EBEN (*harshly*): I don't want t' be happy—from yew!

ABBIE (*helplessly*): Ye do, Eben! Ye do! Why d'ye lie?

EBEN (*viciously*): I don't take t'ye, I tell ye! I hate the sight o' ye!

ABBIE (*with an uncertain troubled laugh*): Waal, I kissed ye anyways—an' ye kissed back—yer lips was burnin'—ye can't lie 'bout
that! (*Intensely*) If ye don't care, why did ye kiss me back—why
was yer lips burnin'?

EBEN (*wiping his mouth*): It was like pizen on 'em (*Then tauntingly*) When I kissed ye back, mebbe I thought 'twas someone
else.

ABBIE (*wildly*): Min?

EBEN: Mebbe.

ABBIE (*torturedly*): Did ye go t' see her? Did ye r'ally go? I thought
ye mightn't. Is that why ye throwed me off jest now?

EBEN (*sneeringly*): What if it be?

ABBIE (*raging*): Then ye're a dog, Eben Cabot!

EBEN (*threateningly*): Ye can't talk that way t' me!

ABBIE (*with a shrill laugh*): Can't I? Did ye think I was in love with
ye—a weak thin' like yew? Not much! I on'y wanted ye fur a
purpose o' my own—an' I'll hev ye fur it yet 'cause I'm stronger'n
yew be!

EBEN (*resentfully*): I knowed well it was on'y part o' yer plan t'
swaller everythin'!

ABBIE (*tauntingly*): Mebbe!

EBEN (*furious*): Git out o' my room!

ABBIE: This air my room an' ye're on'y hired help!

EBEN (*threateningly*): Git out afore I murder ye!

ABBIE (*quite confident now*): I hain't a mite afeerd. Ye want me,
don't ye? Yes, ye do! An' yer Paw's son'll never kill what he wants!
Look at yer eyes! They's lust fur me in 'em, burnin' 'em up! Look
at yer lips now! They're tremblin' an longin' t' kiss me, an' yer
teeth t' bite! (*He is watching her now with a horrible fascination.*

She laughs a crazy triumphant laugh.) I'm a-goin' t' make all o' this hum my hum! They's one room hain't mine yet, but it's a-goin' t' be tonight. I'm a-goin' down now an' light up! (*She makes him a mocking bow.*) Won't ye come courtin' me in the best parlor, Mister Cabot?

EBEN (*staring at her—horribly confused—dully*): Don't ye dare! It hain't been opened since Maw died an' was laid out thar! Don't ye . . . ! (*But her eyes are fixed on his so burningly that his will seems to wither before hers. He stands swaying toward her helplessly.*)

ABBIE (*holding his eyes and putting all her will into her words as she backs out the door*): I'll expect ye afore along, Eben.

EBEN (*stares after her for a while, walking toward the door. A light appears in the parlor window. He murmurs*): In the parlor? (*This seems to arouse connotations for he comes back and puts on his white shirt, collar, half ties the tie mechanically, puts on coat, takes his hat, stands barefooted looking about him in bewilderment, mutters wonderingly*) Maw! Whar' air yew? (*Then goes slowly toward the door in rear.*)

SCENE III

(*A few minutes later. The interior of the parlor is shown. A grim, repressed room like a tomb in which the family has been interred alive.* ABBIE *sits on the edge of the horsechair sofa. She has lighted all the candles and the room is revealed in all its preserved ugliness. A change has come over the woman. She looks awed and frightened now, ready to run away.*

The door is opened and EBEN *appears. His face wears an expression of obsessed confusion. He stands staring at her, his arms hanging disjointedly from his shoulders, his feet bare, his hat in his hand.*

ABBIE (*after a pause—with a nervous, formal politeness*): Won't ye set?

EBEN (*dully*): Ay-eh. (*Mechanically he places his hat carefully on the floor near the door and sits stiffly beside her on the edge of the sofa. A pause. They both remain rigid, looking straight ahead with eyes full of fear.*)

ABBIE: When I fust came in—in the dark—they seemed somethin' here.

EBEN (*simply*): Maw.

ABBIE: I kin still feel—something'. . . .

EBEN: It's Maw.

ABBIE: At fust I was feered o' it. I wanted t' yell an' run. Now—since yew come—seems like it's growin' soft an' kind t' me. (*Addressing the air—queerly*) Thank yew.

EBEN: Maw allus loved me.

ABBIE: Mebbe it knows I love yew too. Mebbe that makes it kind t' me.

EBEN (*dully*): I dunno. I should think she'd hate ye.

ABBIE (*with certainty*): No. I kin feel it don't—not no more.

EBEN: Hate ye fur stealin' her place—here in her hum—settin' in her parlor whar she was laid— (*He suddenly stops, staring stupidly before him.*)

ABBIE: What is it, Eben?

EBEN (*in a whisper*): Seems like Maw didn't want me t' remind ye.

ABBIE (*excitedly*): I knowed, Eben! It's kind t' me! It don't b'ar me no grudges fur what I never knowed an' couldn't help!

EBEN: Maw b'ars him a grudge.

ABBIE: Waal, so does all o' us.

EBEN: Ay-eh. (*With passion*) I does, by God!

ABBIE (*taking one of his hands in hers and patting it*): Thar! Don't git riled thinkin' o' him. Think o' yer Maw who's kind t' us. Tell me about yer Maw, Eben.

EBEN: They hain't nothin' much. She was kind. She was good.

ABBIE (*putting one arm over his shoulder. He does not seem to notice —passionately*): I'll be kind an' good t' ye!

EBEN: Sometimes she used t' sing fur me.

ABBIE: I'll sing fur ye!

EBEN: This was her hum. This was her farm.

ABBIE: This is my hum! This is my farm!

EBEN: He married her t' steal 'em. She was soft an' easy. He couldn't 'preciate her.

ABBIE: He can't 'preciate me!

EBEN: He murdered her with his hardness.

ABBIE: He's murderin' me!

EBEN: She died. (*A pause.*) Sometimes she used to sing fur me. (*He bursts into a fit of sobbing.*)

ABBIE (*both her arms around him—with wild passion*): I'll sing fur ye! I'll die fur ye! (*In spite of her overwhelming desire for him, there is a sincere maternal love in her manner and voice—a horribly frank mixture of lust and mother love.*) Don't cry, Eben!

I'll take yer Maw's place! I'll be everythin' she was t' ye! Let me kiss ye, Eben! (*She pulls his head around. He makes a bewildered pretense of resistance. She is tender.*) Don't be afeered! I'll kiss ye pure, Eben—same 's if I was a Maw t' ye—an' ye kin kiss me back 's if yew was my son—my boy—sayin' good-night t' me! Kiss me, Eben. (*They kiss in restrained fashion. Then suddenly wild passion overcomes her. She kisses him lustfully again and again and he flings his arms about her and returns her kisses. Suddenly, as in the bedroom, he frees himself from her violently and springs to his feet. He is trembling all over, in a strange state of terror.* ABBIE *strains her arms toward him with fierce pleading.*) Don't ye leave me, Eben! Can't ye see it hain't enuf—lovin' ye like a Maw—can't ye see it's got t' be that an' more—much more—a hundred times more—fur me t' be happy—fur yew t' be happy?

EBEN (*to the presence he feels in the room*): Maw! Maw! What d'ye want? What air ye tellin' me?

ABBIE: She's tellin' ye t' love me. She knows I love ye an' I'll be good t' ye. Can't ye feel it? Don't ye know? She's tellin' ye t' love me, Eben!

EBEN: Ay-eh. I feel—mebbe she—but—I can't figger out—why—when ye've stole her place—here in her hum—in the parlor whar she was—

ABBIE (*fiercely*): She knows I love ye!

EBEN (*his face suddenly lighting up with a fierce triumphant grin*): I see it! I sees why. It's her vengeance on him—so's she kin rest quiet in her grave!

ABBIE (*wildly*): Vengeance o' God on the hull o' us! What d'we give a durn? I love ye, Eben! God knows I love ye! (*She stretches out her arms for him.*)

EBEN (*throws himself on his knees beside the sofa and grabs her in his arms—releasing all his pent-up passion*): An' I love yew, Abbie! —now I kin say it! I been dyin' fur want o' ye—every hour since ye come! I love ye! (*Their lips meet in a fierce, bruising kiss.*)

SCENE IV

(*Exterior of the farmhouse. It is just dawn. The front door at right is opened and* EBEN *comes out and walks around to the gate. He is dressed in his working clothes. He seems changed. His face wears a bold and confident expression, he is grinning to himself with evident satisfaction. As he gets near the gate, the window of the parlor is heard opening and the shutters are flung back and* ABBIE *sticks her head out. Her hair tumbles over her shoulders in disarray, her face is flushed, she looks at* EBEN *with tender, languorous eyes and calls softly.)*

ABBIE: Eben. (*As he turns—playfully*) Jest one more kiss afore ye go. I'm goin' to miss ye fearful all day.

EBEN: An' me yew, ye kin bet! (*He goes to her. They kiss several times. He draws away, laughingly.*) Thar. That's enuf, hain't it? Ye won't hev none left fur next time.

ABBIE: I got a million o' 'em left fur yew! (*Then a bit anxiously*) D'ye r'ally love me, Eben?

EBEN (*emphatically*): I like ye better'n any gal I ever knowed! That's gospel!

ABBIE: Likin' hain't lovin'.

EBEN: Waal then—I love ye. Now air yew satisfied?

ABBIE: Ay-eh, I be. (*She smiles at him adoringly.*)

EBEN: I better git t' the barn. The old critter's liable t' suspicion an' come sneakin' up.

ABBIE (*with a confident laugh*): Let him! I kin allus pull the wool over his eyes. I'm goin' t' leave the shutters open and let in the sun 'n' air. This room's been dead long enuf. Now it's goin' t' be my room!

EBEN (*frowning*): Ay-eh.

ABBIE (*hastily*): I meant—our room.

EBEN: Ay-eh.

ABBIE: We made it our'n last night, didn't we? We give it life—our lovin' did. (*A pause.*)

EBEN (*with a strange look*): Maw's gone back t' her grave. She kin sleep now.

ABBIE: May she rest in peace! (*Then tenderly rebuking*) Ye oughtn't t' talk o' sad thin's—this mornin'.

EBEN: It jest come up in my mind o' itself.

ABBIE: Don't let it. (*He doesn't answer. She yawns.*) Waal, I'm a-goin' t' steal a wink o' sleep. I'll tell the Old Man I hain't feelin' pert. Let him git his own vittles.

EBEN: I see him comin' from the barn. Ye better look smart an' git upstairs.

ABBIE: Ay-eh. Good-by. Don't fergit me. (*She throws him a kiss. He grins—then squares his shoulders and awaits his father confi-*

dently. CABOT *walks slowly up from the left, staring up at the sky with a vague face.*)

EBEN (*jovially*): Mornin', Paw. Star-gazin' in daylight?

CABOT: Purty, hain't it?

EBEN (*looking around him possessively*): It's a durned purty farm.

CABOT: I mean the sky.

EBEN (*grinning*): How d'ye know? Them eyes o' your'n can't see that fur. (*This tickles his humor and he slaps his thigh and laughs.*) Ho-ho! That's a good un!

CABOT (*grimly sarcastic*): Ye're feelin' right chipper, hain't ye? Whar'd ye steal the likker?

EBEN (*good-naturedly*): 'Tain't likker. Jest life. (*Suddenly holding out his hand—soberly*) Yew 'n' me is quits. Let's shake hands.

CABOT (*suspiciously*): What's come over ye?

EBEN: Then don't. Mebbe it's jest as well. (*A moment's pause.*) What's come over me? (*Queerly*) Didn't ye feel her passin'—goin' back t' her grave?

CABOT (*dully*): Who?

EBEN: Maw. She kin rest now an' sleep content. She's quits with ye.

CABOT (*confusedly*): I rested. I slept good—down with the cows. They know how t' sleep. They're teachin' me.

EBEN (*suddenly jovial again*): Good fur the cows! Waal—ye better git t' work.

CABOT (*grimly amused*): Air yew bossin' me, ye calf?

EBEN (*beginning to laugh*): Ay-eh! I'm bossin' yew! Ha-ha-ha! see how ye like it! Ha-ha-ha! I'm the prize rooster o' this roost. Ha-ha-ha! (*He goes off toward the barn laughing.*)

CABOT (*looks after him with scornful pity*): Soft-headed. Like his Maw. Dead spit 'n' image. No hope in him! (*He spits with contemptuous disgust.*) A born fool! (*Then matter-of-factly*) Waal—I'm gittin' peckish. (*He goes toward door.*)

CURTAIN

$$\ll \gg$$

PART III

SCENE I

(*A night in late spring the following year. The kitchen and the two bedrooms upstairs are shown. The two bedrooms are dimly lighted by a tallow candle in each.* EBEN *is sitting on the side of the bed in his room, his chin propped on his fists, his face a study of the struggle he is making to understand his conflicting emotions. The noisy laughter and music from below where a kitchen dance is in progress annoy and distract him. He scowls at the floor.*

In the next room a cradle stands beside the double bed.

In the kitchen all is festivity. The stove has been taken down to give more room to the dancers. The chairs, with wooden benches added, have been pushed back against the walls. On these are seated, squeezed in tight against one another, farmers and their wives and their young folks of both sexes from the neighboring farms. They are all chattering and laughing loudly. They evidently have some secret joke in common. There is no end of winking, of nudging, of meaning nods of the head toward CABOT *who, in a state of extreme hilarious excitement increased by the amount he has drunk, is standing near the rear door where there is a small keg of whisky and serving drinks to all the men. In the left corner, front, dividing the attention with her husband,* ABBIE *is sitting in a rocking chair, a shawl wrapped about her shoulders. She is very pale, her face is thin and drawn, her eyes are fixed anxiously on the open door in rear as if waiting for someone.*

The musician is tuning up his fiddle, seated in the far right corner. He is a lanky young fellow with a long, weak face. His pale eyes blink incessantly and he grins about him slyly with a greedy malice.)

ABBIE (*suddenly turning to a young girl on her right*): Whar's Eben?

YOUNG GIRL (*eyeing her scornfully*): I dunno, Mrs. Cabot. I hain't seen Eben in ages. (*Meaningly*) Seems like he's spent most o' his time t' hum since yew come.

ABBIE (*vaguely*): I tuk his Maw's place.

YOUNG GIRL: Ay-eh. So I've heerd. (*She turns away to retail this bit of gossip to her mother sitting next to her.* ABBIE *turns to her left to a big stoutish middle-aged man whose flushed face and staring eyes show the amount of "likker" he has consumed.*)

ABBIE: Ye hain't seen Eben, hev ye?

MAN: No, I hain't. (*Then he adds with a wink*) If yew hain't, who would?

ABBIE: He's the best dancer in the county. He'd ought t' come an' dance.

MAN (*with a wink*): Mebbe he's doin' the dutiful an' walkin' the kid t' sleep. It's a boy, hain't it?

ABBIE (*nodding vaguely*): Ay-eh—born two weeks back—purty's a picter.

MAN: They all is—t' their Maws. (*Then in a whisper, with a nudge and a leer*) Listen, Abbie—if ye ever git tired o' Eben, remember me! Don't fergit now! (*He looks at her uncomprehending face for a second—then grunts disgustedly.*) Waal—guess I'll likker agin. (*He goes over and joins* CABOT *who is arguing noisily with an old farmer over cows. They all drink.*)

ABBIE (*this time appealing to nobody in particular*): Wonder what Eben's a-doin'? (*Her remark is repeated down the line with many a guffaw and titter until it reaches the fiddler. He fastens his blinking eyes on* ABBIE.)

FIDDLER (*raising his voice*): Bet I kin tell ye, Abbie, what Eben's doin'! He's down t' the church offerin' up prayers o' thanksgivin'. (*They all titter expectantly.*)

MAN: What fur? (*Another titter.*)

FIDDLER: 'Cause unto him a—(*He hesitates just long enough.*)— brother is born! (*A roar of laughter. They all look from* ABBIE *to* CABOT. *She is oblivious, staring at the door.* CABOT, *although he hasn't heard the words, is irritated by the laughter and steps forward, glaring about him. There is an immediate silence.*)

CABOT: What're ye all bleatin' about—like a flock o' goats? Why don't ye dance, damn ye? I axed ye here t' dance—t' eat, drink an' be merry—an' thar ye set cacklin' like a lot o' wet hens with the pip! Ye've swilled my likker an' guzzled my vittles like hogs, hain't ye? Then dance fur me, can't ye? That's fa'r an' squar', hain't it? (*A grumble of resentment goes around but they are all evidently in too much awe of him to express it openly.*)

FIDDLER (*slyly*): We're waitin' fur Eben. (*A suppressed laugh.*)

CABOT (*with a fierce exultation*): T'hell with Eben! Eben's done fur now! I got a new son! (*His mood switching with drunken suddenness*) But ye needn't t' laugh at Eben, none o' ye! He's my blood, if he be a dumb fool. He's better nor any o' yew! He kin do a day's work a'most up t' what I kin—an' that'd put any o' yew pore critters t' shame!

FIDDLER: An' he kin do a good night's work, too! (*A roar of laughter.*)

CABOT: Laugh, ye damn fools! Ye're right jist the same, Fiddler. He kin work day an' night too, like I kin, if need be!

OLD FARMER (*from behind the keg where he is weaving drunkenly back and forth—with great simplicity*): They hain't many t' touch ye, Ephraim—a son at seventy-six. That's a hard man fur ye! I be on'y sixty-eight an' I couldn't do it. (*A roar of laughter in which* CABOT *joins uproariously.*)

CABOT (*slapping him on the back*): I'm sorry fur ye, Hi. I'd never suspicion sech weakness from a boy like yew!

OLD FARMER: An' I never reckoned yew had it in ye nuther, Ephraim. (*There is another laugh.*)

CABOT (*suddenly grim*): I got a lot in me—a hell of a lot—folks don't know on. (*Turning to the* FIDDLER) Fiddle 'er up, durn ye! Give 'em somethin' t' dance t'! What air ye, an ornament? Hain't this a celebration? Then grease yer elbow an' go it!

FIDDLER (*seizes a drink which the* OLD FARMER *holds out to him and downs it*): Here goes! (*He starts to fiddle "Lady of the Lake." Four young fellows and four girls form in two lines and dance a square dance. The* FIDDLER *shouts directions for the different movements, keeping his words in the rhythm of the music and interspersing them with jocular personal remarks to the dancers themselves. The people seated along the walls stamp their feet and clap their hands in unison.* CABOT *is especially active in this respect. Only* ABBIE *remains apathetic, staring at the door as if she were alone in a silent room.*)

FIDDLER: Swing your partner t' the right! That's it, Jim! Give her a b'ar hug! Her Maw hain't lookin'. (*Laughter.*) Change partners! That suits ye, don't it, Essie, now ye got Reub afore ye? Look at her redden up, will ye! Waal, life is short an' so's love, as the feller says. (*Laughter.*)

CABOT (*excitedly, stamping his foot*): Go it, boys! Go it, gals!

FIDDLER (*with a wink at the others*): Ye're the spryest seventy-six ever I sees, Ephraim! Now if ye'd on'y good eye-sight. . . ! (*Suppressed laughter. He gives* CABOT *no chance to retort but roars.*) Promenade! Ye're walkin' like a bride down the aisle, Sarah! Waal, while they's life they's allus hope, I've heerd tell. Swing your partner to the left! Gosh A'mighty, look at Johnny Cook high-steppin'! They hain't goin' t'be much strength left fur howin' in the corn lot t'morrow. (*Laughter.*)

CABOT: Go it! Go it! (*Then suddenly, unable to restrain himself any longer, he prances into the midst of the dancers, scattering them, waving his arms about wildly.*) Ye're all hoofs! Git out o' my road! Give me room! I'll show ye dancin'. Ye're all too soft! (*He pushes them roughly away. They crowd back toward the walls, muttering, looking at him resentfully.*)

FIDDLER (*jeeringly*): Go it, Ephraim! Go it! (*He starts "Pop Goes the Weasel," increasing the tempo with every verse until at the end he is fiddling crazily as fast as he can go.*)

CABOT (*starts to dance, which he does very well and with tremendous vigor. Then he begins to improvise, cuts incredibly grotesque capers, leaping up and cracking his heels together, prancing around in a circle with body bent in an Indian war dance, then suddenly straightening up and kicking as high as he can with both legs. He is like a monkey on a string. And all the while he intersperses his antics with shouts and derisive comments*): Whoop! Here's dancin' fur ye! Whoop! See that! Seventy-six, if I'm a day! Hard as iron yet! Beatin' the young 'uns like I allus done! Look at me! I'd invite ye t' dance on my hundredth birthday on'y ye'll all be dead by then. Ye're a sickly generation! Yer hearts air pink, not red! Yer veins is full o' mud an' water! I be the on'y man in the county! Whoop! See that! I'm a Injun! I've killed Injuns in the West afore ye was born—an' skulped 'em too! They's a arrer wound on my backside I c'd show ye! The hull tribe chased me. I outrun 'em all—with the arrer stuck in me! An' I tuk vengeance on 'em. Ten eyes fur an eye, that was my motter! Whoop! Look at me! I kin kick the ceilin' off the room! Whoop!

FIDDLER (*stops playing—exhaustedly*): God A'mighty, I got enuf. Ye got the devil's strength in ye.

CABOT (*delightedly*): Did I beat yew, too? Wa'al, ye played smart. Hev a swig. (*He pours whisky for himself and* FIDDLER. *They drink. The others watch* CABOT *silently with cold, hostile eyes. There is a dead pause. The* FIDDLER *rests.* CABOT *leans against the keg, panting, glaring around him confusedly. In the room above,* EBEN *gets to his feet and tiptoes out the door in rear, appearing a moment later in the other bedroom. He moves silently, even frightenedly, toward the cradle and stands there looking down at the baby. His face is as vague as his reactions are confused, but there is a trace of tenderness, of interested discovery. At the same moment that he reaches the cradle,* ABBIE *seems to sense something. She gets up weakly and goes to* CABOT.)

ABBIE: I'm goin' up t' the baby.

CABOT (*with real solicitude*): Air ye able fur the stairs? D'ye want me t' help ye, Abbie?

ABBIE: No. I'm able. I'll be down agen soon.

CABOT: Don't ye git wore out! He needs ye, remember—our son does! (*He grins affectionately, patting her on the back. She shrinks from his touch.*)

ABBIE (*dully*): Don't—tech me. I'm goin'—up. (*She goes.* CABOT *looks after her. A whisper goes around the room.* CABOT *turns. It ceases. He wipes his forehead streaming with sweat. He is breathing pantingly.*)

CABOT: I'm a-goin' out t' git fresh air. I'm feelin' a mite dizzy. Fiddle up thar! Dance, all o' ye! Here's likker fur them as wants it. Enjoy yerselves. I'll be back. (*He goes, closing the door behind him.*)

FIDDLER (*sarcastically*): Don't hurry none on our account! (*A suppressed laugh. He imitates* ABBIE) Whar's Eben? (*More laughter.*)

A WOMAN (*loudly*): What's happened in this house is plain as the nose on yer face! (ABBIE *appears in the doorway upstairs and stands looking in surprise and adoration at* EBEN *who does not see her.*)

A MAN: Ssshh! He's li'ble t' be listenin' at the door. That'd be like him. (*Their voices die to an intensive whispering. Their faces are concentrated on this gossip. A noise as of dead leaves in the wind comes from the room.* CABOT *has come out from the porch and stands by the gate, leaning on it, staring at the sky blinkingly.* ABBIE *comes across the room silently.* EBEN *does not notice her until quite near.*)

EBEN (*starting*): Abbie!

ABBIE: Ssshh! (*She throws her arms around him. They kiss—then bend over the cradle together.*) Ain't he purty?—dead spit 'n' image o' yew!

EBEN (*pleased*): Air he? I can't tell none.

ABBIE: E-zactly like!

EBEN (*frowningly*): I don't like this. I don't like lettin' on what's mine's his'n. I been doin' that all my life. I'm gittin' t' the end o' b'arin' it!

ABBIE (*putting her finger on his lips*): We're doin' the best we kin.

We got t' wait. Somethin's bound t' happen. (*She puts her arms around him.*) I got t' go back.

EBEN: I'm goin' out. I can't b'ar it with the fiddle playin' an' the laughin'.

ABBIE: Don't git feelin' low. I love ye, Eben. Kiss me. (*He kisses her. They remain in each other's arms.*)

CABOT (*at the gate, confusedly*): Even the music can't drive it out— somethin'. Ye kin feel it droppin' off the elums, climbin' up the roof, sneakin' down the chimney, pokin' in the corners! They's no peace in houses, they's no rest livin' with folks. Somethin's always livin' with ye. (*With a deep sigh*) I'll go t' the barn an' rest a spell. (*He goes wearily toward the barn.*)

FIDDLER (*tuning up*): Let's celebrate the old skunk gittin' fooled! We kin have some fun now he's went. (*He starts to fiddle "Turkey in the Straw." There is real merriment now. The young folks get up to dance.*)

SCENE II

(*A half hour later—exterior—*EBEN *is standing by the gate looking up at the sky, an expression of dumb pain bewildered by itself on his face.* CABOT *appears, returning from the barn, walking wearily, his eyes on the ground. He sees* EBEN *and his whole mood immediately changes. He becomes excited, a cruel, triumphant grin comes to his lips, he strides up and slaps* EBEN *on the back. From within comes the whining of the fiddle and the noise of stamping feet and laughing voices.*)

CABOT: So har ye be!

EBEN (*startled, stares at him with hatred for a moment—then dully*): Ay-eh.

CABOT (*surveying him jeeringly*): Why hain't ye been in t' dance? They was all axin' fur ye.

EBEN: Let 'em ax!

CABOT: They's a hull passel o' purty gals.

EBEN: T' hell with 'em!

CABOT: Ye'd ought t' be marryin' one o' 'em soon.

EBEN: I hain't marryin' no one.

CABOT: Ye might 'arn a share o' a farm that way.

EBEN (*with a sneer*): Like yew did, ye mean? I hain't that kind.

CABOT (*stung*): Ye lie! 'Twas yer Maw's folks aimed t' steal my farm from me.

EBEN: Other folks don't say so. (*After a pause—defiantly*) An' I got a farm, anyways!

CABOT (*derisively*): Whar?

EBEN (*stamps a foot on the ground*): Har!

CABOT (*throws his head back and laughs coarsely*): Ho-ho! Ye hev, hev ye? Waal, that's a good un!

EBEN (*controlling himself—grimly*): Ye'll see!

CABOT (*stares at him suspiciously, trying to make him out—a pause—then with scornful confidence*): Ay-eh. I'll see. So'll ye. It's that's blind—blind as a mole underground. (EBEN *suddenly laughs, one short sardonic bark: "Ha." A pause.* CABOT *peers at him with renewed suspicion.*) Whar air ye hawin' 'bout? (EBEN *turns away without answering.* CABOT *grows angry.*) God A'mighty, yew air a dumb dunce! They's nothin' in that thick skull o' your'n but noise—like a empty keg it be! (EBEN *doesn't seem to hear—*CABOT's *rage grows.*) Yewr farm! God A'mighty! If ye wa'n't a born donkey ye'd know ye'll never own stick nor stone on it, specially now arter him bein' born. It's his'n, I tell ye—his'n arter I die—but I'll live a hundred jest t' fool ye all—an' he'll be growed then—yewr age a'most! (EBEN *laughs again his sardonic "Ha." This drives* CABOT *into a fury.*) Ha? Ye think ye kin git 'round that someways, do ye? Waal, it'll be her'n, too—Abbie's—ye won't git 'round her—she knows yer tricks—she'll be too much fur ye—she wants the farm her'n—she was afeerd o' ye—she told me ye was sneakin' 'round tryin' t' make love t' her t' git her on yer side . . . ye . . . ye mad fool, ye! (*He raises his clenched fists threateningly.*)

EBEN (*is confronting him choking with rage*): Ye lie, ye old skunk! Abbie never said no sech thing!

CABOT (*suddenly triumphant when he sees how shaken* EBEN *is*): She did. An' I says, I'll blow his brains t' the top o' them elums—an' she says no, that hain't sense, who'll ye git t'help ye on the farm in his place—an' then she says yew'n me ought t' have a son —I know we kin, she says—an' I says, if we do, ye kin have anythin' I've got ye've a mind t'. An' she says, I wants Eben cut off so's this farm'll be mine when ye die! (*With terrible gloating*) An' that's what's happened, hain't it? An' the farm's her'n! An' the dust o' the road—that's you'rn! Ha! Now who's hawin'?

EBEN (*has been listening, petrified with grief and rage—suddenly laughs wildly and brokenly*): Ha-ha-ha! So thats her sneakin' game—all along!—like I suspicioned at fust—t' swaller it all—an' me, too . . . ! (*Madly*) I'll murder her! (*He springs toward the porch but* CABOT *is quicker and gets in between.*)

CABOT: No, ye don't!

EBEN: Git out o' my road! (*He tries to throw* CABOT *aside. They grapple in what becomes immediately a murderous struggle. The old man's concentrated strength is too much for* EBEN. CABOT *gets one hand on his throat and presses him back across the stone wall. At the same moment,* ABBIE *comes out on the porch. With a stifled cry she runs toward them.*)

ABBIE: Eben! Ephraim! (*She tugs at the hand on* EBEN'S *throat.*) Let go, Ephraim! Ye're chokin' him!

CABOT (*removes his hand and flings* EBEN *sideways full length on the grass, gasping and choking. With a cry,* ABBIE *kneels beside him, trying to take his head on her lap, but he pushes her away.* CABOT *stands looking down with fierce triumph*): Ye needn't t've fret, Abbie, I wa'n't aimin' t' kill him. He hain't wuth hangin' fur—not by a hell of a sight! (*More and more triumphantly*) Seventy-six an' him not thirty yit—an' look whar he be fur thinkin' his Paw was easy! No, by God, I hain't easy! An' him upstairs, I'll raise him t' be like me! (*He turns to leave them.*) I'm goin' in an' dance!— sing an' celebrate! (*He walks to the porch—then turns with a great grin.*) I don't calc'late it's left in him, but if he gits pesky, Abbie, ye jest sing out. I'll come a-runnin' an' by the Etarnal, I'll put him across my knee an' birch him! Ha-ha-ha! (*He goes into the house laughing. A moment later his loud "whoop" is heard.*)

ABBIE (*tenderly*): Eben: Air ye hurt? (*She tries to kiss him but he pushes her violently away and struggles to a sitting position.*)

EBEN (*gaspingly*): T'hell—with ye!

ABBIE (*not believing her ears*): It's me, Eben—Abbie—don't ye know me?

EBEN (*glowering at her with hatred*): Ay-eh—I know ye—now! (*He suddenly breaks down, sobbing weakly.*)

ABBIE (*fearfully*): Eben—what's happened t' ye—why did ye look at me 's if ye hated me?

EBEN (*violently, between sobs and gasps*): I do hate ye! Ye're a whore—a damn trickin' whore!

ABBIE (*shrinking back horrified*): Eben! Ye don't know what ye're sayin'!

EBEN (*scrambling to his feet and following her—accusingly*): Ye're
nothin' but a stinkin' passel o' lies! Ye've been lyin' t' me every
word ye spoke, day an' night, since we fust—done it. Ye've kept
sayin' ye loved me. . . .

ABBIE (*frantically*): I do love ye! (*She takes his hand but he flings
hers away.*)

EBEN (*unheeding*): Ye've made a fool o' me—a sick, dumb fool—a-
purpose! Ye've been on'y playin' yer sneakin', stealin' game all
along—gittin' me t' lie with ye so's ye'd hev a son he'd think was
his'n, an' makin' him promise he'd give ye the farm and let me eat
dust, if ye did git him a son! (*Staring at her with anguished,
bewildered eyes*) They must be a devil livin' in ye! 'Tain't human
t' be as bad as that be!

ABBIE (*stunned—dully*): He told yew . . . ?

EBEN: Hain't it true? It hain't no good in yew lyin'.

ABBIE (*pleadingly*): Eben, listen—ye must listen—it was long ago—
afore we done nothin'—yew was scornin' me—goin' t' see Min—
when I was lovin' ye—an' I said it t' him t' git vengeance on ye!

EBEN (*unheedingly. With tortured passion*): I wish ye was dead! I
wish I was dead along with ye afore this come! (*Ragingly*) But I'll
git my vengeance too! I'll pray Maw t' come back t' help me—t'
put her cuss on yew an' him!

ABBIE (*brokenly*): Don't ye, Eben! Don't ye! (*She throws herself on
her knees before him, weeping.*) I didn't mean t' do bad t'ye!
Fergive me, won't ye?

EBEN (*not seeming to hear her—fiercely*): I'll git squar' with the old
skunk—an' yew! I'll tell him the truth 'bout the son he's so proud
o'! Then I'll leave ye here t' pizen each other—with Maw comin'
out o' her grave at nights—an' I'll go t' the gold fields o' Californi-a
whar Sim an' Peter be!

ABBIE (*terrified*): Ye won't—leave me? Ye can't!

EBEN (*with fierce determination*): I'm a-goin', I tell ye! I'll git rich
thar an' come back an' fight him fur the farm he stole—an' I'll kick
ye both out in the road—t' beg an' sleep in the woods—an' yer son
along with ye—t' starve an' die! (*He is hysterical at the end.*)

ABBIE (*with a shudder—humbly*): He's yewr son, too, Eben.

EBEN (*torturedly*): I wish he never was born! I wish he'd die this
minit! I wish I'd never sot eyes on him! It's him—yew havin' him
—a-purpose t' steal—that's changed everythin'!

ABBIE (*gently*): Did ye believe I loved ye—afore he come?

EBEN: Ay-eh—like a dumb ox!

ABBIE: An' ye don't believe no more?

EBEN: B'lieve a lyin' thief! Ha!

ABBIE (*shudders—then humbly*): An did ye r'ally love me afore?

EBEN (*brokenly*): Ay-eh—an' ye was trickin' me!

ABBIE: An' ye don't love me now!

EBEN (*violently*): I hate ye, I tell ye!

ABBIE: An' ye're truly goin' West—goin' t' leave me—all account o' him being born?

EBEN: I'm a-goin' in the mornin'—or may God strike me t' hell!

ABBIE (*after a pause—with a dreadful cold intensity—slowly*): If that's what his comin's done t' me—killin' yewr love—takin' yew away—my on'y joy—the on'y joy I've ever knowed—like heaven t' me—purtier'n heaven—then I hate him, too, even if I be his Maw!

EBEN (*bitterly*): Lies! Ye love him! He'll steal the farm fur ye! (*Brokenly*) But 'tain't the farm so much—not no more—it's yew foolin' me—gittin' me t' love ye—lyin' yew loved me—jest t' git a son t' steal!

ABBIE (*distractedly*): He won't steal! I'd kill him fust! I do love ye! I'll prove t' ye . . . !

EBEN (*harshly*): 'Tain't no use lyin' no more. I'm deaf t' ye! (*He turns away.*) I hain't seein' ye agen. Good-by!

ABBIE (*pale with anguish*): Hain't ye even goin' t' kiss me—not once —arter all we loved?

EBEN (*in a hard voice*): I hain't wantin' t' kiss ye never agen! I'm wantin' t' forgit I ever sot eyes on ye!

ABBIE: Eben!—ye mustn't—wait a spell—I want t' tell ye. . . .

EBEN: I'm a-goin' in t' git drunk. I'm a-goin' t' dance.

ABBIE (*clinging to his arm—with passionate earnestness*): If I could make it—'s if he'd never come up between us—if I could prove t' ye I wa'n't schemin' t' steal from ye—so's everythin' could be jest the same with us, lovin' each other jest the same, kissin' an' happy the same's we've been happy afore he come—if I could do it—ye'd love me agen, wouldn't ye? Ye'd kiss me agen? Ye wouldn't never leave me, would ye?

EBEN (*moved*): I calc'late not. (*Then shaking her hand off his arm —with a bitter smile*) But ye hain't God, be ye?

ABBIE (*exultantly*): Remember ye've promised! (*Then with strange intensity*) Mebbe I kin take back one thin' God does!

EBEN (*peering at her*): Ye're gittin' cracked, hain't ye? (*Then going towards door*) I'm a-goin' t' dance.

ABBIE (*calls after him intensely*): I'll prove t' ye! I'll prove I love ye
better'n. . . . (*He goes in the door, not seeming to hear. She
remains standing where she is, looking after him—then she finishes desperately:*) Better'n everythin' else in the world!

SCENE III

(*Just before dawn in the morning—shows the kitchen and* CABOT'S
bedroom. In the kitchen, by the light of a tallow candle on the table,
EBEN *is sitting, his chin propped on his hands, his drawn face blank
and expressionless. His carpetbag is on the floor beside him. In the
bedroom, dimly lighted by a small whale-oil lamp,* CABOT *lies asleep.*
ABBIE *is bending over the cradle, listening, her face full of terror yet
with an undercurrent of desperate triumph. Suddenly, she breaks
down and sobs, appears about to throw herself on her knees beside the
cradle; but the old man turns restlessly, groaning in his sleep, and she
controls herself, and shrinking away from the cradle with a gesture of
horror, backs swiftly toward the door in rear and goes out. A moment
later she comes into the kitchen and, running to* EBEN, *flings her arms
about his neck and kisses him wildly. He hardens himself, he remains
unmoved and cold, he keeps his eyes straight ahead.*)

ABBIE (*hysterically*): I done it, Eben! I told ye I'd do it! I've proved I
love ye—better'n everythin'—so's ye can't never doubt me no
more!

EBEN (*dully*): Whatever ye done, it hain't no good now.

ABBIE (*wildly*): 'Don't ye say that! Kiss me, Eben, won't ye? I need ye
t' kiss me arter what I done! I need ye t' say ye love me!

EBEN (*kisses her without emotion—dully*): That's fur good-by. I'm a-
goin' soon.

ABBIE: No! No! Ye won't go—not now!

EBEN (*going on with his own thoughts*): I been a-thinkin'—an' I
hain't goin' t' tell Paw nothin'. I'll leave Maw t' take vengeance on
ye. If I told him, the old skunk'd jest be stinkin' mean enuf to take
it out on that baby. (*His voice showing emotion in spite of him*)
An' I don't want nothin' bad t' happen t' him. He hain't t' blame
fur yew. (*He adds with a certain queer pride*) An' he looks like
me! An' by God, he's mine! An some day I'll be a-comin' back
an'. . . !

ABBIE (*too absorbed in her own thoughts to listen to him—pleadingly*): They's no cause fur ye t' go now—they's no sense—it's all

the same's it was—they's nothin' come b'tween us now—arter what I done!

EBEN (*something in her voice arouses him. He stares at her a bit frightenedly*): Ye look mad, Abbie. What did ye do?

ABBIE: I—I killed him, Eben.

EBEN (*amazed*): Ye killed him?

ABBIE (*dully*): Ay-eh.

EBEN (*recovering from his astonishment—savagely*): An' serves him right! But we got t' do somethin' quick t' make it look s'if the old skunk'd killed himself when he was drunk. We kin prove by 'em all how drunk he got.

ABBIE (*wildly*): No! No! Not him! (*Laughing distractedly*) But that's what I ought t' done, hain't it? I oughter killed him instead! Why didn't ye tell me?

EBEN (*appalled*): Instead? What d'ye mean?

ABBIE: Not him.

EBEN (*his face grown ghastly*): Not—not that baby!

ABBIE (*dully*): Ay-eh!

EBEN (*falls to his knees as if he'd been struck—his voice trembling with horror*): Oh, God A'mighty! A'mighty God! Maw, whar was ye, why didn't ye stop her?

ABBIE (*simply*): She went back t' her grave that night we fust done it, remember? I haint felt her about since. (*A pause.* EBEN *hides his head in his hands, trembling all over as if he had the ague. She goes on dully*) I left the piller over his little face. Then he killed himself. He stopped breathin'. (*She begins to weep softly.*)

EBEN (*rage beginning to mingle with grief*) He looked like me. He was mine, damn ye!

ABBIE (*slowly and brokenly*): I didn't want t' do it. I hated myself fur doin' it. I loved him. He was so purty—dead spit 'n' image o' yew. But I loved yew more—an' yew was goin' away—far off whar I'd never see ye agen, never kiss ye, never feel ye pressed agin me agen—an' ye said ye hated me fur havin' him—ye said ye hated him an' wished he was dead—ye said if it hadn't been fur him comin' it'd be the same's afore between us.

EBEN (*unable to endure this, springs to his feet in a fury, threatening her, his twitching fingers seeming to reach out for her throat*): Ye lie! I never said—I never dreamed ye'd—I'd cut off my head afore I'd hurt his finger!

ABBIE (*piteously, sinking on her knees*): Eben, don't ye look at me

like that—hatin' me—not after what I done fur ye—fur us—so's
we could be happy agen—

EBEN (*furiously now*): Shut up, or I'll kill ye! I see yer game now—
the same old sneakin' trick—ye're aimin' t' blame me fur the
murder ye done!

ABBIE (*moaning—putting her hands over her ears*): Don't ye, Eben!
Don't ye! (*She grasps his legs.*)

EBEN (*his mood suddenly changing to horror, shrinks away from
her*): Don't ye tech me! Ye're pizen! How could ye—t' murder a
pore little critter—Ye must've swapped yer soul t' hell! (*Suddenly
raging*) Ha! I kin see why ye done it! Not the lies ye jest told—but
'cause ye wanted t' steal agen—steal the last thin' ye'd left me—
my part o' him—no, the hull o' him—ye saw he looked like me—
ye knowed he was all mine—an' ye couldn't b'ar it—I know ye! Ye
killed him fur bein' mine! (*All this has driven him almost insane.
He makes a rush past her for the door—then turns—shaking both
fists at her, violently.*) But I'll take vengeance now! I'll git the
Sheriff! I'll tell him everythin'! Then I'll sing "I'm off to Californi-
a!" an' go—gold—Golden Gate—gold sun—fields o' gold in the
West! (*This last he half shouts, half croons incoherently, suddenly
breaking off passionately.*) I'm a-goin' fur the Sheriff t' come an'
git ye! I want ye tuk away, locked up from me! I can't stand t' luk
at ye! Murderer an' thief 'r not, ye still tempt me! I'll give ye up t'
the Sheriff! (*He turns and runs out, around the corner of house,
panting and sobbing, and breaks into a swerving sprint down the
road.*)

ABBIE (*struggling to her feet, runs to the door, calling after him*): I
love ye, Eben! I love ye! (*She stops at the door weakly, swaying,
about to fall.*) I don't care what ye do—if ye'll on'y love me agen
— (*She falls limply to the floor in a faint.*)

SCENE IV

(*About an hour later. Same as Scene III. Shows the kitchen and
CABOT's bedroom. It is after dawn. The sky is brilliant with the
sunrise. In the kitchen, ABBIE sits at the table, her body limp and
exhausted, her head bowed down over her arms, her face hidden.
Upstairs, CABOT is still asleep but awakens with a start. He looks
toward the window and gives a snort of surprise and irritation—
throws back the covers and begins hurriedly pulling on his clothes.*)

Without looking behind him, he begins talking to ABBIE *whom he supposes beside him.*)

CABOT: Thunder 'n' lightnin', Abbie! I hain't slept this late in fifty year! Looks 's the sun was full riz a'most. Must've been the dancin' an' likker. Must be gittin' old. I hope Eben's t' wuk. Ye might've tuk the trouble t' rouse me, Abbie. (*He turns—sees no one there—surprised*) Waal—whar air she? Gittin' vittles, I calc'late. (*He tiptoes to the cradle and peers down—proudly*) Mornin', sonny. Purty's à picter! Sleepin' sound. He don't beller all night like most o' 'em. (*He goes quietly out the door in rear—a few moments later enters kitchen—sees* ABBIE—*with satisfaction*) So thar ye be. Ye got any vittles cooked?

ABBIE (*without moving*): No.

CABOT (*coming to her, almost sympathetically*): Ye feelin' sick?

ABBIE: No.

CABOT (*pats her on shoulder. She shudders*): Ye'd best lie down a spell. (*Half jocularly*) Yer son'll be needin' ye soon. He'd ought t' wake up with a gnashin' appetite, the sound way he's sleepin'.

ABBIE (*shudders—then in a dead voice*): He ain't never goin' to wake up.

CABOT (*jokingly*): Takes after me this mornin'. I ain't slept so late in . . .

ABBIE: He's dead.

CABOT (*stares at her—bewilderedly*): What . . .

ABBIE: I killed him.

CABOT (*stepping back from her—aghast*): Air ye drunk—'r crazy—'r . . . !

ABBIE (*suddenly lifts her head and turns on him—wildly*): I killed him, I tell ye! I smothered him. Go up an' see if ye don't b'lieve me! (CABOT *stares at her a second, then bolts out the rear door, can be heard bounding up the stairs, and rushes into the bedroom and over to the cradle.* ABBIE *has sunk back lifelessly into her former position.* CABOT *puts his hand down on the body in the crib. An expression of fear and horror comes over his face.*)

CABOT (*shrinking away—trembling*): God A'mighty! God A'mighty. (*He stumbles out the door—in a short while returns to the kitchen—comes to* ABBIE, *the stunned expression still on his face—hoarsely*) Why did ye do it? Why? (*As she doesn't answer, he grabs her violently by the shoulder and shakes her.*) I ax ye why ye done it! Ye'd better tell me 'r . . . !

ABBIE (*gives him a furious push which sends him staggering back and springs to her feet—with wild rage and hatred*): Don't ye dare tech me! What right hev ye t' question me 'bout him? He wa'n't yewr son! Think I'd have a son by yew? I'd die fust! I hate the sight o' ye an' allus did! It's yew I should've murdered, if I'd had good sense! I hate ye! I love Eben. I did from the fust. An' he was Eben's son—mine an' Eben's—not your'n!

CABOT (*stands looking at her dazedly—a pause—finding his words with an effort—dully*): That was it—what I felt—pokin' round the corners—while ye lied—holdin' yerself from me—sayin' ye'd a'ready conceived— (*He lapses into crushed silence—then with a strange emotion*) He's dead, sart'n. I felt his heart. Pore little critter! (*He blinks back one tear, wiping his sleeve across his nose.*)

ABBIE (*hysterically*): Don't ye! Don't ye! (*She sobs unrestrainedly.*)

CABOT (*with a concentrated effort that stiffens his body into a rigid line and hardens his face into a stony mask—through his teeth to himself*): I got t' be—like a stone—a rock o' jedgment! (*A pause. He gets complete control over himself—harshly*) If he was Eben's, I be glad he air gone! An' mebbe I suspicioned it all along. I felt they was somethin' onnateral—somewhars—the house got so lonesome—an' cold—drivin' me down t' the barn—t' the beasts o' the field. . . . Ay-eh. I must've suspicioned—somethin'. Ye didn't fool me—not altogether, leastways—I'm too old a bird—growin' ripe on the bough. . . . (*He becomes aware he is wandering, straightens again, looks at* ABBIE *with a cruel grin.*) So ye'd liked t' hev murdered me 'stead o' him, would ye? Waal, I'll live to a hundred! I'll live t' see ye hung! I'll deliver ye up t' the jedgment o' God an' the law! I'll git the Sheriff now. (*Starts for the door.*)

ABBIE (*dully*): Ye needn't. Eben's gone fur him.

CABOT (*amazed*): Eben—gone fur the Sheriff?

ABBIE: Ay-eh.

CABOT: T' inform agen ye?

ABBIE: Ay-eh.

CABOT (*considers this—a pause—then in a hard voice*): Waal, I'm thankful fur him savin' me the trouble. I'll git t' wuk. (*He goes to the door—then turns—in a voice full of strange emotion*) He'd ought t' been my son, Abbie. Ye'd ought t' loved me. I'm a man. If ye'd loved me, I'd never told no Sheriff on ye no matter what ye did, if they was t' brile me alive!

ABBIE (*defensively*): They's more to it nor yew know, makes him tell.

CABOT (*dryly*): Fur yewr sake, I hope they be. (*He goes out—comes around to the gate—stares up at the sky. His control relaxes. For a moment he is old and weary. He murmurs despairingly*) God A'mighty, I be lonesomer'n ever! (*He hears running footsteps from the left, immediately is himself again.* EBEN *runs in, panting exhaustedly, wild-eyed and mad looking. He lurches through the gate.* CABOT *grabs him by the shoulder.* EBEN *stares at him dumbly.*) Did ye tell the Sheriff?

EBEN (*nodding stupidly*): Ay-eh.

CABOT (*gives him a push away that sends him sprawling—laughing with withering contempt*): Good fur ye! A prime chip o' yer Maw ye be! (*He goes toward the barn, laughing harshly.* EBEN *scrambles to his feet. Suddenly* CABOT *turns—grimly threatening*) Git off this farm when the Sheriff takes her—or, by God, he'll have t' come back an' git me fur murder, too! (*He stalks off.* EBEN *does not appear to have heard him. He runs to the door and comes into the kitchen.* ABBIE *looks up with a cry of anguished joy.* EBEN *stumbles over and throws himself on his knees beside her—sobbing brokenly.*)

EBEN: Fergive me!

ABBIE (*happily*): Eben! (*She kisses him and pulls his head over against her breast.*)

EBEN: I love ye! Fergive me!

ABBIE (*ecstatically*): I'd fergive ye all the sins in hell fur sayin' that! (*She kisses his head, pressing it to her with a fierce passion of possession.*)

EBEN (*brokenly*): But I told the Sheriff. He's comin' fur ye!

ABBIE: I kin b'ar what happens t' me—now!

EBEN: I woke him up. I told him. He says, wait 'til I git dressed. I was waiting. I got to thinkin' o' yew. I got to thinkin' how I'd loved ye. It hurt like somethin' was bustin' in my chest an' head. I got t' cryin'. I knowed sudden I loved ye yet, an' allus would love ye!

ABBIE (*caressing his hair—tenderly*): My boy, hain't ye?

EBEN: I begun t' run back. I cut across the fields an' through the woods. I thought ye might have time t' run away—with me— an' . . .

ABBIE (*shaking her head*): I got t' take my punishment—t' pay fur my sin.

EBEN: Then I want t' share it with ye.

ABBIE: Ye didn't do nothin'.

EBEN: I put it in yer head. I wisht he was dead! I as much as urged ye t' do it!

ABBIE: No. It was me alone!

EBEN: I'm as guilty as yew be! He was the child o' our sin.

ABBIE (*lifting her head as if defying God*): I don't repent that sin! I hain't askin' God t' fergive that!

EBEN: Nor me—but it led up t' the other—an' the murder ye did, ye did 'count o' me—an' it's my murder, too, I'll tell the Sheriff—an' if ye deny it, I'll say we planned it t'gether—an' they'll all b'lieve me, fur they suspicion everythin' we've done, an' it'll seem likely an' true to 'em. An' it is true—way down. I did help ye—somehow.

ABBIE (*laying her head on his—sobbing*): No! I don't want yew t' suffer!

EBEN: I got t' pay fur my part o' the sin! An' I'd suffer wuss leavin' ye, goin' West, thinkin' o' ye day an' night, bein' out when yew was in—(*lowering his voice*)—'r bein' alive when yew was dead. (*A pause.*) I want t' share with ye, Abbie—prison 'r death 'r hell 'r anythin'! (*He looks into her eyes and forces a trembling smile.*) If I'm sharin' with ye, I won't feel lonesome, leastways.

ABBIE (*weakly*): Eben! I won't let ye! I can't let ye!

EBEN (*kissing her—tenderly*): Ye can't he'p yerself. I got ye beat fur once!

ABBIE (*forcing a smile—adoringly*): I hain't beat—s'long's I got ye!

EBEN (*hears the sound of feet outside*): Ssshh! Listen! They've come t' take us!

ABBIE: No, it's him. Don't give him no chance to fight ye, Eben. Don't say nothin'—no matter what he says. An' I won't neither. (*It is* CABOT. *He comes up from the barn in a great state of excitement and strides into the house and then into the kitchen.* EBEN *is kneeling beside* ABBIE, *his arm around her, hers around him. They stare straight ahead.*)

CABOT (*stares at them, his face hard. A long pause—vindictively*): Ye make a slick pair o' murderin' turtle doves! Ye'd ought t' be both hung on the same limb an' left thar t' swing in the breeze an' rot— a warnin' t' old fools like me t' b'ar their lonesomeness alone—an' fur young fools like ye t' hobble their lust. (*A pause. The excitement returns to his face, his eyes snap, he looks a bit crazy.*) I couldn't work today. I couldn't take no interest. T' hell with the farm! I'm leavin' it! I've turned the cows an' other stock loose! I've druv 'em into the woods whar they kin be free! By freein' 'em, I'm freein' myself! I'm quittin' here today! I'll set fire t' house an' barn an' watch 'em burn, an' I'll leave yer Maw t' haunt the ashes, an' I'll will the fields back to' God, so that nothin' human kin never touch 'em! I'll be a-goin' to Californi-a—t' jine Simeon an' Peter— true sons o' mine if they be dumb fools—an' the Cabots'll find Solomon's Mines t'gether! (*He suddenly cuts a mad caper.*) Whoop! What was the song they sung? "Oh, Californi-a! That's the land fur me." (*He sings this—then gets on his knees by the floorboard under which the money was hid.*) An' I'll sail thar on one o' the finest clippers I kin find! I've got the money! Pity ye didn't know whar this was hidden so's ye could steal . . . (*He has pulled up the board. He stares—feels—stares again. A pause of dead silence. He slowly turns, slumping into a sitting position on the floor, his eyes like those of a dead fish, his face the sickly green of an attack of nausea. He swallows painfully several times— forces a weak smile at last.*) So—ye did steal it!

EBEN (*emotionlessly*): I swapped it t' Sim an' Peter fur their share o' the farm—t' pay their passage t' Californi-a.

CABOT (*with one sardonic*): Ha! (*He begins to recover. Gets slowly to his feet—strangely*) I calc'late God give it to 'em—not yew! God's hard, not easy! Mebbe they's easy gold in the West but it hain't God's gold. It hain't fur me. I kin hear His voice warnin' me agen t' be hard an' stay on my farm. I kin see his hand usin' Eben t' steal t' keep me from weakness. I kin feel I be in the palm o' His hand, His fingers guidin' me. (*A pause—then he mutters sadly.*) It's a-goin' t' be lonesomer now than ever it war afore—an' I'm gittin' old, Lord—ripe on the bough. . . . (*Then stiffening*) Waal—what d'ye want? God's lonesome, hain't He? God's hard an' lonesome! (*A pause. The* SHERIFF *with two men comes up the road from the left. They move cautiously to the door. The* SHERIFF *knocks on it with the butt of his pistol.*)

SHERIFF: Open in the name o' the law! (*They start.*)

CABOT: They've come fur ye. (*He goes to the rear door.*) Come in, Jim! (*The three men enter.* CABOT *meets them in doorway.*) Jest a minit, Jim. I got 'em safe here. (*The* SHERIFF *nods. He and his companions remain in the doorway.*)

EBEN (*suddenly calls*): I lied this mornin', Jim. I helped her to do it. Ye kin take me, too.

ABBIE (*brokenly*): No!

CABOT: Take 'em both. (*He comes forward—stares at* EBEN *with a trace of grudging admiration.*) Purty good—fur yew! Waal, I got t' round up the stock. Good-by.

EBEN: Good-by.

ABBIE: Good-by. (CABOT *turns and strides past the men—comes out and around the corner of the house, his shoulders squared, his face stony, and stalks grimly toward the barn. In the meantime the* SHERIFF *and men have come into the room.*)

SHERIFF (*embarrassedly*): Waal—we'd best start.

ABBIE: Wait. (*Turns to* EBEN.) I love ye, Eben.

EBEN: I love ye, Abbie. (*They kiss. The three men grin and shuffle embarrassedly.* EBEN *takes* ABBIE'S *hand. They go out the door in rear, the men following, and come from the house, walking hand in hand to the gate.* EBEN *stops there and points to the sunrise sky.*) Sun's a-rizin'. Purty, hain't it?

ABBIE: Ay-eh. (*They both stand for a moment looking up raptly in attitudes strangely aloof and devout.*)

SHERIFF (*looking around at the farm enviously—to his companion*): It's a jim-dandy farm, no denyin'. Wished I owned it!